LIVING IN LOVE & FAI†H

Christian teaching and learning about identity, sexuality, relationships and marriage

CHURCH HOUSE PUBLISHING

official publisher of the Church of England

Church House Publishing
Church House
Great Smith Street
London SW1P 3AZ

www.chpublishing.co.uk

Commissioned and commended for study
by the House of Bishops of the Church of England.

Published for the House of Bishops
of the General Synod of the Church of England
by Church House Publishing 2020

ISBN 978 0 7151 1167 3 (Paperback)
ISBN 978 0 7151 1168 0 (Kindle Edition)
ISBN 978 0 7151 1169 7 (CoreSource eBook)

British Library Cataloguing in Publication Data

A catalogue record for this book is available from the British Library

Cover and internal design by Narrative Design
Typeset by Helen Jones Editorial
Indexed by Meg Davies
Printed in the UK by Ashford Colour Press

Welcome

Welcome to this book about living in love and faith. It begins with an invitation from the Bishops of the Church of England to embark on a learning journey: each of the book's five Parts is intended to guide you as you proceed from one to the next. But where you begin your journey might depend on who you are and how you prefer to learn.

If you're someone who likes to start by thinking about life and God and how it is that the church is the way it is, then **Part One** might be your starting point. These chapters are about receiving, more than questioning – for now.

Or you may be someone who likes to start by taking a good look at the world we find ourselves in. You might want to head straight for **Part Two**. These chapters are about noticing what is going on without drawing any conclusions – just yet.

Maybe you are the kind of person who wants to make sense of things first from the perspective of faith. **Part Three** puts theology to work. These chapters are about wrestling in faith with some hard questions.

How do we know what is true? How do we know what God is saying? If you like to think about 'how' and 'why' questions, then **Part Four** may be a good place for you to start. These chapters are about analysing how Christians come up with different answers to the questions we are asking.

But maybe you are someone who likes a good discussion. Then **Part Five** might be your entry point. These chapters are about inspiring you to learn more and to have similar conversations with others.

Real life stories might be the key to drawing you in. The **Encounters** are about bringing the questions to life as you meet people who are followers of Christ. These can be found in between each of the Parts.

Wherever you choose to start we hope that you will want to read the other parts of the book too – each one is a crucial part of the learning journey. We hope you'll also want to explore the **LLF Course**, the **films**, the **podcasts** and the **online library** all of which can be accessed at **www.churchofengland.org/LLF**.

Don't forget to read the **Appeal** at the end, which gives an idea of the way ahead and your part in it. The more you engage with the whole book, the more the Appeal and the journey beyond it will make sense.

Contents

Foreword

by the Archbishops of Canterbury and York

'There is no fear in love, but perfect love casts out fear' (1 John 4.18).

Yet, because our love is imperfect, it is often fear that casts out love when we, as individuals and as a church, seek to discern how the church should act on matters that are central to our identity. God in perfect love has created us. In Jesus Christ, God became human and a servant to save us from our sins and to restore in us the image of God. As followers of Jesus we are called to have 'the same mind ... that was in Christ Jesus' so that we may have relationships of love that look not only to our 'own interests, but to the interests of others' (Philippians 2.4-13) and so reflect the holy love of Jesus Christ. Walking in love and holiness means walking together with God, open to the Holy Spirit who keeps God at the heart of our thoughts and desires (Romans 8.5-17).

We seek to understand the mind of God revealed in Scripture, our final authority in which we find all things necessary for salvation. We listen to the Church present and past and universal. We use our reason and understanding, drawing on the best thinking of the natural and human sciences. In that process of threefold listening we commit to learning, from God and through each other, in the spirit and light of that perfect love.

In February 2017, the General Synod of the Church of England debated a Report from the House of Bishops called 'Marriage and Same Sex Relationships after the Shared Conversations (GS 2055)'. In a very unusual moment, the General Synod declined to take note of the report. Such an exceptional action by the Synod required an equally exceptional response by the Bishops. A few weeks after the vote a joint letter from the Archbishops of Canterbury and York said that 'we need a radical new Christian inclusion in the Church. This must be founded in Scripture, in reason, in tradition, in theology and the Christian faith as the Church of England has received it; it must be based on good, healthy, flourishing relationships, and in a proper twenty-first century understanding of being human and of being sexual.' Every word of that sentence was carefully weighed and was, and remains, essential. Inclusion must be radical because the grace of God as expressed in Jesus Christ is radical beyond our imagination. It must be Christian because inclusion has become a term which has become a means of exercising power over one another. And it must be new because we must learn from the mistakes of the past, and not simply reproduce models from secular society.

This is an Anglican method of theological reflection, based around Richard Hooker's pattern of Scripture, reason and tradition: Scripture read together in the wide and long life of the church, with all the skills that God has given to us. Discernment of the mind of Christ necessitates careful, prolonged and deep reflection. This is especially true in an area that is a source of intense controversy in Christian churches as well as across society here and around the world.

At the same time, we are not discussing abstract concepts, but matters that are of immense sensitivity and often pain to almost every human being. In the Ignatian tradition, discernment involves two key principles: consolation and desolation. We are treading amongst people's deepest hopes and dreams, where they experience profound consolation and intense desolation. Therefore, the work of discernment has to include the actualities of human experience.

The supreme and unique beauty of the person of Jesus of Nazareth is found not only in that he is the Truth, but also that his truth abounds in grace and love (John 1.14). In Christ, God demonstrated that truth need not damage and hurt, and is not to be used to threaten those who are vulnerable. Truth may often be challenging, but it transforms us 'from one degree of glory to another' (2 Corinthians 3.18) as we see the face of the Lord who is the Spirit.

As soon as we begin to consider questions of sexual identity and behaviour, we need to acknowledge the huge damage and hurt that has been caused where talk of truth, holiness and discipleship has been wielded harshly and not ministered as a healing balm. Especially amongst LGBTI+ people, every word we use – quite possibly including these in this very foreword, despite all the care we exercise – may cause pain. We have caused, and continue to cause, hurt and unnecessary suffering. For such acts, each of us, and the Church collectively, should be deeply ashamed and repentant. As archbishops, we are personally very sorry where we have contributed to this.

At the heart of our failure is the absence of a genuine love for those whom God loves in Christ, knowing as God does every aspect of all of our lives. Such lack of perfect love causes us at times to fear and act out of fear. Defensiveness is felt, and aggression is experienced, both by those who long for change and by those who believe, sincerely, that change would be wrong and damaging.

This book arises from the extraordinary efforts of more than forty people, from all dimensions of the debates, with very different life experiences and theological convictions, as well as the close involvement of the bishops of the Church of England. Discernment requires time. Many people wish that we could jump to a quick decision as a church in England. However, in this process, we have been committed to listening to people's life stories, to being open to questions, and to understanding each other's views. We acknowledge that we in the Church of England are just one small part of the Anglican Communion and the universal Christian Church, and of the wider human family.

In taking time, and yet moving comparatively quickly (at least in terms of the average speed of change in church history), we have sought both to respect the enormous importance of the questions discussed in this book and the fears, anxieties and pastoral impact on those who have been anticipating its outcomes with growing impatience. Even now, this book does not represent the end of the process, although it is a very significant step. It is intended to enable all those in the Church of England who wish to take part by using this book – and the other Living in Love and Faith resources – to learn and reflect together to help the entire church in its task of discernment.

A model for such engagement has come from the Pastoral Advisory Group under the leadership of Bishop Christine Hardman. The group has established six principles for living well together: to acknowledge prejudice, to speak into silence, to address ignorance, to cast out fear, to admit hypocrisy and to pay attention to power. This careful work gives us a tool to help us to love one another more perfectly, not only in the areas discussed in this book but in all our differences within the church.

Inevitably, many people will read this work with trepidation. They will be anxious in case it causes them more pain or betrays, or seems to them to betray, principles they hold as essential. You will hear testimonies of spiritual growth from people whose convictions and lived experiences seem incompatible. God seems to be present in these opposing circumstances and people of divergent convictions.

This book will be deeply uncomfortable in different places for everyone who reads it sincerely and honestly. It will bring you face to face, as it has us, with Christian people who have been hurt or harmed by the words and actions of the church. It will confront each of us with the realities of the depth and breadth of disagreement that is the experience of all churches, including our own, today. It will remind us of the depth of commitment to holiness that the gospel and the cross call us to, and how short all of us fall from it. We must not pretend otherwise. Only in looking honestly at the fact that we have sisters and brothers in Christ who have vehemently opposed views to ours, can we come in humility before God and seek the guidance of the Holy Spirit.

Our vision must be that which Jesus prays for in John 17.21, 'that they may all be one. As you, Father, are in me and I am in you, may they also be in us, so that the world may believe that you have sent me.' Being one is not in the sense of being the same, but being one in love and obedience and holiness, so that the world may find the knowledge of Christ as Saviour and the peace of God in the experience of God's Kingdom. There will probably never be a time when we all agree exactly what that looks like, but our prayer for the Church through this work is that collectively we demonstrate the same love to one another that we have experienced from God; the grace that includes everyone whom Jesus Christ is calling to follow him; the holiness that changes the world and the unity that calls others to faith in Christ. The gift of that kind of love for God, for each other, and even for those who oppose us, is, in the words of 1 Peter, a love that covers a multitude of sins and thus leads us to be holy as God is holy (1 Peter 4.8 and 1.16).

Finally, we need to express thanks beyond words to those who have participated in this project. Their names are listed in **www.churchofengland.org/LLF**. But we are especially aware of the work of the Coordinating Group, led by Bishop Christopher Cocksworth, and of the working groups, led by Bishops Tim Dakin, Sarah Mullally, Martin Warner and Pete Wilcox. We particularly would like to pay tribute to Bishop Christopher and to Dr Eeva John. The journey they have gone through has been immensely painful at times, challenging beyond description, and yet has produced something which, like all human work, will not be perfect but is, nevertheless, an exceptional and unique contribution to the thinking of the church. We offer our appreciation, our love and our thanks.

✠ Justin Cantuar: ✠ Stephen Ebor:
Lambeth Palace, London   Bishopthorpe Palace, York

September 2020

Note to the reader

The Glossary at the end of the book contains definitions and brief discussions of words relating to identity, sexuality and gender. We recognize that while it is particularly important to use words with care when we are talking about sex and gender, there are no neutral words. For the sake of flow and consistency, we have generally adopted the formulation 'LGBTI+' (Lesbian, Gay, Bisexual, Trans, Intersex), except when quoting or referring to work which uses other formulations (such as LGB or LGBT). We recognize that 'LGBTI+' brings together a variety of people whose interests, characteristics and perspectives are not the same. Some people might wish to use other formulations or words to describe themselves – such as 'queer', 'same-sex attracted', or having a 'difference of sex development', for example. Using 'LGBTI+' is not intended to signal a preference for one or other formulations or descriptors.

'Encounters' sections appear at the end of each of the book's five Parts. The people that you will meet and the stories that you will read in them are the result of real encounters that have taken place all around the country. They are taken from transcripts of recorded conversations with people who have risked sharing their stories and their lives with us. The stories offer us a chance to listen in on those conversations and to allow these encounters to take root in our hearts and prayers. Each story has been agreed by the person or people concerned. All the names and places are fictitious. There are many more stories on the website – on film as well as in written form. We are immensely grateful to each person who has given of themselves in this way to the Living in Love and Faith project.

Bible quotations are from the New Revised Standard Version (NRSV) throughout. On the handful of occasions when a different translation is used, the version is given after the quotation.

For simplicity, we have adopted the convention of using 'Church' to refer to the universal Church and 'church' to refer to the Church of England and to local congregations.

'Living in Love and Faith' has been abbreviated to 'LLF' in Part Five's conversations, in the Endnotes and in the website address.

An invitation
from the Bishops of
the Church of England

We, the Bishops of the Church of England, invite you to join us in using this book and its accompanying resources to learn together about how the Christian understanding of God relates to questions of identity, sexuality, relationships and marriage.

These are questions that touch all of us deeply. They are about our lives and the loves that sustain them. They are about experiences and convictions that bring both joy and pain. And so this invitation is about learning together as human beings, each one of us created in the image of God and equally precious in God's sight.

This book has come about because there is disagreement within the people of God, including among us, the Bishops of the Church of England. There are disagreements about same-sex relationships and the Christian understanding of marriage as the Church of England has received it. There are also disagreements about pastoral practice in relation to gender identity, sexuality and relationships more generally. The roots of these disagreements relate to Scripture, doctrine, ethics and the nature of the Church, including the Church of England.

Accepting the invitation to join us – with all our differences – is about embarking on a venture of learning and discovery. Our prayer is that as all of us, the people of God, take time to listen and learn together, our love for one another will be deepened and our faith in Jesus Christ strengthened so that his joy will be made complete in us.

An invitation with a challenge

This book begins (in Part One) and ends (in an Appeal) with some reflections from the Gospel of John. So here, too, we turn to John's account of the story of the feeding of the 5,000. As John so often does, he tells the story in a way that leaves us in no doubt that Jesus, the source of our salvation, is in charge. It is Jesus who confronts the disciples with the problem of the hungry crowd at the end of the day. And it is Jesus who distributes the loaves and the fish after giving thanks. It is Jesus who feeds the large crowd, a sign pointing back to creation and to the feeding of Israel in the desert and forward to his giving of himself as food that endures to eternal life to those who believe in him. It is a sign that Jesus is 'the bread of life' (John 6.27,35). All that the disciples have to do is to 'Make the people sit down' (John 6.10).

That is the very thing that this book and its accompanying resources seek to do in the life of the Church of England:[1] the book and its accompanying resources invite us all to sit down together with each other, and, like the crowds, to be nourished by Christ. It is an invitation made in faith: that God will provide the nourishment that we need to better understand God's purposes in relation to human identity, sexuality, relationships and marriage. It is an invitation that carries with it the power of God's love: the love of the one who created us and cares for us in the seemingly impossible dilemmas we face as a church with regard to our different perspectives on these matters.

As you leaf through this book it may be that you identify with the disciples in the story of the feeding of the 5,000. The disciples must have been wearied and worried by the relentlessness of the needy crowd and frustrated by the seemingly impossible challenge that Jesus puts to them, 'Where are we to buy bread for these people to eat?' (John 6.5).

It may be that you are weary of the decades of attempts by the church to engage seemingly fruitlessly or superficially with questions of sexuality and marriage. Maybe you are overwhelmed by your own experience and pain in relation to these matters and do not have the capacity or even the desire to attend to a church that seems to have been deaf to your cries.

It may be that all you can see is the impossibility of the task: the depth of disagreement within the church. So, like the disciples, you are already poised and even planning to find another way out.

It may be that you feel the pressure of the crowds watching and waiting to see what will happen as the church deliberates and hesitates. Maybe you share Jesus' compassion for the crowd and want the church to respond, but you are held back by the inadequacy of what the church has to offer.

It may be that what you really want is to 'get on with the real task of the church'. Maybe you are disappointed and frustrated by a church that keeps being derailed from its core mission by having to expend precious resources talking about sexuality and marriage.

So it may be that, like the disciples, you can't see the sense of getting everyone to 'sit down'. And yet, this book is an invitation to do just that: to sit down to learn, listen and pray together. This is neither easy nor comfortable and is itself a step of love and faith. When Jesus ordered the disciples to make the crowd sit down, they had no hard evidence that everyone would be fed. In fact, quite the contrary. In the same way, this book offers no recommendations or guarantees of an agreed way forward for the church in relation to human identity, sexuality, relationships and marriage. But it does challenge all of us to believe that God is at work among us as we sit together to learn, to study, to listen, to talk and to receive; and, in so doing, to follow Christ together in his way, truth and life.

An invitation offered in hope

So this book is intended to nourish the people of God. It is not a comprehensive account of all that can be known about identity, sexuality and relationships and is, in that sense, inadequate, as were the five loaves and two fish. However, we offer it to the church in hope.

We hope that engaging with the book will deepen our sense of being a church that is a learning community – or a community of learning communities. We hope that the book will draw together people with different views and experiences, so that we do our learning in the unity of the body of the church, not in factions or silos. We hope that we will hold each other's pain as we touch on matters that are deeply personal. We hope that we will honour each other as beloved disciples of Christ.

We hope that together we will be led to deeper understanding from Scripture and the church's tradition. We hope that we will be enlightened by exploring new areas of knowledge. We hope that we will be transformed into greater Christlikeness by our attentiveness to and involvement with each other and the communities we serve.

We dare to hope that as together we study this book and its accompanying resources we will become a church that has good news to bring to society on matters of identity, sexuality, relationships and marriage.

An invitation to examine ourselves

The sobering truth, however, is that we, the people of God, are not always good at living in love and faith or being a beacon of God's love in the world. Many of us do not experience our own church – the Church of England – as a welcoming and safe environment where the fulness of the love of Christ is manifest. Many of us in our church communities have not always experienced the unconditional love of Christ. Indeed, some have experienced outright rejection, homophobia, transphobia or other unacceptable patterns of behaviour. Some have experienced hostility, scorn and demeaning accusations because of their convictions. Some have been subjected to sexual abuse.

As we gather to sit and learn together, we need to do our part in creating safe spaces where we can relate honestly, graciously and lovingly to one another. This will involve admitting and addressing the realities of our past failures if we are to hear God in and through our study and prayer. It will involve repenting of the ways in which our attitudes and behaviours cause these sins, rooted as they are in fear.

That is why the House of Bishops commended the 'Pastoral Principles for Living Well Together'.[2] These principles help us to examine ourselves as we use this book and its accompanying resources in ways that build up our common life and help us to discern together 'what the Spirit is saying to the churches' (Revelation 2.11,17,29; 3.6,13,22). The Living in Love and Faith Course that accompanies this book provides more detail about how we can put these principles into practice. This is available at **www.churchofengland.org/LLF**.

They will help us

...to address ignorance

> by learning together about identity, sexuality, relationships and marriage in the light of our call to be faithful to both Scripture and the Church's tradition;

> by learning together with people who have different perspectives and lived experiences in relation to identity, sexuality, relationships and marriage.

...to acknowledge prejudice

> by welcoming people as they are, loving them unconditionally and seeking to see Christ in them;

> by reflecting deeply on our attitudes and behaviour in order to nurture understanding and respect between people who disagree.

...to admit hypocrisy

> by not condemning certain behaviours and attitudes while turning a blind eye to others, remembering that we are all weak, fallible, broken and equally in need of God's grace;

> by learning from one another about the challenge to holy living and the wideness of God's mercy as the Spirit moves within, among and between us.

...to cast out fear

> by consciously demonstrating and living out what it means for perfect love to cast out fear even in situations of disagreement;

> by modelling openness and vulnerability as each of us wrestles prayerfully with the costliness of Christian discipleship.

...to speak into silence

> by remembering that we are the Body of Christ, called to relate deeply and openly with one another, sharing what is on our hearts as well as in our minds;

> by practising deep listening, without a hidden agenda, that encourages conversations about questions of human identity, sexuality, relationships and marriage.

...to pay attention to power

> by being alert to attempts to control others, remembering that God's Spirit alone can bring transformation into our lives and the lives of others;

> by following Christ's example of service and compassion as we accompany one another in following the way of the cross.

An invitation to perceive the love of Christ among us

Only the gospel of John recounts the crowd's reaction to the miraculous abundance of food that they had received: 'This is indeed the prophet who is to come into the world' (John 6.14). This sign revealed the truth about Christ. It was a sign of love: an authoritative and compassionate love that responds to human need; a self-giving and sacrificial love, shown in Christ's actions of giving thanks, which point to the Last Supper (John 6.47-51); and an overflowingly abundant love, as the baskets of leftovers were gathered and counted, 'so that nothing may be lost' (John 6.12).

This love reminds us that the book is not primarily about abstract ideas and controversies, but about all of us and the many ways we live in love and faith with hope. It is about our lives and passions, our struggles and delights – the everyday substance of our lives. Crucially, for many it is about pain and suffering, sometimes made more acute by the church. Engagement with this project will be more costly for some than others, especially LGBTI+ people, and so it is an invitation to exercise utmost kindness and patience as we seek truth together, all the while listening deeply to one another's experiences and convictions.

This book is trying to create a space for us all to rediscover the compassionate, self-giving and abundant love of Christ in and among us as we learn together. It is about being led deeper into the truth about the God we encounter in Scripture: the God who has spoken in love to our broken world in the life, death and resurrection of Jesus; the God who, in renewing all things (Matthew 19.28), is calling us to the hope in which we were saved, a hope for what we do not yet see, but wait for with patience. It is about proclaiming the kingdom of God and making Christ known in the world he came by grace to save and bring to fulness of life.

We hope you will accept the invitation to read this book, explore the accompanying resources that can be found on the Living in Love and Faith website (**www.churchofengland.org/LLF**) and make use of the Living in Love and Faith Course.

Here are some suggestions to help you begin.

- Whenever possible, consider studying the book together with people who have different convictions and experiences from your own, using the Living in Love and Faith Course together to help you to engage lovingly, sensitively, generously and respectfully with one other.

- Wherever you choose to enter the book, make sure you cover the whole route of the learning journey that it takes you on, which might mean going back to parts that you skipped.

- Be prayerfully open to learning from understandings and perspectives that differ from your own, even when this is uncomfortable.

- Be active in your reading: engage with the Bible verses that are referred to, use the Living in Love and Faith Course and read the lived experience stories – the Encounters – that can be found in between each Part of the book.

- Listen to your own inner responses – intellectual, emotional, spiritual – to what you are reading and become aware of how they might be shaping your understanding.

- Read prayerfully and expectantly in love and faith with hope. Why not pray the following prayer each time you meet with others to learn together?

O Holy Spirit,
Giver of light and life,
Impart to us thoughts higher than our own thoughts,
and prayers better than our own prayers,
and powers beyond our own powers,
that we may spend and be spent
in the ways of love and goodness,
after the perfect image
of our Lord and Saviour Jesus Christ.
Amen.

from *Daily Prayer* (1941)
edited by Eric Milner-White and G.W. Briggs

Eternal God and Father,
you create and redeem us
by the power of your love:
guide and strengthen us by your Spirit,
that we may give ourselves
in love and service
to one another and to you;
through Jesus Christ our Lord.
Amen.

Common Worship Daily Prayer

Reflecting: what have we received?

The purpose of Part One is to set our questions about human identity, sexuality, relationships and marriage in the context of God's gift of life.

Chapter 1 invites us to wonder at the gift of abundant, eternal life that is offered to us through the redemptive life, death and resurrection of Jesus Christ.

Chapter 2 shows us that this gift of life is a gift of relationship. It explores some of the characteristics of our relationships that flow from God's gift of life, a gift renewed through the reconciling work of Jesus Christ and made known in the community of love formed around him.

Chapter 3 explores one element of this life of love and faith. It explains the biblical and historical roots of the church's understanding of marriage as a lifelong, faithful relationship between one man and one woman.

Chapter 4 draws Part One to an end with an explanation of how, in the rest of the book, we will go about learning together – being taught together by Christ – about human identity, sexuality, relationships and marriage. It explains the rationale for engaging with the Bible, the church's tradition, history and the sciences in the search for truth. It explores how and why we also need to be good observers of the world in which God has placed us, and of the lived experiences which call us to understand God's presence in human experience.

CHAPTER 1

The gift of life

A meditation on the Gospel of John

From void and darkness, from utter nothingness, comes life (Genesis 1.2). An explosion of life: light, land, water, vegetation, living creatures of every kind, all of them created by God.

Among them is humankind, male and female, made in God's 'image' and 'likeness' to be faithful and fruitful (Genesis 1.26-31).

God speaks life into being, and it is good: abundantly, breathtakingly good and wonderfully diverse. God gives life.

The Bible begins with God and the life that God gives. It ends with 'the grace of the Lord Jesus' (Revelation 22.21) and an invitation from the Spirit and the bride: 'Let anyone who wishes take the water of life as a gift' (Revelation 22.17). It ends with life again, and with God. But this is not the old life, the life with which the story began, the life soon to be spoiled. It is *new* life, life in a new heaven and a new earth where death, the very antithesis of life, is no more (Revelation 21.4). God renews life.

The first chapter of the Gospel of John is a pivotal moment in this biblical journey from life to life. It begins where the first book began, 'In the beginning' (John 1.1). It tells of the Word that was spoken there – the Word that 'was with God and was God', bringing 'all things…into being' (John 1.3). The Word spoken with God's breath that gives life. The Word that brings light to all and overcomes the dark. The Word, the Gospel tells us, that 'became flesh and lived among us' (John 1.14).

This Word was sent in love from the source of life to renew and restore all life, all that has been stained by tears and lost in death. 'We have seen his glory', says the Gospel, a glory that is 'full of grace and truth' (John 1.14). This Word-made-flesh is, in other words, true life, life in all its fulness, from which we receive 'grace upon grace' (John 1.16).

It is this very fulness of life that those who became Jesus' first disciples recognize in him when, in his first spoken words in the Gospel, he asks them a question. 'What are you looking for?' he says (John 1.38), a question that is full of grace, searching out the truth that is in them. What are you seeking? What are you longing for? What is it that you desire? 'Rabbi' they respond (John 1.38). (John, in an aside to the reader, tells us that a Rabbi is a teacher.) They instinctively perceive, in other words, that Jesus is someone with something to teach them. In Jesus there is something to be found, some truth, some grace, some life.

'Where are you staying?', they ask (John 1.38), recognizing that to take hold of this life that is in Jesus they will need to be with him. Jesus' reply is startlingly simple. 'Come and see', he says (John 1.39). Come and see that I dwell with God as I dwell with you. Come and see the life of heaven living on earth. Come and see God's life renewing and restoring human life, giving 'power to become children of God' (John 1.11). Come to be – to dwell – with me.

'I came that they may have life, and have it abundantly', said Jesus (John 10.10). But to bring this life to us will cost him dearly. People prefer darkness to light. We choose hate over love. We reject life and court death. 'I am the good shepherd', promises Jesus (John 10.11). He is no 'hired hand' (John 10.12) who deserts the sheep when the wolves come to snatch them away or when thieves come to steal their lives. Jesus is ready to lay down his life for the life of others, and steal away death, for ever. Jesus knows 'the ruler of this world is coming' (John 14.30), turning people away from the truth that will set them free, turning them in upon themselves in ways that will enslave and destroy them. Jesus is ready to confront every evil that deprives us of life and to conquer it.

'Father, the hour has come', Jesus prays (John 17.1). Soon we see him as he said we would, lifted high (on the cross): flesh given for 'the life of the world' (John 6.51), blood poured out that we may no longer live in hate and perish in death. Truly, said John the Baptist, 'Here is the Lamb of God who takes away the sin of the world!' (John 1.29).

Mary of Magdala, whose life had been scarred by evil but whom Jesus had befriended and delivered, meets him at his tomb. She hears a question through her tears, a familiar sort of question, 'full of grace and truth' (John 1.14). 'For whom are you looking?' (John 20.15). And then she hears her name, 'Mary'. 'Rabbouni', she responds (John 20.16). Once again John reminds us of the importance of this word: *teacher*. And once again the truth Jesus makes known to her is something thoroughly new, a truth she proclaims down through the ages: 'I have seen the Lord' (John 20.18). God's life has defeated death. God's light has overcome darkness. God's love triumphs. The enemy of death that has drawn the life out of life through lies and enmity, betrayal and hate, injustice and conflict is overwhelmed. Truly, Jesus said, 'I am the resurrection and the life' (John 11.25).

'This is eternal life, that they may know you, the only true God, and Jesus Christ whom you sent' (John 17.3). Jesus has spoken of a new kind of life throughout his ministry. He has lived out this new sort of life, the life that comes 'from above' (John 8.23), life that is called eternal. He has brought that life to the world: water into wine, sickness into health, paralysis into movement, doubt and fear into faith and joy, lack of bread into abundance, blindness into sight, even death into life. Now, close to his own death, Jesus prays that we may know what lies at the heart of this new life.

Righteous Father, the world does not know you, but I know you; and these know that you have sent me. I made your name known to them, and I will make it known, so that the love with which you have loved me may be in them, and I in them. (John 17.25,26)

This is the love we yearn for, the love we thirst for: the love of God that is the heart of God's life, the love that can flow through us like 'rivers of living water' as we come to Christ and drink of God's Spirit (John 7.37-39).

John tells us at the beginning of the Gospel that it is 'God the only Son, who is close to the Father's heart, who has made him known' (John 1.18). Here, in Jesus' prayer, he prays that the eternal love with which he has been loved by his eternal Father may be in us.

Jesus' prayer that we may be where he is makes sense of what Jesus has said before about believing in him and following him. Will we believe in – trust and put our faith in – the love that God has for us in Jesus – love that God has opened up for us in sending Jesus? This love is the truth of Jesus, and 'whoever believes in the Son has eternal life' (John 3.36). Will we truly and fully entrust ourselves to this love by receiving the one through whom it has come? This love, this 'grace upon grace' (John 1.16) is the way of Jesus, and 'whoever disobeys the Son will not see life' (John 3.36). Will we live this way of love, obeying Jesus' command to love as he loves, laying down our lives for our friends as Jesus laid down his life for those he called no longer servants but friends (John 15.15)? And will we refuse, as one of John's letters puts it, to hate our brother or sister (1 John 4.20)? Believing Jesus' truth, living Jesus' way is life: 'I came that they may have life, and have it abundantly' (John 10.10).

'Choose life so that you and your descendants may live', says the Old Testament (Deuteronomy 30.19). 'Take hold of the life that really is life', says the New (1 Timothy 6.19). The invitation to live fully runs through John's Gospel. Nicodemus wrestles with it in the cool of the night and finds that God has done a new thing with him and with his people (John 3.1-6). The Samaritan woman rejoices in it in the heat of the day and finds a new dignity in herself and in her community. A crowd learns to see a sinner differently because of it, and to give her space to live again, differently (John 4.7-42). Martha and Mary are astounded by it, and believe it, *believe him*, and their family is renewed (John 11.1-53). Pontius Pilate interrogates and condemns it, *condemns him*, and turns away. He turns in the same direction as many do in every age and culture when they cannot see the truth God sets before their eyes, taking another step in the way of darkness and death (John 18.28-38). The greater power of light and life is demonstrated when God raises Jesus from the tomb and as the risen Christ breathes the Spirit of life – the breath of God – on his disciples (John 20.1-23).

The life that God has for us is shown in profound acts of humility as feet are washed and lives recast to serve. It is demonstrated in gestures of acceptance and words of forgiveness that heal and set free. It is shaped in a new community of friendship as people, very different people, gather around the same teacher, and learn to love each other as he loves them. God's eternal love – love that brings life, eternal life – is experienced in Christ's community of love. It is experienced in a community bound together in a hard-won friendship and led into the truth of love by the Spirit, the advocate of God's love in Christ. It is a new community of faith and love that has placed its hope in Jesus Christ, and found that 'All who have this hope in him purify themselves, just as he is pure' (1 John 3.3). It is here we find that very life about which the Spirit and the bride – the heavenly people of God gathered from all tribes and peoples and languages – say, 'Let anyone who wishes take the water of life as a gift' (Revelation 22.17). This is the life that brings all things into being (John 1.3), the life that enlightens all people (John 1.4,9), the life that binds creation together in a shared existence (Colossians 1.15-17).

So the gift that God gives to all creation is life. It is a gift generated in each of us as we are brought to birth and live out our lives. It is a gift that Christ came to raise into a fulness of life that continues beyond death. This gift of life that is for everyone and is without limit can only be fully known together – together with God and each other, together in families and communities, together in relationships, friendships and marriages, together in the life of Jesus' body, the Church. For the life that God gives is life *together*.

CHAPTER 2

The gift of life in relationship

We began with God's gift of life in creation. It is a gift God reaffirms, renews and restores through the work of redemption in which everything that came to spoil the good in creation is redeemed in Jesus Christ.

It is a gift that shall be fully known at the end of time as we know it, when God's purposes are fulfilled. Yet it can be experienced now in a real and tangible form.

This gift of life is given and received in and through many kinds of relationship: ways of togetherness, with God, with each other, and with the whole created order. God's gift of life brings life – it brings us to life. And because we are made in the image and likeness of the God of life, this gift makes us life-givers. Through our gift of life we bring life to the world as we relate to other people and take up our responsibilities to the whole community of creation.

The gift of life that is given and received through relationship is a gift of love. God loves us into life and calls us to live life in love. To love God and be loved by God, to love others and to let others love us, to love this creation of which we are part and to receive God's love through it, is at the heart of what it means to dwell with God and to be indwelt by God.

When Jesus was asked a question about marriage he spoke about 'the beginning' (Matthew 19.8). He rooted marriage in the characteristics of God's gift of life in creation. God's gift of love, the gift that brings us life in God's likeness, enables us to share life with others and to give life to others. We will reflect more on what this might mean in relation to marriage in the next chapter. But for now it is important to see the sharing of life in love – we might call it *mutuality* – and the bringing of life through love – we might call it *fruitfulness* – are also to be found in other forms of relationship and human connection.

Jesus was not married, neither was he a parent, but he lived his life with others in mutuality and fruitfulness. He lived with his mother Mary – whose 'spirit rejoices in God' (Luke 1.47) because of the gift of her child – and Joseph and the family that grew up around them, along with the people of the towns and communities in which they lived. In adult life, Jesus gathered a community of disciples around him who travelled with him, sharing their lives together. There were many other relationships too, beyond those circles of formative companionship, some of them ready to receive life from Jesus, others determined to take life from him.

We too live our lives in an array of relationships, some of them, especially those made possible by the mobility and technolo modern life, unimaginable in Jesus' time. And in the wa COVID-19 pandemic this technology, despite its lim to be a lifeline for many during the lockdown per imposed. At the same time intimacies of to as well as great distances, and the ordinary closeness of gathering, were all marked by a danger we were not aware of before. This loss of physical connectedness that the lockdown imposed heightened our longing for it.

In different degrees, many of our relationships are marked by mutuality and fruitfulness. We are bound together in ties of family, friends and neighbours, companions, colleagues and those with whom we share a common purpose. These relationships shape our lives and through them we affect the lives of others and, in some genuinely creative ways, the world around us. We face each other bearing the scars caused by the absence of love, yet through the exchange of truth about ourselves, which is the gift of stable and more long-lasting relationships, we are given the chance to heal what has been hurt. The greater our commitment to the constancy of loving, on which such mutuality ultimately depends, the greater the fruitfulness in lives freed to 'look not to [their] own interests, but to the interests of others' (Philippians 2.4).

One form of togetherness, one that underlies the sorts of life-bringing relationships we are describing here, is friendship. Friendship is close to the heart of God's work. God calls Israel the one 'I have chosen' and 'the offspring of Abraham, my friend' (Isaiah 41.8). God speaks to Moses 'face to face, as one speaks to a friend' (Exodus 33.11).

Jesus speaks words of friendship to the people he meets, describes qualities of friendship in his parables, reaches out to those estranged from society, becoming known as 'a friend of tax collectors and sinners' (Luke 7.34), bringing people to the deepest truth about themselves. A new community of friends forms around Jesus (John 15.15). 'No one has greater love than this, to lay down his life for his friends', Jesus tells his disciples (John 15.13) as he sends them 'to bear fruit, fruit that will last' (John 15.16). When one of their number approached him in a threatening crowd 'with words and clubs' (Matthew 26.47) on a dark night of betrayal, Jesus ⁀d out to him '*Friend*, do what you are here to do' (Matthew ⁀anding at the foot of his cross, when many other friends of ⁀tered, Mary, Jesus' mother, and 'the disciple whom ⁀ 21.20), were bound together in a new family of ⁀nduring support. After Jesus' resurrection, ⁀d come upon them and the rest of Jesus' ⁀ed words of life with those to whom they were sent and, through their common life and actions, drew people from many places into this life of friendship with God.

Some of Jesus' friendships seem to have had a physical intensity about them. There is 'one of his disciples – the one whom Jesus loved' (John 13.23) reclining very close to Jesus (the King James Version says, 'leaning on Jesus' bosom') as Jesus speaks to his followers of the betrayal he will soon endure. There is Mary of Bethany, sister to Martha and Lazarus, who poured costly oil over Jesus' feet, wiping them with her hair, preparing him – as Jesus told those shocked at the extravagance, emotional and financial – for his burial (John 12.1-8). In happier times, she also sat near to him, listening intently to every word he spoke (Luke 10.39). And there is the other Mary, of Magdala, who did not abandon Jesus but stayed near his cross watching him die. The first to arrive at his tomb, distraught that his body is gone, she weeps over his grave. Even angels cannot console her (John 20.1,11-18).

We hear of other close friendships and relationships in the biblical story where fierce loyalty and fearless devotion between two people speak of the God 'abounding in steadfast love and faithfulness' (Exodus 34.6). 'Deal kindly with your servant', says David to Jonathan, 'for you have brought your servant into a sacred covenant' (1 Samuel 20.8). Jonathan replies, 'If I am still alive, show me the faithful love of the Lord' (1 Samuel 20.14). Jonathan loves David 'as he loved his own life' (1 Samuel 20.17). Jonathan steps into danger, ready to lay his life down for his friend. As they part, 'they kissed each other, and wept with each other'; and 'David wept the more' (1 Samuel 20.41). Ruth, the Moabite, clings to Naomi, her mother-in-law, refusing to be parted from her. Famine had driven Naomi and Elimelech from Bethlehem to Ruth's land beyond the Dead Sea. Now the death of her husband and sons sends her back to Bethlehem. 'Do not press me to leave you or turn back from following you!', says Ruth, vowing to her 'where you die, I will die – there will I be buried' (Ruth 1.16,17). She determines that her life will be bound to Naomi's, that the one shall protect and preserve the other.

For more about Ruth and Naomi, see Chapter 11, pages 224-225. For further discussion about friendship, see Chapter 5, pages 75-78; and for a discussion about the friendship of Jonathan and David see Chapter 9 pages 180-181.

In the early centuries of the Church, all of these biblical examples, the example of Jesus' community of friends, and supremely Jesus' own example, inspired the rise of monastic communities. Men and women covenanted themselves to communities of Christian friendship, exploring intense experiences of togetherness in different forms of common life. 'The Pastoral Prayer' of Aelred, the Cistercian Abott of Rievaulx in the twelfth century, shows how his life was given over to a community of people and how his one concern was the good of those whom Christ had 'appointed this blind guide to lead'. He desired 'to be subject to them in humility' and 'always one of them in sympathy'. And so he prayed:

> You know my heart, O Lord;
> whatever you have given to your servant,
> it is my will that it be bestowed upon them in its entirety
> and entirely used up for their benefit.
>
> Through your indescribable grace, O Lord,
> grant me patience in supporting their weaknesses,
> compassion in my love for them,
> and discernment in helping them.
> Let me learn, let your Spirit teach me,
> to console the sorrowing,
> to strengthen the fainthearted,
> to set the fallen upright,
> to be weak with the weak,
> to be indignant with the scandalized,
> to become all things to all people
> in order to win them all.[3]

Patterning himself on Jesus' life of love and service, Aelred committed not only to live with others throughout his life but to devote himself to the fulness of their lives, so that together they would become a community of love, and be at peace with God and each other. For this peace, as Augustine said, 'is perfectly ordered and wholly concordant fellowship in the enjoyment of God, and of each other in God'.[4]

We see that sort of enjoyment of God and others supremely in Jesus who, according to modern definitions, was single. In a culture where marriage was almost mandatory, as a religious responsibility and a service to society, this was unusual. Jesus' life, though, was lived in togetherness. Close to God whom he called *Abba* (his Father), born of Mary, adopted by Joseph, shaped by home and synagogue, growing into adulthood in Nazareth, calling the 'twelve' (Luke 9.1), sending the 'seventy' (Luke 10.1), drawing them and others into a new community, Jesus' life was lived with others. Jesus gave himself to others – teaching his disciples, bringing good news to the poor, healing the sick, delivering the oppressed, touching the outcast, befriending the stranger, welcoming the rejected, meeting opposition and eventually dying at their hands.

Jesus spent his life with and for others. It was through others that Jesus' understanding of his truest identity and deepest vocation grew. It is in Jesus that our creation for relationship, fellowship and communion with others comes to fulfilment. It is through him that we are redeemed from our propensity, distorted as we are by sin, to turn in on ourselves and away from God, from each other, and from the creation in which we are placed. It is through him, and through the community of friends that he gathers, that we can be drawn deeper into mutuality and fruitfulness and so deeper into God's life.

Today, some Christians, patterning themselves on Jesus' life, devote themselves to the single life as a free expression of their loving response and faithful service to God. They find that their readiness to forsake sexual intimacy and the opportunity to have children is received by God in a particular kind of intimacy and relationship with Christ, the Church and the world.

Others, though, through a variety of circumstances, find themselves single through no choice of their own and without any sense of being called by God into such a life; and for them the relationships of the church generally fail to provide the sort of mutuality and way of fruitfulness they yearn for. Their loss is real and painful. They call the church to shape its life in ways that allow the intimate love of God to be experienced more fully in the relationships of our common life.

For more discussion about singleness see Chapter 5, pages 67 and 70. For further discussion about celibacy and the consecrated life, see Chapter 12, pages 238-241.

Some Christians find themselves drawn into relationships of deep love for another person of the same sex. They find that these relationships bring them life-giving gifts of knowing and being known by another person, but that they are not affirmed and celebrated by the church. Sometimes those relationships have been sealed through the commitment of vows recognized by state and society as marriage, but not embraced by the church's teaching and practice of marriage described in the following chapter. Their loss is also real and painful. It is at least one of the reasons for what follows in Parts Two to Five of this book where we will explore further the will and way of God for all of our relationships.

> Questions about same-sex relationships and same-sex marriage are discussed in a number of places in the book. See, for example, Chapter 5, pages 71–72; Chapter 6, pages 107–109 and 115–119; Chapter 7, pages 140–144; Chapter 13, pages 279-283; and the conversations in Part Five, Scene 1, pages 381-387 and Scene 2, pages 389–396.

CHAPTER 3

The gift of marriage

God is love,
and those who live in love
live in God
and God lives in them.[5]

So begins the service of marriage
celebrated in countless churches
across the country. Believing that
God is love, Christians have seen
marriage as a gift of God in which
God's life-giving love can be known.

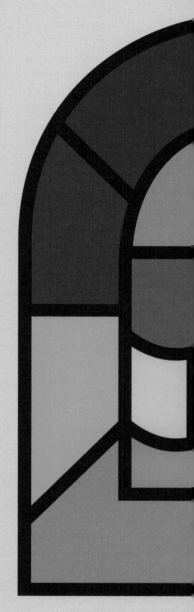

Marriage is 'an honourable estate',[6] a way and state of life that supports and brings good not only to those who enter into it but also to the lives of the children who belong to it and the life of society as a whole. It is one of the forms or conditions of human living in which God's gift of life and love is communicated to the world.

In this chapter we explain the form and content of the Christian understanding of marriage as the Church of England has received it, drawing particularly on some of the texts that shape its common life – the formularies, canons and liturgies of the church, and other key sources of influence, as well as the Bible from which they all derive their inspiration and authority.

We are conscious that, as 'part of the one, holy, catholic and apostolic Church',[7] the Church of England's doctrine of marriage shares in a common tradition among the churches. We are also conscious that some Anglicans, and some Christians in other churches, contend that this understanding of marriage is ripe for developments that allow people of the same sex also to receive its blessings and disciplines; and we recognize that in some churches developments in doctrine and practice are taking place. We will be engaging with such proposals, as well as different perspectives on sexuality more generally, and on the place of gender in human identity itself, in the rest of this book. In this chapter, however, attention is focused on the tradition the Church of England has received: its scriptural basis, and as it is set out in its liturgical and other texts.

> Marriage is discussed from a variety of perspectives in the book. For example, marriage in contemporary society is described in Chapter 5 (pages 66–72). Chapter 10 (pages 194–195) considers marriage and the experience of women. Chapter 12 (pages 244–252) explores marriage as a rule of life as well as Jesus' teaching on marriage. A discussion of marriage and the Bible can be found in Chapter 13 (pages 280–283). And in Part Five, Scene 1 there is a conversation about marriage (pages 381–387).

The foundations of marriage

The story of God's people in the Bible shows that marriage, as the church came to understand it, had a long history of development. For example, while the marriage of Ruth and Boaz (Ruth 4) may look in some respects fairly familiar to us, Jacob's marriage to both Leah and Rachel at the same time (Genesis 29.15-35) looks strange. We will see later in the book how the practice of distinctively Christian marriage has changed over history. The Church discerned in the Hebrew Scriptures a stable form of marriage even amidst the changing practices of Israel. Secure in its roots, the Christian understanding of marriage has been sufficiently supple to respond to changing cultures, and suitably rich in meaning to allow God's gift to be received in different ages, even if its purposes have been lived out with greater clarity at some times more than others. Like every form of life, it needs always to be shaped more deeply by the liberating gift of God's love that brings us into fulness of life.

Jesus, quoting the Book of Genesis, traced the roots of marriage to 'the beginning' (Matthew 19.4,8).

Have you not read that the one who made them at the beginning 'made them male and female', and said, 'For this reason a man shall leave his father and mother and be joined to his wife, and the two shall become one flesh'? So they are no longer two but one flesh. Therefore what God has joined together, let no one separate. (Matthew 19.4-6)

This is why the church's liturgy describes marriage as 'a gift of God in creation'.[8] It is a gift given to bring life and to give life. God wants us to live fully and offers us ways to live that draw on God's life of love. The joining of a man and woman in marriage is a gift given together with the gift of humanity itself. It is a gift given 'at the beginning' – before God's people Israel were formed, before the law arrived and even before sin came. It is a gift given to all peoples. The Church of England has resisted practising marriage in a way that is inaccessible to those who are not baptized and active followers of Jesus Christ. Rather it has wanted to help everyone who enters into marriage to do so more truly and deeply – to receive more fully the gift that God has given.

Marriage's form, as described by Jesus, is the union of a man and a woman, and one that is intended to last for life. That is why the church's 'canons' (its laws), echoing the liturgies which have been heard in our land for centuries, say that 'Marriage is in its nature a union permanent and lifelong, for better for worse, till death them do part, of one man with one woman, to the exclusion of all others on either side'.[9] Marriage is defined by *mutuality* (sharing life) and *fruitfulness* (bringing life), characteristics belonging also to the wider framework of relationships we explored in the last chapter. As the 1958 Lambeth Conference affirmed, marriage is 'a vocation to holiness, through which men and women share in the love and creative purpose of God'.[10]

This description of marriage is very close to one offered in the fifth century by St Augustine. Augustine spoke of *fides*, faithfulness, and *proles*, offspring, as the goods or gifts of marriage, believing that they belong to the character of marriage and are the gifts that it brings for the good of humanity. He also spoke of marriage as *sacramentum*, referring to the lifelong pledge between husband and wife, which echoes or points to God's love for the Church – a theme we will explore more fully below.[11] The Church's teaching and liturgies over the years, including those of the Church of England, have worked with these three foundational goods of marriage in different ways, sometimes emphasizing one more than others. Nevertheless, in one way or another they have remained the basis of the Christian understanding of marriage.

Mutuality – sharing life through love

The Homily on the State of Matrimony published soon after the Reformation described marriage as 'a perpetual friendship'.[12] It reflected one of 'the causes for which Matrimony was ordained'[13] set out in *The Book of Common Prayer* in its service of 'Solemnization of Matrimony': 'the mutual society, help, and comfort, that the one ought to have of the other'.[14]

'Mutual society, help and comfort'[15] run like a golden thread through the liturgies of the Church, ancient and modern, especially in the Western Church where the couple themselves are 'the ministers of the marriage'. In a public act with legal status, they marry themselves in the presence of a congregation who witness their marriage, and before a member of the clergy who proclaims that, having married each other in the sight of God, 'they are husband and wife'. Echoing the words of Jesus, the minister then declares to all:

Those whom God has joined together let no one put asunder.

The couple's marriage is effected through three interrelated stages. The first is where they consent to marry. It sounds strange that they should be asked to state very clearly and publicly at this late stage that they want to marry. Nevertheless, freely choosing to marry is an essential mark of the Christian understanding of marriage.[16] The couple make a free decision not only *to be* married but to undertake *to do* all that marriage involves: to 'love, comfort, honour and protect' each other, 'forsaking all others'.[17] They each declare their readiness to dedicate themselves to the one they have chosen to love and serve for the rest of their lives. 'Forsaking all others', they make it known that they are giving themselves over to the endless mystery of another person, determined to 'be faithful' to each other 'as long as they both shall live'.[18]

In the second stage, the couple turn their decision to marry into vows of marital commitment – promises of love, care and fidelity – as the bridegroom, taking the hand of the bride, says to her, 'I take you to be my wife'; and as the bride, taking his hand, says to the bridegroom, 'I take you to be my husband':[19]

> to have and to hold
> from this day forward;
> for better, for worse,
> for richer, for poorer,
> in sickness and in health,
> to love and to cherish,
> till death us do part;
> according to God's holy law.
> In the presence of God I make this vow.[20]

In the third stage, these solemn vows are sealed by the giving and receiving of rings and by the joining of hands. The rings are signs of their pledge to honour each other, give all that they are to each other, share all that they have with each other, and to do so 'within the love of God, Father, Son and Holy Spirit'.[21]

In this love of God, a man and woman have become bound to each other, each promising to seek not their own good, benefit or fulfilment but the very best for the other whether their resources are plenty or few, whether their health is strong or weak, when they are young with life ahead of them and when they are old with memories of their lives together. They make a solemn undertaking to serve another human being in faithful love throughout that person's life. Stability is the foundation of their mutuality. They have chosen to be 'one flesh'[22] not only in sexual union but in the giving of their whole selves to an interdependent life together (Genesis 2.24; Matthew 19.6; 1 Corinthians 11.10,11) They will often fail each other and fall from everything they are reaching for on this day. They will need to rely in the days and years that follow on each other's costly love, and so it is prayed that they may be

> **Gentle and patient, ready to trust each other, and, when they fail, willing to recognize and acknowledge their fault and to receive forgiveness.[23]**

For all this, the couple will need the help of God. After their consent, vows and exchange of rings, the blessing of their marriage therefore calls down all 'the riches of his grace' upon them.[24] God's blessing is great for those who make the promises of love, care and fidelity that marriage requires of them. God's promise of steadfast love and care is sure for them as they live out their marriage. Marriages made 'in the sight of God, and in the face of this Congregation'[25] are sustained through all the means of grace God makes available to those who seek God's help.

Fruitfulness – bringing life to others and bringing others to life

God, the source of life, gives creation the capacity to bring forth life, a gift in which human beings share. As we have seen, procreation is one of the goods of marriage identified by St Augustine. It is celebrated in the church's liturgy as God is thanked for the 'gift of sexual love by which husband and wife may delight in each other and share with [God] the joy of creating new life'.[26]

The creation of male and female and their union in 'one flesh' brings the capacity to conceive new life and to receive not only 'the gift of children'[27] but also the responsibility for 'the care of children'. The intrinsic relationship between sexual union and procreation is one of 'the causes for which Matrimony was ordained' in the church's teaching and it is at least one of the reasons why the non-consummation of a marriage is regarded as grounds for its dissolution in law. The Prayer Book's liturgy includes a prayer that carefully weaves together the themes of marital mutuality and fruitfulness, asking that the couple may be both 'fruitful in procreation of children' and – so that they can provide the environment in which their children will flourish as God wills – faithful in 'godly love and honesty'.

Nevertheless, since the first of the Reformation liturgies, the marriage services of the Church of England have recognized that not every marriage will produce children. The 1549 rite notes that some women are 'past childbearing'.[28] The Common Worship service allows for the omission of a reference to children being born, and not only for reasons of age. There are other ways than bearing children in which marriages 'share in the creative purpose of God'.[29] Through the adoption of children, the love of husband and wife can embrace a child born of other parents and provide the nurture and care the child needs to flourish. A couple can create an environment of care for those in need and of hospitality to the lonely as they find 'such fulfilment of their affection that they … reach out in love and concern for others'.[30] Theirs is to be a love that overflows to 'neighbours in need' and embraces 'those in distress'.[31]

As 'a sign of Christ's love',[32] the love that husband and wife have for each other will not remain closed within the circle of their marriage. It will go out from them to reach others, bringing 'refreshment and joy to all around them'.[33] Openness to life, not only to enjoying life together but also enabling life in others and bringing the world into fuller life, belongs to the character of marriage because that is the way of God's love. It is a love that at its truest is never self-contained but always self-giving, always generative of life, good life, in others. 'The mutual society, help, and comfort that the one ought to have of the other' does not find its end in their own self-fulfilment but rather in the good it brings to the wider society of families, communities and nations.

For many couples who have married, the desire for the gift of children seems to come from deep within them, sometimes surprising them with its strength. They long for the sexual union of their marriage to bear the fruit of a new life that they can love together, love into fulness of life, love for ever. The strength of this desire can be reflected in the pain experienced by some who find themselves unable to bear children. For other couples the gift of children comes unaccompanied by such intensity of feeling or intention and yet they find themselves receiving the gift of new life with unexpected joy and fulfilling the responsibility that has come to them with untold devotion.

For many couples a pregnancy or the decision to 'start a family' is the cause of their marriage. They believe, with the liturgy of the church, that marriage is 'the foundation of family life in which children are born and nurtured'.[34] They want their love – God's love – to 'bestow on them … the heritage and gift of children and the grace to bring them up'.[35] For others the arrival of children in their relationship will prompt them to choose to be joined in marriage for the good of their children. They believe – again with the liturgy of the church – that marriage will help them 'to nurture their family with devotion'.[36]

Tragically, in some circumstances, the gift a couple has been given is a gift they neglect or otherwise abuse with great consequences of harm for their children, for society and for themselves.

Family life has taken many shapes over human history and there are different forms of family life in our own culture and throughout the world where love and care are to be found and where people flourish. Nevertheless, the church sees in marriage the form of human life provided by God for children to receive the secure love, protection and nurture of their parents, and to learn to love. For the strength of the family 'lies in its capacity to teach us how to love',[37] and that is one of its many gifts to society. Hence, the church promotes the virtues of sustained, committed loving through marriage so that

> Each member of the family,
> in good times and in bad,
> may find strength, companionship and comfort,
> and grow to maturity in love.[38]

While the mutuality of mother and father in marriage brings good to their children, there are families that through various, and sometimes difficult, circumstances have only one active parent. Such families undoubtedly also embody love and care with great strength, and enable children to thrive. Indeed, in Christian tradition Mary, Jesus' mother, is usually depicted as a lone parent following the death of her husband Joseph.

Marriage as a sign

The liturgy of the Church of England describes marriage as 'a means of [God's] grace'.[39] It is not a sacrament in the way that baptism and the Eucharist are, but it is sacramental nonetheless. It is a form or state of life, 'instituted of God'[40] in which God promises to be found, a way in which God acts, and a place in which God is present in the ordinary, physical, tangible and sometimes messy conditions of human life. In the midst of humanity, divinity is made known to us, to make us more fully alive in God's life.[41]

There are three particular places in the New Testament that point to the way that marriage is associated with the presence and action of God in Jesus Christ – from whom 'we have all received, grace upon grace' (John 1.16).

The first is the story of a wedding in Cana, a small town in Galilee, that is told by John very near the beginning of Jesus' ministry. In the words of the Prayer Book, it was a wedding that Jesus 'adorned and beautified with his presence and first miracle that he wrought'.[42] Water is turned into wine, lavishly. Divine glory transforms ordinary human possibilities, the supernatural suffuses the natural, and Jesus, in John's carefully chosen word, provides a *sign* of who he is and what he does (John 2.11).

The second is in the Letter to the Ephesians. There, marriage is described as 'a great mystery' (Ephesians 5.32) – *mysterion* in Greek, translated *sacramentum* in Latin – 'signifying unto us', as the Prayer Book puts it, 'the mystical union that is betwixt Christ and his church'.[43] We find this reference in a profound passage that relates marital love to the love of Christ. It calls on husbands to love their wives 'just as Christ loved the church and gave himself up for her' (Ephesians 5.25). By patterning their love on the love of Christ, a love given over for the good of the other person, they grow in Christlikeness and bring good to the world. Leaving parents and others behind, and cleaving to each other, husband and wife become 'one flesh',[44] as Christ is one with his Church, the body that he cares for and nourishes as his own.

In the Eastern Church the service of marriage culminates in a crowning of the couple. This anticipates the 'crown of life' given to Jesus' followers who, as witnesses to Christ – signs, living sacraments of his ennobling love – have been 'faithful until death' (Revelation 2.10). With similar imagery, the Common Worship marriage service describes the couple's 'love for each other' as 'a crown upon their heads'.[45] Marriage enables two people, through their covenant of love, to mirror the steadfast covenant love of God described by the Hebrew prophets in vivid nuptial imagery. In Jeremiah's prophecies, for instance, God is bound to Israel as a husband to a bride. (See, for example, Jeremiah 2.1,2,31,32; 31.31-

34.) For Malachi, marriage reflects the 'covenant of life and well-being' (Malachi 2.5) made with God's people through which God's desire for 'godly offspring' (Malachi 2.15) is fulfilled.

The third place where the New Testament especially associates the work of God with the imagery of marriage is towards the close of the Book of Revelation, the last book of the Bible, echoing some of Jesus' own imagery of the coming of the Messiah and the kingdom of God (for example, Matthew 9.15; 22.1-14; John 3.29). God's people, the bride, and Christ, the bridegroom, are brought together in the vision of 'the marriage supper of the Lamb' (Revelation 19.9). In anticipation of that time when all God's people are gathered 'from every tribe and language and people and nation' (Revelation 5.9) in one communion of love with God, some couples choose to celebrate their marriage in the setting of the Eucharist, the Lord's Supper – a foretaste of that greater marriage feast.

In the age to come, said Jesus, we 'neither marry nor are given in marriage' for we will be 'children of the resurrection' (Luke 20.35,36) and death will be no more. The creative work of God in which marriage gives us a share will be done. The new creation which does not fade will have come and the covenant of which marriage is a sign will be fulfilled. Fulness of life will flow eternally from 'the spring of the water of life' (Revelation 21.6). The mutuality of man and woman in marriage will be consummated in the new heaven and new earth where God dwells with us and we – all the peoples together – dwell with God.

In these references to abundance and transformation, the imaging of Christ's union with the Church, and the final consummation of God's purpose for humanity, Scripture speaks of the ways in which the marriage of husband and wife signifies God's relation with the world.

Marriage and the gift of sex

The Bible's Song of Solomon celebrates the intensity of love between a man and a woman, its feelings of overwhelming desire and its consummation in physical delight. The love between them, the desire they have for each other, and the physical intimacy for which they yearn, awakens every dimension of their being and they are filled with life. 'Set me as a seal upon your heart, as a seal upon

your arm; for love is strong as death, passion fierce as the grave'
(Song of Solomon 8.6). These words sing to us from an ancient
society in a way that rings true with couples today, many of whom
choose these words for a reading in their own wedding and receive
them in the blessing prayed upon them.

'I am my beloved's and my beloved is mine' (Song of Solomon 6.3),
she says, her soul and spirit joined to the force of her body. 'You
have ravished my heart, my sister, my bride' (Song of Solomon 4.9),
he says with equal passion, longing for their love to lead into life
shared together.

God's good gifts of sexual desire and intimacy, with all their power
and potential for good and harm, find their proper place and freest
space in marriage. Here, the 'natural instincts and affections' that
God has planted within us are 'hallowed' and to be 'rightly directed'
for the purposes of love:[46]

> Marriage is given,
> that with delight and tenderness they may know each other in love,
> and through the joy of their bodily union,
> may strengthen the union of their hearts and lives.[47]

The Song of Solomon rejoices in love, desire and sexual expression
without any obvious reference to procreation. Although we
should not lose sight of the likely consequences of intercourse in
conception, and all its implications for the family and community
which the Song's ancient world would have known, the primary
reference in its poetry of love is to sex as God's gift for the
expression of the couple's love and the deepening of their life
together.

As we will see later in this book, after a long journey of deliberation
in the Anglican Communion, the 1930 Lambeth Conference agreed
that 'other methods [than abstinence] may be used' in order 'to limit
or avoid parenthood'.[48] Nevertheless, the Conference emphasized
the intrinsic connection between intercourse and procreation,
making clear that as well as sex serving the love between the
couple, its generative capacities for the life of another belong also
to its character and function, as indeed is implied by the practice
of contraception itself. So if sex serves mutuality, it clearly, under
many conditions, serves fruitfulness. The imagery of husband and
wife becoming 'one flesh' (Matthew 19.5,6) which Jesus lifts from

Genesis 2, echoes the original creation and commission of humanity in Genesis 1 where:

God created humankind in his image,
in the image of God he created them;
male and female he created them.
God blessed them, and God said to them,
'Be fruitful and multiply, and fill the earth.' (Genesis 1.27,28)

The action of sexual intercourse joins a man and woman together for the purposes of both love and procreation.

The life-giving joining of bodies in sexual intimacy also serves the sacramental character of marriage. We can see this mirrored in the giving and receiving of a ring each to the other as 'a sign of our marriage', symbols of 'unending love and faithfulness',[49] physical signs carrying great emotional and spiritual value. This exchange of rings points to the sharing of bodies – a profound physicality of mutuality that demands great trust (1 Corinthians 7.3,4). The 'delight and tenderness of sexual union',[50] as the liturgy describes it, powerfully conveys the reality signified by the rings: the giving of all that a man and woman are, the sharing of all that they have, honouring, adoring, revering and respecting each other as they receive and return a hallowed gift. Where this 'vow and covenant'[51] is honoured and enacted, bodies are not commodified (as by some forms of commerce) or idolised (as they are by some forms of religion), enslaved (as they are by some forms of criminality), weaponised (as they are by some forms of war and conflict) or just objectified (as they are in many forms of human practice). They are dignified with immense worth. Joined by God, sanctified by God's grace, they are created for life and life-giving together.

More than that, bodies joined in this kind of passionate, tender, faithful mutuality are an icon that opens to us a reality beyond themselves. As Jewish and Christian readers of the Song of Solomon have seen over the centuries, its story of desire and faithful loving points beyond the couple's yearning for each other to the human longing for God and God's delight in humanity: 'I am my beloved's and his desire is for me' (Song of Solomon 7.10).

Further discussions about the gift of sex, including an exploration of the Song of Solomon, can be found in Chapter 12 (pages 256-257). Chapter 5 (pages 78-85) considers sex in contemporary society and Chapter 6 (pages 114-115) explores the relationship between sex and well-being. Chapter 7 (page 148) reviews the development of ideas about sex and contraception within the wider context of the Anglican Communion.

Marriage – the gift that can be lost

Christian life in all its forms is called to witness to the faithfulness of God. Marriage is a particular form of witness resonant in many distinctive ways of the steadfast love of God. But it is not the only one. We looked in the last chapter at monastic life with its own particular form of vowed togetherness that speaks of God's fidelity. Other relationships witness in their own way to the faithfulness of God – relationships of responsible loving and caring, serving and supporting; commitments of family and friendship; and other conditions of life lived truly and faithfully. Paul's encouragement to the married and the unmarried can be applied to many of our relationships in life: 'each has a particular gift from God, one having one kind and another a different kind' (1 Corinthians 7.7).

All forms of human witness to God's faithfulness, however, are only as strong as their share in the perfect obedience and fidelity of Christ. For most of us, most of the time, our share in Christ's strength is thin, and we remain weak. Marriages miss their mark in many ways every day. They do not always bring life and give life. At times they corrode and corrupt life. Sometimes spouses drain life from each other and suppress life in others, even damaging the children they have received into their lives. That is why in the liturgies of marriage, after the vows and blessing come the prayers, with the Lord's Prayer as their summation:

> **Forgive us our sins**
> **as we forgive those who sin against us.**
> **Lead us not into temptation**
> **but deliver us from evil.**[52]

When Jesus challenged the ease with which husbands could divorce their wives in his culture, the disciples were disgruntled. 'It is better not to marry' (Matthew 19.10), they responded. Divorce was a dangerous thing for women in Jesus' day, often leaving them destitute, victims of the arbitrary decisions of men. It was right for the disciples to be faced with the intentions of God 'in the beginning' (Matthew 19.4,8). It is also right for us today, in our very different culture, to acknowledge that divorce carries heavy consequences for those involved, and that children in particular can pay a high cost. So we too can be overwhelmed by the serious commitments expected of two people in marriage, especially when we set them against the fragility of human loving and the longevity and complexity of modern life. We know that marriages run into trouble, regularly. We may accept that marriage is 'an honourable estate instituted at the time of man's innocency'[53] but we may wonder with Jesus' first disciples whether the loss of that innocency makes the Christian understanding of marriage an impossible ideal.

For most of us that sort of questioning is far from theoretical but is born of our own experience of life or our involvement in the life of others. The Bishops' 1999 Teaching Document on Marriage speaks wisely and is worth quoting quite fully:

> God often meets us when we come to the edge of our own capacities and stand on the brink of unknown possibilities and dangers. He meets us as free and generous mercy, and as demanding holiness; these two characteristics are not in tension or contradiction, but complementary. The scope of God's holiness is the scope of his mercy, and the more we are ready to open ourselves to the demand, the more we will know of his generosity, forgiving us where we have failed and granting us success where we thought we were bound to fail. The reason that the church continues to insist on the highest expectations of married couples, when so many of our contemporaries are content to treat the matter lightly, is that much more than marriage is lost if we let the scope of the demand and generosity of God slip from our sight. But if we respond to them seriously, we are changed by them; and our lives acquire hopefulness and patience in the knowledge of his love.[54]

That is why the prayers for the newly married couple in the Common Worship service ask God to:

> Give them patience with their failures
> and persistence with their hopes.
> In gentleness let them be tender with each other's dreams
> and healing of each other's wounds.[55]

It is also why the family and friends of the couple are asked in the service whether they will:

> Support and uphold them in their marriage
> now and in the years to come.

What happens, though, where there is such betrayal in a marriage (such as the 'unchastity' (Matthew 19.9) that Jesus describes) or desertion (such that Paul describes when one partner is abandoned by another (1 Corinthians 7.15)) or breakdown (such that the marriage has reached a point where it is deemed beyond repair) or some other causes of damage (such as those that are so serious they are abusive)? Although with all Christians, the Church of England believes that the marriage 'promises are made unconditionally for life',[56] it accepts that marriages that have been made can also be broken, sometimes by one partner and sometimes by both. It respects the view of couples who believe that their marriage has come to its own end and that the marital gift of love and commitment has been lost. It recognizes circumstances where fuller life may come only when that is formally acknowledged, and the possibility of a new beginning is opened up.

The Church of England – where the conditions are right – allows clergy – where their consciences allow them – to solemnize the marriage of those who choose, with due regard to the past and full responsibility to the future, to marry again and for their bishops to support them, praying to the God who is 'rich in mercy' (Ephesians 2.4):

> **Pour out your blessings upon [them]**
> **that may be joined in mutual love and companionship,**
> **in holiness and commitment to each other.**[57]

In this way, the church seeks to witness to the biblical call for marriage to reflect God's 'covenant of life and well-being' (Malachi 2.5), to the challenges of human life known so well to the biblical writers, and to the God who, 'rich in mercy', is always ready to redeem and make new.

Christian faith, realistic as it is about the reality of sin in human life and our tendency to turn in on ourselves, believes in the greater power of divine love at work in our relationships, including 'this man and this woman' about to be joined together in 'holy Matrimony'.[58] The church rejoices that it is an 'honourable estate instituted of God'[59] and 'a means of his grace':[60] a form of human living and loving in which God dwells and where two people, their family and their society receive 'grace upon grace' (John 1.16). When received well and cherished, nourished and nurtured, supported by others and sustained by God's other means of grace in the life of the church, the gift of marriage brings life with fulness and gives life with abundance.

CHAPTER 4

The gift of learning

We have seen that God's gift of life is given and received in and through relationships, ways of togetherness with God, with each other, and with the whole created order. We have seen how Jesus models what it means to be a friend, and we have explored the Christian understanding of marriage as the Church of England has received it.

We are now ready to think about the many questions that we have as individuals and as a church about human identity, sexuality, relationships and marriage.

How do we go about living this gift of life together in the everyday realities of today? To whom or to what do we go for wisdom, insight and guidance when faced with new contexts and new realities? How do we respond to the questions, challenges and alternative interpretations which the received understanding of marriage now faces? And how do we, as the Church of England, go about learning together about these things in love and faith? In this chapter we describe the thinking behind the learning journey that this book invites readers to make.

In Chapter 1, with the help of John's Gospel, we met Jesus, the teacher, who teaches us how he will give his own life in order that we might have this abundant, eternal life. But 'when many of the disciples heard it, they said, "This teaching is difficult; who can accept it?"' (John 6.60) and many stopped following him. When Jesus asks the twelve whether they, too, wish to leave him, they reply: 'Lord, to whom can we go? You have the words of eternal life' (John 6.68). As far as the disciples were concerned, there was only one teacher to whom they could or would entrust themselves.

The cornerstone: sources of authority

**See, I am laying in Zion a stone,
a cornerstone chosen and precious;
and whoever believes in him will not be put to shame. (1 Peter 2.6)**

It is to the living Word, Jesus Christ, the 'chief cornerstone' (Psalm 118.22; Matthew 21.42) that we too go to be taught, and from whom we learn, by the power and guidance of the Holy Spirit. Jesus is the one who offers us the gift of learning: 'Take my yoke upon you, and learn from me; for I am gentle and humble in heart, and you will find rest for your souls. For my yoke is easy, and my burden is light' (Matthew 11.29,30).

So it is to the Bible that we turn to find what Christians agree is a uniquely authoritative account of who Jesus is, how he lived and what he taught. It sets the story of Jesus in the story of God's revelation and saving activity through the people of Israel and celebrates God's work in the creation of the world. The Bible is central to the life of the whole church community and to the lives of individual Christian disciples. This collection of history books, poetry, wisdom literature, stories and letters contains everything that we need for salvation, for receiving the gift of abundant life together. It show us how to flourish truly as human beings in the complex, confusing and changing realities of our everyday lives.

Just as the Bible permeates the life of the Church and the lives of Christian believers as it is read, taught, studied, sung and prayed, so the Bible permeates this book. Telling the story of the God of Israel who becomes flesh in Jesus Christ, it becomes the cornerstone of our learning together as we return to it again and again, confident that in its pages we will find the resources that we need for perceiving together the mind of Christ for his Church.

As we do so we will discover that making connections between what we read in the Bible and the questions we bring to it about identity, sexuality, marriage and relationships is not a simple matter. We will need to explore how the identities and contexts of the Bible's many human authors shape the texts we read and how our own contexts and the questions we put to the Bible affect our interpretation of it. As with all human understanding, our knowledge of the Bible is provisional and our understanding partial. We need to read it responsibly, paying attention to the voices of reason and mercy. We need to read it together as the people of God, listening to the wisdom and perspectives of others, including those who have spent their lives studying the Bible. We need the help of experts to understand the complexities of translating the Bible and of appropriating its historical context to that of our contemporary world. We need help to understand how the Church has interpreted the Bible through the ages. Above all, we need to listen to the Spirit of Christ as together we search the Scriptures for wisdom and guidance.

Much more will be said in Part Four about the different ways in which Christians interpret the Bible in relation to human identity, sexuality, relationships and marriage, and about the different conclusions we reach. These differences are important precisely because of the particular place that the Bible has in our Christian faith: we profess a 'faith that is uniquely revealed in the Holy Scriptures'.[61] They are deeply felt because the subject matter is so personal to our understanding of who we are and who God is. And they make new demands on us in calling us to listen well to voices that we may not have attended to before as we seek together to follow Christ, especially the voices of LGBTI+ people. This book will challenge us to not shy away from these differences. It invites us to find the courage to explore our different and inevitably partial perspectives and biases, of which we will not be aware, with humility and with love, trusting in the faithfulness of the God who travels alongside us. Engaging with this book invites us to find God afresh within and amidst our differences.

The Bible is central to the life of the Church. It was the Church that saw how some early Christian writings seemed to be so God-given that they could be received in the same way as the God-breathed Scriptures (2 Timothy 3.16 (NIV)) of their Hebrew heritage. A living tradition of interpretation of these writings soon emerged, expressed in rules of faith and creedal statements, giving rise to liturgies, canons and formularies, explored in the Church's worship, witness and common life. Our learning in this book, therefore, is set against this backdrop of centuries of Spirit-inspired wisdom as we seek to live faithfully as the body of Christ in the twenty-first century. This is about more than being true to the past: it is about the belief that the same God who has been faithfully active among his people through the centuries continues to be so today. As with the Bible, however, disagreements are likely to arise about the nature and interpretation of this inheritance of faith – and these disagreements will have consequences for the way that Christian faith is lived out in the life of every church today.

As we attend to the Bible and to the Church's living tradition, we use God's gift of reason to help us understand and find meaning in both the Bible and the doctrines of the Church. This, too, is integral to our learning, enabling us to read and analyse texts, making connections between one text and another, and between texts and our observations, knowledge and experience of the world around us. Reason infused with the Spirit of Christ, applied to the Bible and accompanied by the godly reflection of Christian believers past and present, leads us into the wisdom that we seek for our particular situations and circumstances. We desire nothing less than to 'be transformed by the renewing of [our] minds, so that [we] may discern what is the will of God – what is good and acceptable and perfect' (Romans 12.2).

All this was articulated in the originating documents of the Living in Love and Faith initiative which committed those involved

> to work prayerfully, attending faithfully to holy Scripture and acknowledging its authority, within the community, tradition and pastoral practice of the church in the reality of the world using God's gifts of reason and wisdom shaped by the Spirit, in order to seek and discern the mind of Christ for the church and the world.

See Chapters 13 and 14 (pages 273-330) for more detailed discussions about the place of the Bible and the church in Christian deliberations about identity, sexuality, relationships and marriage.

Touchstones: the pursuit of truth

The biblical narrative is cosmic in its scope. The triune God preceded anything that we know or could imagine. All space, time, matter and knowledge come from God. As we have seen, this is the message of Genesis 1 and 2 and of the opening chapter of John's Gospel: 'All things came into being through [the Word], and without him not one thing came into being' (John 1.3). All reality is God's reality and so we apply that same reason that we mentioned above to the pursuit of truth through the sciences, history, and the arts. That is why in our learning together we also draw on the insights and knowledge of other disciplines which enrich our understanding of human identity, sexuality, marriage and relationships. This book is an invitation to engage in this interdisciplinary learning with confidence, wonder and humility because we are accompanied by the God who is the source of all life and truth.

History

The birth and resurrection of Jesus were pivotal moments in the history of the universe: God became incarnate at a particular time and place, the culmination of God's continuing involvement in the world since it began. In the resurrection of Jesus, the new creation, the kingdom of God, was inaugurated, transforming our understanding of history.

In Jesus, we are given a foretaste of God's purposes for the whole world, and we long for the fulfilment of those purposes in the new creation. For now, however, we live 'between the times'. We look around us for signs that point us to the power of God's redeeming love, and that can help us imagine and understand that love more fully. We also look around us to see the ways that love has been misunderstood, ignored, and betrayed, seeking to understand more fully our own propensity to turn away from that love. And the study of history is part of this. As we pursue our questions about human identity, sexuality and relationships, we can learn a great deal from the ways in which those realities were experienced and lived out by people in the past. We can find new perspectives and role models which act as signposts to God's new creation. We can find abuses of power which point in quite the other direction. We can see how marginalized and excluded voices have contributed to redemptive change in the course of history. We can learn to understand better the dynamics that have shaped our own cultural worlds.

Learning from history is not straightforward, however. How history is told depends on who is telling it and what questions are asked of it. Historical evidence is always incomplete, provisional and open to different interpretations. We have to ask who produced the evidence, why and for whom. New evidence may change our picture of particular events. Equally, we need to be aware of our own subjectivity as we project our fears or value systems onto other ages and cultures. Nevertheless, studying history invites us to see our own questions and struggles within the longer arc of time and to look for traces of God's transforming love at work.

Science

The Christian faith is a faith that rejoices in the material world. The world's seemingly infinite diversity and intricate interdependence reflect the glory of its creator. The work of the sciences, therefore, is a means of enlarging and enriching our understanding of the cosmos and therefore of the God who made it. The sciences' questions are not so much about meaning or purpose, but about how and why things are as they are in the material world: the sciences help us to interpret the Bible and to see how they and theology are complementary pursuits of truth that deepen our understanding of God, ourselves and the world. Science and theology belong together and need to be pursued together.

But, as we have seen from our learning from the Bible, from the church's tradition and from history, our knowledge is always incomplete and seeking greater understanding. There is always more to learn, and what we think we know may be interpreted differently by different people or in different circumstances. This is the case for science just as much as it is for other disciplines. Scientific knowledge is always provisional not only because there is always more to know but because scientists are constantly questioning whether what seems right today is really the full picture. Scientific knowledge is structured around hypotheses, models and concepts that may be invalidated by empirical evidence. New models need to be made to fit 'unexpected' observations, until they, too, are discarded by new evidence.

As with other areas of knowledge, our scientific understanding of the world may be skewed by the questions we choose to ask, by what we choose to observe, or by how we interpret those observations. Scientific findings can unwittingly be used as 'proof' of a particular viewpoint, when, in fact, the evidence is far from clear because it is not replicable or because it makes cause and effect claims on shaky evidence. The social and psychological sciences are particularly vulnerable to such misuse because they may challenge not only our understanding but our behaviours as individuals or as a society. They therefore may be even more prone to biased interpretations or inferences about cause and effect.

Another reason why scientific research may not offer the kinds of definitive answers we might be hoping for is because scientific investigations often uncover greater complexity and diversity which lead to the need for further research before conclusions can be reached. This is what makes scientific endeavour so fascinating and awe-inspiring – but frustrating for people who want simple or authoritative answers where none are to be found. Think, for example, about the question of whether sexual orientations are genetically or environmentally determined. Most psychological traits are determined by a complex interplay of genes and environment, and sexual orientation would appear to be no exception. It is not an either/or question.

This is not to say that nothing can be said: far from it. As peer-reviewed scientific investigations progress, a weight of evidence emerges in one direction or another, and it is this weighted evidence that we rely on when discussing scientific matters in this book. The sciences reveal things concerning the world and human nature which we can be confident about, and which we need properly to bear in mind when thinking theologically.

While neither history nor the sciences alone yield the wisdom for leading Christlike lives of love and faith, respectful and informed engagement with them is vital for the theological task. This book invites us to a humble, informed and respectful engagement with a range of disciplines in the belief that this will enhance and deepen our learning together.

> For a discussion about the place of the biological and behavioural sciences in the study of human identity, sexuality and relationships see Chapter 6 (pages 103–120). The role of science and natural knowledge in Christian understanding is explored in Chapter 15 (pages 333–340).

Stepping stones: connecting with context

Jesus was born in a particular place, with its particular culture, politics and religion. Into this context he proclaimed the coming of the kingdom of God. The Gospel of John invites us to notice Jesus' relationship with the world. It is a world of darkness into which Jesus brings light and life (John 1.3-5), a world he loves and for which he dies (John 3.16). It is a world that he has conquered (John 16.33) which yet remains distinct from the kingdom of God (John 18.36). The disciples do not belong to the world but are called to be in it (John 17.14,15). As children of the kingdom they are called to live in a world that contains weeds as well as wheat (Matthew 13.38).

How does Jesus navigate a world that is a complex mix of justice and injustice, of power and oppression, of truth and falsehood and everything in between? How does he negotiate proclaiming the kingdom of God and the call to repentance while living alongside the practices and powers of secular and religious authorities? The Gospel accounts are full of surprises: a Roman centurion is praised for his faith (Luke 7.9); Jesus welcomes a corrupt tax official (Luke 19.1-10); Jesus accepts physically intimate expressions of devotion that defy social mores (John 12.3-8).

In this book we seek the wisdom of God for life together in the twenty-first century. How are we to negotiate the world in which we find ourselves? What are the prevailing visions of a flourishing life in our world? How are these enacted in people's relationships and sexual behaviour? Where is there darkness and where do we see light? Where is power being abused and where are the values and virtues of God's kingdom being lived out? Whose voices are we listening to or silencing? How far should the gospel be at home in this culture? How can we communicate our Christian vision for human flourishing in ways that are meaningful? How can we inhabit the gospel authentically and faithfully as communities of Christian believers in our culture today?

In order to begin to address these questions we need to look carefully at the world we inhabit, remembering that it is a world in which we ourselves are embedded. So while we will try to describe what is going on in our society as objectively as we can, we will need to be attentive to our own tendencies to make judgements or draw conclusions which may or may not be shaped by our Christian faith. We may, for example, find ourselves overwhelmed by the pace of change around us or by our anger about the church's resistance to change. The visceral and intimate nature of the subject may trouble us in a way that arouses powerful emotions we find hard to express. We may find ourselves silenced because the 'political' nature of the conversation prohibits us from saying what we think or feel. We may find ourselves threatened by the findings of biological or social sciences or by technologies that can change our bodies in previously unimagined ways.

And yet our task now, as always, is to see the culture we inhabit through the lens of the gospel. We are seeking a way of living in the world as citizens of heaven (Philippians 3.20; 1 Peter 2.9-12). We are seeking to live together as a church, faithfully and prophetically. For this we need to listen to the perceptions of Christians whose lives have been shaped differently from us in order to begin to tease out together what is truly good and what is bad, what is creative and what is destructive, what is and what isn't conformed to God's kingdom in our culture today. The Church is international, so we will also need the help of disciples from other parts of the world, who live in other cultures and situations, and who can speak with fresh insight into our own. The Church is universal, so we will need the guidance of other Christians living out their faith in other churches. The Church is not isolated: there are others who seek to walk the path of God. We always have more to learn from 'the true light, which enlightens everyone' (John 1.9) and which came into the world: Jesus Christ.

> For further discussion about the place of cultural context in Christian deliberations about identity, sexuality, relationships and marriage, see Chapter 16 (pages 341–352).

Living stones: lived experience

The gospels tell us about the historically pivotal events of Jesus' birth, life, death, resurrection and ascension. And they tell of a Jesus whose teaching is repeatedly described as astounding and authoritative (Matthew 7.28, 13.54, 22.33, Mark 1.22, 6.2, Luke 4.32). But in amongst these accounts of momentous events and transcendent wisdom, the gospel writers draw our attention to a multitude of details about Jesus' encounters with people and the stories he tells. They reveal a Jesus who was a keen observer of human behaviour. He notices how guests behave at dinner parties (Luke 14.7), how much money they give away (Luke 21.1,2), what children do when they play (Luke 7.32), how frazzled people can get when entertaining (Luke 10.41) or how happy they are when they've found something they had lost (Luke 15.9). They tell of a Jesus who is instinctively compassionate when faced with the suffering of illness (Mark 6.56), of social exclusion (Luke 19.1-10), of regret (Luke 7.38-50), or of grief (John 11.33). They tell of a Jesus who asks questions: 'What are you looking for?' (John 1.38), 'Why do you call me good?' (Luke 18.19), 'Do you want to be made well?' (John 5.6), 'Is it lawful to do good or to do harm on the sabbath, to save life or to destroy it?' (Luke 6.9).

This book, too, invites us to notice the particularity of people's lived experiences by telling their stories. Much as in the gospels, these 'Encounters' – clustered in between the different parts of the book – interrupt and disrupt the flow of biblical, theological, historical and scientific exploration. They are the stories of real, contemporary disciples of Christ who are seeking to live in the abundant life that Jesus offers. They are stories of people who are trying to enact their faith, to live their lives in Christ and set their hope on Christ. They are stories told as each has chosen to tell it and they are stories that raise questions that form part of our learning journey together. They are stories asking us to discern where God is active in human lives.

The stories remind us that as we explore what it means to be human, to be sexual, to belong to the people of God, we are exploring questions that have real-life consequences. Our learning is not just in our heads, but it is also in our hearts and in the living of our lives. Our discussions are not just about ideas or concepts, theories or theologies. They are not about disembodied biblical texts, but about the holy ground of people's real lives. We do our theology and learning in one another's company as disciples of Christ.

The stories invite us to step out of ourselves, out of our own world and concerns into those of another. They invite us to listen actively and attentively, laying down for a moment our own anxieties and fears in order to be present to another. In so doing we create a space for the work of God's Spirit in us. We are exercising *faith* in the reality of Christ in each person, and in the possibility of Christ addressing us through the life of another. By paying attention to the stories of people who have different, and even opposing, understandings of abundant life, we are taking a first step towards something that we do not yet see and cannot perhaps even imagine: a community of believers whose love for one another testifies to the living Christ. The book invites readers into this act of hopeful, attentive listening as an act of holy *love*.

Without exception, these lived experience stories encompass both joy and pain. They tell of the joy of human love and of being made new in Christ. And they tell of wounds, sin and failure. Some wounds are inflicted by others, perhaps even by others in the Church. They may be wounds caused by rejection, prejudice, ignorance or the abuse of power. Other wounds are internal. They are harder to identify or name, but they are none the less real and are the source of confusion, pain and mental distress. All the stories are about people seeking to be transformed into the likeness of Christ (2 Corinthians 3.18). As we'll see in chapter 10, the Bible, too, tells many stories of complexity, diversity, imperfection and messiness – and often without passing explicit judgements.

The stories remind us that we are learning together as a community of disciples in all its complexity and diversity and its imperfection and messiness. They call us to be courageously honest about the diversity that exists among the people of God in the Church of England while resisting the temptation to simplify or to control, holding back from the impulse to judge and to exclude. Instead, they call us to receive one another as gifts, gifts through whom God is at work refining and shaping those who seek to follow Christ. We look for the living Christ in the midst of the complexity, imperfection, messiness and glory of our lives and life together.

Stories are powerful and memorable. Our purpose, however, is not to use them as a basis for validating a particular way of life. They are not by themselves the means by which the church will arrive at a Christian ethic of sexuality or of gender identity. Rather they are testimonies of how people have understood their lives in relation to God – understandings that have been honed in the course of a life, but which are, of course, always incomplete and in need of fuller truth. We are invited to attend to them seriously and to allow the Holy Spirit to question our assumptions and raise possibilities for what faithfulness can look like: possibilities that we will need to reflect on and test in our hearts and minds.

Attending to the stories – both in this book and in the films that form part of the resources – has the potential to transform us. They can help us to follow the way of Christ, in being truly human in our deliberations and learning and discernment as we engage with these resources. These 'Encounters' are there to drive us deeper into Christ, to make us hungrier for the living bread and thirstier for the living water that Christ offers. They are there to deepen our desire to be more Christlike in our life together as individuals and as a church.

'If you keep my commandments, you will abide in my love' (John 15.10). By listening to lived experiences we acknowledge that theology that isn't lived isn't theology, for 'the Word became flesh and lived among us' (John 1.14). The authenticity of our faith is in our lived obedience together as followers of Christ.

Stories of people's lived experience are introduced on page 51 and can be found at the end of each Part of the book. Questions about how experience, conscience, prayer and guidance relate to the way we approach these subjects can be found in Chapters 17 and 18 (pages 353–368).

In these opening chapters we began with God. We were reminded that all of creation, and all of life, are gifts from God. All of creation is made by God's love, and it is made for the purposes of God's love. As creatures of a loving God, we are called into relationship – with one another, with the created order, and with God. In Part Three we will explore further how this gift of relationship fits within the Christian story.

We saw how the particular relationship called marriage is also a gift from God. We traced the origins of the Church of England's received teaching on marriage as a lifelong union between a man and a woman. We saw that marriage is a gift that is rooted in creation and in the history of the relationship between God and the people of God both before and after Jesus' life on earth. We saw that its hallmarks are mutuality and fruitfulness – and that they both unite marriage with, and distinguish it from, other kinds of relationship. We saw how it is a sign that enlarges and deepens our understanding of God's love in Jesus Christ for us, the people of God, the church. We noticed its modulations in response to context and human weakness. We will look much more closely at some of this material later in the book – exploring Jesus' teaching on marriage in **Part Three** and other biblical teaching about marriage in **Part Four**.

We also began to see some of the ways the Bible, theology, the sciences and experience support and equip us, as we seek to learn about all these topics. We will delve into these questions more deeply in **Part Four**.

Part One has provided, therefore, the backdrop for our explorations about identity, sexuality, relationships and marriage.

In **Part Two**, we will continue that journey by paying attention to developments in the world around us.

Encounters

Meet DAMON, CHERRY, JORDAN AND DAN

This group gathers regularly to support each other in their emerging leadership roles in various estate churches around the city. On this occasion, they used their time together to talk about identity, sexuality, relationships and marriage.

They began by sharing stories of encounters at church where they have extended welcome to people who expected rejection or had experienced it elsewhere. Jordan helped a young girl rejected by her family for being bisexual: 'We just prayed about it. And I think she went out a bit calmer and relaxed.' She goes on: 'I'm not called to judge her. I'm just called to give her some compassion and some love and friendship.'

'It's a conversation you've got to have; you cannot hide what's going on in the world.'

Cherry describes a gay young man working as a carer who brought congregation members to church as part of his job. 'One week he said "I don't think I'd be welcome in your church." I said, "Oh, you would. You'd be made really welcome here."'

Damon says: 'However kind or nice we all are individually, or not, somehow we're in an institution which isn't perceived in that way ... and has rules which exclude people at different levels.'

Talk moves to the importance of not judging and of 'meeting people, not their issues', citing stories when this approach led to individuals coming to faith and being embedded in church life – a single mum wanting her son baptized but afraid of rejection because each of her three children had a different father; a divorced couple who came to Jesus after being invited to be part of church life rather than just use the church building for getting married.

A few people – single and divorced – comment on the assumption within church that marriage is the norm, and the pressure associated with that. Dan observes that Jesus was single and 'no one told him to join Dateline!'

The group discusses how it's important for the church to be pastorally equipped to support all kinds of people and be ready to actively participate in society. Jordan puts it like this: 'It's a conversation you've got to have; you cannot hide what's going on in the world. It's out there.'

They observe what a privilege and opportunity it would be if young people, those struggling and in difficulty, felt they could come into church, be accepted and talk.

Meet some people at ALL HALLOW'S CHURCH

I was met at the railway station by Mary. We struck up a lively conversation about mutual Africa interests: Mary has been a Church Mission Society mission partner for decades. The vicar welcomed us into the vicarage, where we found the others already ensconced in the comfortable sofas ready for our conversation. The vicar wished us well and left the room.

The conversation begins with Scripture. 'Everything that happens in life falls under Scripture,' says Clare. Mary refers us to a recent sermon series which included titles such as 'Who am I?' 'Is gender fluid?' 'Who can I marry?' 'Is following Jesus good news for the LGBTI+ community?' and talks about how the sermons were 'done with such love. We're all sinners in need of the love of Jesus and the transforming work of the Holy Spirit.'

But the conversation quickly moves on to what genuine welcome means in practice. Everyone is eager to express their deep desire for people to feel truly welcomed. 'Please come and talk to us; let us know what it's like to be you. We want you to be here.' 'That doesn't of course, compromise what we believe the Bible says,' notes Amy. 'And actually, I think those two things are held together really well. The Bible wants us to speak the truth as God's given it to us in his word. But we must do it in a genuinely loving way; we are going to put action behind those words and really seek to help you in whatever struggle it is that you have.' 'The point is no one is good enough. And that's why we are all here.'

> 'We're all sinners in need of the love of Jesus and the transforming work of the Holy Spirit.'

Samuel verbalises a concern about how welcome is perceived not as 'how friendly and polite and welcoming and warm we are to people, but whether or not we accept their lifestyle choices.' That doesn't, of course, mean demanding a change in lifestyle choices as a condition of welcome. But it might mean being challenged at some point – and challenge is never comfortable for anyone.

Samuel reminds them that this isn't easy. 'It's been helpful for us as a church just to be clear that, in saying we wouldn't promote or celebrate same-sex marriages or gender transitions, we are doing that out of love for people, out of a genuine desire to see them flourish. Because it's really easily misinterpreted as bigotry, and not without some foundation, because lots of churches are quite unwelcoming.'

Mary puts the conversation within the context of her own experience as a single woman. 'And if we really care, as a people of God, here in this community, we don't want them to carry on feeling that being free to define ourselves as we want is the way ahead. That's building your life on sand. I've been single all my life, and sometimes that's a struggle. The world says, "Go and have fun. Have any relationships you like." No, if I'm single, I'm celibate for the Lord. And that's where my identity is [in Christ], and that's who I am, and I'm totally at peace and content with that situation.'

Nigel identified the church's tendency to put married family life on a pedestal, which means single people or married couples without children are easily diminished. Both ways of life are gifts to be celebrated, he says. All of this, he reflects, points to the uncomfortableness of too easily talking about them and us in relation to LGBTI+ people. Everyone is included in 'them' and 'us'. 'Perhaps some of my discomfort,' says Nigel, 'is that we're making the LGBTI+ issue special [...] which troubles me.'

The discussion concluded on one more area that the group agreed the church could improve on: prayer – both 'prayer that we would be welcoming to people, but also prayers for the issues in the Church of England surrounding it.'

Meet ESTHER

Esther grew up in a fishing town, one of ten children with a dad who worked on the fish docks and a mum who stayed at home 'looking after all of us' – hard physical labour. Esther remembers her mum talking about God and praying during the many crises they faced as a family. She also learnt about God and Jesus by attending Sunday School.

The family had to contend with one tough situation after another. Esther recalls that her dad would be violent towards her mum if he drank too much. This ended when her mum threatened to leave if it ever happened again. Terrible tragedy struck when one of Esther's brothers died at the age of four after taking their father's medicine. A short time later Esther's niece died of pneumonia. In addition two of Esther's sisters had abusive husbands.

It was important for the whole family to be near each other and see each other a lot. Esther's boyfriend, Bill, was a help in crises: 'He was a great support at a very difficult time. [He] used to come and visit me. He was really a godsend.'

She and Bill had a January wedding followed by their first child in December the same year, and another pregnancy straight away. They were very hard up – with few resources and just managing with food. They had three children in all and it was important to Esther to thank God for the safe deliveries and also to have the babies christened – although she describes this as being 'superstitious' and the 'done thing', saying 'Although I went to church as a child, I didn't really understand what church was really about, if I'm honest.'

> 'There was a strength in me and I know now it was the Holy Spirit.'

They moved, getting a new house on a new estate and finding new friends. 'We were all in the same boat, none of us had much money, but we all helped each other, and it was a really good community.' As the children grew up their fortunes changed for the better. 'My husband got a good job at the gas board, and then I got a job with social services. We were getting a bit more affluent. I did have a happy marriage.'

Esther's mum died suddenly which was a shock: 'I thought, my goodness, how am I going to cope without my mum? And then, my world seemed to cave in.' This led to Esther seeking God more, with the support of a local vicar. She remembers a 'fight within herself' that she later identified as spiritual warfare. She also remembers 'There was a strength in me and I know now it was the Holy Spirit.'

The churchwarden gave her a Bible: 'I just used to open it up at random and it [read] "Do not be afraid, trust me." I thought that's not a coincidence, I know it isn't. I'm going to try my utmost not to be afraid.' She asked God to come into her life and Christ to be her Saviour at this time. 'I can honestly say I'm not ashamed to say that I love Jesus.'

As she talks, Esther recounts many stories of God's faithful protection and goodness in difficult circumstances. Perhaps the greatest trauma

Esther went through was when she learnt of her husband's conviction and imprisonment. It was a profound shock, especially as 'everybody thought the world of him; he'd do anything for anybody'. It was their eldest son who had to report his father, who subsequently was in prison for ten years.

'I was angry at myself because I thought "Why didn't I see this?" I used to bend God's earhole something chronic. It was a horrendous time but by the grace of God I got through it.' When her husband was in prison, Esther neither wrote nor visited. If her husband contacted her, she ignored it. However, she did not divorce him. 'If I didn't have my faith, I don't know what I'd have done. Through all the traumas, God's still there. Although we've had our moments, God has certainly blessed us.'

Meet JOSH

Josh grew up in a Christian household and describes himself as an introvert who was 'a bit socially anxious' when he was younger. Annual camps in Wales shaped and grew his faith, when young people from around the UK met up 'for a week of Christian worship and unwinding'. Josh particularly enjoyed 'being away from the world' and talking to people his own age. These days he's involved in youth ministry at his church in the north of the country.

He describes his faith as a lifelong journey of discovery, trying daily to become more like Christ, 'which is an uphill struggle! I still make mistakes. I still find myself slipping back down the hill. But I keep picking myself up and trying again, which is, I think, all anyone can do.'

Josh is bisexual, something he describes as 'just part of my journey as a human being. I think, for a long time, I tried to ignore it because of my Christian upbringing. When you're attracted to women and men, if the thoughts of men pop up you just push it aside and go, "Oh, it's just my brain being silly." You don't know how to confront it because you can just focus on the part of your sexuality that's more socially acceptable. But eventually you realize that there's no point trying to run away from it. It's just who you are.'

He feels happier now he's accepted that part of himself and no longer avoids it, and notes that 'accepting it hasn't meant that I've run away from Christianity'. He's tried that but has always been drawn back: 'Once you let Jesus in, it's like a magnetic force.' That Christians recognize they are sinful and need Jesus Christ 'is true of everyone, regardless of whether you're bi, gay, trans, cis or straight. It seems strange that so many people in the church don't seem to see it that way. They'll be willing to forgive a murderer if they show repentance but they won't show that same kind of forgiveness to someone who was just born different to them, which is frustrating.'

'I don't necessarily hide or pretend to be someone else. I just don't mention certain things'

Josh hopes attitudes will change as people of different orientations and backgrounds become more outspoken. But he observes it's quite difficult to speak up in church: 'I don't necessarily hide or pretend to be someone else. I just don't mention certain things that might aggravate the wrong people. But then the longer you avoid that, the less interaction they have with people who are different from them. Until you have that difficult conversation with them, they're never going to change their views.'

He thinks that pornography is a big problem that the church would also benefit from talking about and tackling. It is particularly pernicious because it is so addictive, so accessible and so hidden from view, especially in Christian circles.

Josh has had struggles with anxiety and depression, but prayer helps him keep going every day: 'My experience of prayer is that it actually works! You don't expect that to be the case when you first start. But I've had enough experiences to make me keep on trying.'

He would encourage Christians to confront things that are uncomfortable, because 'we're all on a journey together. We're all sinners saved by Jesus Christ. People of different sexualities are just human beings. We deserve as much empathy as you'd give to anyone else.'

Christ be with me, Christ within me,
Christ behind me, Christ before me,
Christ beside me, Christ to win me,
Christ to comfort and restore me.
Christ beneath me, Christ above me,
Christ in quiet, Christ in danger,
Christ in hearts of all that love me,
Christ in mouth of friend and stranger.

Common Worship Daily Prayer,
from St Patrick's Breastplate

PART TWO

Paying attention: what is going on?

The purpose of Part Two is to take a careful look at what is happening in the world around us with regard to identity, sexuality, relationships and marriage. We describe, as dispassionately as possible, what is going on in God's world with its mix of goodness and fallenness, of glory and human weakness. In this Part of the book we are not seeking to interpret these observations from the perspective of the Christian faith. That will be the task of Part Three, when we will begin to discern what aspects are signs of God's kingdom drawing nearer, and what aspects seem to be pulling us further away.

Chapter 5 begins by setting out social trends concerning singleness, marriage, friendship and loneliness. It considers the place of sexual activity in relationships, including issues of commodification, freedom and consent. An exploration of how identity is perceived in relation to sexual orientation and gender is followed by a brief timeline of how society has responded to these trends.

The focus of **Chapter 6** is on scientific understandings of sexuality and gender. We begin by exploring the complexity and difficulty of scientific studies of sexuality before offering brief overviews of the science of sexual orientation, gender identity and variations in sexual characteristics. The chapter concludes with scientific findings about well-being, mental health, procreation and sexual orientation change efforts.

In **Chapter 7** we turn to look at the place of religious faith in society. We notice how other religions and other Christian churches have responded to matters of identity, sexuality, relationships and marriage, before turning to the Church of England and the Anglican Communion. These brief overviews provide a backdrop for the theological engagement that is the focus of Part Three.

A social revolution seems to be taking place. Across British society, we are seeing changes in the patterns of people's relationships, in sexual activity and attitudes, and in understandings of identity.

Relationships are changing. We are seeing changes in the proportion of people who remain single. We are seeing changes in the number and duration of people's sexual relationships. We are seeing changes in patterns of cohabitation, marriage, and divorce. We are seeing changes in when and where people marry, in what they hope for when they do, and in whether children are part of the picture. We have seen legal changes allowing same-sex couples to marry, and we are seeing different types of family appearing. More recently, we have seen how the COVID-19 pandemic has influenced how we think about, value and conduct our relationships; although it is too early to tell how deep or permanent that impact will be, it is likely that no part of British social life will be untouched.

Attitudes to sex are changing. We seem to be caught between expanding ideas of sexual freedom and increasing concern about freedom's proper limits. Questions about sexual consent and power are becoming more prominent. Questions about sexual abuse have risen to the top of the agenda. Technology, often a harbinger of change in sexual practice, is raising new questions, such as those about the prevalence of online pornography and its continuing development, as well as the use of AI in various ways.

The ways in which we approach identity are changing. More and more of us are coming to recognize ourselves, or people we know and love, as trans, as lesbian or gay or bisexual, as asexual, as intersex. We are asking new questions about what that means, and about how anybody's identity works, whichever words we might choose to describe ourselves. We are also asking what are the best terms to use (see also the Glossary), and about whether 'identity' is even the right category for thinking about all this.

For an explanation and discussion of the terms used in this paragraph, see Chapter 5, 'Identity and self-understanding' on pages 88–97 and the Glossary on pages 425–427.

These changes are visible in all our lives, in the stories we tell and hear, in the questions we ask, in the arguments that we fall into. Related discussions fill our news, our online debates, our public forums, and our legislature. There are arguments about the public acceptance of same-sex marriage, or transgender identity in the very young, or the handling of cases of child sexual abuse, or what sex education in schools should cover, or the effect upon people of ubiquitous online pornography, of the impact of #MeToo – the list is endless.

All of this poses questions to us as a society. Should we focus on encouraging particular kinds of relationship? Or should we be enabling many different kinds of relationship, and many different kinds of family, to flourish? Are we able to be honest about the consequences of our choices? Do we have good ways of talking together about sex, about the good and the harm involved? Or do we need to learn to talk about it a whole lot less? Is identity something that we are given and need to discover, or are we free to define it? How are our identities, our bodies, our sex lives and our relationships connected?

All of this also poses questions to the Church of England as it does to other churches. What challenges do these changes pose to existing teaching and practice? What new possibilities and opportunities do they suggest? How are we to respond? What teaching, what forms of care, what rites, what disciplines, what ways of relating do we need? How do we respond as followers of Jesus? How do we respond as readers of the Bible, as inhabitants of a tradition, as members of a worldwide Church? How do we live and share the gospel – God's good news for the world in Christ – amidst all these changes?

Chapter 3 provided an outline of the Church of England's teaching on marriage and the place of sex within it, setting these in the context of God's gift of life and of the many relationships in which that life can flourish. Chapter 5 surveys some of the social changes that surround us in these areas, highlighting some that seem to pose the most urgent questions. In Chapter 6 we look at recent scientific developments that can contribute to our understanding of all these topics. In Chapter 7 we ask what responses there have been to these topics so far in the Church of England, in other churches, and in other religious communities. In each of these chapters, we do not have the space to provide more than a brief description of recent developments, but you can find more detail in the Living in Love and Faith Online Library (**www.churchofengland.org/LLF**).

The whole of Part Two is only one step in our journey, and these chapters are not themselves meant to offer answers. They aim to provide preliminary descriptions, and to pose some questions, in order to set the scene for later Parts. In those later Parts we will explore Christian responses to these questions.

Before we begin, however, there are some important caveats to offer. First, British society is diverse, and always has been. It includes people of different religions, ethnicities, cultures, classes and genders. It is constantly being remade by people who bring other inheritances into it, and influenced by all the societies that surround it. It is also shaped by capitalism and its values, by modern technology, by a history of colonialism, by democratic politics, by a globalized market economy – and so on. We don't have enough space here even to name all the many forces that shape the world we live in, let alone argue about which are the most significant.

We have not had the space to tease out how the social changes we describe differ across ethnic groups, social and economic backgrounds, or regions – either in society as a whole, or within the church. There will be many exceptions to all of the trends we describe. There will be many ways in which those trends are tangled up with class structures and other uneven distributions of power. The descriptions we offer are only rough and partial characterizations – a broad brush picture – to serve as a backdrop to our explorations.

Second, none of the changes we discuss in these chapters is completely new. Even if we are living through a revolution, it is one that has been brewing for a long time – and there are all kinds of historical parallels to most of the elements that we now think of as new. The present situation may pose questions with a new urgency, or in new terms, but none of those questions is completely unprecedented. Whatever response the church gives to these questions now, that response will be one more episode in a long history of deliberation and decision. As we will be seeing in later Parts, the church has all sorts of resources to draw on as it responds – even if it also has all sorts of disagreements about the value and best use of those resources.

Third, we have had to choose which topics to cover and what words to use and not one of those decisions is neutral. We are talking about topics that people care about passionately and the words we use are likely to trigger strong emotions. They have the capacity to bless or to harm. They can certainly all be argued about – and those

arguments abound in church and society. We will highlight below
some of the main instances where there is dispute about the terms
we have chosen to use.

The way we have arranged our material is not neutral, either. Think,
for instance, about your own reactions to the opening paragraphs
above. They describe complex social changes and suggest that
those changes might amount to a social revolution. Did you hear this
as a story of progress – however uneven and fragile that progress
might be? Did you hear it as a story of decline – of the erosion of
important institutions or the forgetting of important truths? Did
you hear it as describing something too messy to be thought of
as either progress or decline? Did you hear it and think that, in a
wider historical view, this is not really a revolution, just the ongoing
process of change? All of these perspectives, and more, have fed
into the production of this book – and, however much we have tried
to smooth them out in the pages below, you will still hear echoes of
them.

Finally, all of the questions that we raise throughout this Part are
questions posed to us by real people's lives. They are posed by our
own lives, the lives of all the people in our churches, the lives of our
families, friends and neighbours. None of those people is a problem
to be solved, or an issue to be argued about. This book is about *us* –
all of us in our society and in the church. It is about our relationships,
our identities, our experience in all our conditions of life. It is about
the influence that our patterns of living have on others, for good
or ill. It is about the questions that all of us pose to one another:
questions about how we can live together in love and faith.

CHAPTER 5

Society

We begin by paying attention to
what is happening in the society of
which we are a part. We describe the
kinds of relationships that people
form today. This involves looking at
singleness, marriage, partnerships,
families and friendships. We rely
on a variety of statistics to help us
see some of the overarching trends
and to remind us of the diversity of
people's lives and relationships.

We then move on to consider the
place of sex in relationships and
draw out some trends and issues
that affect people's lives. Finally, we
turn to questions of identity: what is
happening in our society with regard to
sexual orientation and gender identity?

Our purpose in this chapter is to observe and notice rather than comment or evaluate. It is also to widen our field of vision from our own lives and those whom we know to society as a whole.

Relationships

A changing picture

The patterns of relationships in our society are changing. It is easy to slip into grand generalizations when discussing this, so before reading on take a moment to think about the people around you. What kinds of story of singleness, of marriage, of living together, of divorce, of remarriage do you see? What shape is taken by the families you know – not in media representations and church reports, but amongst your own family, friends, and colleagues? Behind every statistic there are always real people – and every one of them has a story as complex as the people you know, driven by as many different factors. That complexity can get washed out when we focus on society-wide trends.

The statistics in the infographic on pages 68–69 illustrate some of the trends to which all those individual stories and decisions contribute. More people are living alone. Fewer are marrying, and those who do marry tend to marry later in life. As a result, 'the proportions of men and women in recent years ever married by age 25 are the lowest on record over the last 100 years.'[62] More people cohabit prior to, or instead of, marrying, to the extent that 'marriage without first living together is now as unusual as premarital cohabitation was in the 1970s'.[63] Fewer children are being born to married couples. Divorce is beginning to become less common – not just in absolute terms, which you might expect given the smaller number of marriages, but proportionally: the lifetime risk of divorce for people who marry today is the lowest since 1969. The number of same-sex couples is growing, as is the proportion who have married. More children are being born and nurtured in families headed by couples of the same gender.

English society has never been uniform, but the spectrum of relationships visible in our society (and in all our media) does seem to be broader than ever before. There are wide variations in practice and expectation. No simple explanation covers the changes that have taken place. The story needs to include changes to marriage law; technological and medical changes affecting birth control and life expectancy; the emancipation of women, which has brought with it educational and professional opportunities and new possibilities of financial and legal independence; the evolution of the welfare state and changes to tax regimes; altered distributions of wealth and changing patterns of employment; shifts in immigration; growing awareness of domestic abuse and the need to escape it; changing patterns of religious commitment; changes to the kinds of behaviour that get stigmatized; changes to the ways in which human fulfilment tends to be imagined; and changes to people's attitudes to a wide variety of institutions. There is no one story to tell – no simple narrative of progress or decline.

Singleness

Look, for example, at singleness. The word 'single' can be used to describe someone who is not married, someone who is neither married nor cohabiting, or someone who is not currently in a significant romantic or sexual relationship. Up until the late twentieth century, singleness (in the first of these senses) tended to be deprecated in many English contexts. Unmarried people – especially women – have often been seen primarily as people who lack something: they have not managed to find a partner, or they have somehow been prevented from marrying. Unmarried women were often marginalized, stigmatized and pitied. Countless novels, plays and films have reinforced this popular view, captured in pejorative phrases such as 'old maid', 'spinster' and 'on the shelf'. Yet, however invisible they have sometimes been, we know that there have, since the Middle Ages, been large numbers of unmarried people, both women and men, in both rural and urban contexts.

All of the kinds of change listed above have affected the prevalence, the variety and the perception of single people in our society. And singleness today – in any of the senses given above – is far more complex than it first appears. It includes the widowed, the separated, the divorced, and those who have never married. It also includes those who defer marriage until later, waiting until they have obtained occupational and financial security. It can include people living in a variety of family contexts, some who live in other kinds of shared accommodation, and some who live alone. For some, singleness is a choice; for others, it is a result of circumstance; for most, it might be something in between. For some, it may be

– MARRIAGE –

The proportion of people who marry has been decreasing since the 1970s. Marriage rates for opposite-sex couples have fallen to the lowest on record (since 1862) for both men and women.

75%↓ since 1972 69%↓ since 1972

In 2017, there were 21.2 marriages per 1,000 unmarried men and 19.5 marriages per 1,000 unmarried women aged 16 years and over. Since 1972, marriage rates have fallen by three-quarters for men (75%) and by 69% for women.

50.5%

of the UK population over 16 were married in 2018

In 2018 50.5% of the total UK population over 16 were married, a percentage which has been broadly stable for a decade, though is now declining slightly. Roughly 0.5% are same-sex spouses. A further 13.1% are cohabiting. Just over a third (35%) of people over 16 in England and Wales have never been married.

38 years old 35 years old

In 2017 the average age of men at first marriage in England and Wales was 38 years and for women it was 35. These figures have been rising steadily since the 1970s.

– SINGLE PEOPLE –

8.2m

living alone

In 2019 there were 8.2 million people living alone, more than half of them aged between 16 and 64. The number has increased by a fifth over the last twenty years.

2.9m

living as lone parents

A further 2.9 million people lived as lone parents with children, which is 14.9% of families in the UK.

– DIVORCE –

35%

lifetime divorce risk

More people have experienced divorce. The number of divorces in England and Wales exceeded 50,000 in 1969 and 100,000 in 1972, never falling below that figure until 2018 when there were 90,871 divorces of opposite-sex couples, a decrease of 10.6% compared with 2017 and the lowest number since 1971. Most of this decline is accounted for by the decline in the number of marriages, but the proportion of marriages that end in divorce appears now to be falling too. The Marriage Foundation estimates the lifetime divorce risk for today's newlyweds is 35% – the lowest level since 1969.

– COHABITATION –

25.8%↑

between 2009–2019

The number of cohabiting couples in the UK continues to grow, with an increase of 25.8% between 2009 and 2019.

. . . .

90% (civil) **80%** (religious)

In 2017, almost 90% of opposite-sex couples were cohabiting when they married in a civil ceremony, as were over 80% of those marrying in a religious ceremony.

– SAME-SEX COUPLES –

40%↑

increase since 2015

More people are living as same-sex couples and more of these are married. In 2019 there were 212,000 same-sex couple families, having increased by 40% since 2015.

19% **28%** **53%**

married couples civil partnerships cohabiting couples

27% of these couples were married, 52% cohabiting and 21% were in civil partnerships. The same figures for 2015 were 19% married, 53% cohabiting and 28% in civil partnerships.

– CHILDREN –

48.4%

children born outside marriage

More children are born outside of marriage. The proportion of children born outside marriage has risen steadily since the 1960s to reach 48.4% (in England and Wales) in 2018, a year which also saw the 'largest percentage decrease in the rate [of live births within marriage] since 1973'.

15.3%

21.1%

63.5%

Children grow up in a range of family structures. The latest (2019) study shows that, for the UK, 'Married or civil partner couples remain the most common family type in 2019. They represent two-thirds of families in the UK' in which dependent children live (63.5%). 21.1% of families are lone parent families and 15.3% are cohabiting couple families.

1.3m

cohabiting couple families in 2018

The study also notes that 'Cohabiting couple families have had the largest statistically significant percentage increase of those families with dependent children at 23.9% in the decade 2008 to 2018, rising to 1.3 million in 2018.'

The statistics above are drawn from the Office of National Statistics, with the exception of the 'Divorce' infographic where information was also sourced from the Marriage Foundation. For full source references see endnote 64 on page 431.

empowering, for others painful; for most it will be as complex as any other kind of status. For some Christians, as we will discuss later, singleness may be part of a calling or vocation which may take different forms, including the joining of a monastic community and the life lived with others that this brings.

The forms of companionship and intimacy possible for married and cohabiting people are not the only forms of companionship and intimacy available. A single life is a life shaped by different possibilities of relationship, not by an absence of relationships. Nevertheless, the church has often mirrored negative cultural attitudes towards singleness, including tacit assumptions that to be single is to lack completeness and to be lonely. Many single people in the church and across society would insist that their single status is not what defines them. It does not dictate their capacity for fulfilment or the contributions that they are capable of making.[65]

Marriage, relationships and fulfilment

There remains a very high level of expectation placed on marriage and other long-term relationships. In May 2019, Radio 4's *Analysis* devoted a programme to *Love Island*. The presenter, Shahidha Bari, talked about the culture of sexual encounter in Britain today. '*Love Island* dramatizes love as a market place,' she said.[66] The programme suggested that, for most participants in this market place, the end to which sexual activity tends is 'self-fulfilment'.

Multiple sexual encounters are seen as a necessary, even sometimes an irksome, means towards that end. People are seeking the holy grail: a person truly worthy of becoming their permanent romantic partner – and they expect to take time to find the right person.[67]

For many, there is an aspiration that, having found the right person, marriage will, sooner or later, follow. The anthropologist Helen Fisher told Bari that modern dating behaviour was in effect a prudent 'extension of the pre-commitment stage of partnerships.' Permanent union is not out of fashion, she explains, but marriage is not now seen as the beginning of a long exploration of commitment. Instead, it is the possible end of a long period of research and experimentation.

Who wants to be married, and how and where?

A large survey undertaken in 2003 tells us that

- monogamous marriage was a current 'relationship ideal' for a little under half the population, though women were keener (48.5% against men's 40.9%);

- a further 21% said they would like a permanent monogamous partner but wished to live independently;

- a further 18% said they would opt for monogamous cohabitation; and

- when asked what their ideal relationship for five years' time would be, two-thirds said they wanted to be 'married with no other partners' (62.5% of men, 69.3% of women), and another fifth chose 'cohabiting with no other partners' (20.4% of men, 18.0% of women).[68]

More recently, in 2017, when the Church of England Life Events team asked 1,000 unmarried 18- to 35-year-olds whether they planned to get married in the future, 72% said yes.[69] The number of people hoping for a permanent monogamous relationship remains high.

Following the Marriage (Same-Sex Couples) Act in 2013, same-sex couples were able to marry from 29 March 2014 onwards; same-sex couples who had been in a civil partnership were able to convert their partnership into a marriage from 10 December 2014. On 31 December 2019, heterosexual couples were granted the same rights to enter civil partnerships and to convert these into a marriage.

- In the nine months of 2014 when same-sex marriage was legal, 4,850 couples were married. In the three weeks at the end of that year when it became possible, a further 2,411 couples converted their civil partnerships into marriages.[70]

- In 2015, 6,493 same-sex couples were married; 9,156 couples converted their civil partnerships into marriages.[71]

- In 2016 (the most recent year for which full statistics have been published), 7,019 same-sex couples were married; 1,663 couples converted their civil partnerships into marriages.[72]

- By 2019 there were 212,000 married same-sex couples in the UK, having increased by 40% since 2015.[73]

The number of weddings taking place in church has dropped.

- In 2017, less than a quarter of all marriages were religious ceremonies, having fallen from less than a half in the late 1970s.[74] The fastest growing choice of venue for civil marriages is in 'approved premises' like hotels and country houses: in 2015, 89% of opposite-sex couple and 88% of same-sex couples married in approved premises.[75] Weddings in holiday settings are increasingly popular.

- The number of weddings taking place in the Church of England has fallen by 27% from 2007 to 2017. In 2018, there were 35,000 Church of England marriages (none of them for same-sex couples) and 2,500 services of prayer and dedication after civil marriages in 2018, down from 38,000 and 3,000 respectively in 2017.[76]

If marriage is indeed now seen as the end rather than the start of commitment, a great deal is being asked of it. It is looked to for romantic permanence, and as the place where the needs of the self may be met by its soulmate. 'It's not that we don't believe in love anymore, but that love means everything', claimed Bari. 'This is why the modern couple fails', agreed the philosopher Pascal Bruckner. 'It is like an overloaded boat that sinks under its own weight.'

This idea of marriage as the end of a search for the true romantic partner goes deep in our culture. It is the basic plot, for instance, of the classic novel – one of the most influential genres in modern history, with a mass of other narrative forms growing from it in film and TV, from sitcoms to romcoms. Yet this idea sets the bar for a successful marriage extremely high, and the result is often a never-ending quest: a pattern of serial monogamy in which each partner in turn fails to match the ideal.

We should be careful not to caricature people's reasons for marrying, however. One recent study indicated that those reasons can include a desire to comply with convention (especially religious and parental expectations); to express and celebrate publicly an already formed relationship; to confirm commitment to a relationship now understood to be permanent; to set up 'a framework within which a process of deepening commitment would take place', especially as a context for raising children; or for financial reasons or reasons related to immigration.[77]

For many in our society, marriage holds out an attractive promise of security, intimacy, and mutual care, legally protected and culturally valued. Data repeatedly show it to be the most positive context for the flourishing of children, although there is debate about how much of this is due to the parents being married and how much to other factors.[78] It is not surprising to find groups who have in the past been excluded from marriage longing for its benefits, or simply longing to live in a society where they are not automatically excluded from a widely valued ideal.

Marriage, procreation and the well-being of children

The overall birthrate, inside and outside marriage, is falling fast in the UK. In 2018 it was 1.7 per woman, whereas a 'replacement rate' of 2.1/2.2 would be needed for population numbers to be stable. This is a major trend in the Western world, and it gives rise to an ageing population. Women are having fewer children (one per family is now more common) and women tend to be starting child-bearing later in life.

The percentage of live births outside marriage continues to increase: 48.4 per cent of live births were outside marriage in 2018. There is evidence across a number of measures that 'children born to parents who are cohabiting are more likely to see their parents separate than those children born within marriage'.[79]

A question that arises from these statistics is the relationship between marriage and the well-being of children. An in-depth US study (corroborated by a more recent UK study) of the link between marriage and child well-being asserts that 'children raised by two biological parents in a stable marriage do better than children in other family forms across a wide range of outcomes'.[80] There are many possible factors that may account for this seemingly consistent phenomenon, such as family income, parents' physical and mental health, and parenting quality. The study concludes that 'studies of child well-being that attempt to control the indirect effects of these mechanisms typically find that a direct positive association remains

– BIRTH RATE –

1.7↓

**live births per woman
in England and Wales**

In 2018 the number of live births in England and Wales decreased for the third year in a row. The total fertility rate decreased from 1.76 to 1.7 children per woman in 2018; this is lower than all previous years except 1977 and 1999 to 2002. A 'replacement rate' of 2.1/2.2 would be needed for population numbers to be stable.

– RELATIONSHIPS –

80.5

live births per 1,000 married women

In 2018, there were 80.5 live births within marriage per 1,000 married women aged 15 to 44 years, which was a 5.8% decrease compared with 2017. This was the largest percentage decrease in the rate since 1973.

. . . .

48.4%

live births outside of marriage

Meanwhile 48.4% of live births were outside of marriage in 2018. This continues the long-term increases in the percentage of live births outside of marriage, since the 1960s. Conceptions in England and Wales have also shown a similar trend where most conceptions in 2017 occurred outside marriage or civil partnership.

– AGE GROUPS –

40+

Fertility rates decreased in all age groups except for women aged 40 years and over.

Fertility rates for women aged 40 years and over have generally increased since the late 1970s until 2017. However, in 2018, the fertility rate for this age group remained the same as 2017, at 16.1 births per 1,000 women aged 40 years and over. This ended a four-year period of consecutive increases and was the only age group for which the fertility rate did not decrease in 2018.

. . . .

<20↓

In contrast, since the turn of the century, there has been a long-term decrease in fertility rates for women aged under 20 years. This trend continued in 2018, when the fertility rate for this age group decreased by 6.3% compared with 2017, to 11.9 births per 1,000 women aged under 20 years.

. . . .

30-34

Women aged 30 to 34 years have had the highest fertility rate of any age group since 2004. Prior to this, women aged 25 to 29 years generally had the highest fertility rate. This indicates women are delaying childbearing to older ages.

The statistics above are drawn from the Office of National Statistics. For full source references see endnote 81 on page 433.

between child well-being and marriage, strongly suggesting that marriage is more than the sum of these particular parts'. In other words, the author of the paper suggests that there is something about marriage that is able to have a further and particular influence, which is difficult to replicate in other forms of relationship.

These and other studies indicate that relationship stability is a key aspect of child well-being, but that a causal link between marriage and relationship stability cannot be proven. A recent study shows that, although cohabiting couples are more likely to separate than married couples, once cohabiting couples have children, the difference between married and cohabiting couples is significantly reduced.[82] The interaction of mechanisms impacting child well-being both inside and outside of marriage are complex, as are the individual life experiences of the parents themselves.

These studies also suggest that same-sex couples are as good at parenting as different-sex couples. They argue that any differences can be explained by the fact that children being raised by same-sex couples have, on average, experienced more family instability. This may be, for example, because many children being raised by same-sex couples were born to heterosexual parents, one of whom is now in a same-sex relationship. Furthermore, it is suggested that those same-sex couples who raise children are now 'more likely to be raising their children from birth' than they were ten years ago, and therefore such differences of instability may be expected to decrease. Recent findings of longitudinal research – which follows lesbian mothers and their children who were conceived by donor insemination during the 1980s – concludes that '25-year-olds born into planned lesbian families did not differ from reports on emerging adults generally in these predictors of mental health: education; having an intimate relationship; or quality of relationships with intimate partner, friends, and parents. However, offspring affected by associative homophobic stigma had higher rates of behavioral/emotional problems.'[83]

Friendship and loneliness

According to Kate Leaver's study, *The Friendship Cure*, many contemporary Western people regard friendship as more reliable than marriage.[84] While there are overlaps, friendship is often distinguished from couple relationships in a number of ways. First, friendships can be picked up and let go of, and may therefore be less intense than couple relationships.[85] Friendship represents a commitment to stay in each other's lives by choice more than by obligation: the notion of freedom is inherent in popular understandings of friendship. One of the appeals of friendships over family relationships is the way that they enable people to define and identify themselves in ways that are under *their* control, in what might be called 'families of choice'.[86] Friendships tend to be relationships of equality rather than hierarchy. Because of the voluntary nature of friendships, and the equality at their centre, they also require a different kind of ongoing reciprocity and effort. Some sociologists have argued that friendship is a particularly 'ethical kind of love'.[87]

Secondly, friendships tend not to become institutionalized in the ways that exclusive couple relationships do. Where couples over time tend to subordinate individual goals to those of the unit, friends remain autonomous agents, pursuing their own lives and bringing their distinct life experiences to the relationship in a creative act in which each party is enriched.[88] The absence of formal contracts means that friendship is comparatively 'weak' as a social bond. Yet despite the informal, voluntary and non-institutionalized nature of friendships, they are increasingly perceived to offer alternatives to more traditional social models based on the sexual couple relationship and the raising of children. For those choosing to remain single or not to have children, living arrangements organized around friendships are increasingly common.[89]

Research suggests that human beings can sustain relationships with a maximum of around 150 people, of whom 15 are close friends, 35 are friends and the rest are acquaintances.[90] In contemporary society there are many types of friendship: legacy friends from early life, family friends, college and work friends, neighbourhood friends, casual friends and social media friends. Friendships within and between genders are much more fluid today than in traditional societies.

Friendships and friendship groups alter considerably over time as different stages of life draw people into different environments and spaces, forging new encounters and relationships. For example, a significant shift in friendship patterns happens when people have children. Parents suddenly find themselves in antenatal groups, play groups and at school gates, mixing with a whole new cohort of other parents. The friendships that emerge around child-rearing are often anchored by mothers, who find in other mothers solidarity and support in the responsibility of caring for and raising children. These friendships are characterized by mutual caregiving – for the children, for each other and for each other's families – and are time-bound and contingent on the life-stage of the children.[91]

According to Leaver, modern female friendships tend to involve more intense sharing than male friendships. Male friendships tend to be about doing things together and being there for each other. Friendships between genders have become more prevalent, as work and social life bring the genders more regularly into contact with each other. However, the nature of such friendships may be challenged by the different social rules for friendships between genders, particularly where both parties are heterosexual, and questions of sexual attraction may arise.

The mixing of friendships with sex – 'friends with benefits' or 'erotic friendships' – seeks to incorporate the benefits of sexual intimacy without elements of romance or commitment. However, some sociologists have argued that friendships which incorporate sexual elements involve hidden power dynamics which work against the equality at the heart of the relationship because it remains the case that there are different social rules that inform male and female intimacy.[92]

A major and new feature of friendship in society today is the phenomenon of online friendships, which can themselves come in a variety of forms, and that interact with offline friendship in complex ways that are not yet well understood. The nature of online encounters – often fleeting and transient – pose challenges to the very ways that 'friendship' has been defined and understood. Online spaces both foster the development of entirely new friendships and help deepen connections within existing friendships through the regular sharing of experiences and feelings. Whilst there can be negative consequences to online expressions of friendship – such as people unfavourably comparing themselves and their lives with the (curated) lives of their friends, or feeling the pressure to present well-liked content – the benefits of technology for friendship are well evidenced. Online friendships can be a very important or even primary route to friendship, not least because the Internet can enable the elderly, widowed, introverted, isolated, disabled and hard of hearing to keep in touch with friends and indeed to find friendships. Further they enable the development and sustenance of relationships across geographical contexts in increasingly mobile populations. During the COVID-19 pandemic an increasing number of people connected with family and friends in this way. This was particularly significant for some older people who would not have relied on virtual ways of connecting prior to the lockdown.

Friendships can be life-affirming because they imply likeability and worth. They represent emotional investment in each other's lives. They are generally good for health, especially as people get older.[93] One of the effects of the pandemic was, for some, a renewed sense of mutual care manifested in the forging of local, neighbourly relationships.

They can, however, be an arena for problems. Friendships tend to form between people who are like one another, and so tend to reinforce social silos rather than bridging social divides. Like other forms of relationship, friendships can be arenas for social anxiety, for manipulation, and for bullying. They can be sites for the negotiation of prestige: the more 'friends' a person has, especially on social media, the more influence and significance that person is perceived to enjoy.

Alongside changing patterns of friendship, our society has also seen a growth in loneliness, to the extent that many now speak of a 'loneliness epidemic'. The incidence of loneliness was exacerbated, especially among some young people, during the pandemic. Loneliness is not the same as living alone – though the massive growth in solo living is one of the factors in the growth in loneliness. Loneliness is a matter of felt isolation, an experience of lacking rich contact with others – lacking friendship. The causes are multiple: demographic, economic, and cultural, involving everything from lengthening life expectancy to urban planning, and from divorce rates to changing patterns of employment.[94] The consequences are serious: as well as itself being a painful experience, loneliness appears to be bad for our mental and physical health in a wide variety of ways.[95]

Sex

The first section of this chapter was about relationships; this section is about sexual activity: both intercourse and other kinds of sexual interactions and experiences. We have thought carefully about how to do justice to the reality of sex in what we write. There are, perhaps, other kinds of literature better suited than a book like this to capturing the passion and the pleasure of it, as well as the dangers and disasters. It is important, however, as we start to describe cultural trends and behavioural statistics, not to lose sight completely of what all these words are about.

Facts about sexual behaviour are notoriously difficult to establish securely, since much research relies on people being willing to tell the unvarnished truth about their sexual histories and habits. We have highlighted some research findings in the infographic below, but in general it seems that in recent decades people are having sex with more partners, and starting earlier in life, but that they are not necessarily having more sex. More women are having same-sex sexual experiences. Few people now think that sex before marriage is wrong, but most think that married people should only have sex with their partner.

> See Chapter 3 (pages 32–34) for a discussion about marriage and the gift of sex, and Chapter 12 (pages 256-257) for a reflection on the Song of Solomon. For a conversation about sex and relationships see Part Five, Scene 2 (pages 389-396).

Sex and fulfilment

Sexual activity in our society is shaped by some widespread – though not universal – assumptions. One set of assumptions has to do with the benefits of sexual activity. Studies show that sex can contribute to individual happiness and perhaps to other aspects of health.[96]

In the twentieth century, sexual desire became increasingly important to our understanding of how human beings work.[97] The idea developed that, if sexual fulfilment makes you flourish, sexual repression must be inappropriate. The recent rise in those identifying as asexual – that is, as people who do not experience sexual attraction to others – is just one way in which assumptions about the centrality of sex to human existence have been challenged. Nevertheless, the idea that sex is necessary is still widespread, although as we have noted, people are actually having less sex now than in previous decades. Sex is often, perhaps, seen as analogous to food: perhaps marvellous, perhaps boring, occasionally toxic; but always vital for survival – and heterosexual intercourse is, of course, vital for the continued existence of the

The National Survey of Sexual Attitudes and Lifestyles (Natsal) covers various different kinds of sexual activity: vaginal, oral, anal, and other genital contact. The survey takes place approximately every 10 years. The latest survey, Natsal-3, took place between September 2010 and August 2012.

– WHO –

average lifetime sexual partners in 2012

In the 1990s, the average number of opposite-sex sexual partners people report having had over their lifetime went up for both men and women; more recently the increase has continued only for women. The average for men aged between 16 and 44 in 2012 was 11.7, for women 7.7.

same-sex sexual experiences

Over the same period, the number of men reporting same-sex sexual experiences rose slightly, from 6 to 7%, whereas the number for women rose significantly, from 4 to 16%.

– WHEN –

first had sex before age 16

The numbers reporting that they first had sex before they were 16 has gone up. Among those aged 16–24 at the time of the 2010–12 survey, those figures had risen to 31% of men and 29% of women.

average times people had sex over four weeks

On average over the past two decades the median number of times that people aged between 16 and 44 say they have had sex over the past four weeks has decreased from 5 to 3.

– SEX & MARRIAGE –

The idea that sexual intercourse should be reserved for within marriage has not characterized the behaviour of the majority of any cohort born since 1935, and has been growing less prevalent for each successive cohort.

5%
considered pre-marital sex wrong in 2003

84.4%
– men –

88.7%
– women –

considered extra-marital sex wrong in 2003

Few people surveyed in 2003 considered pre-marital sex to be wrong (5%); but most considered extra-marital sex to be wrong (84.4% of men, 88.7% of women).

A more recent 'British Social Attitudes' survey, with a different methodology, suggested that in 2018:

– SEX & MARRIAGE –

74% of people considered pre-marital sex to be 'not wrong at all'.

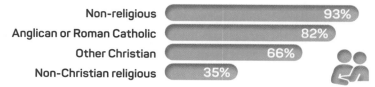

Non-religious	93%
Anglican or Roman Catholic	82%
Other Christian	66%
Non-Christian religious	35%

The vast majority (93%) of those who identify as non-religious consider premarital sex to be "rarely wrong" or "not wrong at all", falling to 82% among those who identify as Anglican or Roman Catholic, 66% among those who identify as other Christian and 35% of those who are affiliated with non-Christian religious groups.

We do not have statistics on the proportion of sexual activity that is undertaken for the sake of, or with openness to, the birth of children. The statistics on abortion, however, suggest that considerably more sexual activity leads to conception than people expect or want:

– ABORTION –

205,295

abortions in England and Wales in 2018

There were 205,295 abortions for women in England and Wales in 2018. This is the highest number recorded.

17.4↑

per 1,000 women in 2018

The abortion rate – the number of abortions per 1,000 women – rose to 17.4 in 2018 from 16.4 in 2017, but it is down slightly from 17.5 in 2008.

8.1↓ 9.2↑

per 1,000 <18 **per 1,000 35+**

The abortion rate for women under 18 has been decreasing steadily; at 8.1 per 1,000 it is now less than half the 18.9 rate of 2008. The rate for women aged 35 and over has increased from 6.7 to 9.2 in the same period.

In 2018, 97.7% (196,083) of abortions in England and Wales were performed on the legal ground that 'continuance of pregnancy would involve risk, greater than if the pregnancy were terminated, of injury to the physical or mental health of the pregnant woman' rather than on other grounds.

The information above is drawn from the most recent *National Survey of Sexual Attitudes and Lifestyles* and the Department of Health and Social Care *Abortion Statistics*. For full source references see endnote 98 on page 434.

human race. In many contexts, adults are assumed to be sexually active, so that those who are not (whether by calling, choice, chance, imposed constraint or because they identify as asexual) can feel unnervingly invisible. To be implicitly defined, or dismissed, as deviantly abstinent – even if the facts show that it might not be as unusual as all that[99] – is painful and difficult. On the other hand, adults with some kinds of disability are often assumed to be sexually inactive, which can be no less of a stereotype.

Commodification

Sex is an activity between people who are both (or should both be) agents. It is an activity between people who are both subjects as well as objects. Being an 'object' of sexual desire certainly matters. That is, it matters to most people that others can desire them and be aroused by them. But being a subject matters too: people are not simply desired but desiring, not simply arousing but aroused. Sex involves not just the entangling of bodies, but the entangling of subjectivities. That is, in a healthy sexual relationship, each partner needs to have a sense of what the other wants and needs; the feelings, pleasure and excitement of each partner will be dependent on those of the other. We speak of 'objectification' when this is absent – when the subjectivity is all on one side, the objectivity all on the other. In a situation of objectification, the only desire that matters to me in a sexual encounter is *my* desire – and the only question to be asked of the other person is whether they match my desire. The other person becomes a commodity, used for my gratification.

Freedom and consent

Another set of widespread assumptions about sexual activity in our culture has to do with freedom and consent. It is often assumed that people's decisions about sex are their own. People are free, within certain limits, to make decisions about whether and when to have sex, with whom, in what ways – and whether and when to abstain. Accordingly, nobody can demand sexual activity (or sexual abstinence) from someone else – and the need for the consent of the other people involved is the primary limit on anyone's sexual freedom.

The age at which people in England are deemed legally capable of consenting to sexual acts was raised from 12 to 13 in 1875, and to 16 in 1885. Across Europe, the age of consent varies from 14 to 18.

Pornography

Since the rise of the Internet, pornography – generally understood as visual depictions of sexual behaviour intended to arouse the viewer – is nearly all digital. 'Mainstream' porn is usually offered as free-to-use; it is easy to access, despite restrictions about advertising. It is also big business with ongoing investment in developing technologies. In 2018 one of the world's biggest free-to-use digital sites, Pornhub, had 33.5 billion visits worldwide, an increase of 5 billion on the previous year, with daily visits up at almost 100 million per day and a volume of content provided to match demand. The UK is second after the US in the top 20 countries using Pornhub's services. And Pornhub is only one of about ten major porn sites.

Preferences within digital porn sites are navigated through search term categories. Some are unvarying categories provided by the site, others are generated through the analysis of users' search keywords. Search patterns follow the ordinary world of media: cinema, videogames, sports events, and celebrities, as well as terms of sexual preference. 'Lesbian' is the top search term for women and men; 'trans' has risen fast as a search term during 2018.

Although porn sites primarily cater for men, women users are catching up. In 2018 29% of Pornhub's users were women. No data is offered by the sites about usage by under-18s.

'Free' porn makes profits through advertising based on algorithms of user preferences. The free content therefore directs users to more 'specialised' pay-to-use offers based on digital analysis of their usage. As with other algorithmic models, this can mean that the tastes of users are being shaped, directed and sharpened by the commercial imperatives of the business.

There are few checks upon the age or employment conditions for porn actors.[100]

In order to be able to consent, someone also needs the mental capacity to make a choice: they need, in particular, to understand what they are being asked to do. Some people with some mental disorders may therefore not be in a position, legally, to consent.[101]

The idea of the need for consent may seem obvious now, but that has not always been the case and not just in the ancient world. You only need to think of Britain's very deep involvement in the slave trade. Until the nineteenth century, it was possible for all kinds of people to claim absolute rights, including sexual rights, over another person simply by paying a price for them. Nor is that reality now safely confined to history. Modern slavery, where people are confined economically and physically and their bodies and labour used for others' gain, is widespread and difficult to counter, especially with people who are in a country illegally. The UK government estimated in 2018 that there were between 10,000 and 13,000 victims of slavery in the UK, and that the number was increasing. Thousands of those people are suffering sexual exploitation.[102]

Marriage was another context in which, until recently, people did not have the kind of freedom that we are discussing here. Men could not be convicted of marital rape in the UK until 1991, because it was deemed that marrying someone automatically implied consent. Marital rape was only established as an international human rights violation in 1993. In 2018, a YouGov survey of nearly 4,000 people, commissioned by the End Violence Against Women coalition, stated that 'Almost a quarter (24 per cent) of the people we asked thought that in most cases it isn't rape if non-consensual sex occurs within a long-term relationship.'[103]

In recent years, much more attention has been paid in our society to protecting people from unwanted sexual behaviour. Intervention in cases of domestic abuse has become more common. More attention has been paid to the many forms that rape can take, even though public awareness of these developments is patchy. Rates of conviction for rape remain distressingly low, however, in part because of arguments about what constitutes consent, or the perception of consent.[104] The #MeToo movement and similar developments have contributed to increased awareness of many other forms of unwanted sexual behaviour, and of the harm that they do. A narrative of steadily increasing permissiveness is much too simplistic to capture the changes taking place in our culture.

One of the consequences of the #MeToo campaign has been to expose problems with consent when one party is significantly more powerful than the other. Someone might be coerced into having sex in any number of overt ways, but the coercion can also be far more subtle. Someone might agree to have sex only because of an implied threat, or because they have been subject to psychological pressure. They might agree only because refusing will have other social or professional consequences for them, or even because they are intimidated by the other person's importance or forcefulness. While guidelines on consent, such as those given by the #Consentiseverything project, are very important, and work well in the absence of significant power dynamics, they are not enough.[105]

Domestic abuse

'Domestic violence' is defined as any act or omission that causes psychological, physical, sexual or economic harm, or that restricts a person's freedom and development by means of control or coercion,[106] and that takes place between adults within the context of an intimate relationship, whether dating, cohabiting, married, separated or divorced.[107] It might be an isolated act of physical violence, but it could equally well be an ongoing process of coercion. Violence or the threat of violence is often used by one partner to control the other, and, rather than a series of isolated incidents, forms the shape and substance of the relationship.

One in four women in England and Wales, experience some form of domestic violence in their lifetimes.[108] Although both men and women commit and suffer from domestic violence, the vast majority of victims are women. Women are more likely to suffer from sustained, serious forms of violence. For many women, domestic violence is thus an everyday, persistent, and sometimes deadly experience.

There is no single cause of domestic violence. Instead, a wide range of factors increases the likelihood of violence taking place in a marriage or other intimate relationship.[109] If families are forced to live for extended periods at close quarters, as in the lockdown imposed during the COVID-19 pandemic, for example, the risk of domestic violence increases. If a society is marked by violence and insecurity, the risk increases. If there is poverty, exclusion and inequality in a community, the risk increases. If men and women's cultural identities and social roles are rigidly established, and there is little tolerance of change, the risk increases. And if marriage is so protected that divorce is difficult to access, the risk increases.

A particularly stark statistic relates to the proportion of sexual assaults on men and women. In a survey carried out in 2016-17, 20 per cent of women and 4 per cent of men had experienced some type of sexual assault since the age of 16. This is equivalent to 3.4 million female and 631,000 male victims.[110]

We have highlighted above some changes in attitudes to sex across the twentieth century. Those changes were bound up, in part, with attempts to liberate people from situations in which sexual consent was absent or undermined. They accompanied the development of new forms of analysis – such as feminist critique – which could be used to identify the power dynamics affecting sexual relationships. The same processes, however, often led to sex being valued in its spontaneity, to be enjoyed in the moment, quite possibly with no binding promises made for the future. It has taken a long time to notice that such an approach to sex can itself work to the advantage of the most powerful in society and leaves the less powerful (women, children, the poor, the young, and those whose sexuality has given them no legal redress) vulnerable.

We should not ignore or downplay another horrific reality. As the Interim Report of the Independent Inquiry into Child Sexual Abuse says:

> No-one knows, or will ever know, the true scale of child sexual abuse in England and Wales. It will always be hidden from view...
>
> According to the 2015–16 Crime Survey for England and Wales, 7 per cent of people aged between 16 and 59 reported that they were sexually abused as a child. Although this survey did not include young children or all forms of sexual abuse, this still equates to over two million victims and survivors in that age bracket across England and Wales, a substantial proportion of the population.[111]

It is also worth noting the existence of 'peer sexual abuse', in which children are abused by other children. The National Society for the Prevention of Cruelty to Children reports that more and more children are contacting its Childline service to ask for advice after having been coerced by another child into unwanted sexual activity.[112]

The Church of England and the Independent Inquiry into Child Sexual Abuse

The Independent Inquiry into Child Sexual Abuse highlighted the fact that the Church of England's record on protecting people from harm, ensuring sexual safety, and upholding sexual consent, has at times been shockingly poor. There have been similar failures in the church's protection of vulnerable adults, and its responses to domestic abuse. As a result, many do not regard the Church of England as a body that one can look to for good news in the area of sexual relationships.

This book and its accompanying resources were commissioned for the specific purpose of providing the Church of England with teaching and learning resources about human identity, sexuality, relationships and marriage, with a particular focus on the questions raised by LGBTI+ people among us. The process of creating the Living in Love and Faith resources has involved the Church of England in sustained and serious conversations about human sexuality among the bishops, members of General Synod and the Living in Love and Faith groups. Furthermore, the purpose of this book and its accompanying resources is to promote church-wide engagement, undergirded by the Pastoral Principles, that, it is hoped, will lead to a new culture of openness and mutual respect.

Questions surrounding child sexual abuse in the church relate to these overall themes. While acknowledging the reality of abuse in the church, it is important that the specific work of theological reflection on IICSA be carried out separately from the Living in Love and Faith project, and, importantly, together with victims, with great pastoral sensitivity and only after the full published findings of IICSA have been carefully assessed. However, whatever the church's response to the changes that we are describing in this chapter, it is clear that it must be accompanied by ongoing humility, scrutiny and repentance.

There are also other questions to ask about children and consent
– some of which relate to topics we will turn to later in this chapter.
Who decides what action to take when children identify as trans?[113]
Whose responsibility is it when children are sexually active before
the age of consent? Who decides how to respond to a child born
with what are called 'Variations in Sexual Characteristics' (VSC),
commonly known as intersex characteristics? We see children
as needing adult protection and adults' help to make decisions
about their bodies, and yet the most fleeting look at the history of
children's treatment within families and by institutions, including the
church, shows how vulnerable this leaves them to adult abuse – and
how patchy, painful and difficult is their redress.

In today's online-dominated world whole new dimensions to
these concerns have emerged. Protecting the images of children's
bodies is a vital aspect of the current safeguarding agenda.
Adults, too, need similar protection: images and videos of people
can proliferate online and ruin lives.[114] Some of the pressures on
freedom are more subtle: people's online choices and preferences,
including the choices and preferences of children, are nudged
by algorithms processing their mined data, until the question of
who has actually made a particular choice becomes extremely
problematic.[115]

Identity and self-understanding

Having looked at relationships and sex, we now turn to a set of
developments that come under the broad heading of 'identity' or
'self-understanding'. In this context, 'identity' refers to a person's
deeply rooted sense of themselves: their habitual, often seemingly
automatic, ways of understanding who they are and how they fit
into the wider world around them. It refers to deep patterns of
feeling, imagination and understanding that colour the whole
of someone's experience. Those patterns emerge through the
interaction between a person's inheritance and their environment,
from the first moment in which their cells start developing in the
womb. They are shaped by a person's whole history, by all the
people around them, by all the ways in which they have been
classified and positioned. They are shaped by all the ways in

which a person has responded to all of that, and all that they have discovered about themselves in the process.

To understand people's identities, one needs to listen to their stories – and that is one of the reasons why this book has stories woven through it. That is not to say that the way people tell their own stories automatically does justice to who they are. People might not have a clear sense of their own capacities and limitations. They might not see the ways in which they are influenced by others, or the impact they have on those around them. They might miss the ways in which they fit into the power structures that shape our world, or the larger stories of which they are a part. To understand people's identities demands critical attentiveness to the stories people tell about themselves, and to all the stories that are woven around them.

Our more abstract discussions of identity are not meant to divert attention from those stories or push them to the sidelines. One could think of them, instead, as a commentary on those stories – not just the stories given explicitly in the book, but the stories of all the people in our church and in our society, whatever their sexual orientation or their gender. Our abstract discussions are a commentary that might help us listen to those stories more closely, ask deeper questions of them, and see more clearly what questions they ask of us.

There can be many different aspects of identity, including class, race, and nationality, but in this section we are going to discuss sexual orientation and gender. Here more than anywhere else in this chapter we recognize that there is no neutral language to use. Even using the term 'identity' as the heading for the chapter is controversial. The word 'identity' can be heard as meaning something like 'the deepest story that can be told about a person' – and so it can tip us into a competitive argument over what the deepest story about a person should be. We recognize that controversy, but have tried to use the word 'identity' more loosely and descriptively. All kinds of factors can be part of a person's 'deeply rooted sense of themselves', to differing degrees and in differing ways. We are not trying, simply by using the heading 'identity', to pre-empt discussion of how much all these different components matter, how they might interact, or what difference they might make.

Many of the other terms that we use in this section are similarly controversial. We have tried to indicate some of the main areas where contention and questions arise for some, while also paying close attention to those of us who find the language we have used an important and liberative way of articulating our experience.

> See Chapter 10 (pages 201–211) for a discussion of identity in the Christian narrative.

Sexual orientation

The first area of identity that we want to cover is sexual orientation. A person's orientation is their tendency to feel sexual interest in, or attraction to, people of particular sexes or genders, or to feel such interest or attraction to people regardless of sex or gender. Asexuality, which describes people who are not sexually attracted to anyone, is not a 'sexual orientation' as such, but a reality that is important to bear in mind in these discussions.

Some resist the language of 'orientation', or resist describing it as a matter of 'identity', preferring to keep the focus on patterns of attraction, behaviour, and sexual relationships, without making assumptions about how central these are to a person's identity.

Various terms are commonly used to name different kinds of orientation. To give a list that is certainly not exhaustive: a person might be called

- 'heterosexual' to the extent that they are predominantly attracted to people of the 'opposite' sex;

- 'homosexual' (normally lesbian or gay) to the extent that they are predominantly attracted to people of the same sex as themselves;

- 'bisexual' to the extent that they find themselves attracted to both men and women and possibly other gender categories (and since this is about the experience of attraction, someone might be in a lifelong monogamous sexual relationship and still be bisexual).

As mentioned above, the word 'asexual' is not a sexual orientation, nor is 'gender fluidity', which is discussed in the next section.

In 2020, the Office for National Statistics Annual Population Survey published data on sexual orientation in the UK which had been gathered in 2018. The survey captured the self-perceived orientation of respondents over the age of 16 at the time of the survey and extrapolated the data to give indicative figures for the whole UK population. It found that:

– IDENTITY –

94.6%↓

identified as heterosexual

94.6% of the UK population identify as heterosexual or straight – a decline from 95.3% in 2014.

2.2%↑

identified as LGB

In 2018, 2.2% (approximately 1.2 million people) identified as lesbian, gay or bisexual (LGB), an increase from 1.6% in 2014. 1.4% identified as lesbian or gay, and 0.9% as bisexual.

2.5%   2.0%

identified as LGB

Men (2.5%) were more likely to identify as LGB than women (2.0%).

– SINGLE –

68.7%

More than two thirds (68.7%) of people who identified as LGB were single (never married or in a civil partnership).

– AGE –

They noted that people in older age groups were less likely to identify as LGB than those in the younger age groups:

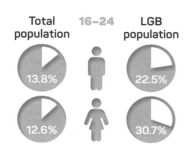

Total population	16–24	LGB population
13.8%		22.5%
12.6%		30.7%

Of the total population aged 16 years and over, 13.8% men and 12.6% women were aged between 16 and 24. However, of the total population of people who identified as LGB, 22.5% of men and 30.7% of women were aged between 16 and 24.

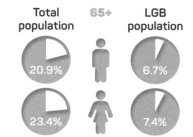

Total population	65+	LGB population
20.9%		6.7%
23.4%		7.4%

Of the total population aged 16 years and over, 20.9% of men and 23.4% of women are aged 65 years and over. However, of the total population of people who identified as LGB, only 6.7% of men and 7.4% of women were aged 65 years and over.

The statistics above are drawn from the Office of National Statistics. For full source references see endnote 116 on page 435.

Sexual orientation from a historical perspective

It is very difficult to line up any of our terminology with the experience of people in the past – or, indeed, with that of other cultures. There is a tendency either to assume people have had the same kinds of feelings over the whole of human history, or to regard some forms of orientation as specific to our times. This is part of a wider approach to past societies, in which we either search the past for possible allies or instead emphasize their difference from 'us'. So, considering relationships in ancient Greece between an older man and a much younger one, some people would see this as homosexuality (although the word 'homosexual' was only created in the late nineteenth century), others as sexual abuse, and – because the older man was also supposed to have a female wife and to have children with her – others would see it as bisexuality. The use of many of these terms – in this example, and in countless others – is contested.

Gender identity

The second aspect of identity that we want to explore is gender. Before going any further, however, it is important to recognize that almost every part of the discussion below is controversial. There is no neutral terminology available. Every way of talking about this material is 'theory-laden': it assumes a particular way of understanding the subject matter. We have therefore had to make choices. We have chosen to use a set of terms and distinctions that are used in many scientific and academic discussions in this area, and that are important to many trans people (that is, people who identify as transgender – see below).[117] They are regarded by many trans people as necessary to do justice to their experience, and as avoiding assumptions that are seen as discriminatory. There are, nevertheless, serious discussions about many of these terms and distinctions. Some in the church, and in wider society, defend them; others dispute the understandings of gender that they appear to assume. We will highlight some of the questions this raises along the way, and return to them later in the book. We don't want the choices we have made in this section to pre-empt those discussions.

Since the 1970s, it has become common to distinguish gender from sex. In this context, 'sex' has to do with biology, and specifically to the ways in which bodies are sexually differentiated. 'Gender', on the other hand, has to do with culture and experience, and specifically to the ways in which sexual differentiation is responded to and experienced. It can refer to someone's sense of their own identity, or to other people's ways of categorising them.

When we look more closely, all the parts of these initial definitions quickly get more complicated. On the biological side, to talk about 'the ways in which bodies are sexually differentiated' can refer to a number of different things. To give a simplified list, it can refer to:

- a person's chromosomes;

- aspects of their body that develop while they are in the womb, including: genitals, internal reproductive organs, brain structure, balance of hormones;

- the ways in which any of these aspects of their bodies develop through childhood and beyond, especially during puberty.

The relationship between these different aspects of sexual differentiation is sometimes more complicated than people expect – as we will be discussing in the material on intersex in the next chapter.

Gender can be similarly complicated. In recent discussions, the word 'gender' can refer to any of the following:

- The way in which a person is categorized at birth. Parents or medical professionals typically identify where a baby fits within the standard gender categories prevalent in the society around them: 'It's a girl!' It is increasingly common to call this 'gender assigned at birth'.

- The way that someone currently understands themselves: their sense of where, if anywhere, they currently fit within their society's gender categories, or of their lack of fit with those categories. This is often referred to as 'gender identity'.

- The ways in which someone expresses or performs gender, in behaviours and adornments that have gender associations. This is often referred to as 'gender role'.

- A society's expectations for how people will look and behave, and the conscious and unconscious evaluations that will tend to be made of people, based on what is known or believed about those people's gender.

With all of these, there are complex discussions about where the distinctions people use come from. When we categorize babies at birth, when we develop an understanding of our own gender identity or perform gender roles, when we make stereotypical assumptions about people, we are always responding to what we see and know in ways that are shaped by our whole history and all our social interactions, in the way outlined at the start of this section on identity.

The first of the points above illustrates something of the controversy that exists in this area. It has only fairly recently become common to speak about gender being 'assigned at birth'. Some would argue that what happens at birth, except in relation to some intersex individuals, is a straightforward recognition of biological sex. Others insist that what is happening is the assigning of an individual, on the basis of just some of their biological features, to one of the two gender categories that we stereotypically divide our world into.

Gender and sex

The third place where things get complicated is precisely in the distinction between sex and gender – because the two are tangled together. One connection between sex and gender is obvious. The way in which a baby is categorized at birth is typically a response to that baby's visible genitals – though we will see in the next chapter that the picture is not always so straightforward. There are other connections between gender and the body, however. It has been argued, for instance, that someone's sense of their own gender, whether or not it is the one assigned to them at birth, might emerge in part from the way their body has developed. It might, for instance, emerge from the ways their brains and nervous systems have developed. That might have to do with development that took place while they were still in the womb, but it can go beyond that. There are, in other words, complex two-way flows between sex and gender, some aspects of which are not yet well understood. Some now therefore refer to 'gender/sex' as a single complex reality, rather than try to sustain a neat distinction between biology and culture.[118]

History of trans identities

What we understand as trans (in all its different forms) has been understood very differently in different cultural settings and periods of history. Many societies have had ways of categorising gender that don't divide everyone up into 'male' and 'female'. In some societies people who we might today identify as trans have had a special status as shamans or priests. For example, North American tribal cultures often recognized 'Two-Spirit' people – a term which overlaps with what we are calling trans, as well as with lesbian, gay, bisexual, and intersex. In different ways, in different contexts, such people have been treated with reverence and sometimes have a role as leaders of the community.[119] The word 'transsexual' was first used in German in 1923 and in English in 1949, framing as a medical issue the experience of those who don't identify with the gender that they were assigned to at birth.

The word 'transgender' is more recent, and was coined in part to avoid this medical framing. It can be traced back to the 1970s, when it was popularised by an American activist, Virginia Prince. She used it to describe the way in which she lived full-time in a gender role different from the gender to which she had been assigned at birth, but without surgical intervention. Since then, usage of the term has evolved to cover all those who don't identify with their assigned gender.

The adjective 'trans' (or 'transgender') can be used to refer to any individual whose sense of their own gender identity does not match the gender that they were assigned to at birth. The adjective 'cis' (or 'cisgender') can be used to refer to any individual whose sense of their own gender identity does match the gender that they were assigned to at birth. ('Cis' is a Latin prefix, often contrasted with the prefix 'trans'. It has been used, for instance, in geographical contexts: 'cisalpine' meaning 'on this side of the Alps' and 'transalpine' 'on the other side of the Alps'. It was adopted in discussions of gender in the 1990s, simply in order to have words to use for people on both sides of the distinction we are discussing.)

The adjective 'trans' is increasingly used to name a wide range of different kinds of identity. It is perhaps most commonly used for someone who was assigned female at birth but who identifies as male, or vice versa. It can also be used of someone who was assigned female or male at birth but who does not identify as either. Amongst various other possibilities, someone may identify as 'non-binary' if they don't identify either as fully male or fully female; they may identify as 'gender-fluid' if they experience their gender identity as fluctuating or as context-specific; they may identify as 'agender' if they don't identify at all as either male or female.

Gender identity can change with time. Gender fluidity is a term which is used in different ways. Often it describes non-binary gender identity, or a person's understanding of themselves as gender fluid, having transitioned from one (binary) gender to another. It may also refer to change in gender identity across time, or to the recognition of a multiplicity or continuum of gender categories. Discussions about sex, gender and gender identity are ongoing and there is still much to learn about these matters.[120]

Some people who identify as trans (but not all) experience gender dysphoria. Dysphoria is a deeply rooted discomfort or distress. A person can experience it towards bodily features that are not typically regarded as matching their identified gender ('physical dysphoria'). It can also be experienced towards the ways in which other people respond to and categorize those bodily features ('social dysphoria'). Identifying as trans does not necessarily bring with it these kinds of visceral discomfort, but many trans people do experience them with differing levels of severity. This experience can lead to anxiety, depression, and an increased risk of suicide.[121] ('Gender incongruence' is the term now suggested by the World Health Organization for 'a marked and persistent incongruence between an individual's experienced gender and the assigned sex', which need not manifest as dysphoria.[122])

Some trans people transition. That is, either temporarily or permanently, they express a different gender identity from the one they have previously expressed. Such transitioning can be social: changing some or all of one's name, the pronouns one uses, one's clothing, make-up, hairstyle, voice, deportment, and social roles. It can be legal: seeking recognition of one's gender identity on legal documents such as passports, as allowed under the 2004 Gender Recognition Act (though relatively few people take advantage of this[123]). It can also be medical: pursuing various different kinds of hormonal or surgical treatments designed to align some aspects of the body more closely with a person's identified gender.

Transitioning is normally understood as a way for someone to do justice to a gender identity that they have been aware of for a long time (perhaps for as long as they can remember), or that they have slowly discovered – though some also experience their gender identity as changing over time.

Transgender: statistics

It is very difficult to know how many trans people there are in the UK. The Government Equalities Office tentatively estimated in 2018 that there are currently between 200,000 and 500,000 trans people in the UK. Recent studies in the United States suggested that trans people make up between 0.5 and 2.7% of the population – with this very wide variation reflecting significant differences in the definition used.[124]

The situation is changing rapidly, however, and these numbers may turn out to be too low. The growth in public awareness of trans people, the prevalence of social media sites and online trans forums, the spread of new vocabularies for naming trans experience, seem to be leading to increased numbers of people identifying as trans.

These increases are reflected in referrals reported by gender clinics in a number of countries. In the UK, referrals of young people to the Gender Identity and Development Service (GIDS), part of the Tavistock-Portman NHS Trust, have been rising steadily, growing from 678 in 2014–15 to 2,590 in 2018–2019. The average age at time of referral has also dropped over the last decade. The treatment of children and young people continues to be a source of significant controversy.[125] In 2018/19, 1,740 of the referrals were for young people assigned female at birth, and 624 for those assigned male at birth, though this may simply be a matter of a correction to an earlier under-diagnosis of people in the former category.

It is important to remember, however, that not all trans people seek this kind of medical treatment, and only some of those who do are referred to clinics like this. The number of referrals is only one indication of the number of people identifying as trans in the population more widely.[126]

Society's response

There have been enormous changes in the way that society has responded to LGBTI+ people over the past half century, and these have been mirrored in numerous changes to law and policy.

1967: Male same-sex acts in certain circumstances were decriminalized, but full legal equality remained a long way off: according to a Guardian article published in 2007, between 1967 and 2003, 30,000 gay and bisexual men were convicted for behaviour that would not have been a crime had their partner been a woman.[127] In the 1970s, in particular, there were still frequent prosecutions for homosexual activity, often following entrapment by the police.[128]

1988: The Conservative Government passed the Local Government Act. Section 28 ruled that local authorities 'shall not intentionally promote homosexuality or publish material with the intention of promoting homosexuality'.

1994: The male homosexual age of consent, which had been set at 21 in 1967, was lowered to 18.

2000: Following the election of a Labour government in 1997, there was an increased liberalization of the laws concerning homosexual activity. The age of consent was reduced again to 16. The bar to LGBT people serving in the armed forces was removed. Until then, military personnel found guilty of same-sex activity could be immediately discharged for gross misconduct. The army, navy and air force subsequently introduced many changes to their procedures, including representation on Pride marches and recruitment advertisements in LGBT magazines.

2003: Section 28 was repealed.

2004: The Civil Partnership Act was passed with overwhelming support in the House of Commons. The first civil partnerships were created in 2005.

2004: In the same year, the Gender Recognition Act passed into law. It enabled, for the first time, trans people to achieve legal recognition of their affirmed gender.[129]

2010: The Equality Act both combined and extended earlier anti-discrimination legislation. It introduced the concept of 'protected characteristics' and made discrimination illegal on the grounds of age, disability, gender reassignment, marriage and civil partnership, pregnancy and maternity, race, religion and belief, sex, and sexual orientation.[130]

2013: The Marriage (Same Sex Couples) Act 2013 was introduced by the Conservative Government. The Act passed with large majorities in both Houses of Parliament.

2018 A consultation about a Reform of the 2004 Gender Recognition Act was undertaken by the Conservative Government.[131]

2019: The law on civil partnerships was changed to include heterosexual couples.

2019: The Conservative Government's requirements on relationship and sex education in schools – 'we expect all pupils to have been taught LGBT content at a timely point as part of this area of the curriculum'[132] – encountered opposition, mainly on the grounds of religious belief. Guidance on how to respond to 'disruption' over LGBT teaching/relationship education was issued by the government in October 2019.[133]

These legal changes, which overall mean that LGBTI+ people are more able to be open about their identities and relationships, have been accompanied by a growth in the visibility of those minorities, and by rapidly changing social attitudes to them.

The first march for gay equality took place in London's Highbury Fields in November 1970, attended by only 150 people.[134] Two years later, London's first Gay Pride march was attended by between 700 and 2000 people. The controversy over Section 28 led to increased numbers attending Pride marches in protest. In 1983 the march was renamed 'Lesbian and Gay Pride', and in the 1990s it became more of a carnival, with large park gatherings and a fair after the marches. In 1996 the event was renamed 'Lesbian, Gay, Bisexual and Transgender Pride'. An estimated 1.5 million joined the London Pride March in 2019.[135]

The Government's LGBT Action Plan, published in 2018, says that

> The existing evidence base shows that acceptance of same-sex relationships among the general public is at a record high and continues to increase, with 64% of the British public saying same-sex relationships were 'not wrong at all' in 2016, up from 47% in 2012, and 11% in 1987.[136]

A more recent report suggests a slight decline in acceptance of premarital sex and same-sex sexual relationships.[137]

In recent years there has been a significant growth in public awareness of trans people, helped in part by such celebrities as Caitlyn Jenner, Andreja Pejic, and Laverne Cox. This has prompted some critical reactions. Controversy has surrounded issues such as the access to women's bathroom facilities,[138] or to women's sporting events,[139] by trans women, as well as about treatment of children and young people experiencing gender dysphoria.[140] There have also been debates amongst feminist thinkers.[141] Some focus on the differences between the socialisation and experience of cis women and of trans women before they transition, and on that basis question whether trans women are truly women. Others have argued that women's experience is very diverse, and that the experience of trans women is part of that diversity. Public debate on these matters is often polarised and strongly expressed, especially in social media.

The growth in public awareness of LGBTI+ people has not made life safe for LGBTI+ people. Reported LGBT hate crimes doubled between 2014 and 2018, and reported transphobic crimes more than trebled.[142] Recent data obtained by the BBC indicates that the number of reported hate crimes against trans people recorded by police in England, Scotland and Wales has risen by 81 per cent from 1,073 crimes in 2016/17 to 1,944 in 2018/19. Reported crimes are likely to be only a fraction of all incidents, however, and it is unclear what proportion of these increases reflects greater awareness and higher rates of reporting, and what proportion reflects an increase in the number of incidents themselves.

Drawing on a YouGov poll of more than 5,000 LGBTI+ people in Britain, the charity Stonewall estimated in 2017 that 'Two in five trans people have experienced a hate crime or incident because of their gender identity in the last 12 months.'[143] In the same year, the Government Equalities Office received over 108,000 responses to a survey of LGBTI+ people:

- More than 70 per cent of those surveyed said they had 'avoided being open about their sexual orientation for fear of a negative reaction from others'

- 68 per cent said that they had avoided holding hands with a partner in public for fear of a negative response from others.

- Two out of every five reported that they had experienced an incident such as physical violence or verbal harassment in the last twelve months – the vast majority of which were left unreported, because the respondents believed that such things 'happen all the time'.[144]

Although LGBTI+ people are now free from fear of prosecution, there is a long way to go before they are free of fear from harassment.

All the discussion above of statistics, medical interventions, and cultural trends can obscure the fact that we are always talking about *people*. We are talking about real individuals, each with their own rich and varied history of experience. We are often talking about people who have had to endure high levels of bullying and exclusion, in society and in the church. And we are talking about people who have too often been treated – including by the church – as problems to be resolved or issues to be debated.

CHAPTER 6

Science

In Chapter 5 our primary focus was on social trends relating to relationships, sex and identity.

In this chapter the focus is on developments in our understanding of sexuality and gender through the biological, medical and behavioural sciences.

In order to illustrate how scientific research impacts this area of our lives, it is worth thinking about some of the scientific and technological developments that have completely changed our thinking about sex and gender in relation to child bearing. Consider, for example, the advent of reliable and effective contraception in the early 1960s which allowed the reproductive element of heterosexual relationships to be separated from that which promotes bonding of the couple in mutual affection. Developments in reproduction technologies, such as in vitro fertilisation and artificial insemination, have enabled female same-sex couples to conceive and bear children through known donors or sperm banks. Recent legal, technical, and social changes have produced new possibilities and opportunities for gay men to become fathers and create their families through surrogacy.[145]

All of these developments, made possible through scientific research, have significantly influenced the social and psychological ways in which human beings behave sexually and how they view their sexuality and sexual relationships. They also raise moral and legal questions which science alone cannot answer. A legal case in 2019, for example, raised the issue of whether a trans man, Freddie McConnell, who gave birth to a child can be identified as the child's father. The case was lost in the Family Division Courts and in the Court of Appeal.[146]

So with these examples as a backdrop, we begin by thinking in some detail about how science expands our understanding of what is going on in human bodies - while not necessarily either addressing or providing simple or clear-cut answers to some of the questions we have. We will then go on to offer brief overviews of the status of current scientific understanding of key topics of relevance to human identity, sex, sexuality and gender.

See Chapter 15 (pages 333-335) for a discussion of how science helps us to hear God in relation to matters of identity, sexuality and relationships.

Scientific study of sexuality and gender

We reflected in Chapter 4 on how learning about science enriches our understanding of God's world. Matters relating to human identity, sexuality and relationships are about bodies, how we experience them and what we do with them. They raise questions that the sciences can legitimately ask and explore, such as, 'What factors influence sexual orientation or gender identity?' and 'How is sexual activity related to mental well-being?' Furthermore, technological developments have not only opened up whole new areas of research, such as genetics, but have also made possible medical interventions that affect what we can do with our bodies in relation to sexuality, gender identity and procreation. A vast array of different but interconnected branches of science feed into these complex areas of study: medicine, genetics, epigenetics, psychiatry, physiology, endocrinology, neuroscience, epidemiology, psychology and other social and behavioural sciences. That is one reason why there are no simple answers to some of the questions we may want to put to science.

Knowledge of the human body has developed enormously in the past 500 years. In 1543, Andreas Vesalius' *On the Fabric of the Human Body* set in train a revolution in our understanding of anatomy. Darwin's *On the Origin of Species*, published in 1859, made us more aware than ever before of the closeness of our relationship to the other living species on our planet. Only in the twentieth century have psychology and the social sciences emerged as scientific disciplines in their own right. The task of identifying and mapping all the genes of human DNA was not completed until 2003. So another reason why there are no simple answers is because many of the scientific fields to which we turn to explore gender and sexuality are relatively new and developing rapidly.

Many scientific studies of the kind that are needed in relation to sexuality and gender ideally require randomized and large sample sizes in order to produce robust evidence. This can be difficult when relying on an already small proportion of the population who may be self-selecting or who may have reasons not to wish to participate or to continue to participate in research. Practical and ethical considerations also make randomization difficult in this area, and so all of these methodological issues also contribute to the difficulty of producing evidence for definitive conclusions.

This doesn't mean that the results of scientific research in these areas are unreliable, but it does mean that coming to firm conclusions takes time. It takes time because some research is longitudinal: it involves making observations over many years. It also takes time because of the scientific community's commitment to peer review and the replicability of research. All scientific findings must be scrutinized by other scientists in the field before they can be published to ensure, as far as possible, that they are not anomalous or influenced by human bias. An example of possible bias would be in relation to research into the causes of human sexual orientation. People who believe that the free expression of some sexual orientations is morally questionable may seek to find social causes for sexual orientation. People who see nothing wrong with the expression of sexual orientations may be more likely to seek biological causes. Cultural trends, social norms and political agendas can also influence what and how scientific research is carried out. The availability of funding, for example, is likely to shape the research agenda of the scientific community. Thus research into the causes of sexual orientation (like all scientific research) needs to be scrutinized for how these factors influence the focus and methodology of scientific work and the interpretation of its results.

A case study: scientific studies into the causes of sexual orientation

In order to get some insight into the multidisciplinary complexities of scientific work in sexuality and gender, consider what might be involved in the search for a definitive answer to the question, 'What causes sexual orientation?'.[147] A first step would be defining what is meant by sexual orientation. Is sexual orientation about the *sexual activity* between people of the same sex, of opposite sexes, or both sexes? Or is it about a person *choosing to identify* as homosexual, heterosexual or bisexual, for example? Or is it about a degree of *sexual attraction* to the same sex, both sexes or the other sex? Or is it about *physiological sexual arousal* to men or women or both? In any research, it is important to define exactly what phenomenon is being studied, if findings are to be corroborated with other research.

If we were to define sexual orientation as being about physiological arousal, then how would we go about measuring this? We could ask people to self-report, but this would have certain inbuilt inaccuracies: some people may be conflicted about their patterns of sexual arousal, for example, and may not wish to report a true answer. Some people's responses may be affected by the stigma associated with particular answers. An alternative way forward would be to carry out experiments that measured changes in a subject's genitals in response to male or female images as stimuli. Such measurements offer a level of consistency of findings among men and (to a lesser extent) among women, but it would be difficult to compare them given the different physiological and anatomical changes that occur in male and female genitals.

Once we have established what we mean by sexual orientation, then the work of defining the question of causation begins. Not all questions are valid starting points for scientific exploration. The question, 'Is sexual orientation a choice?', for example, does not make scientific sense if we accept the definition of sexual orientation as being about sexual attraction and / or arousal. It is not possible to choose our sexual desires or arousal, but it is, of course, possible to choose how we act on them. The possibility of changing one's pattern of desire or arousal *can* be scientifically addressed and will be discussed when we consider the issue of what has become known as conversion therapy.

The question 'To what extent is sexual orientation determined by genetics or the environment?' is a valid question and has led to studies on twins on the one hand, and molecular genetics on the other. Another question is, 'What is the relationship between hormones and sexual orientation?'. This has led to studies about the different levels of hormones in individuals of different sexual orientations and, more importantly, the irreversible effects of early hormones in individuals' development.

Another way of exploring the question of causation might be to ask, 'Are different sexual orientations affected by different postnatal social experiences?'. 'Social experiences' in this question are experiences involving other people, rather than what might be called 'innate' factors, such as hormones or genes. A major difficulty with any scientific research of this kind is that finding a correlation between two bodies of data does not necessarily imply causation.

Our discussion about the challenges of scientific enquiry into sexuality and gender would be incomplete without drawing attention to the fact that some research simply cannot be carried out on ethical grounds. It would not be ethically possible to inject adults with hormones to test hypotheses about sexual orientation, or to subject people to social influences – such as sexual seduction or abuse – to determine whether or not this affects sexual orientation.

Hopefully this brief detour into just one area of scientific research illustrates the complexity, breadth and provisionality of contemporary scientific enquiry. It will be important to bear this in mind as we now turn to a number of topics that are the subject of contemporary scientific enquiry and that form a backdrop to many of the perceptions and discussions about human identity, sexuality and gender in our society today.

The science of sexual orientation

One of the ways of defining sexual orientation is concerned with the sex and gender of those to whom we are sexually attracted. It is usually construed in terms of attraction to the same or opposite sex, or either/both – and thus as homosexual, heterosexual or bisexual respectively. An alternative approach is to consider it in terms of attraction to male or female – thus as androphilic or gynephilic respectively – without reference to the sex/gender of the person experiencing the attraction. Helpful though this is in terms of research, and in terms of helping us to think about what exactly the important differences and variations in sexual orientation are, it does presume a binary understanding of gender.

Genetic research has employed a variety of methods to attempt to ascertain the extent to which sexual orientation is influenced by genes as opposed to biological or social environment and exactly what that influence might be.[148] Research is further complicated by environmental and genetic influences which modify the *expression* of genes, so that the same gene may have different effects in different circumstances.

The conclusion would seem to be that approximately one-third of the variation appears to be due to genetic factors, with the rest due to environment.[149] There is scope for future research to provide better evidence, and the figure may be higher or lower than this, but this is the best evidenced estimate currently available. Studies of genetic markers to try to identify particular genes that might be affecting sexual orientation have not produced consistent results, although various genes have been suggested in particular studies in relation to homosexuality. Given the likely complexity of the genetic influence on homosexuality, this is not surprising. A recent large-scale study concluded:

> Same-sex sexual behavior is influenced by not one or a few
> genes but many. Overlap with genetic influences on other traits
> provides insights into the underlying biology of same-sex sexual
> behavior, and analysis of different aspects of sexual preference
> underscore its complexity [...]. Nevertheless, many uncertainties
> remain to be explored, including how sociocultural influences on
> sexual preference might interact with genetic influences.[150]

Sociocultural influences are not the only ways in which environment
might contribute to variation in sexual orientation. The word
'environment' is far-reaching and means different things to
scientists working in different disciplines. The two-thirds of variation
that is made up by non-genetic factors is all understood to be
'environment' in one way or another, but this might include the
influence of non-social as well as social factors. Hormones and
other biochemical/physiological influences within the womb, for
example, as well as non-social environmental influences after birth
might be important. A large amount of research, from different
scientific disciplines, has attempted to establish what these diverse
environmental influences might be.

Amongst non-social environmental influences that have been
studied, the hormonal influences exerted upon the foetus in
the womb during pregnancy have been of particular interest.
It is possible that variant levels of male sex hormones acting
differentially upon sexual organ development and certain brain
regions during crucial periods of development might sometimes
result in adult males who experience androphilia (attraction to
males), or adult females who experience gynephilia (attraction to
females). This theory is supported by evidence from animal studies
and from clinical studies of humans. It is highly likely that there is
some degree of pre-birth biological influence of this kind.[151]

One of the best-studied and well-attested observations in research
in this field has been that of the fraternal birth order effect (FBOE).
Statistically speaking, gay men are more likely than heterosexual
men to have more older (biological) brothers.[152] This effect has been
observed around the world, independent of cultural context. It is
important to emphasize that this is a *statistical* finding, which means
that exceptions occur which do not invalidate the trend but show
that other factors may also be involved. For example, some firstborn
sons are homosexual, and some identical twins have different
sexual orientations despite both having the same number of older
brothers. While the exact mechanism of the FBOE is still debated,

it is almost certainly due to environmental influences within the uterus.[153]

The scientific research that has been published to date suggests that the *social* environment does not appear to exert any significant impact on the development of sexual orientation. There has been extensive debate over various theories that have suggested that it is important. For example, it has been proposed that the development of same-sex sexual orientation might be unhelpfully influenced by encounters with older homosexuals. In fact, most non-heterosexual people recall experiencing same-sex attraction, on average, three years before their first sexual encounter. Psychoanalytic theories concerning difficulties in relationship with parents have relied on evidence based on therapists' observations which are of limited value and significance. Rearing by homosexual parents has also been offered as a cause for increasing the likelihood of becoming homosexual, but there is little evidence that this is the case, although the research is of limited scope.

It is important to remember that all these areas of research are vulnerable to political, moral and religious aspirations of scientists themselves or of agencies which fund research.

The science of gender identity

Origins of gender identity

The origins and nature of gender identity are currently poorly understood. For all of us, our sense of our own gender identity will have emerged from the ways our bodies and brains have developed, the ways people have behaved towards us, and the ways we have responded, and the ways we have learnt to negotiate the gendered assumptions, practices and institutions of our society. Both biological and psycho-social factors are likely to be involved.

Much appears to be learnt before the age of two years, but it is only by the age of six years that most children can understand the relationship between genitalia and gender, and the typical constancy of gender. It is possible that there is a period during which the brain is maximally sensitive to formative experiences concerned with gender identity.

It is possible that gender identity is more directly influenced by genes and/or hormones, or indirectly influenced by biologically determined traits of personality and temperament. Psychosocial factors influencing development of gender identity may include verbal and non-verbal gender labelling and reinforcement, and issues related to parental attachment.

Gender transition

Gender transition can mean different things for different people. Some people may choose to dress and live in the gender with which they identify, while some opt to take hormones or also have surgery. Current guidance emphasizes commencing with reversible steps related to social presentation of gender and only later progressing to irreversible treatments.

Currently, treatment through the NHS, for example, begins with an in-depth assessment leading to a diagnosis of gender dysphoria that involves several consultations with two or more specialists over a number of months. These sessions may involve close family members. A treatment plan may vary considerably from individual to individual. Hormone treatment requires regular monitoring, and genital reconstructive surgery is only made available after a person has socially transitioned to the gender with which they identify, by dressing and behaving in ways associated with that gender for at least a year. It should be emphasized, however, that this is an area that is evolving rapidly.

A recent review of peer-reviewed primary research carried out between 1991 and 2017 reported that the evidence in 52 out of 57 studies pointed to improved well-being of trans people following gender transition treatments.[154] Four studies had mixed or null findings, and no studies conclude that gender transition causes overall harm. The review suggests that only a very small proportion of people (0.3 to 3.8 per cent) regret gender transition and that such regret is likely to be caused by a lack of social support or poor surgical outcomes. There are anecdotal accounts of transgender individuals who do regret having had gender reassignment treatment and even seek to detransition. A Swedish study that followed up the long-term effects of gender transition concluded that people who had undergone hormone treatment and surgery showed considerably higher risks for mortality, suicidal behaviour, and psychiatric morbidity than the general population.[155] However, as the authors of this research emphasize, a properly controlled trial of the benefits/harms of gender reassignment is not possible. Their findings do suggest that even though medical treatments may alleviate gender dysphoria, they do not completely remedy the high rates of mental health problems that many transgender people experience prior to treatment.

Transgender and gender diverse (TGD) children and adolescents

An increasing number of children and adolescents identifying as gender nonconforming or transgender are seeking help with gender dysphoria, and/or achieving a social and/or medical change that would bring their physical and personal appearance, and their behaviour, in line with their gender identity.[156] Furthermore, the sex ratio is changing. Until about 2006, the majority of young people who sought clinical help were children assigned male at birth who identify as girls. However in the US and in Europe, this ratio has changed with more girls who are expressing gender non-conformity or who are seeking help to live as the opposite sex.[157] This may be because gender dysphoria among girls has been under-diagnosed in the past. There also appears to be some co-occurrence of gender dysphoria and autism.[158] Studies from the United States and Netherlands suggest that more children are socially transitioning before puberty.[159]

Not all children and young adolescents who express concern or distress about their gender continue to do so into late adolescence and young adulthood.[160] In relatively recent studies it would appear that 40 per cent or more of TGD young people continue in the longer term to express a wish to change to the opposite sex. [161]

To date, no evidence exists that can be used clinically to predict how individuals will develop in relation to their gender identity. In particular, it is not possible to predict which children with concerns about their gender identity as they approach puberty will continue to experience these concerns into adult life. Treatment is controversial. The purpose of puberty blocking medication is to prevent the development and progression of unwanted sexual characteristics that the body's own sex steroids would produce. It is argued that this provides some breathing space in which the young person and their family can decide about treatment options later in adolescence. However, little is known about the short- or long-term physical or psychological impacts of such treatments. Blocking or delaying puberty is a serious step to take for young people and their families and there is a need for better evidence on its wider impact, including bone development and cognition[162]. Although guidelines on management of young people experiencing gender dysphoria have recently been published in Australia, [163] [164] we still need better scientific evidence on which to base clinical management.[165]

The science of variations in sexual characteristics: intersex

We listed above various different ways in which people's bodies show sexual differentiation. In some people's bodies, those various aspects don't align as 'all male' or 'all female' (if we label them in conventional ways).[166] Chromosomes, for example, exist not just as XX (female) or XY (male), but in various other combinations (e.g. XY chromosomes in a body which looks female; one single X chromosome; a mixture of XX and XY cells in the same individual). Males typically have testes and females ovaries, but sometimes someone will have one testis and one ovary in the same body, or a combined ovotestis containing both testicular and ovarian tissue. A person's genital anatomy may appear female, male, somewhere in between, or not particularly like either: it is possible to have a female vulva (and, after puberty, breasts, hips, and a generally female morphology) in combination with testes and XY chromosomes.

Terminology is controversial. While we will refer here to 'intersex', some people prefer to use other terms, like 'differences in sex development' or 'variations in sex characteristics', that reflect the numerous combinations and possibilities that exist. Some do not prefer any of these umbrella terms.[167]

It has been very common for babies who display such intersex characteristics at birth to be conformed to standard male or female features by means of surgery. For instance, surgery on an XX child with fused labia and a large clitoris might include clitoral reduction or recession, and surgery to open the vagina. Children with XY chromosomes and testes, but very small external genitalia, may have the penis and testes removed altogether and a rudimentary vaginal opening constructed in their place.[168]

Sometimes such medical surgery is a one-off intervention; often, it is the beginning of a longer – perhaps life-long – process of medical treatment. Such surgery tends now to be practised less frequently, and more cautiously, than before.

A recent government report notes that

> There is no robust estimate of the number of people with variations in sex characteristics in the UK. There are several reasons for this. Firstly, as outlined above, for some, the variation may never be apparent. Secondly, some people may not disclose information when asked, for example via a survey. Thirdly, there is no consistent definition or approach to collecting data of people with variations in sex characteristics.[169]

Existing clinical research estimates that the 'birth prevalence of atypical genitalia may be as high as 1 in 300 births, but the birth prevalence of a condition that may lead to true genital ambiguity on expert examination may be as low as 1 in 5,000 births'.[170]

Different intersex people understand, describe, and respond to their bodies in different ways. Some consider their intersex characteristics as elements of a medical condition: something to be diagnosed and, where possible, treated or ameliorated. Some are therefore happy with the medical interventions that they underwent, whether as babies or subsequently. Others regard these interventions as a form of violence: they have (often literally) been cut, without their consent, to fit society's assumptions about what counts as normal. They might regard their intersex characteristics simply as part of the complex variety in which natural human bodies appear.

Depending on the type of intersex characteristics a person has, they can be at risk of experiencing various forms of bullying and discrimination. The United Nations Office of the High Commissioner for Human Rights noted in a recent document that:

> Because their bodies are seen as different, intersex children and adults are often stigmatized and subjected to multiple human rights violations, including violations of their rights to health and physical integrity, to be free from torture and ill-treatment, and to equality and non-discrimination.[171]

The medical sciences, sexuality and gender

Sex and well-being

Research carried out in the US[172] and China[173] shows that frequency of sexual activity is linked to reported happiness. According to the former, it seems to make no difference whether someone is homosexual or heterosexual for this benefit to hold true. However, both studies reported lower levels of happiness for people who had paid for sex and who had had sex outside marriage. Feeling ashamed during sex, feeling dirty about sex or about genital secretions during sex, and fantasizing about having sex with others during intercourse were also associated with lower levels of happiness.

It is difficult to be sure about the direction of causality in these studies. Happy people may simply have more sex! Studies suggest that people who had had treatment for depression were far more likely to have sexual dysfunction or sexual dissatisfaction.[174] This might be a consequence of the depressed mood itself, the antidepressant medication or both.

A recent report highlights the striking increase in the incidence of sexually transmitted diseases (STIs) in the UK.[175] New diagnoses increased by 5 per cent in 2018 from 2017. While there has been some progress with declines in rates of some STIs, other STIs are increasing rapidly. Syphilis and gonorrhoea have increased by 165 per cent and 249 per cent respectively in the past decade. Men who have sex with men, young people and some ethnic minority communities are among those disproportionately impacted by STIs. The report states

> Behaviours associated with STI risk include condomless sex, increased number of sexual partners, and concurrent sexual partners. In addition, chemsex and the use of dating apps are changing behaviours and associated risk. However, surprisingly, there is limited up-to-date research on behaviours – even in men who have sex with men who have seen the biggest volume of research to date.[175]

There is no evidence that the form of genital expression is a factor in the relationship between sex and well-being in either homosexual or heterosexual relationships. However, attitudes to homosexual

sexual acts may be a significant contributing factor to the phenomenon of homophobia. Disgust about sexual acts between two people of the same sex and, particularly in the case of men, anal penetration, correlates with conservative sexual attitudes.[176] Early epidemiological studies suggested that anal sex was largely a gay male phenomenon.[177] This idea persists despite the fact that more recent studies report that one third of heterosexual couples report having anal sex.[178] This proportion is not very different to the proportion of gay men who report having anal sex, and in actual numbers it is far greater.

Questions of sexual health also have a bearing on attitudes towards anal sex. For example, there is evidence that unprotected anal intercourse is a key risk factor associated with HIV transmission.[179] There is also some evidence for an increased risk of anal cancer as a result of anal intercourse.[180]

Sexual orientation and gender identity as diagnoses

In this section we consider how sexual orientation and gender identity have, in the past, been understood as mental disorders. This is different from considering how the mental health of LGBTI+ people may be affected by social stigma, which is discussed in the next section.

Understanding and therefore classifying health conditions changes as scientific knowledge increases. The International Classification of Diseases (ICD), produced by the World Health Organization, is the international standard for defining and reporting all kinds of diseases and health conditions. The Diagnostic and Statistical Manual of Mental Disorders (DSM) is the handbook used by health care professionals in the United States and much of the world as the authoritative guide to the diagnosis of mental disorders. These two manuals are useful indicators of internationally agreed understandings of health and illness within the medical and psychological professions, which is why medical practitioners turn to them for current scientific perspectives on mental well-being in relation to sexuality and gender.

Questions about the nature of sexual orientation in relation to medical diagnosis are sensitive and can cause hurt. In 1974, in the sixth printing of the DSM-II, homosexuality was declassified by the

American Psychiatric Association as a psychiatric disorder. It was removed from ICD-10 in 1992.[181] There has been much debate about the political pressures that influenced these changes, and there are wider questions about the basis for classifying mental disorders as medical diagnoses. The fundamental questions here are concerned with the confinement of diagnostic categories to conditions associated with pain or distress and impairment of functioning directly due to the condition itself. It is now widely recognized in the clinical and scientific community that, on this basis, homosexuality is not a psychiatric disorder.

Transgender identity has similarly undergone a process of de-medicalization, although this has not thus far been as complete as the comparable process for homosexuality. What was termed 'Gender Identity Disorder' in DSM-IV in 1994 and ICD-10 in 1992 has been replaced by 'Gender Dysphoria' in DSM-5 in 2013 and 'Gender Incongruence' in ICD-11 in 2018. In this latest ICD, gender incongruence is included with 'conditions related to sexual health' and is no longer classified with mental disorders. Gender incongruence is defined as a marked and persistent incongruence between the gender felt or experienced and the gender assigned at birth and, as we shall see at the end of this chapter, there are a range of medical procedures that can be accessed to enable people to transition physically and physiologically to their identified gender.

The trend in the medical profession, therefore, has been towards understanding that neither homosexuality nor gender incongruence are, in themselves, psychiatric diagnoses. Homosexuality is no longer understood as a diagnosis and is affirmed as a part of the normal variation of sexual experience and behaviour encountered within any population. Transgender people may or may not experience gender dysphoria. The origins of this distress are a separate consideration to the origins of gender identity.

Mental health and social stigma

A large body of research demonstrates an excess burden of mental ill health experienced by LGBT people.[182] LGB people experience up to six times the rate of common mental disorders such as depression and anxiety, substance misuse, deliberate self-harm, and completed suicide[183] as compared with heterosexuals. Bisexuals appear to be at particular risk. Transgender people experience similarly increased risk in comparison with cisgender people.

There are many reasons why this increase in mental ill health might be expected. In particular, it is known that stigma, prejudice and bullying are all risk factors for mental ill health. Sexual minorities have suffered particularly in this regard. Growing up in an intolerant society is stressful, and homophobia is commonly internalized. LGB people experience less social support for their intimate relationships than the heterosexual majority, and families, churches and faith communities are often not supportive, and may be actively rejecting.

The effects of social stigma became particularly apparent during the COVID-19 pandemic. Some LGBTI+ young people, for example, lacked family support or faced violence and homelessness as a result of social distancing and lockdown measures.[184]

There is evidence that distress arises as a result of the stigma and disapproval expressed by adults and others in relation to incongruent expression of gender roles. Distress may resolve or be reduced when children are allowed to freely express their gender identity. For some, gender dysphoria resolves with puberty, whereas for others it is exacerbated.

Attitudes to homosexuality vary widely around the world, with North American and Western European countries being most tolerant and African and Middle-Eastern countries most intolerant.[185] Where states in the USA banned same-sex marriage, rates of common mental disorder and alcohol related problems increased amongst LGB people.[186] In British schools in 2012, 55 per cent of LGB young people had experienced homophobic bullying, and 6 per cent had been subject to death threats.[187]

Studying the mental well-being of people with differences of sex development (DSD or dsd[188]) is complex. This is partly because DSD, or intersex, is an umbrella term for the anatomical, chromosomal and hormonal variations which can occur during sexual development.[189] Nevertheless, a picture emerges of psychosocial harm caused to some by repeated genital examinations, genital interventions and poorly managed negotiation of difference. These can result in shame and secrecy. In recent years genital interventions that are not considered 'vital for health' have come to be seen as harmful and, in some cases, a breach of human rights. There is a growing consensus that a less medicalized and more psychosocially focused approach improves quality of life and mental well-being of intersex people.[190]

Sexual orientation and gender identity change efforts

A broad consensus of clinical and scientific research and professional opinion supports the view that sexual orientation change efforts (SOCE), sometimes called 'conversion therapies', for homosexual orientation are both ineffective and potentially harmful.[191] In 2017 the Church of England's General Synod endorsed the 2015 'Memorandum of Understanding on Conversion Therapy' calling for a ban on the practice of Conversion Therapy aimed at altering sexual orientation. It defines conversion therapy as

> the umbrella term for a type of talking therapy or activity which attempts to change sexual orientation or reduce attraction to others of the same sex. It is also sometimes called 'reparative' or 'gay cure' therapy.[192]

A new 'Memorandum of Understanding' was published in 2017. It developed the 2015 MoU in a number of ways. For example, it extended its definitions to gender identity and gave fuller advice to therapists working with those who 'experience conflict or distress regarding their sexual orientation' as well as their 'gender identity'. It defines 'conversion therapy' as

> an umbrella term for a therapeutic approach, or any model or individual viewpoint that demonstrates an assumption that any sexual orientation or gender identity is inherently preferable to any other, and which attempts to bring about a change of sexual orientation or gender identity, or seeks to suppress an individual's expression of sexual orientation or gender identity on that basis.[193]

Its primary purpose is to ensure that counsellors avoid harmful and unethical practices by seeking appropriate training and adhering to appropriate guidance regarding good practice. The document is careful to assert that there is no intention to 'deny, discourage or exclude those with uncertain feelings around sexuality or gender identity from seeking qualified and appropriate help' or

> to stop psychological and medical professionals who work with trans and gender questioning clients from performing a clinical assessment of suitability prior to medical intervention. Nor is it intended to stop medical professionals from prescribing hormone treatment and other medications to trans patients and people experiencing gender dysphoria.

Some continue to argue against this view, arguing for the possibility of successful SOCE.[194] Little of this work is peer reviewed and it reflects the scientific difficulties entailed in research in this area: there have been no randomized controlled trials in this area. It is possible to present case studies which appear to show successful sexual orientation change, in some people, at least in the short term.[195] However, carefully constructed longitudinal and controlled studies would be needed to demonstrate whether such changes are enduring and deeply effective. Given the potential for harm that would arise to many (if not all) of the people involved, such research would be unethical. Research subjects are generally people of a religious conviction who have experienced distress at same-sex attraction and who are strongly motivated to report change. While it is clear that some people who do not wish to express their same-sex attraction in genital sexual activity, for religious and other reasons, are able to find patterns of life and practice that work for them, the attraction itself usually persists.

Gender transition procedures

Developments in endocrinology and surgical medicine have enabled people with gender dysphoria to undergo a range of hormonal and anatomical interventions in order to make a physical and physiological transition to their identified gender. Some people choose only to have hormone therapy as a means of enabling them to live with reduced gender incongruence. Others undergo a range of surgical interventions. Trans men may undergo removal of both breasts, of the womb, the fallopian tubes and ovaries, and a construction of the penis, scrotum and testes. Surgery for trans women may involve breast implants, the removal of the testes and penis, and the construction of a vagina, vulva and clitoris. Other interventions for both trans men and women may involve facial surgery, body hair removal or hair transplantation, voice therapy or voice modifying surgery. These medical procedures have developed in sophistication since the first known UK gender reassignment surgery in 1951 and are now available through the NHS.

It is important to note that while there is evidence of benefit, controversy among some scientists about the risks, morality and therapeutic desirability and effectiveness of these procedures continues.[196] More research needs to be carried out using robustly randomized trials, larger sample sizes and over longer periods, while finding ways to avoid recruitment bias and high subject dropout rates.

The administration of puberty suppressants and sex hormones to children who are diagnosed with gender dysphoria is proving to be very controversial.[197] The National Health Service has recently announced an independent review 'to make evidence-based recommendations about the future use of these drugs'.[198]

Conclusion

We began this chapter by thinking about how scientific and technological developments have changed the way we think about relationships, sexuality and identity. We have seen how scientific research offers new insights and understanding about the origins of gender identity and sexual orientation. We have begun to understand how questions of well-being intersect in complex ways with social, behavioural and biological sciences. As we turn to explore the place of religion in society, we ask different kinds of questions. In the light of our growing scientific understanding and of the new possibilities that technology offers, where do people find the wisdom to live well, to live in a way that is faithful to their religious beliefs while interacting with the social and scientific realities of our world? This is the focus of the next chapters.

CHAPTER 7

Religion

Chapters 5 and 6 described developments in UK society in the areas of relationships, sex, and identity, and some relevant scientific findings. This chapter completes this scene-setting by looking at the place of religion in society.

We will not at this point be digging deeply into the long histories of different religions' thought and practice. Nor will we be discussing at any length the reasons that these communities have given for their policies and practices.

This chapter is simply meant to help us to be aware of the wider religious context of our present discussions.

We begin with the multireligious context within which we find ourselves, noting the presence of Muslim, Jewish, Sikh, Hindu and Buddhist communities in the UK. We then look at Christian Churches (other than the Church of England) before moving on to describing developments in the Church of England and its role in the life of the nation and as part of the wider Anglican Communion.

All of these developments and findings provide the broad context for this book. They pose many questions, and in the rest of the book we will be exploring and trying to answer at least some of them.

A multireligious society

The Church of England is part of a multireligious society and addresses questions of identity, sexuality, relationships and marriage within the broader British religious landscape. The British Social Attitudes survey indicates that, in 2018, 52 per cent of the British population identified as having 'no religion' (up from 31 per cent in 1983); 38 per cent identified as Christian (down from 66 per cent in 1983) and within that 12 per cent as Anglican (down from 40 per cent in 1983). Six per cent of the population identified as Muslim, and 3 per cent as being of other non-Christian religions.[199] The Church of England's deliberations about identity, sexuality, relationships and marriage don't happen in isolation, but alongside and entangled with the conversations of many other religious and non-religious communities.

The Church of England has strong relationships at all levels with people and communities of different faiths. All of our religious communities are dealing with questions of identity, sexuality, relationships and marriage, and we have found it important to listen to each other during the Living in Love and Faith process. Our discussions are enriched as we learn how others interpret their scriptural texts about sexuality, for example, or negotiate tensions between religious requirements and those of British law.

The most common view of religious authorities within the minority religious traditions of Britain, apart from some denominations within Judaism, is that sexual activity belongs only within heterosexual marriage. Traditional teaching is therefore mostly negative towards homosexuality and forbids homosexual activity. As within the

Church, it can be very difficult and painful for LGBTI+ people within these traditions. This formal teaching does not, however, necessarily translate into intolerance at a community level.

There is also an increasing presence of self-organized LGBTI+ grassroots movements and their allies which affirm people's religious as well as sexual and gender identities and support those who choose to come out as LGBTI+. These groups are offering emotional support and security especially to younger people in facing questions of sexuality, and in recognizing their experiences within the language and practices of their faith traditions.

It is important to note that although there is much that our religious traditions have in common, there are also substantial differences. We may, as Christians, claim, with Muslims and Baha'is, the inheritance of Abraham and therefore an understanding with Jews of God as creator and judge. But different Jews, let alone different Muslims, Christians and Baha'is, have different ways of understanding the authority and interpretation of different texts including texts about sexual relationships.

When a Reform Jewish rabbi, Jeff Goldwasser, reads the description in Leviticus 18.22 of homosexual intercourse as an 'abhorrence', he does not read it as applying to loving, committed homosexual relationships today. He points out that there is no word in the Hebrew Bible for 'homosexual' (just as there was no word in English for it until the late nineteenth century). Instead, he argues, sexual activity between people of the same gender in the Hebrew Bible is either a form of violence designed to humiliate, or a form of sexual excess so unbridled that it doesn't discriminate between male and female. He also explains that the word translated, 'abhorrence' is the one used of 'bad table manners' in the story of Joseph in the Book of Genesis, explaining why Egyptians won't eat with Hebrews.[200]

Orthodox Jewish rabbi Norman Lamm takes a different reading of those same texts. Commenting on Leviticus 18.22 in the light of Genesis 2.18 in which God says, 'It is not good that Adam should be alone; I will make the human a help meet / partner', Rabbi Lamm writes, 'Homosexuality imposes on one an intolerable burden of differentness, of absurdity and of loneliness, but the biblical commandment cannot be put aside solely on the basis of sympathy for the victim of these feelings.'[201]

In 2018, the British Orthodox Chief Rabbi, Ephraim Mirvis, used
a different verse from Leviticus in producing groundbreaking
guidance for Orthodox Jewish schools. This included detailed
teaching from the Hebrew Bible and the Talmud making clear
that the command in Leviticus 19.16 to 'not stand idly by your
fellow's blood' is an absolute obligation and directly applies to the
protection of LGBT+ school children with specific examples given of
homophobic, biphobic and transphobic bullying.[202]

Among Sikhs, liberal and conservative views about homosexuality
cannot be drawn directly from the main Sikh scripture, the Guru
Granth Sahib, because it does not mention homosexuality. Dr
Jagbir Jhutti-Johal describes how Sikhs were drawn into the
controversy around same-sex marriage in Canada. The bill
being debated in the Canadian Parliament stated that same-sex
marriages would be allowed in places of worship where the religion
does not object to same-sex marriages. The head Priest at the Akal
Takht, the highest seat of authority for Sikhs worldwide, issued an
edict in response to the bill denouncing same-sex marriages and
urging the worldwide Sikh community not to allow such marriages
to take place in any Gurdwara. Same-sex relationships were
condemned as being anti-Sikh.

In the ensuing debate, more conservative Sikhs drew on the
example and teaching of the Sikh Gurus about the importance
of the traditional heterosexual family as the context for raising
children to guide their views on homosexuality. More liberal Sikhs,
however, drew on the emphasis that the Sikh Gurus place on
the universal equality of people created as God's children, and
the divine 'jot' [light] being present in everyone, which was then
applied to people of different sexual orientations.[203] The LGBT
support group for Sikhs, Sarbat, claims that homophobic attitudes
within Sikhism are rooted in conservative Punjabi culture rather
than in Sikh philosophy.[204]

Differences between religious traditions concerning sexuality
and marriage include not only the range of sources out of which
differences emerge, whether scriptural or cultural, but also
differences about how important questions of sexuality are for
religion in the first place. There may be a variety of texts and
teachings about sexual practices in the different schools of Buddhism,
for example, but for many lay Buddhists in the West at least,
religious practice is primarily an individual pursuit which emphasizes

overarching values of compassion and tolerance. These values are important in marriage, but marriage is not considered a sacrament or religious act as such, and clergy do not carry out weddings.

Even when questions of sexual ethics are important within the tradition, there is often great reserve when talking about an area of life that has been considered very private, historically and culturally. In such a climate where sexuality is not openly discussed, people are often not aware of the trauma and pain of those suffering from persecution, prejudice and discrimination.

While British Churches are learning a new vocabulary for sexual orientations and gender identities, Hindu epics such as the Mahabharata as well as Indian temple sculptures such as those at Khajuraho have celebrated gender variance and diverse sexual practices for hundreds of years. Official attitudes hardened under British rule, and colonial history is still cited as being part of the reason for ambivalent attitudes towards questions of sexuality and gender identity within India and the Hindu diaspora. [205] In 2009, the Hindu Council UK welcomed the Delhi High Court's ruling decriminalizing same-sex conduct between consenting adults.[206] That ruling was, however, overturned by the Indian Supreme Court in 2013.

Across the Indian Subcontinent, *Hijras* are people recognized in law within Hindu-majority as well as Muslim-majority states as being of a third gender. Drawing on narratives in the Mahabharata and popular in Bollywood films, they are widely regarded as givers of blessings through rituals performed at weddings and when a child is born. *Hijras* were labelled as a 'criminal caste' under British rule and while they are welcomed for their blessings, they continue at times to suffer ridicule and violence.

While prevailing UK attitudes and world politics are now very different, British colonial rule still casts a shadow over attitudes within minority religious communities towards questions of sexuality and marriage. The Indian Penal Code, for example, which made 'carnal knowledge against the order of nature' a crime was introduced in 1860 and was applied over time to colonies in East Africa and Malaysia. Today 40 Commonwealth countries and 70 countries in total have laws that criminalize homosexuality.[207]

There is a perception within some minority religious communities in the UK, as well as among some African-heritage and Asian-heritage churches in the UK, that the promotion of LGBTI+ rights is a Western and colonial agenda, and that the widespread acceptance of homosexuality in the West is a symptom of its spiritual malaise. Common threads would suggest that many minority religious community attitudes towards questions of sexuality and marriage have been impacted by both colonial history and societal and legal changes in the countries of origin subsequent to colonial rule.

LGBTI+ people, historically and today, bring to society and to faith communities great gifts. They also often experience great suffering. As has been the case in churches, many LGBTI+ people within other religious communities in the UK experience traumatic struggles in relation to their faith, and with friends, families and the wider community. A project by the Universities of Cambridge, Exeter and Westminster brought scholars, activists and community leaders from across Britain's Muslim communities together to discuss what it means to live faithfully as a Muslim in contemporary Britain. Their report includes an acknowledgement that LGBT Muslims,

> may not know whom to turn to and may suffer in silence; some experience depression and other mental health conditions and may even be driven to suicide. They often experience a double sense of alienation and threat, being stigmatised by Islamophobic attitudes when in LGBT spaces and by homophobic reactions when in Islamic spaces... They also face constant fear of loss of employment and estrangement from family if their sexuality comes to light.[208]

These pressures and the changing of attitudes and the law more widely in British society have led to a growing acceptance of LGBTI+ people within minority faith communities and a greater willingness among some LGBTI+ members of these faith communities to come out and to tell their stories. Stories in the media such as that of Abby Stein, a descendant of Ultra Orthodox Hasidic Judaism's founder The Baal Shem Tov, and the increasing number and popularity of celebrities such as Tan France and Rav Bansal are providing role models for LGBTI+ people from a range of religious communities to be more open about their sexuality. The Internet has also opened up many of these conversations. The Inclusive Mosque Initiative,[209] for example, has flourished partly because it is now much easier for people to find alternative approaches to sexuality within religious traditions.

Organizations within these communities, as within churches, are arguing for changes in attitudes towards LGBTI+ people, the interpretation of religious texts concerning sex, relationships and marriage, and in religious practices such as same-sex marriage. These organizations are often relatively small and fragile, but are growing and making their voices heard, often amplified by a sympathetic media.

The first Jewish gay and lesbian organization was formed in 1972, followed by others. In 2011 a number of these organizations and groups created a forum, now known as KeshetUK, to share information and resources for British LGBTI+ Jews. They are involved in a wide range of activities including training and consultancy work. Their website lists a number of Jewish LGBTI+ support groups, British and international.[210] GALVA-108 is an international organization offering support and information to LGBTI+ Hindus. It developed particularly within the ISKON (Hare Krishna) movement in the early 2000s.[211] Sarbat, mentioned earlier in this section, is a British-based support group for LGBT Sikhs, founded in 2007.[212]

In 1998, Faisal Islam founded the Al-Fatiha Foundation in the USA, which operated until 2011. From this emerged groups in other countries including Imaan in the UK which offers support for LGBT Muslims and their families and promotes an interpretation of Islam which is positive about homosexuality through projects like 'Demystifying Shariah', offering different perspectives on key texts.[213] In the early 2000s a group called the Safra Project was also active, focused specifically on issues facing gay Muslim women.

Increasingly LGBT inclusion is being addressed as part of broader developments within Islam, typified by New Horizons in British Islam and the Inclusive Mosque Initiative. The former seeks to nurture a positive vision of what it means to be a Muslim in Britain today, while the latter addresses LGBT inclusion as part of a movement for progressive Islam and hosts Friday prayers and events which intentionally include people of all genders, sexualities and abilities.

In addition, concerns about Islamophobia mean that Muslim groups are finding common ground with LGBTI+ activists with regard to equality legislation and the prevention of hate crime. These groups and others point to dissenting scholarly voices which promote alternative readings of the relevant Quranic passages[214] and call for a rediscovery of *ijtihad* – the notion of using independent reasoning to find a solution to a legal question, in contrast with *taqlid* – imitation or conformity to legal precedent. Other arguments for an inclusive position are drawn from Islamic principles of justice, love, compassion and *tawhid* – the doctrine of God's absolute unity.

The religious and non-religious landscape of England is not divided up into neatly distinct territories, each a separate world. It is held together by a dense stitching of relationships, of influences, and of reactions. We are very aware that we in the Church of England do not deliberate and decide alone. Even when we don't realize it, our arguments and decisions are affected by what we see and hear from our friends, relatives, neighbours and colleagues in other communities, and we in turn affect them. We are not islands.

At a multireligious gathering marking Her Majesty's Diamond Jubilee, hosted by the Archbishop of Canterbury in 2012, The Queen spoke about the role that she saw for the Church of England:

> Here at Lambeth Palace we should remind ourselves of the significant position of the Church of England in our nation's life. The concept of our established Church is occasionally misunderstood and, I believe, commonly underappreciated. Its role is not to defend Anglicanism to the exclusion of other religions. Instead, the Church has a duty to protect the free practice of all faiths in this country.[215]

There is, therefore, an awareness within the Church of England that how it responds to the changing legal and cultural situation within England often has a particular significance for other faith communities and organizations nationally.

It is true that our approach in the remainder of this book is to dig deeply into the resources of the Christian tradition as the Church of England has received them. We will be looking at the stories that Christians tell about God and the world and asking how our questions about identity, sexuality, relationships and marriage relate to those stories. We will be looking at the way in which, as we try to answer these questions, Christians in the Church of England read the Bible and learn from the Christian tradition. We will, in other words, be focusing on approaches to these questions that make sense in distinctively Christian terms. That is not, however, a turn away from engagement with our neighbours. We trust that it is instead a contribution to it – to a rich conversation where members of different religious and non-religious communities can each speak in their own distinctive voices, draw on their own distinctive resources, and display something of the complexity and diversity of their own reasoning to others.

Relationship and sex education in schools

In September 2020, the curriculum in English schools changed to require all primary schools to teach relationships education and all secondary schools to teach relationships and sex education (RSE).[216] This change has led to widespread anxiety among some religious communities about how age-appropriate the teaching will be, and particularly how LGBTI+ relationships will be taught. Parkside, a primary school in a largely Muslim area of Birmingham, became a flashpoint in 2019 as hundreds of parents and others protested outside, with parents claiming that the new curriculum offends their Islamic faith because it promotes homosexuality as normal and morally correct. Teachers supporting the new curriculum argue that unless children are taught about families with same-sex parents, there is a risk of homophobic and transphobic bullying. They also want to make sure that children know how to respond to unwanted sexual advances. The controversy has been a lightning conductor for concerns about education and safeguarding on the one hand, and freedom of conscience on the other. The 2018 Orthodox Jewish publication cited on page 124 provides an example of how one minority religious community has been able to affirm a conservative doctrinal stance on questions of sexuality while offering a resource of teaching material that responds to the challenge of learning *about* different family structures. Allowing individual schools to decide with parents how to introduce and teach the curriculum has helped to ease the controversy, but concerns remain among other religious groups and the issue continues to divide.

Christian churches

All British churches have had to respond to the profound social and cultural changes described in the first two chapters of this Part of the book.

Remarriage after divorce remains a divisive issue among Roman Catholics, for instance, while current discussion within the Methodist Church about church services to celebrate civil partnerships, now available for opposite as well as same-sex couples, raises long-standing questions about heterosexual partners in faithful, long-term relationships who choose not to marry. The recognition of gender transition generates a range of reactions in the churches as indeed within wider society. The challenge to inherited Church teaching and practice is sharpest, however, in relation to same-sex relationships.

Three broad types of response might be identified among the churches to the growing social acceptance of same-sex relationships. The first, which could be called 'pastoral accompaniment', focuses on pastoral ministry to the individual.[217] It would perhaps best characterize the response in many churches which consistently teach that sexual activity outside heterosexual marriage is sinful. That would include, in the British context, the Roman Catholic Church, the Orthodox Church, churches in the diverse Pentecostal family and churches affiliated with the Evangelical Alliance. In most – though not necessarily all – of these churches, a person seeking to participate in congregational life would not be turned away if they acknowledged to those in positions of responsibility that they identify as gay, lesbian or bisexual.

On the other hand, the welcome and care offered to that person would need to include some recognition that entering or continuing in a same-sex sexual relationship would be out of line with that church's teaching.

One way to frame the relationship of ministers, and perhaps of others in the congregation, to the individual in this context would be as one of 'pastoral accompaniment' (a phrase used in the Roman Catholic Church in particular). Such accompaniment implies a genuine 'coming alongside' and listening, but with an understanding that this will be on a journey in which the person involved should gradually become more able to discern the way forward in the practice of their faith, taking into account Scripture and the church's teaching, with prayer and the action of the Holy Spirit. In the meantime, questions may arise as to where the limits might be on this person's participation in congregational life and leadership, – in areas such as receiving communion, or joining the choir or the worship band, or sitting on the church council, or convening a home group.

A second type of response is associated with churches where there has been long-running public disagreement, extending to contexts of church governance, between those who maintain the inherited teaching that sexual activity outside heterosexual marriage is inevitably sinful and those who make the case for the acceptance of same-sex relationships. The evident reality of different views within the church on this matter leads to formal public processes of reflection and deliberation. Reports are written, theological commissions assembled, consultations held, and recommendations for change discussed at all levels of the church. As a result, it is agreed that it is possible for both views to be held and – crucially – acted on within the church: the traditional position, and an acceptance of faithful same-sex relationships, including civil partnerships and now marriage. Action in this context could include either freedom to hold services of blessing and / or marriages for same-sex couples, or freedom for ministers to enter into civil partnerships and marriages with a person of the same sex, or both. The challenge then becomes how to manage the difference in theology and practice institutionally.

This kind of response characterizes some of the historic Protestant churches in Britain. In various ways, though with very significant distinctions, it can be seen in the Baptist Union of Great Britain, the Church of Scotland and the United Reformed Church. Managing difference institutionally is perhaps easier in church contexts where a 'congregationalist' understanding of the church is influential, as it is with the Baptist Union (which is a union of churches rather than a church) and, to a lesser extent, with the United Reformed Church. The choice of which approach to follow lies with the 'congregation', that is, with those who are part of the worshipping community in a particular place, and their minister, while the denomination itself may continue to hold one view as normative. In the case of the

Baptist Union and the Church of Scotland (where the decision lies with the Presbytery), this is broadly speaking the traditional position.

This second type of response – managing difference institutionally – rests on agreement that the question of public affirmation of same-sex relationships can be answered differently in different local churches and does not require a consistent answer from the Church as a whole. That does require that there be nothing in that church's or denomination's shared rules and documents that rules out such local variation. Although that may sound straightforward, there may be some debate, not least around the question of whether the inherited understanding of marriage and relationships belongs to the church's doctrine or not, and therefore the extent to which some parts of the church are free to act in ways that may be contrary to it. The introduction of civil marriage for same-sex couples has sharpened the issue here: to make it possible for such marriages to take place in a denomination, a church might have to remove gender difference from its theology of marriage, as from the liturgical texts it uses – in some cases at least – and that pushes towards the third type of response.

A third type of response, then, is for the church to revise its formal teaching on marriage, whether or not this is regarded as a formal development in the church's doctrine. That might be expressed in official teaching documents, or in agreed resolutions from authoritative bodies, or in revision of liturgical texts – though the latter have different statuses in different churches. The proposals put forward in a recent report from the Methodist Church, for instance, which were being considered in preparation for decisions to be made at the Methodist Conference in July 2020 (though the process was subsequently extended because of the COVID-19 pandemic), would enable same-sex marriages to take place as part of its life.[218] They pivot on what the report explicitly calls a significant development of the Methodist Church's 'teaching' and 'theology'. As noted in the previous paragraph, there may be a question as to whether this should be considered a change in the church's doctrine, depending on how that is defined. One factor here may be how the relationship between liturgy and doctrine is conceived: Canon B 30 of the Church of England, for instance, having affirmed that 'marriage is in its nature a union permanent and lifelong, for better for worse, till death them do part, of one man with one woman' and stated that this teaching 'is expressed and maintained in the Form of Solemnization of Matrimony contained in The Book of Common Prayer', then refers to it as 'the Church's doctrine of marriage'. Churches who locate their doctrine exclusively in formal statements of belief are less likely to consider marriage as a 'doctrinal' matter.

The three types of response are not wholly separate from one another. As has already been indicated, the boundary between managing difference institutionally and revising church teaching may be blurred, and indeed disputed. In a church which has changed its formal teaching on the marriage of same-sex couples, for instance, it is still entirely possible that people whose sexual relationships lie outside the range of what the church advocates will become regular members of a congregation, and so some element of pastoral accompaniment may be part of the picture here too. Nonetheless, a broad distinction can be drawn between (a) churches where such pastoral accompaniment is the primary response to those who are, or express a desire to be, in a same-sex relationship, (b) churches where in some congregations same-sex relationships can be publicly affirmed without such an affirmation being made by the church or denomination as a whole, and (c) churches that have revised their formal teaching so that the gender of a couple ceases to be relevant to the moral and theological evaluation of their relationship.

How, then, might the current position of the Church of England fit within these responses of British churches over the past 40 years to growing acceptance of same-sex relationships? It is evident that it does not belong with the third type of response, in which the church's doctrine of marriage has been revised, as was made clear in the first part of this book and in earlier sections of this chapter. There is substantial common ground between the understanding of marriage in the Anglican Communion as it was then, which the Church of England's teaching about marriage remains aligned with, and the understanding of marriage in the Roman Catholic Church. This was set out in *Life in Christ*, a document of the Anglican – Roman Catholic International Commission[219] which we refer to in Chapter 14.

One might see some evidence of the second category of responses – managing difference institutionally – in the diversity of practice across the Church of England's worshipping communities, for instance with regard to including prayers for same-sex couples who wish to mark their commitment to one another within public worship. Such diversity, however, remains essentially informal, by contrast with the position in some of the historic Protestant churches in this country. There is no official provision of practices that reflect different views regarding same-sex relationships. There is no such provision, for example, with regard to holding or blessing same-sex marriages, or permitting ordained ministers to be in same-sex marriages.

In fact, the Church of England's current position – as described earlier in this chapter and set out in reports like *Issues in Human Sexuality* – might best be characterized as belonging within the first category of responses, that of pastoral accompaniment. In *Issues in Human Sexuality*, the Church of England established a framework for pastoral accompaniment in the case of faithful, stable same-sex relationships that is both far-reaching in its effects and publicly acknowledged. Not least, they insisted that where same-sex couples come to the conclusion in conscience that sexual activity has a proper place in their committed and faithful relationship, they should continue to be welcomed as full participants in congregational life.[220] The nature of that framework, however, makes the Church of England distinctive in some respects among the other churches within the first category of responses.

The divergence between these three responses is undoubtedly placing relationships between churches under some pressure. Ecumenical relations in England have been remarkably strong in recent decades, and Churches Together in England has been very effective in providing a meeting point for the growing diversity of churches in this country, including Pentecostal and Orthodox churches, with its membership having more than tripled since its inception in 1990, from 16 to 50 (with more churches currently applying). Nonetheless, in 2019, Hannah Brock Womack, nominated by one grouping of the member churches to be their President alongside the other five was asked by the Enabling Group not to take her place, because she had recently married her female partner. Quite properly, the question was asked of why difference and disagreement on so many other issues could be handled without precipitating conflicts of this kind.

Many factors are involved here, but part of the picture is the nature of the bonds that exist between churches in this country and churches elsewhere in the world, where the social and cultural context may be significantly different. The historic Protestant churches by and large belong to global communions within which it has come to be accepted that national churches are free to make their own decisions on same-sex relationships. The exception here is the Moravian Church, where the international body, the Unity, has final authority on matters of doctrine, including marriage.

Nevertheless, all churches are aware that how they respond to the social changes we are considering in this book may have profound effects on their ecumenical relationships in the UK and globally. None of us makes our decisions in a vacuum.

The Church of England

The years after the Second World War marked a major transition in the relationship between the Church of England and wider society.

In 1945 the Church of England was still widely regarded as one of the guardians of moral authority for the nation, and indeed for the British Empire. Bishops retained a degree of political power and worked closely with government to ensure that the interests of the church were represented in law and policy. In the 1950s, at least in relation to the areas we are focusing on, there was little sign of this changing. A desire for stability and security after the immense disruption of the war led to a renewed emphasis on the centrality of marriage and the family, reinforcing the position of the church. Yet dramatic changes were in the pipeline. Following the war, the state took over the initiative from the church in education and welfare. Social developments of the kinds we discussed in Chapter 5 began to widen the gap between church teaching and wider social beliefs and practices. The numbers of people actively involved in church life began to drop dramatically.

The Church of England is still established by law. It plays a significant role in education, the provision of care, the nurturing of local communities through its parochial structure and civic involvement, the shaping of local, regional and national commemorations and celebrations through its churches and cathedrals, and national politics through bishops in the House of Lords. It also continues to occupy a distinctive role in relation to marriage. With some exceptions, opposite-sex couples throughout England have a right to be married in their local parish church, or one with which they have a qualifying connection.[221] There are still many who welcome the church's moral teaching in the areas of relationships, sex, and identity, and call for the church to communicate that teaching clearly in response to some of the societal changes outlined in Chapter 5.

Nevertheless, you are far less likely today than in 1945 to encounter the idea that the Church of England is a moral legislator for the nation, especially in the area of sexual relationships. It is not simply the case that fewer people pay attention to, or follow, the church's traditional teaching. Rather, that teaching has increasingly come to be seen by many in our society as itself morally questionable.

For some, this is because the church's teaching is seen as a denial of freedom. Human beings can find happiness and fulfilment in sexual activity of different kinds at different stages of life. To impose restrictions on such activity beyond those relating to consent and the avoidance of harm is therefore sometimes understood to be damaging to human fulfilment and an offence against human freedom.

For some, the problem with the church's teaching relates specifically to its attitude to same-sex relationships. In our society, equality with regard to sexual orientation is becoming a litmus test for moral competence. Distinctions made between acceptable sexual behaviour for gay or lesbian and straight people are seen to render the Church of England, and other religious bodies of the same mind, untrustworthy moral guides not only in this but in other areas of human life.

For some, the deepest problem is that of sexual abuse. Members of the Church of England, clergy and lay, have been responsible, shamefully, for perpetrating abuse, for mistreating survivors of abuse, and for covering up the activities of abusers. Some of the relevant practices and attitudes have had deep roots in the church's institutional structures and culture – and some believe that the situation was made worse by aspects of the church's moral teaching. Many people's attitudes to the church have been shaped by the very deep betrayal of trust involved in this abuse.[222]

It is also clear that opinions within the church on many moral matters are divided. There are committed Anglicans who have reached very different understandings about appropriate Christian responses to questions about identity, sexuality, relationships and marriage.

Many of the changes described earlier in this Part happened within, as well as outside, the churches. Christians have engaged with the Bible and the Christian tradition in new ways in the light of changing experience, and developed new understandings and practices. One of the questions facing the Church of England is, at least in part, where the boundaries of acceptable diversity ought to be drawn, a matter that we will explore in Chapters 11 and 14.

In recent decades, there have been many debates and developments in the Church of England that relate to our themes of identity, sexuality, relationships and marriage. We do not have space to survey all of the relevant developments in the church's life, but have sketched below some of the most prominent, focusing on the church's official teaching rather than on changing opinions amongst clergy and laity.

Marriage

Divorce and remarriage

From the late nineteenth century onwards, pressure grew in English society for a change in the divorce laws. Divorce could only be granted on the grounds of proven adultery, and this was increasingly understood to create hardships and injustices, particularly for women and the poor. Attempts at legal reform began in the late nineteenth century and continued with greater regularity in the first decades of the twentieth century. The church, however, remained opposed. This opposition to divorce was reflected in regular resolutions during these years from the Lambeth Conferences – gatherings of bishops from around the Anglican Communion held roughly once every ten years. In 1888 the Conference had stated that

> inasmuch as our Lord's words expressly forbid divorce, except in the case of fornication or adultery, the Christian Church cannot recognize divorce in any other than the excepted case.[223]

Twenty years later this was reaffirmed with the statement that 'no view less strict than this is admissible in the Church of Christ'.[224] By 1920, the Conference was calling marriage 'a life-long and indissoluble union', language it reaffirmed in 1930.[225] It was as a result of this teaching that the Church of England played such an important role in the events leading to the December 1936 abdication of Edward VIII because of his wish to marry Wallis Simpson, a woman who had two former husbands still living.

The legal grounds for divorce were extended in 1937. By then, however, only one bishop in the Lords voted against the Bill, and in 1938 the bishops explained their position in terms which clearly distinguished English law from Church of England teaching. They resolved

> That while convinced that Christ's principle of a lifelong and exclusive personal union provides the only sure ground on which to base the relations of man and woman in marriage, and that the Church should therefore commend that principle as the true foundation for legislation by the State, this House nevertheless recognizes that its full legal enactment may not always be possible in a State which comprises all sorts and kinds of people, including many who do not accept the Christian way of life or the means of grace which the Church offers to its members.[226]

In 1957, the Canterbury Convocation (the synod of bishops and clergy for Canterbury Province) reaffirmed that

> according to God's will, declared by Our Lord, marriage is in its true principle a personal union ... indissoluble save by death; ... as a consequence ... remarriage after divorce during the lifetime of a former partner always involves a departure from the true principle of marriage as declared by Our Lord.[227]

The convocation concluded that the church should not allow the use of the marriage service in the case of anyone who has a partner still living and that 'no public Service shall be held for those who have contracted a civil marriage after divorce'. Clergy were, however, permitted to say private prayers with couples, and free to decide where and when to say such prayers. The same decision also required explicit written permission of the bishop before baptizing, confirming, or admitting to communion anyone who in civil law was in a marriage while a former partner was still living. This requirement was not formally lifted until 1982.

The distinction created in 1937 between English law and the church's official teaching made it possible for clergy to ignore the latter. They retained the legal right, as registrars, to marry anyone who could marry in civil law. Continued debate in the church about the issue was driven, in part, by the fact that a number of clergy exercised that right.

The 1969 Divorce Reform Act made divorce much more accessible through expanding the grounds for divorce to include the irretrievable breakdown of the marriage. This led to a massive rise in the number of divorces. The Church of England, through its *Putting Asunder* report,[228] had supported these legislative changes, again distinguishing between the church's own more restrictive 1957 teaching and how the law and the state should act.

In 1971 the Root Report unanimously concluded that, in certain circumstances, the marriage in church of divorced persons was compatible with reason, the Word of God in Scripture, and theological tradition, and should be allowed.[229] There followed many years, and numerous reports and Synod debates, attempting to get consensus on this principle and on practical procedures to implement it. Finally, in 1981, Synod agreed in principle that while 'marriage should always be undertaken as a lifelong commitment' nevertheless 'there are circumstances in which a divorced person may be married in church during the lifetime of a former partner'. Even then, however, it proved impossible to agree on processes to implement this stance.

In 1985, General Synod allowed a public service for those marrying who have a surviving spouse from a previous marriage – although it maintained the 1957 call not to use the marriage service in such a situation. The bishops commended a Service of Prayer and Dedication after a Civil Marriage which became quite widely used and, in a lightly revised form, is still an authorized liturgy.

In 1990, a process was created for ordaining someone who was divorced and had a former spouse still living. Those who are already ordained are permitted to divorce and remarry. However, a divorced person who has a surviving spouse or who is married to someone with a surviving spouse cannot be ordained deacon or priest without formal permission from the archbishop of the province. In 2010 a similar process was made available for those becoming bishops.

It was not until July 2002, following another working party and report, that Synod formally approved a structure for remarriage in church after divorce. It reaffirmed that marriage should always be undertaken as a 'solemn, public and life-long covenant between a man and a woman' but stated that 'there are exceptional circumstances in which a divorced person may be married in church during the lifetime of a former spouse'. Finally, in November 2002, Synod rescinded the historic resolutions which had exhorted clergy not to use the marriage service for anyone who had a former partner still living.[230]

Marriage and civil partnerships

As noted earlier, in December 2019 changes in the law allowed heterosexual couples to form civil partnerships. The House of Bishops responded to this legal change and in January 2020 issued *Civil Partnerships – for same-sex and opposite-sex couples. A pastoral statement from the House of Bishops of the Church of England*.[231] This drew on the 2005 pastoral statement on the introduction of same-sex civil partnerships (that we will consider in the next section), its conclusion that civil partnerships were not marriage, and the church's traditional teaching. Although welcomed by some, it was widely criticized by others for its content, tone and timing. Following a meeting of the College of Bishops, the Archbishops issued a statement in which they said, 'We as Archbishops, alongside the bishops of the Church of England, apologise and take responsibility for releasing a statement last week which we acknowledge has jeopardised trust. We are very sorry and recognise the division and hurt this has caused.'[232]

Same-sex relationships

There was little discussion of the question of homosexuality in the Church of England at either an official or unofficial level before the Second World War. However, from the late 1930s on, there was a considerable increase in prosecutions for homosexual activity, and increasing recognition of the harm being caused by the law. The penalty for men committing sexual acts with each other, whether committed in public or private, was two years hard labour. The Church of England became a significant supporter of homosexual law reform. Sir John Wolfenden chaired a government committee which produced a report under his name in 1957 and the Church Assembly voted in November of that year, by 155 to 138, to support its call for the decriminalization of homosexual acts in private[233] – though the law was not changed until 1967. Archbishop Michael Ramsey was a strong supporter of decriminalization, although clear that the distinction between sin and crime should be maintained: 'Amidst the modern talk about the new morality I would uphold the belief that … homosexual acts are always wrong.'[234]

Decriminalization created a new context, and began a long process of deliberation and argument within the Church of England, punctuated by the production of reports – and by the controversy that each report in turn generated. It began in the late sixties, with a report from the Board for Social Responsibility that set out divergent views on whether homosexual relationships could be accepted by the Church.[235] There was another report from the Board in the seventies (the 'Gloucester Report'), and then another in the eighties (the 'Osborne Report'). The last of these was sent to the bishops in 1989 but never officially published. It described four broad viewpoints in the church in the following terms:

1. Those who wish to uphold the tradition in a way which is hostile to homosexual people involved in any homosexual practice.

2. Those who uphold the tradition but who recognize the need for pastoral care and sensitivity in meeting the needs of all homosexual people in the church.

3. Those who believe the tradition needs to be developed to be more accommodating of what we now know about homosexuality and those who are homosexual people.

4. Those who want to make a positive affirmation of homosexual relationships … and who therefore wish to question large parts of the tradition and its use in the history of the church.

It also warned that 'In the church the growing conflict around the issue is felt at both personal and corporate levels…. It would seem that this conflict will persist for some time to come.'[236]

Meanwhile, General Synod in 1987 debated a motion proposed by Tony Higton. In amended form it was passed by 403 votes to 8, with 13 abstentions, and stated that sexual intercourse properly belonged only within a 'permanent married relationship' and that fornication and adultery and 'homosexual genital acts' are sins against this ideal and 'are to be met by a call to repentance and the exercise of compassion.' This remains the last substantive motion on sexual behaviour passed by General Synod.

In 1991 the House of Bishops produced its own document, entitled *Issues in Human Sexuality*, which effectively became the church's official working policy. (It was defended in a further report, *Some*

Issues in Human Sexuality, in 2003.[237]) Its final chapter (which sought unsuccessfully to introduce the term 'homophile' for 'same-sex') set out 'two fundamental principles of equal validity and significance':

> Homophile orientation and its expression in sexual activity do not constitute a parallel and alternative form of human sexuality as complete within the terms of the created order as the heterosexual. The convergence of Scripture, tradition and reasoned reflection on experience, even including the newly sympathetic and perceptive thinking of our own day, make it impossible for the church to come with integrity to any other conclusion...

> Homosexual people are in every way as valuable to and as valued by God as heterosexual people. God loves us all alike, and has for each one of us a range of possibilities within his design for the universe ... Every human being has a unique potential for Christlikeness, and an individual contribution to make through that likeness to the final consummation of all things. [238]

In its application of these principles, the bishops commended those homosexuals who embraced abstinence, and also committed themselves to offer friendship and understanding and to stand alongside those in the fellowship of the church who

> are conscientiously convinced that this way of abstinence is not the best for them, and that they have more hope of growing in love for God and neighbour with the help of a loving and faithful homophile partnership, in intention lifelong, where mutual self-giving includes the physical expression of their attachment.[239]

Such faithful and loving sexual same-sex relationships, however, are not open to clergy and ordinands, who should uphold the ideal, although the bishops say they 'do not think it right to interrogate individuals on their sexual lives'.[240] We will return in Chapter 17 to the use of conscience made in *Issues in Human Sexuality*.

Shortly after the Civil Partnerships Act came into law in 2004, the bishops issued a Pastoral Statement, setting out the church's response. 'What needs to be recognized', the bishops said

> is that the Church's teaching on sexual ethics remains unchanged. For Christians, marriage – that is the lifelong union between a man and a woman – remains the proper context for sexual activity. In its approach to civil partnerships the Church will continue to uphold that standard, to affirm the value of

committed, sexually abstinent friendships between people
of the same sex and to minister sensitively and pastorally to
those Christians who conscientiously decide to order their lives
differently.[241]

The Bishops affirmed 'that clergy of the Church of England should
not provide services of blessing for those who register a civil
partnership' but said that 'Where clergy are approached by people
asking for prayer in relation to entering into a civil partnership
they should respond pastorally and sensitively in the light of the
circumstances of each case.'[242] They also explained that 'Members
of the clergy and candidates for ordination who decide to enter into
partnerships must … expect to be asked for assurances that their
relationship will be consistent with the teaching set out in *Issues in
Human Sexuality.'*[243]

In 2011, Sir Joseph Pilling was asked by the bishops to chair a
working group to review the current position of the church in the
light of recent developments – the sixth report produced by the
Church of England since 1967. The Pilling Report was published
in November 2013 and included a number of recommendations
beginning with what it described as the report's 'foundation', that
'we warmly welcome and affirm the presence and ministry within
the church of gay and lesbian people, both lay and ordained'. It
made several recommendations 'on the church's pastoral response'
including that 'there can be circumstances where a priest … should
be free to mark the formation of a permanent same-sex relationship
in a public service'. The report was not unanimous, however. One
of the Working Group's episcopal members asked for a dissenting
statement to be included, setting out various reasons for his
decision, including his belief that the report did not do justice to
'the biblical witness on same-sex attraction'. [244]

The recommendations were never formally approved by the bishops
or Synod, but one proposal was implemented: to set up a process of
'Shared Conversations' the aim of which was

> that the diversity of views within the church would be expressed
> honestly and heard respectfully, with the hope that, in so doing,
> individuals might come to discern that which is of Christ in those
> with whom they profoundly disagree.[245]

From 2014 to 2016 this process of Shared Conversations took place
across the Church of England.

In 2014, the Marriage (Same Sex Couples) Act became law. The Act included a series of legal guarantees for religious groups opposed to same-sex marriage, meaning that the church was not required to change its teaching or practice. The House of Bishops again responded with Pastoral Guidance reaffirming the church's position, while explaining that

> Those same-sex couples who choose to marry should be welcomed into the life of the worshipping community and not be subjected to questioning about their lifestyle. Neither they nor any children they care for should be denied access to the sacraments.[246]

As with civil partnerships, the bishops said that 'clergy should not provide services of blessing', but that 'more informal kind of prayer, at the request of the couple, might be appropriate in the light of the circumstances'.[247] They maintained, however, that those who are in a same-sex marriage could not be ordained, and that those who are ordained could not enter into same-sex marriages.[248]

Following the completion of the Shared Conversations, the Bishops asked the General Synod in February 2017 to take note of a report outlining its policy intentions for the future: *Marriage and Same Sex Relationships after the Shared Conversations*.[249] The content, style and tone of the report were criticized in the House of Laity and, even more, in the House of Clergy. Some who had been hoping for more acceptance of same-sex relationships were disappointed by what was seen as a lack of movement following the extensive engagement in the Shared Conversations process. On a vote by Houses, a motion to 'take note' of the report fell, failing to win a majority among the clergy.

Immediately after the debate, the Archbishop of Canterbury spoke, calling for the Church of England to seek a 'a radical new Christian inclusion in the Church … founded in Scripture, in reason, in tradition, in theology and the Christian faith as the Church of England has received it', and initiating the Living in Love and Faith project.[250]

Responses to trans people

In contrast to the extensive studies and debates about same-sex relationships, discussions of the church's understanding of, and response to, trans people have featured little in Church of England discourse until very recently.

The first priest to continue to serve in her parish following gender assignment surgery, was in 2000, and in 2004 a trans person was ordained. This followed a discussion and decision in the House of Bishops in 2002 concerning transgender ordinands. The current policy of the Church of England in relation to transgender ordinands is that

> Transgender candidates are welcome to be considered for selection for ordained ministry in the Church of England

and that

> any Bishop intending to sponsor a transgender person for a BAP [Bishops' Advisory Panel] will certify that they have decided that they would be prepared to ordain and offer a title to that person if during the course of training and formation they were deemed to have a vocation to ordained ministry.[251]

The Evangelical Alliance produced a report, *Transsexuality*, in 2000, and the House of Bishops drew on this and other materials in *Some Issues in Human Sexuality* in 2003,[252] although the bishops did not come to conclusions on trans questions. It suggested two questions as of importance in ongoing reflection. Firstly, whether obedience to Christ for trans Christians meant 'learning to accept and live with their given biological identity because this is the identity which God has given them' or 'seeking a new post-operative identity on the grounds that it is this which will enable them to more fully express the person God intends them to be'. Secondly, on the basis of belief in bodily resurrection, it was noted that the traditional understanding was that 'our bodies are integral to who we are before God' and so the report asked about 'the theological grounds for saying that in the case of people with gender dysphoria their "true" identity is different from that of the body in which they were born'.[253]

Although these contributions were welcomed by some, they were seen by others as not engaging seriously with the lived experience of trans people, or with the theological explorations it has generated.

In 2004, the Gender Recognition Act included a 'conscience clause', allowing clergy to refuse to marry persons, one or both of whom they reasonably suspect to have transitioned gender. This had been sought by the Church of England after the House of Bishops issued a memorandum in early 2003 which acknowledged that 'there was a range of views within the Church on transsexualism [sic]'. In response to the first question subsequently raised in *Some Issues in Human Sexuality*, the bishops

> accepted that (as matters stood at present) both the positions set out below could properly be held:
>
> a   some Christians concluded on the basis of Scripture and Christian anthropology, that concepts such as 'gender reassignment' or 'sex change' were really a fiction. Hormone treatment or surgery might change physical appearance, but they could not change the fundamental God-given reality of 'male and female he created them'.
>
> b   others, by contrast, whilst recognizing that medical opinion was not unanimous, were persuaded that there were individuals whose conviction that they were 'trapped in the wrong body' was so profound and persistent that medical intervention, which might include psychiatric, hormone and surgical elements, was legitimate and that the result could properly be termed a change of sex or gender.[254]

In the light of this conclusion, bishops sought to safeguard 'the position of bishops unwilling to ordain transgendered [sic] candidates and, once marriage of transsexuals became possible in law, securing an exemption for clergy not willing to solemnise such marriages'.

In recent years, the level of discussion and debate has increased substantially, not least because of the recognition of the numbers of people involved. In July 2017 a motion to General Synod from the Diocese of Blackburn was passed by a substantial majority:

> That this Synod, recognising the need for transgender people to be welcomed and affirmed in their parish church, call on the House of Bishops to consider whether some nationally commended liturgical materials might be prepared to mark a person's gender transition.

In December 2018 the House of Bishops published 'Pastoral Guidance for use in conjunction with the Affirmation of Baptismal Faith'. It recommended that the Affirmation of Baptismal Faith be used as the centre of any service to recognize liturgically a person's gender transition, and encouraged such services to be celebratory and welcoming. This pastoral guidance was welcomed by some, including many trans Christians, but was criticized by others.[255]

The Anglican Communion

At the beginning of the twentieth century the Church of England still had a clear, global hierarchical structure that stretched across much of the world. It was centred on the office of Archbishop of Canterbury and ruled by the bishops – and before 1912, with the remarkable exception of Bishop Samuel Ajayi Crowther who had been consecrated Bishop of the Niger Territory in 1864, there was not a single non-white bishop anywhere in the Empire.

The phrase 'Anglican Communion', first used in 1847, became more common following the first Lambeth Conference in 1867. It refers to autonomous but interdependent churches across the globe connected to the Church of England.

As the British Empire experienced an accelerating process of decolonization, the Communion began to radically change. As late as the 1958 Lambeth Conference there were only 15 provinces other than the Church of England (3 in the rest of the UK and 4 in the US, Canada, Australia and New Zealand). More and more local churches started to become self-governing provinces distinct from the Church of England. Today there are 39 other provinces, many of which have grown quickly and dynamically.

These churches are held together by bonds of history and tradition and by four 'Instruments of Communion': the Lambeth Conferences (normally held once a decade), the Anglican Consultative Council (set up in 1968), the Primates' Meeting (first held in 1979), and the symbolic and personal role of the Archbishop of Canterbury. The provinces are autonomous, but they form a distinct family of churches within the body of Christ, and decisions in any one of them can have consequences for the others. This reality of the interdependence of the Communion is perhaps most significant in relation to the decisions of the Church of England as the historic 'mother church' of the Communion.

The dispersal of authority across 40 provinces located in more than 165 countries has created enormous opportunities and challenges for Anglicanism as it has become embedded in cultures and societies across the world, including some, such as Mexico, Brazil and Korea, that were not formerly British colonies. The different parts of the Communion manifest a very wide spectrum of theology and, in several places, practice – so much so that some fracturing of the Communion has happened over recent years.

Changing Anglican views on contraception

At the start of the twentieth century, the churches of the Anglican Communion were firmly opposed to artificial contraception. The 1908 Lambeth Conference urged 'all Christian people to discountenance the use of all artificial means of restriction'.[256] This was reaffirmed in 1920, with the Conference issuing 'an emphatic warning against the use of unnatural means for the avoidance of conception'.[257] By 1930, however, following considerable ethical discussion around the church, the Conference allowed that

> in those cases where there is such a clearly felt moral obligation to limit or avoid parenthood, and where there is a morally sound reason for avoiding complete abstinence, the Conference agrees that other methods may be used, provided that this is done in the light of the same Christian principles. The Conference records its strong condemnation of the use of any methods of conception control from motives of selfishness, luxury, or mere convenience.[258]

Despite continued opposition (both from within the church and from ecumenical partners) the force of change was such that by 1958, the Conference could declare that the responsibility for deciding upon the number and frequency of children has been laid by God upon the consciences of parents everywhere; that this planning, in such ways as are mutually acceptable to husband and wife in Christian conscience, is a right and important factor in Christian family life and should be the result of positive choice before God.[259]

The 1968 Lambeth Conference reaffirmed this position in the immediate aftermath of the Roman Catholic Church confirming its continued opposition to all forms of artificial contraception.

Historically, the Lambeth Conference has often addressed various matters relating to marriage and sexual ethics. Their reports and resolutions over 150 years display both continuity and evolution and development, notably over polygamy, divorce and contraception, sometimes mirroring the changes within Church of England practice as noted above. In recent years, especially since the 1998 Lambeth Conference, differences over same-sex relationships have led to major tensions and divisions within the Communion.

The Lambeth Conference first passed a resolution referring to homosexuality in 1978. This arose because in the churches of some Anglican provinces openly gay and lesbian Christians were beginning to be ordained and to have their relationships blessed. In response to those who began advocating for change, the bishops reaffirmed 'heterosexuality as the scriptural norm' while recognizing 'the need for deep and dispassionate study' which 'would take seriously both the teaching of Scripture and the results of scientific and medical research'. They also encouraged dialogue and pastoral concern.[260]

A similar resolution was passed in 1988 noting 'the socio-cultural factors that lead to the different attitudes in the provinces of our Communion'.[261] Such factors have continued to grow in significance and dissonance. While the predominant culture in some provinces has developed along the lines described in Chapter 5, there are others with social contexts in which homosexuality is widely condemned, and some where homosexual activity is criminalized and therefore punishable by law.

The pattern of global Anglicanism has also continued to change in recent decades. The rapid numerical growth of churches in an area now known as the Global South, which tend to be more theologically and socially conservative, has brought about the birth of new autonomous provinces. Concerned at the increasing conviction of some – particularly in North America – that God was leading their province towards the affirmation of gay and lesbian Christians and their unions, Global South Anglicans started working together with conservative members of some Western provinces. Concerned in particular that the Lambeth Conference of 1998 might approve such developments, they gathered and issued the 1997 Kuala Lumpur Statement which strongly reaffirmed traditional teaching.[262]

At the 1998 Lambeth Conference, the subsection on human sexuality became the focus for these disagreements. Its final report mapped out a diversity of views present among the bishops on homosexuality and stated 'we must confess that we are not of one mind about homosexuality'.[263] In the subsequent plenary meeting of all bishops, the Conference overwhelmingly passed (526 to 70 with 40 abstentions) resolution 1.10.[264] This, while commending the report, stated that 'in view of the teaching of Scripture' the bishops upheld 'faithfulness in marriage between a man and a woman in lifelong union, and believes that abstinence is right for those who are not called to marriage'. While rejecting 'homosexual practice as incompatible with Scripture', such that the Conference could not 'advise the legitimizing or blessing of same-sex unions nor ordaining those involved in same-gender unions', the resolution also called on churches 'to listen to the experience of homosexual persons'. Far from settling the debate or resolving divisions, however, Lambeth 1.10 has remained a continuing focus of contention across the Communion.

For many, it is held as a definitive statement of Anglican teaching, not least given that it has been regularly reaffirmed by the Archbishop of Canterbury and other Instruments of Communion. Early on, however, it was clear that not all Anglicans accepted its authority, and 'A Pastoral Statement to Lesbian and Gay Anglicans' gained support from 185 bishops (including nine primates and some future primates, including Rowan Williams) stating that 'We must not stop where this Conference has left off.'[265] In 2002 the report of the International Anglican Conversations on Human Sexuality identified eight areas of agreement but also revealed major points of disagreement – including an inability 'to reach a common mind regarding a single pattern of holy living for homosexual people'.[266] By then, however, political divisions had widened, with some Global South Primates consecrating conservative American priests as bishops for the new Anglican Mission in America. In 2003 the Episcopal Church in the US elected Gene Robinson – a same-sex partnered priest – as Bishop of New Hampshire, and a Canadian diocese formally authorized a service for blessing same-sex unions. These two developments led to further divisions among North American Anglicans. Many Global South provinces declared themselves in impaired or broken communion with the American and Canadian churches. They subsequently formed further alliances, which included crossing provincial boundaries to consecrate bishops from clergy among those churches.

The Communion's response to this crisis – The Windsor Report – was published in 2004.[267] It did not address issues of sexuality directly but sought to offer a vision for life together and a way forward for the Communion. It recommended various apologies for, and moratoria on, divisive actions, and starkly warned that failure to follow these proposals would mean having to learn to walk apart. Through the following years its specific recommendations largely failed to be enacted by the various parties in conflict. Its longer-term proposal of an Anglican Communion Covenant to help provinces navigate their differences was developed and published in late 2009 but gained limited support across the provinces and was rejected by most dioceses of the Church of England. Alongside these attempts to resolve the divisions, a Listening Process on sexuality was established which helped to clarify the different understandings concerning sexuality found across the Communion and produced a book (*The Anglican Communion and Homosexuality*) for the 2008 Lambeth Conference.[268]

In 2008 the divisions deepened further. A meeting took place in Jerusalem of conservative Anglicans from the Global South (including most bishops from provinces such as Nigeria, Uganda and Rwanda) and the West (including some bishops from Australia, England and North America). This established the Global Anglican Future Conference (GAFCON). In frustration with and challenge to the rest of the Communion, the meeting issued the Jerusalem Declaration and Statement setting out its own statement of the 'tenets of orthodoxy which underpin our Anglican identity'. It included a statement on marriage and sexual ethics. The meeting also created a GAFCON Primates' Council and Global Fellowship of Confessing Anglicans.

The 2008 Lambeth Conference (which many of the 300 Anglican Communion bishops attending GAFCON declined to attend) mainly took the form of smaller group conversations for prayer and study (known as an *Indaba*), without plenary debates or resolutions. Its published reflections described 'competing visions of how the Communion should responsibly handle our current situation'.[269] The format developed into the Communion's *Continuing Indaba Process* which sought to establish new ways of building relationships and

forms of dialogue across difference, including but not limited to
discussions on sexuality.

All the Primates of the Communion (including Nigeria, Uganda,
Rwanda, and the USA and Canada) met together in Canterbury in
January 2016. Referring to the American church's change in their
Canon on marriage and the consecration of a further bishop with
their same-sex partner, they lamented how 'such unilateral actions
on a matter of doctrine without Catholic unity is considered by
many of us as a departure from the mutual accountability and
interdependence implied through being in relationship with
each other in the Anglican Communion'. They said that these
developments 'further impair our communion and create a
deeper mistrust between us' and this 'places huge strains on the
functioning of the Instruments of Communion and the ways in
which we express our historic and ongoing relationships'. While
affirming 'a unanimous desire to walk together' they also spoke
of 'significant distance between us' which was acknowledged by
introducing certain limits on The Episcopal Church's involvement in
Communion affairs.[270]

Tensions remain within the Communion. In October 2019 the
Global South Anglican network, in collaboration with GAFCON,
announced a proposed 'enhanced ecclesial structure' through
a new covenantal framework. The document setting out the
proposal notes that 'The Church of England (CoE) has a historic
role in the life of the Communion. [...] Therefore, decisions it
makes on faith, order and morals impact other Churches and
the well-being of the Communion more deeply than those made
elsewhere.'[271] GAFCON, which met again in Jerusalem in 2018,
called on its bishops not to attend the Lambeth Conference
then planned for 2020 but postponed to 2022, and planned an
alternative gathering of GAFCON bishops in Kigali just before the
Lambeth Conference.

Meanwhile further provinces (including New Zealand and Wales)
have determined a path towards the blessing of same-sex unions
and a number of churches are taking the further step of altering
their approach to marriage to allow the marriage of same-sex
couples. The first province to do this was The Episcopal Church
(USA) in 2015. They have been followed by Scotland and Brazil and
many dioceses within Canada. There are now four serving Anglican

Communion bishops who are in same-sex marriages. Unlike in 1998, they (although not their partners) were invited to the Lambeth Conference then planned for 2020. Significant minorities have continued to uphold traditional approaches within those Anglican provinces that have changed their practice.

In summary, it is clear that issues relating to identity, sexuality, relationships and marriage have had a major impact on global Anglicanism in recent decades. Within the Anglican Communion there are now churches which have fully embraced same-sex marriage, others which are seeking to affirm same-sex unions while upholding traditional marriage doctrine, others which reject such developments but remain in full communion with those pursuing them, and others who see any such changes as a departure from Scripture and Anglican teaching. Many but not all of those who hold to the latter conviction consider it 'communion-breaking'. Divisions within provinces that have moved to affirm same-sex relationships have led (in the US, Canada, Brazil, New Zealand and Europe) to the consecration of bishops and the creation of irregular 'provinces' by those affiliated to GAFCON, causing further breaks of communion. As the Church of England discerns its own way forward within this highly-charged landscape, it is keenly mindful that all decisions will bear great consequence around the wider Communion.

We have raised, across Part Two, a whole host of questions. They may seem like a rather random collection: questions about consent, about bodily features, about marriage law, about the purpose of dating, about the relationship between identity and attraction, about the meaning of sex – and any number of other topics.

All of these questions are, however, intertwined. What you think about the purpose of sex and what you think about the nature of marriage are likely to affect what you think about cohabitation. What you think about gender is likely to affect what you think about same-sex marriage. Pull at any one string in this tangle, and you're likely to find that the whole knot comes along with it. You will almost certainly find that it brings along other topics that we have not covered here. We are very aware that we have only sampled the relevant issues, and that there are many other themes clamouring for attention.

Nevertheless, we hope this Part has at least raised a set of important and interconnected questions. In later parts we explore the kinds of answers that Christian people give to those questions, as they seek to discern the ways of living that lead to the sort of life that God intends for us. In order to understand those answers, we need to turn to the story in which Christians, in all the diversity of their experience and perspectives, find meaning and purpose, shape and hope for themselves and all humanity. This story has at its centre the coming of Jesus Christ to bring the world life – life in all its fulness, the life that is truly worth living. We explore that story, and its implications for identity, sexuality and marriage, in **Part Three**.

Encounters

Meet MAT, NATALIE, JADE, MEGAN AND JEMMA

The scene is a a large Church of England academy in the north of England. Forty-two per cent of pupils in the academy are eligible for pupil premium. A group of five sixth formers have gathered to chat during the lunch hour – four girls and one boy.

Mat begins by highlighting the tensions for those not conforming to societal norms of gender: 'It's not something that you necessarily choose. It's something that you're born with.' He adds that this can lead to 'a sense of alienation and that [you] are "the other"' not to mention loneliness and a struggle to communicate the truth about it. Jemma observes that 'it's hard to understand if you haven't experienced that yourself' and adds that those who don't understand can feel alienated as well.

'Unless you've met somebody that is transgender, how would you actually know anything about it?'

Discussion lights on the fact that those who don't fit into societal norms 'feel like they have to introduce it as a new thing to come out as gay or transgender' says Megan. 'They shouldn't even have to come out to begin with.' Jade agrees: 'No. It should just be who you're allowed to be.'

The group identify ways that some of these barriers could be broken down: education; 'a better understanding'; 'greater respect'; positive media representation; more opportunity to speak about the subject; actual encounters with people – '[because] unless you've met somebody that is transgender, how would you actually know anything about it?' says Natalie.

The group goes on to list things that have helped. Mat says that 'if teachers are educated on these subjects and are able to communicate effectively with students then that changes the perceptions of students greatly'. Jemma talks about the importance of friendships, while Jade says how the environment she was brought up in had a big impact on how she sees things. Everyone agrees that it would help to be able to talk about these topics openly: 'I think sometimes just even speaking to each other can help', says Natalie. For most students in the school, being able to find safe places with access to counselling or therapy is vital.

They talked about things that didn't help. One example is sex education lessons that reinforce societal norms on sexuality and gender. Jemma felt strongly that 'celebratory' events like Gay Pride weren't good because they reinforced gay people as 'other'. Mat talked about tokenism and stereotyping in the media. Megan concluded the conversation: 'It's about actually making [things] equal instead of making it look equal.'

Meet JAMES AND ANNA

James and Anna arrived together but agreed amicably to tell their stories separately, and so James began with his. James sings in the choir in the church where Anna, his Mum, is vicar. He has just finished the first year of sixth form: he's doing maths, further maths and physics. He launches straight in by saying, 'So I suppose the usual place to start [...] would be the point of discovering what your sexuality is. But for me personally, as an asexual and an aromantic asexual, so with no sexual or romantic attraction at all, I'm different from the start, because there is no single point of discovering you don't have an attraction. Which obviously makes me very different to begin with.' James goes on to talk candidly about going through puberty without wet dreams, never having an erection, never having had a 'crush' on anyone.

'My life is exactly what I want it to be, but it's not necessarily what people expect.'

He rarely talks about his asexuality with others, but when he does, he often finds that people try and tell him there's no such thing as asexuality. He finds it strange that people think they can deny his reality, when they wouldn't dream of doing that for someone who was gay, for example. When it comes to Christianity, 'so much of it is about relationships. You look at people in the Bible – Jacob, blessed because he had so many sons; Elizabeth, blessed with children in her old age. God's blessing to his people is so often to do with having children and descendants. So you kind of wonder what that means for an asexual person. Does that mean we don't get God's blessing because we don't have the desire or the ability to have children? Or does that mean we are more blessed, because we are content and happy without the desire for that blessing?' James would love people to understand better what being asexual means and is like. 'I'm perfectly happy. My life is exactly what I want it to be, but it's not necessarily what people expect.'

When it's Anna's turn she talks warmly of her son whom she describes as relational, a 'hugger' and very sensitive to the feelings of others. James had told his Mum about his asexuality when he was 16. As she looked back on his childhood she could see it made sense. What was painful for her to realize was James' feeling of being invisible, alien. 'As a mum and as a vicar, I was heartbroken to think [...] that actually I'm part of [church] – a group of people – who have managed to give the impression to somebody that we simply don't even see them.' She has been wondering about the theological connection between being human and being sexual: 'I've ended up not really forming a theology of sexuality so far, but actually a deeper understanding of what it means to be loved by God and to love one another. That's been a surprise in some ways, but a joy.'

Meet SHARON

Sharon is 23. She was brought up in a single parent Caribbean household by her Christian mother. She has a twin brother and a younger brother. 'I think what was different for me, [was] my mum is Christian and my dad was Muslim." Sharon laughed, 'That was a different way of growing up. My Dad was around and then he left and then he came back and he left, so he was inconsistent in that way. Christianity was pretty much the most consistent thing that's been in our life the whole time. Not to say that [was because of] him being Muslim... it's literally because that was just the situation at the time. Our primary school was linked to the church. Me and my twin brother, we went to the same primary school, same church pretty much...

'So I think identity, Christianity is always going to be a big part because I think it's just who you are; the Bible is the foundation, the fundamental foundation. It's the Word that we live by, do you know what I mean?'

Sharon's mother did not have her children baptized, but had them blessed instead. 'I think from the start, as Caribbeans, we feel like you should grow up and make your own choice.' She would say 'Don't make it because I'm Christian; make it that you want it to be something you're passionate about'. Sharon and her brother got baptized and confirmed in their early teens.

Sharon's view on homosexual relationships is that 'if you can love someone wholly and deeply and not hurt anyone, not get in anyone's way, just do your thing and not judge anyone else, I don't see why that is a problem... you have to remember that Jesus died for our sins – that means none of us are perfect. There's no perfect way of loving someone. If you're going to love them, as long as you're not harming anyone else and you're not bringing in chaos and stress and all that, and you're not judging anyone else, I have never had a problem. Do you know what I mean? I've never really had a problem with it.'

Sharon's view of marriage is that it is complex. 'When it comes to stuff like marriage and sexuality, again, I don't think it's wrong to have sexual intercourse before marriage. I get why people think it's easier to just get married. All my friends are just like, it's just easier, just get married first. I agree as well, but I think there's people that have been able to do that and get married and still be together, some aren't even married and they're still together... But I think relationships... it's just become a lot more difficult, in my age group anyway, in terms of trusting people.

> **'It's the Word that we live by, do you know what I mean?'**

'That's just me, the whole idea of marriage almost like a fantasy. Oh my God, I wish that could be me and it's like, it can but you just think everyone is aiming for the wrong thing – make sure the foundation is right first. Make sure you know them. I think that's what was nice about our youth group. If there was ever going to be a relationship, we knew them from young. We'd known each other for a while, so we kind of know, okay, this could work. I think friendship helps when you're friends first and then you build that up. Then you may have a sexual attraction and then it may become a thing. If it doesn't, you know, that's just life, but that helps, I think.'

Meet EMMA

Emma presented as a woman for the interview. She is an older person, formerly a surgeon who is married to a woman. She describes herself as bigender.

Emma is evangelical by tradition and conviction and had a strong conversion experience in her teens while on a mission in France. 'When I came back I thought, "I've really got to go one way or the other." Either it's God is not for me or I'm all out for God. It wasn't an instant decision but by the time I left school, I knew where I was going. That stayed with me since then'.

**'it was
something I
wished wasn't
there, but we
didn't really
know what to do.'**

Emma was aware of her desire to dress as a female from a very early age, but soon realized it was best to keep this part of her hidden. 'When in my all-boys school, at the age of ten, I was asked to play the part of a girl, which was quite common. I was really embarrassed about it, so I was glad when it was over. But something had sparked in me, and a year later, in the next school play, I was actually wishing I was playing the part of a girl.'

When she (as a man) met her wife, she explained this part of her, and they got married (as man and woman). 'We both thought that my female side would evaporate because we were going to get married and have children. We thought, "God can't like this, can he?"... so it was something I wished wasn't there, but we didn't really know what to do. Of course we were somewhat taken aback, over the ensuing years, when this side of me didn't go away. In fact, it became stronger. We kept it a secret.'

They had three children and Emma generally kept what she describes as the 'trans' side of her hidden. About 12 years ago, following getting to know people at Sibyls [a UK Christian trans spirituality group] and having counselling she decided to let members of the congregation know about this. 'I went to the vicar and... said, "I'm going to write a letter to all our friends in the church." It was around 60 people, mainly couples our age, "to tell them and explain this side of me, and that I felt that God accepted me and that I couldn't keep it secret anymore." The vicar didn't want me to do it. He said, "Let's keep our little secret." But I went ahead and from that moment, I was not allowed to carry out any sort of ministry in the church. For instance, I was due to do a reading in the carol service, and I was told that, "You're not doing that anymore. So, attend church, yes, take communion, yes. We can only restore those things if you seek help, healing, prayer, ministry, to get rid of this sinful side of you." We received about 30 letters from people, in response to my letter... many of them were really bizarre and very negative.'

The couple eventually decided to leave saying, '"We can't stay here any longer. There's no future for us here." So that was it. We left under a cloud basically. There were no thank yous or goodbyes, after 35 years of fellowship.'

They then moved to a different church in the town where they live. Until relatively recently Emma always presented as a man in her new church, but thanks to a new incumbent, she now also presents as a woman. "Two years ago this new vicar immediately latched on and said, 'Why doesn't Emma go to church?'"

Emma does not intend to transition and presents sometimes as a man and sometimes as a woman. She still feels she has quite a strong male identity which she does not want to lose. She and her wife have remained married and she describes her wife as her 'amazing defender' despite the difficulties they have both had to contend with.

Almighty and everlasting God,
who stooped to raise fallen humanity
through the child-bearing of blessed Mary;
grant that we, who have seen your glory
revealed in our human nature
and your love made perfect in our weakness,
may daily be renewed in your image
and conformed to the pattern of your Son
Jesus Christ our Lord.
Amen.

Common Worship:
Collect of the Blessed Virgin Mary

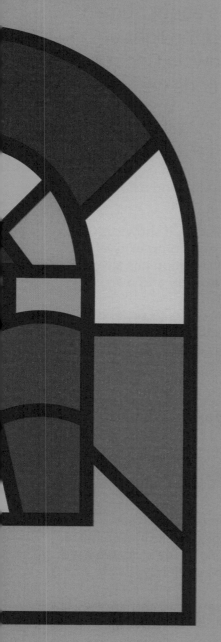

PART THREE

Making connections: where are we in God's story?

The purpose of Part Three is to explore current Christian thinking and discussions about human identity, sexuality, and marriage. In the light of the good news of Jesus Christ, how do Christians understand and respond to the trends we observed in Part Two?

Chapter 8 outlines the story of salvation – the story of God's engagement with the world as its creator, its judge and its redeemer.

Chapter 9 notes that, as the Bible tells us this story, it shows us God engaging with human beings in all the reality and complexity of their lives and their relationships. The story of salvation has always been, in part, a story about human identity, sexuality and marriage.

Chapter 10 looks more closely at what this story has to say about human dignity, diversity and identity. It shows that the way we relate these to our deepest identity – in Christ – gives rise to different understandings about the nature of sin and God's transforming grace.

Chapter 11 turns to the church, a community called to live and proclaim this story of salvation. We look at what the story says about the church's distinctiveness, and about what belongs and what does not belong in its life together. We also ask what it means when disagreements about these matters arise.

Chapter 12 looks at some of the specific patterns of life that Christians understand as responses to this story – including celibacy and marriage. We ask how these patterns relate to the story we have been telling and ask what Jesus had to say about them.

Part One set out the Church of England's current teaching on marriage. It explained how that teaching related to the gift of abundant life in loving relationships offered to the whole of humanity through the life, death, resurrection and ascension of Jesus Christ.

In Part Three, we return to the same territory – but here we explore it differently. Our aim now is not to expound the Church of England's current teaching in these areas. It is, instead, to explore the kinds of thinking that are going on in the church's deliberations and debates about these topics and to see how that thinking relates to the good news of Jesus Christ.

Christians are people who seek to live within, and become defined by, a story – a story which we believe to be true. It is a story drawn from Scripture, reaffirmed in the creeds and celebrated in the liturgies of the church. We try to tell that story in our worship, in our preaching, and in our conversations and actions in the world. We are constantly learning afresh how to inhabit it in all manner of different contexts.

It is a story that begins with God, who in love created humankind in the divine image, so that in communion with one another and with Christ we might mirror God's glory. It is a story about our rebellion, disobedience and refusal to depend on one another and on God – a disorder which has infected the whole of creation. It is a story of our desperate need for the mercy and love of God in the face of this sinfulness. It is a story about Jesus, who embraced our humanity, lived among us, and gave himself to death for us so that we and the whole of creation could be set free from the bonds of sin, the forces of evil and the judgement we deserve. It is a story of forgiveness, which invites us to repent daily and to reflect the love of God by forgiving others with the same measure with which we have been forgiven by God. It is the story of Jesus rising from the dead and ascending into heaven and interceding for us and for the whole creation. It is the story of the Church – his body on earth – inaugurated by the pouring out of the Holy Spirit among us so that we could experience the power of God's transforming love in our human weakness. It is a story about the end of death and the beginning of eternal life here and now. It is a story of faith in Jesus Christ, of hope in a new heaven and a new earth, and of the transforming power of God's love.

The Church of England's deliberations and disagreements about identity, sexuality, relationships and marriage need to be understood in relation to this story. They have emerged as Christians across the church have asked how to inhabit this story in love and faith – and how we can stand together 'firm in one spirit, striving side by side with one mind for the faith of the gospel' (Philippians 1.27). There is much that Christians share as we seek to answer these questions, but there are also differences in the way in which we tell the story and differences in the implications we draw from it. Throughout this Part we will be trying both to show how our deliberations and disagreements about identity, sexuality, relationships and marriage are grounded in a shared story, *and* how they are shaped by some significant differences in our tellings of that story.

Our hope, therefore, is not that readers will agree with everything they find in this Part, nor that they will conclude that everything here represents the recognized teaching of the Church of England. It is, rather, that readers

- will understand better the kinds of claims that Christians around the church make in the areas of marriage, relationships, sexuality, and human identity;

- will understand why these claims matter to Christians committed to following the way of Jesus Christ; and

- will understand how people committed to the same way can nevertheless sometimes come to such different conclusions.

That is certainly not the end of our exploration.

In Part Four, we will be asking in more detail how it is that Christians end up with these different ways of telling the story of salvation. We look, for instance, at the different approaches to Scripture that can be found across the church and the different attitudes to scientific discoveries.

In Part Five we will listen in on some conversations among the people who have been involved in writing this book. They will draw on what we have discussed in Parts Three and Four. Some advocate the reaffirmation of current teaching and practice; some advocate changes of one kind or another. You could think of Parts Three and Four as setting out a range of building blocks: on their own they are a bit fragmentary and inconclusive, so Part Five shows some of the different ways in which they can be put together to make something coherent and striking.

The focus of Parts Three to Five, then, is on helping readers to better understand the various claims being made around the church about, identity, sexuality, relationships and marriage. Understanding this variety is not, however, the same as accepting or approving it. There remains a serious question – which we will point to in these Parts but not fully tackle – of discerning what the proper limits are to the variety of teaching and practice in the church.

In the Appeal at the end of the book, we will hear more directly from the bishops how they hope the Church of England will engage with all the Living in Love and Faith resources and use them to discern the way forward, so that good decisions and right judgements are made about our common life.

CHAPTER 8

A story of love and faith with hope

At the heart of all things is the love of God: 'God is love' (1 John 4.8,16).

The story of salvation that the Bible tells is the story of the never-ending intimacy of love between Father, Son and Holy Spirit.

It is about a way of loving that reaches out in self-giving to the world: 'God so loved the world that he gave his only Son, so that everyone who believes in him may not perish but may have eternal life.' (John 3.16)

The story of salvation is a story that calls humanity to dwell in God's never-ending intimate communion of love in obedience and joy: 'If you keep my commandments, you will abide in my love, just as I have kept my Father's commandments and abide in his love. I have said these things to you so that my joy may be in you, and that your joy may be complete' (John 15.10-11). To become a Christian is to enter this story of God's love. The story of salvation is a love story.

In the story of creation, we discover that human beings exist because God reached out in love and freedom and created humankind as a partner and friend with whom to share love and delight. At each stage of creation God saw that 'it was good' (Genesis 1.4, 10, 12, 18, 21, 25); on the day God created humankind 'it was very good' (Genesis 1.31).

In the story of the fall, we discover that almost from the outset human beings turn away from God's abundant love to the scarcity of their own imagining. They pull up their own roots, turning to selfishness, envy and enmity. We see the whole world affected by this turning away, this sin (Genesis 3). And we learn that judgement is part of this love story: 'The one who rejects me and does not receive my word has a judge; on the last day the word I have spoken will serve as judge' (John 12.48), says Jesus to his disciples. Precisely because God is love, and precisely because God longs to share that love with the world, God stands against all that rejects and betrays that love. The story of salvation speaks of God's grief at the evil inclinations of human hearts (Genesis 6.5,6); it speaks of God's condemnation of that evil and of God's wrath against it (Psalm 90.7-12).

As the story continues, however, we also see the creativity of God's love. God writes new chapters in this love story, finding ways to call human beings away from their rejections and betrayals and re-establish them in love. The story of Noah shows us how God judges the world for the evil of its ways. It also shows us how God calls one man, Noah, and his family, out of that benighted world, to live again as human beings were meant to live. In the story of Abraham, we hear how God calls into being a particular people and promises to be with them in love. In the story of Moses, we hear how God frees that people from slavery, and promises to teach them how to live – how to inhabit and respond to God's love and how to turn away from all that dishonours that love. We hear how God makes a covenant with that people, showing how that love may be sustained forever. As the story of God's people continues, we hear how that love was cultivated, honoured, jeopardised and almost lost – in tales of prophets, priests and kings. Eventually, we hear of Israel going into exile in Babylon, as if the covenant were finally broken and God had turned away. But then we hear how God brings Israel back from Babylon, carrying a renewed sense of who God is and of the trustworthiness of God's loving promises.

And then, at the great turning point of history, God enters the story directly by coming among us, fully God and fully human. Jesus is the God of love incarnate, God's love in the flesh. From a position of intimacy – lying 'close to the Father's heart' (John 1.18) – Jesus lives out the love, tenderness, and compassion of God among us, holding fast to that love all the way through death (Philippians 2.1–11). Jesus shows what love entails by shaping a community of followers. He demonstrates what love requires by spending time with those excluded from the society of his time. He practises what love dictates by challenging the authorities of his time. And because these three commitments bring him into conflict with a world that rebels against and rejects God's love, they lead to his arrest, torture and execution. Jesus suffers the condemnation that should be ours, enduring the consequences of our sin – and refuses to respond with anything but love, all the way to the grave. And God vindicates him, raising him from the dead, lifting him up so that all people can be drawn to him in love and come to share the life of love that he embodies.

And so the last words of the risen Christ to Peter in John's Gospel ring out through the ages as an invitation to all humanity, 'Follow me!' (John 21.22).

Divine and human love

The revelation of the God of love in Jesus is the subject of the First Letter of John.

Beloved, let us love one another, because love is from God; everyone who loves is born of God and knows God. Whoever does not love does not know God, for God is love. God's love was revealed among us in this way: God sent his only Son into the world so that we might live through him. In this is love, not that we loved God but that he loved us and sent his Son to be the atoning sacrifice for our sins. (1 John 4.7–10)

Love is the reason for creation; and sharing love with God is the reason for the creation of human beings. The lavish love that God bestows upon creation is meant to cascade through human lives. 'Beloved, since God loved us so much, we also ought to love one another. No one has ever seen God; if we love one another, God lives in us, and his love is perfected in us' (1 John 4.11,12).

Human love, in all its richness and glory, reflects this prior love of God. Acts of self-giving for the good of the other – gifts of time, attention, nurture and care, the tender touch of lovers, the enduring commitment of friends – are luminous with God's light. If we love one another, God lives in us. Over time, as we learn to love, God's image is perfected in us. Our love can deepen, the more we know ourselves to be the objects of eternal love – a love that is entirely unselfish, entirely attentive, entirely oriented to the flourishing of all God's creatures.

Love is the intersection of God's life and our life. When we love selflessly, devotedly, truly, we come close to perceiving the nature of God's love – indeed, the nature of God who is love. Every moment of conversion is a discovery that love is stronger than hate, than evil, than death. Every process of reconciliation is a statement that love is truer than enmity, estrangement, disharmony. The story of the Church is one in which this love takes earthly, human, institutional form. There are constant setbacks, wrong paths and mistakes, but love is the name for the Spirit that makes something beautiful out of even the worst failure.

Eventually, in God's time, there will only be love. Love is the only thing that lasts forever (1 Corinthians 13). We will find a love untainted by selfishness, unlimited by death and unsullied by unworthy wants and needs. Beyond the last day, when sorrow and sighing and pain are no more and God dwells among humankind, that love, finally fully answering God's love, will abide. Love will never pass away.

Faith in love

Faith is, at root, trust. It is trust expressed in concrete steps into the unknown, through tangible acts that express our convictions about what is true and our confidence in a relationship on which we depend.

But Christianity doesn't begin with our faith in God. It is founded on God's faithfulness to us. God shows unfailing faithfulness, even in the face of human faithlessness and rebellion (Deuteronomy 7.9; Psalm 91.4, 103.15-17; Hosea 11.8,9; 1 Corinthians 1.9; 1 John 1.9; 1 Thessalonians 5.24; 2 Thessalonians 3.3). In the covenant God makes with Israel at Mount Sinai, God's faithfulness to Israel is a given. Israel praises the Lord because the Lord's mercy endures forever. One of the great paradoxes with which Paul wrestles is how the God who made such promises to Israel can be regarded as faithful now that those promises have been extended to the Gentiles – but he remains convinced that God remains true to those promises. God's love abides forever; faithfulness is its form. Where there is faithfulness there is invariably love; but the love that does not issue in faithfulness invariably turns out not to be love at all.

Paul says to the Christians in Corinth that love 'bears all things, believes all things, hopes all things, endures all things. Love never ends' (1 Corinthians 13.7,8). There can be no love without faith, because we cannot know all things about one another, even about God. Instead we must take some things on trust and our word for that trust is faith. Without that faith, we cannot love, because our love would be inhibited, circumscribed and impoverished by suspicion, anxiety and fear. When the First Letter of John says perfect love casts out fear, it means that with love comes trust, and trust is the opposite of fear. Complete trust means no anxiety and no fear.

The story of Adam and Eve eating the fruit of the tree of the knowledge of good and evil is a paradigm of the failure of faith (Genesis 3). The serpent persuades Eve that God's words are not trustworthy. Not trusting God, Adam and Eve behave as if there were no God, or as if they themselves were God, and simply follow their unformed desires. Even with the clear revelation of God's wishes and God's purpose, human beings still fail to trust God. A similar pattern appears when Moses is with God on the mountain and the children of Israel make a golden calf to worship because they have lost trust in God (Exodus 32). Likewise David spots Bathsheba and conspires to make her his own, even though he is well aware of God's abundant faithfulness towards him (2 Samuel 11,12). These stories display the way human beings struggle to trust, and how lack of trust, or of faith, leads to the distortion of love into control and manipulation, and the misconstrual of God's mercy not as a blessing but as a threat.

We were made for love. The rejection of God's offer of love, the gift that brings life, leads us towards death. Yet God continues to offer us love – and Jesus' life, death and resurrection are God's ultimate way of offering this love to the world. In Jesus' life, and in his death on the cross, God takes on the cost of rebuilding love in a world that has turned against it. Refusing, on the cross, our refusal of love, God invites human beings to turn away from our betrayal of love, to be forgiven for that betrayal, and to receive in faith the life of love that steps out from the tomb alive and victorious. This is the work of redemption, the gift of God to fallen humanity, raising us from sin and death and drawing us up into love and on into love's perfection. Faith is believing in this love and entrusting one's life to it.

Love is the grain of the universe, the DNA of creation. Faith is the trust that love is true, that it is indeed at the heart of all things and that it will prevail. Christian faith is trust in Jesus – trust that Jesus truly is fully God and fully human, that he truly does represent everything of God to us and everything of us to God. Faith is trusting that the commandments Jesus gives are the way of life and truth. Faith is trusting that when we stray from God's way of life, Christ's death truly brings about the forgiveness of sins and his resurrection truly is the end of death. Faith is trust in the Holy Spirit to do what we cannot do for ourselves: make Christ present to us until the last day.

Hope of glory

John the Baptist's disciples came to Jesus and on his behalf asked, 'Are you the one who is to come, or are we to wait for another?' (Matthew 11.3; Luke 7.19). Even with Jesus in their midst, those who longed for God's kingdom sometimes struggled to trust in him. Friedrich Nietzsche, arch-critic of Christianity, said 'Better songs they would have to sing to make me believe in their Redeemer: more redeemed would disciples have to appear!'[272] He might also have said, 'I might believe in the Saviour if the world looked more as if it had been saved.'

These two challenges, the shortcomings of the Church and the continuing evil and suffering in the world, are the principal reasons why it is hard to trust that love has been and will finally be the quality that abides forever. If *love* is that which truly reigns, and *faith* is that which trusts in the God who has acted, most of all in Jesus, then we need a third word – for the trust that love will finally prevail. That third word is hope. Hope is the orientation of one's life towards the faith that love alone will abide forever.

Intercessory prayer is an act of hope. In prayer Christians trust that the God whose character has been demonstrated in covenant loyalty and has been fully disclosed in the life, death and resurrection of Jesus, will finally pervade all things with love. Such prayer is often accompanied by lament, the naming of the distance between how God wills things to be and the way they actually are. But intercession is fundamentally a plea that God will bring forward some of the fruits of the final fulfilment so that we may enjoy them now. That's what forgiveness is; that's what healing is; that's what reconciliation is: a taste now of what we shall in Christ enjoy forever. When in the Song of Solomon (8.6) we are told that 'love is strong as death', we affirm the faith that in Christ love has outlasted death and the hope that the victory of God's love will abide forever. That claim in the Song of Solomon is preceded by the words, 'Set me as a seal upon your heart' (Song of Solomon 8.6). This shows that faith, hope and love are always intimate and personal as well as cosmic and perpetual. But it also suggests that what we see today is just the sketchy figure of what will finally be ours. It is the down-payment, engagement ring, or dim reflection in a mirror.

To believe in love despite our personal failings, the sins of the Church and the state of the world takes hope. Hope is not the same as optimism, since hope believes the one who makes things right is *personal being*, not an inanimate force of nature or luck. Hope is not in ourselves, because Christians believe the ultimate future is not something we create; it is the reality God brings to us. Christian hope in the future does not rest upon our assessment of whatever forces seem to be winning in the present, but trust that God's love will have the ultimate victory. It brings people to make remarkable sacrifices for the sake of being faithful. It has been said, 'It is better to fail in a cause that will finally succeed than to succeed in a cause that will finally fail.' That is a succinct summary of hope; and it rests on faith that the God of love has already, in a fundamental way, succeeded. And so as we wait with patience for God to disclose this final purpose across all creation, we work to nurture whatever signs and foretastes of that victory are to be seen in the present.

As Paul tells us, faith, hope and love abide (1 Corinthians 13.13). These are the marks of the intimate and cosmic story that will finally embrace us and all things in joy and peace forever.

CHAPTER 9

A story that embraces all of life

When we open the books of the Old and New Testaments to read this story of salvation – the story of faith, hope and love – we discover that they present just as diverse and complicated a picture of the society of their time as we have observed in ours today (see Part Two).

In the pages of Scripture, we find talk of relationships, friendship, marriage, singleness, sex, faithfulness and romance, as well as stories of betrayal, pain, misuse of power, abuse, infidelity, dysfunctional families and violence. Every aspect of life is drawn together in this picture: public and private, personal and social – from emotions to economics, from social justice to family relationships. It shows us the rich variety and complexity of human life, and it shows us a world marred by the consequences of our rebellion and sin. In its pages, we see all of humanity's beauty and brokenness.

The story of salvation that the Bible tells us is not a story that floats above this complexity and diversity. It shows us God working in the midst of human life – working with all of this rich, dense, messy, beautiful and broken material. This is the world that God loves, despite its rebelliousness. This is the world in which God's plan of salvation is worked out. This is the world in which we see glimpses and foretastes of the love that will abide forever – in the midst of the lives of fallible human beings. And this is the world in which God becomes incarnate, in Jesus of Nazareth, who shows us what it looks like to choose life, to live in perfect communion with God in the midst of this broken and messy world. As the Eucharistic Prayer puts it, 'Embracing our humanity, Jesus showed us the way of salvation.'[273]

In particular, the Bible shows us that the story of salvation is, from its opening, played out in the midst of all the ordinariness and splendour of human bodies and relationships, with all their difficulty and delight. Right at the outset of Genesis, as we saw in Part One, human beings are made for relationship: 'Then the LORD God said, "It is not good that the man should be alone; I will make a helper as his partner"' (Genesis 2.18). Man and woman are made 'in the image of God', to relate to God in a special way. And this image involves something quite extraordinary. Human beings are made as bodies. They are given material existence. The God who made all things, who is beyond our imagination, who is said to be Spirit (John 4.24), places God's image in frail human bodies. God then sets them in the physical world – to care for the world around them, to love one another, and through their relationships to fill the earth and care for it (Genesis 1.27-30). God then surveys creation and declares it 'very good' (Genesis 1.31).

The body

From the beginning, human beings' bodily existence, and the expression of love through their bodies, is valued. Bodies matter in Scripture. They are celebrated for their beauty and their skills, they bear the mark of the promise through circumcision or vows, they express belonging to the community of faith through baptism and the eucharist. Bodies are also a place of vulnerability. They get hurt and maimed, they are open to infection, they age and decay, they are sometimes unruly and troublesome, they can harm others even when we are not aware of it and they can be used deliberately to hurt others. Yet bodies are not an independent entity, separate from the mind or soul. Human beings are a complex whole – hence the insistence, in Paul, on bodily resurrection. To be human is to be embodied, and so while talk of the body changes over the course of Scripture, the value of the body is constant.

Bodies bear the marks of meeting with God: Jacob wrestles with God and his hip is damaged (Genesis 32.24-32), Moses' faces shines with the glory of God (Exodus 34.29-35), Isaiah's mouth is cleansed with a live coal (Isaiah 6.1-7). In the ministry of Jesus, he touches people and heals their bodies (for example, Matthew 8.14,15; 9.27-30; 14.34-36; Mark 5.25-43); Paul is temporarily blinded on the road to Damascus (Acts 9.1-9) and so on. Bodies are significant to spirituality: they can help us get closer to God and other people – or move away from them.

Bodies are the site of loving relationships between people. We see that between friends, such as David and Jonathan who embrace each other (1 Samuel 20.41), or John reclining on Jesus (John 13.23); we see it between parents and their children, with the tenderness of motherly love a constant image of God's care for Israel (Deuteronomy 32.11-18; Isaiah 49.15 and 66.12,13; Hosea 11.3,4); and we see it in sexual relationships between men and women (Song of Solomon).

The significance of intimacy is beautifully explored in the story of Genesis 2. A human being is created, alone, and no amount of relationships with the world around, or indeed with God, satisfies the need for human companionship. Human beings need other human beings, and the longing for intimacy is intrinsic to being human. Here intimacy is also expressed sexually: the man and the woman become 'one flesh'. Sexual union is depicted positively. Human beings are essentially interrelated, social beings, who can form bonded pairs united physically as well as emotionally.

Because bodies matter, what we do with our bodies, and to the bodies of others, also matters. The Old Testament therefore has laws about bodily matters and bodily functions, laws about economics, the land, food, right social relationships, violence towards the body and sexuality. We can see these laws as essentially restrictive or limiting (i.e. trying to contain the excesses of the body), or as protective and affirmative (an acknowledgement that bodies have deep significance, and that to harm the body is to harm the entire human being and society itself), or, indeed, as both.

The importance and value of the body becomes even more striking in the New Testament. The invisible God, who had made human beings in his image, now becomes human himself, in the full bodily reality that we see in Jesus. He worked (Mark 6.3), ate and drank (e.g. Luke 5.29-32; Luke 7.36-50), got tired (John 4.6), wept (John 11.35), was hurt, tortured and died (Matthew 27.26-50; Mark 15.15-37; Luke 23.26-46; John 19.1-37), and his resurrected body, whilst different, still bears the scars of his former body (John 20.24-29), and still moves, stands and eats, before disciples who struggle to believe it is really him (Luke 24.36-43).

In Paul's first letter to the Christians in Corinth he speaks often about the importance of bodies. He reminds us that every time we celebrate Holy Communion we participate in Christ's body and blood (1 Corinthians 10.16). We, the Church, are Christ's body on earth (1 Corinthians 12). Our bodies are described as being 'members of Christ' and 'a temple of the Holy Spirit' (1 Corinthians 6.15, 19). They are destined not for destruction but for resurrection life (1 Corinthians 15). These are remarkable bodily images of intimacy with God and with each other as 'members of Christ'.

The deep significance of human bodies makes what we do with our own bodies and the bodies of others in sexual relationships of great importance: 'You are not your own; you were bought at a price. Therefore honour God with your bodies' (1 Corinthians 6.19,20 (NIV)). As throughout Scripture, Paul here sees sexual immorality as a particularly serious form of sin. We are to flee from it because 'whoever sins sexually, sins against their own body' (1 Corinthians

6.18 (NIV)). This is not necessarily because it is morally worse, but because sex has a specific, particular impact on us. Current discussions around sexual abuse and violence clearly show the differential impact of sexual violence as opposed to other types of violence. When the locus of our deepest intimacy and vulnerability is misused, by ourselves, or by others, it leaves very deep scars, because our bodies are not 'just a body' but temples of the Spirit, members of Christ himself, and a way of becoming deeply joined to others. Sex is never 'just sex' as even in sex with a prostitute 'the two will become one flesh' (1 Corinthians 6.16).

Scripture as a whole therefore directs us to treat our bodies and those of others with respect and care, and not merely as objects. It challenges us to value our bodies far more deeply than simply as instruments, or vessels for our souls, or machines to be used. Our bodies and what we do with them matter to the God who took on a body of his own.

Relationships

The story told in the Bible explores the myriad ways in which human beings conduct relationships. Yet this is no idealized story. It is a story of truth, which allows readers to see the whole of humanity, for good, for bad, and for the many shades of life in-between.

The story of salvation displayed in the Bible is, in one sense, played out amongst people who are just like us. We meet people who are single, some by choice (Paul, 1 Corinthians 7.8), some against their will (Jeremiah, Jeremiah 16.1,2). We meet others who are married, some happily (Isaac and Rebekah, Genesis 24.67; Ruth and Boaz, Ruth 4; Priscilla and Aquila, Acts 18.18, 26; Romans 16.3,4), some less so (Leah and Jacob, Genesis 29.31-35; David and his first wife Michal, 2 Samuel 6.16-23). Some men, including the patriarchs in Genesis, and David and Solomon, had multiple wives and concubines, while, later on, others were in monogamous relationships. Some, like David and his wife Michal, were separated and remarried. Some had children while others struggled with infertility. The practical reality of the lives that we see in the Bible is as varied and diverse as it is now – and we see God at work with people who are struggling, just like us, with the shape of relationships and whose lives, just like ours, are never perfect.

The friendship of David and Jonathan

Scripture is replete with references to friends and companions, and how these relationships sustain, support, and, at times, cause pain to those involved. As we saw in Part One, two striking narrative examples are the friendship between David and Jonathan, and that of Ruth and Naomi. Both relationships involved an explicit commitment between the two partners. Ruth promises loyalty to Naomi, and Jonathan makes a covenant of friendship with David. These relationships of covenanted fidelity in the Lord were capable of overriding conventional family loyalties, and went beyond traditional friendships in being marked by an oath or covenant.

The intensity of mutual affection between Jonathan and David is in no doubt. Their friendship is introduced with the words: 'the soul of Jonathan was bound to the soul of David, and Jonathan loved him as his own soul... Then Jonathan made a covenant with David, because he loved him as his own soul' (1 Samuel 18.1,3). It is clear that the intimacy between Jonathan and David was expressed physically (this was an ordinary aspect of male relationships in biblical culture); though not explicitly sexually, it has been read that way by some. As they parted, 'they kissed each other and wept with each other' (1 Samuel 20.41).

When David later receives the news of Jonathan's death on the battlefield, he grieves profoundly: 'I am distressed for you, my brother Jonathan; greatly beloved were you to me; your love to me was wonderful, passing the love of women' (2 Samuel 1.26). Some have seen a sexual reference in the phrase 'passing the love of women', but while this verb always implies strong affection, it does not typically imply sexual expression. It is used in a wide variety of relationship contexts, and what is stressed here is the unusual intensity of affection. In this case, even allowing for the rhetoric of mourning, it might well mean that this relationship mattered more to David than his marriages.

Saul, Jonathan's father, deeply resented the bond between his son and the man he considered an enemy. Rightly suspecting Jonathan's collusion with David's escape from Saul's court, the king cries out, 'Do I not know that you have chosen the son of Jesse to your own shame, and to the shame of your mother's nakedness?' (1 Samuel 20.30). There are several ways to read Saul's words. They could be a reflection of his anger at Jonathan's choice of his enemy as a friend, which he would consider both an insult and a wilful refusal of family obligations. They could be an accusation, in a traditional patriarchal culture, of a romantic attachment between the two men, which Saul would consider shameful. This accusation, however, could either reflect the truth, or be a calculated insult, insinuating that there is more to their relationship than friendship. In either case, Saul's words are intended as pressure on Jonathan to break an alliance he resents.

This covenant was not simply between the two men. It was a holy thing, which invoked the Lord and assumed the Lord's blessing. Both men felt bound by their oath, to the point that David regarded himself bound by his covenantal fidelity to Jonathan beyond the latter's death (2 Samuel 9.1-7), so he would care for Jonathan's descendants.

The story therefore presents us with an example of covenanted friendship. This covenanted fidelity was not really analogous to marriage. It is clear that almost as soon as the covenant was made, David and Jonathan were parted never to meet again. Both men were already married – in David's case multiply (2 Samuel 2.2, 5.13). However, their story invites some questions. Are male friendships in twenty-first century Britain perhaps as much in need of recovering the capacity for tears as for physical affection? Are there circumstances in which the Church might honour and bless a same-sex relationship of covenanted fidelity today, which is devoted, affectionate, capable of superseding social conventions with regard to family loyalty, capable of being dismissed by those who are threatened by it as a perverse disgrace, and yet holy to the Lord?

The worlds of the text are very different from our own. The patriarchal, rural world of ancient Israel was based around the house of the father. This was an extended household, organized around the male head, and was often polygamous. It included several generations of the extended family: children, aunts, uncles, servants, single relatives and widows. In the more urbanized world of the Exile, the family became increasingly important for ethnic and religious identity. The way in which 'marriage' was understood and practised was very different from the way in which it functions in our society.

There is no description of a wedding ceremony in Scripture, and only a few brief allusions to wedding feasts (Genesis 29.22; Judges 14; Matthew 22.2-4; John 2.1). We know there were some legal protections for married women, and mutual obligations for husbands and wives (see Deuteronomy 24–27; 1 Corinthians 7; Ephesians 5; Hebrews 13.4). But there are no prescriptions for marriage ceremonies, or for vows, or even for blessings of a relationship.

What we do see is the assumption that a healthy sexual relationship between a man and a woman will normally be exclusive, stable and lifelong (with the caveats above concerning polygamy, and the reality of prostitution in Scripture). These relationships are then publicly identified as marriage. But even in Scripture itself, we see the shape of 'marriage' evolve. In Genesis we read of polygamous marriages. The marriage of the prophet Hosea introduces the idea of marriage as a covenant between a wife and her husband that has parallels with the covenant between Israel and God. In the teaching of Paul there is the expectation that deacons should be married only once (1 Timothy 3.12).

The Bible shows us the story of salvation being played out amongst people who are navigating the particular demands, possibilities and dangers of their cultures. When we read the narratives and laws of Scripture, we therefore need to ask, Who are the people of the text? How does their culture influence their life together? How do we see their cultures being challenged, judged and transformed by the love of God? How might the same challenge, judgement, transformation play out in our world?

The family

Families, in the widest possible sense, can be troublesome in Scripture. Husbands and wives disagree. Wives fall out with one another. Rachel and Leah compete for Jacob's attentions, their fertility in competition. Their children are used in household wars, and rivalry between the sons leads to Joseph's slavery in Egypt (Genesis 29–30, 37). Much later on in 1 Samuel, Hannah is the much-loved but childless wife in what would otherwise be a happy relationship with Elkanah, a man who loves her, yet she is consistently bullied by Elkanah's lesser loved but fertile wife (1 Samuel 1).

The vulnerability of women and children in different configurations of relationships often comes through powerfully. Concubines and slaves' wives are most at risk of sexual and other violence, and have a much more precarious place in the household, as we see, for instance, in the story of Hagar in Genesis 16. Women without a male protector, whether widowed, divorced or unmarried, were particularly at risk and widows and orphans are consistently highlighted as needing care from the local community in a highly patriarchal world (e.g. Exodus 22.21-24; Deuteronomy 10.18; Isaiah 1.17; Luke 21.1-4; James 1.27).

Even families organized in socially expected ways struggle in the pages of Scripture: some with the pain of childlessness, some with the moral intricacies of surrogacy, some with wayward children and sibling rivalry. The motif of the wayward child comes up repeatedly in the Old Testament, with Jacob and Esau (Genesis 25.19-34), with the sons of Jacob (Genesis 34, 37, 38), the sons of Eli (1 Samuel 2.22-25), the sons of Samuel (1 Samuel 8.1-3) and the sons of David (2 Samuel 13; 1 Kings 1). It is even applied to the tumultuous relationship between Israel and God (e.g. Jeremiah 3.22).

We see the people in these stories struggling, just as we do, with the vulnerabilities that exist in and around family life; we see them struggling to bring up the next generation faithfully in many different forms and contexts; we see them struggling to provide for one another. We see them, just like us, stumbling and failing and starting again; we see them, just like us, hearing God's judgement, in need of God's forgiveness and responding to God's grace.

Power and pain

The communities and families we meet throughout Scripture would often not be out of place in a Hollywood movie. There is high drama and romance, sex and violence, celebration of love and a realistic look at the dark use of sex in power struggles. David, the great king of Israel, abuses his power as king to enable him to satisfy his lust for another man's wife, and kills her husband in order to secure her for himself (2 Samuel 11). Samson, a judge of Israel, is depicted as promiscuous and abusive, and his actions result in his wife being burnt alive by the Philistines (Judges 13-16). Prostitution, and the vulnerability of the women involved, is depicted in numerous places. Yet prostitutes are also mentioned specifically as people Jesus himself reached out to in grace and love. Adultery and betrayal mar relationships – both on the part of men like David and women like the woman Jesus meets in John 8. The Corinthian church is beset by a whole list of sins, including sexual immorality and a man living with his father's wife (1 Corinthians 5.1). The sons of Eli abuse their position as priests and sleep with women serving in the tent of meeting (1 Samuel 2.22), in a chilling echo of abuse scandals in the church today.

The stories in the Bible that touch on sexual relationships are striking for their careful depiction of the relationship between sex and power. Marriage is often a tool for power in forming political alliances between households and countries. It also provides stability, protection and respectability, as in the story of Ruth. Sex is used to gain political advantage or information, as with the story of Rahab and the spies in Jericho (Joshua 2), or the story of Delilah and Samson (Judges 16). Children, as the fruit of sexual activity, are used in asserting power by some men over others, and some women over others. Certain configurations of family life confer power through reputation and regard: to fit the dominant model means heightened social capital for both men and women. Deviating from the dominant model – as, for example, in the case of widows, prostitutes and those who are single – often meant a much more vulnerable status. We see some of these dynamics at work in the stories of Elijah and Jesus raising widows' sons back to life, so that they are not left utterly powerless (1 Kings 17; Luke 7).

Other stories of abuse and rape are invariably stories of men using sex in order to further their power over individuals and communities. Dinah is raped by a young man from a rival clan (Genesis 34). Tamar, the daughter of David, is raped by her brother Amnon (2 Samuel 13). The Levite's concubine is gang-raped by a murderous crowd and dismembered by her own husband (Judges 19). And whilst all actual victims of rape in the text are women, the possibility of sexual violence against men is raised as well (Genesis 19 and Judges 19). The story of the concubine raises questions of power in all areas of life – in the domestic sphere, with her husband's actions, and the political sphere, where the men of the city use rape as a tool to 'other' and humiliate strangers.

These stories matter deeply: they speak truth about a violent world and expose the ways in which even some of God's most beautiful gifts can become distorted and broken. They invite us to tell the truth in our communities of faith, too: the truth about the world in which we live and about our experiences within it, about the things we do and the things that are done to us. But more than this, these stories matter because they are set within the bigger story of God and his people. They are not the final word on humanity, but are set within the story of a God who responds with grace to our failed attempts to live in the way of salvation. By acknowledging the complexity of life and the pain of brokenness, we find Scripture opens the way for us to acknowledge these also in our worship and life together as a church.

Reality check

The people of Scripture struggled with many of the impulses, desires and sins that we see reflected in our own time. The tension between celebrating the beauty and value of relationships and dealing with the messiness and brokenness of real life and real people is the same then as now. Many of our questions find themselves echoed in some ways in the text. For all the differences in cultural and social context, we see in Scripture people just like us, struggling with similar problems and possibilities.

Yet there are gaps, too, which it is important to acknowledge. Even though some critics point out that the Bible offers significantly more insights and reflections on the lives and perspectives of women and of those with little power than any comparable literature of biblical times, still it often tells the story from the point of view of those who had the power to tell the story. We know less of the lives and perspectives of women, of those with little power. There is also no explicit positive or negative narrative portrayal of same-sex relationships nor of trans people. The few verses that do speak about same-sex matters are all found either in legal material or in lists of sins in Paul's letters, and so the narratives do not enable us to see how the lives of those involved actually played out. People, especially women, who were attracted to those of the same sex and may have been in some sort of relationship are invisible in Scripture, and we know very little of their life of faith in the history of Israel and the Early Church. That has opened the way, as we will see in Part Four, to all kinds of arguments about the lived realities to which those texts might apply.

Nevertheless, Scripture shows people struggling, and failing, and learning, and trying again to live the story of salvation in the midst of the complexity of real lives. It shows us that story played out in people's bodily experience and activity, in their relationships in all their variety and complexity, in the order and struggles of their family lives, and in the tangles of sex and power and vulnerability. When we ask, in the present, how the story of salvation enables us to respond to questions about human identity, sexuality, relationships and marriage, we are pursuing a task bequeathed to us by Scripture.

CHAPTER 10

A story about being human

Christians are people learning to live within the story of salvation – the story of faith, hope and love that we retold in Chapter 8.

Chapter 9 reminded us that all of life is caught up in that story: our bodies, our relationships, all the dynamics of our lives together.

That story provides the context for all of our deliberations.

In the remaining chapters of Part Three, we look more closely at the ways in which Christians relate this story of salvation to questions about human identity, sexuality, relationships and marriage.

There are multiple connections between the story and those questions. For instance, the Bible, in telling us the story of salvation, provides some teaching that directly addresses those questions – teaching about sexual relationships, or about marriage, for instance. We will explore that teaching at various points below, but especially in Chapter 12. In Chapters 10 and 11, however, we focus on another kind of connection: a series of key ideas that are important in the story of salvation and that come up repeatedly in Christian discussions of identity, sexuality, relationships and marriage.

So, for instance, in the story of salvation, all human beings are created in God's image and are the objects of God's unfailing love. That confers on each person a **dignity** that cannot be taken away. How does the distinctive place of human beings in creation play out in our relating and loving?

In the story of salvation God brings about a glorious diversity in creation, a **diversity** that is reflected in humankind. Each person caught up in that story is different, and capable of making a unique and irreplaceable contribution to creation's praise of God's glory. Yet Christians draw different kinds of implications from these sorts of claims, when it comes to thinking about the varieties of human experience and constitution in the areas of gender and sexuality. Here we try to disentangle some of the issues at stake, and clarify the range of answers at which Christians arrive.

The story of salvation also involves claims about human **identity** – and, specifically, about what it means to find our identity in Christ. As we saw in Part Two, discussions about gender and sexuality also involve claims about human identity. Does the word 'identity' mean the same in these two contexts? Is there a conflict here? Do our claims about identity in Christ affect what we can say about gender and sexual identity? We try to sort out some of these strands, to see what issues are at stake and to clarify some of the possible answers.

The story of salvation is a story of sin, of repentance, and of forgiveness – of **dying and rising**. The church's disagreements about gender and sexuality often involve disagreements about how we identify sin and sin's effects. In this chapter, we again try to see what issues are at stake in these discussions and clarify some of the possible answers.

This chapter is not meant to be a cumulative argument for a particular conclusion. It is a series of explorations, in each of which we examine some of the resources that the story of salvation provides for thinking about identity, sexuality, relationships and marriage, and try to untangle some of the knots that tie up discussions in these areas. To change metaphors: we are, here, setting out some of the ingredients that can go into Christian decision-making in this area. We will turn in Part Four to ask where these various ingredients come from, and how judgements can be made about whether they have a place in the Church of England's teaching and practice.

Dignity

The story that Christians tell is one in which human beings have a distinctive place. This is signalled in the creation narrative in Genesis 1. After the light and the water and the land, the plants and the stars and the animals, God creates something new.

Then God said, 'Let us make humanity in our image, according to our likeness; and let them have dominion over the fish of the sea, and over the birds of the air, and over the cattle, and over all the wild animals of the earth, and over every creeping thing that creeps upon the earth.' So God created humankind in his image, in the image of God he created him; male and female he created them. God blessed them, and God said to them, 'Be fruitful and multiply, and fill the earth and subdue it; and have dominion over the fish of the sea and over the birds of the air and over every living thing that moves upon the earth.' (Genesis 1.26-28)

In creating humanity, God is giving a particular and most precious gift to the world: the divine image.

The phrase 'image of God' has been interpreted in the Christian tradition in many different ways. Traditionally, it was often located in human reason: human beings image God because they can mirror or participate in God's intimate knowledge of creation.

More recently, some have argued that when Genesis 1 says 'in the image of God he created him; male and female he created them', the two clauses are meant to be kept closely together. In this view, the image is not something humans possess individually but is expressed in the relationship between male and female and in their capacity together – as the text goes on to say – to 'be fruitful and multiply'.

This interpretation has, however, found little positive reception amongst biblical scholars. It is not required by the Hebrew syntax. Other animals are given the capacity to reproduce sexually without being said to be made in the image of God (though only of humans are the terms 'male and female' specified in connection with both the image of God and the capacity to be fruitful and multiply). In Genesis 5.3 the 'image and likeness' language is used again without reference to the male-female relationship: 'When Adam had lived for one hundred and thirty years, he became the father of a son in his likeness, according to his image, and named him Seth' (Genesis 5.3).

While there continues to be disagreement in Old Testament scholarship about the nature of the image, there is widespread agreement about the functional consequences. The image of God results in humanity's dominion over the created world as described in the first part of the quotation above ('Then God said, "Let us make humankind in our image, according to our likeness; and let them have dominion ..."'). In this understanding, fertility is not itself an aspect or consequence of the divine image, but is part of God's more general blessing upon the entirety of creation. The significance of the line 'male and female he created them' is to make clear that both men and women bear this image.

This line of interpretation can be taken forward in three related ways. First, although some commentators have seen the roots of environmental exploitation in the command to 'have dominion' over the rest of creation, it can also be read to mean that human beings are envoys of God in the midst of creation. And just as God made, ordered and delighted in creation, so human beings are to work with, delight in and care for the world around them. They are to seek its fruitfulness and protect its beauty.

Second, a contrast can be drawn between the images that God provides, and the 'divine images' that filled the ancient world in the form of statues of gods and rulers.[274] There are numerous commands in the Bible not to make and worship such images (e.g.

Deuteronomy 5.8), but the God who issues these prohibitions is the very same one who provides the world with countless divine images. The difference is that God does not make statues: God makes images that live. Human beings receive divine life in the moment of their creation (Genesis 2.7), and unlike all those statues, the human person is an embodied and dynamic image of God. Human beings are able to respond to the divine call, to give voice to creation's prayer and praise of God's glory, to communicate God's love to one another and draw one another closer to God. In the tenderness of a carer's touch, in the embrace of lovers and in the outstretched arms of praise, we see the image of God animating human life.

Third, in the New Testament, Paul writes of Jesus of Nazareth that *he* is the one who is

the image of the invisible God, the firstborn of all creation; for in him all things in heaven and on earth were created, things visible and invisible, whether thrones or dominions or rulers or powers – all things have been created through him and for him. He himself is before all things, and in him all things hold together. He is the head of the body, the church; he is the beginning, the firstborn from the dead, so that he might come to have first place in everything. For in him all the fullness of God was pleased to dwell, and through him God was pleased to reconcile to himself all things, whether on earth or in heaven, by making peace through the blood of his cross. (Colossians 1.15-20)

Jesus is the perfect image of God. In John's Gospel Jesus says, 'Whoever has seen me has seen the Father' (John 14.9). His is a life wholly caught up in God's life and wholly transparent to that life. His entire life is a gift given to the world by God, living out God's nature and purpose in the world. God's reconciling love shines through all his words and deeds, in all his relationships and interactions. Jesus is God made flesh. He is 'Emmanuel', God with us, and he shows us what it looks like to inhabit in full the dignity that is the birthright of all human beings.

As images of God, human beings are given a share in God's life, a distinctive vocation to hear God's voice and respond to God's word, to receive God's light and to reflect God's glory, to experience God's grace and embody God's love. Every human life can become a window through which the love of God shines out to others – and the image of God becomes more fully visible the more that love unites us. As Frances Young puts it, referring to Jesus' parable of the sheep and the goats (Matthew 25.31-45):

> God's glory is seen in the face of Christ, and insofar as we are in Christ, we may reflect that glory, even if only dimly. And sometimes we catch a glimpse in another's face, in an everyday saint who somehow embodies the love of Christ, or in someone who needs us to show the love of Christ – one of those whom neither the sheep nor the goats recognized: someone hungry, or thirsty, a stranger, someone with no adequate clothing, sick or in prison.[275]

Every human person, regardless of their situation or condition, is created in the image of God. Each and every human being comes from God and is the object of God's care and love. Each and every person is therefore a unique and deep mystery of inestimable value and dignity. Whenever we face another, we are seeing a reflection of God's infinite love and glory. The divine shimmers in every human face. As former Archbishop Rowan Williams writes:

> This means that whenever I face another human being, I face a mystery. There is a level of their life, their existence, where I cannot go and which I cannot control, because it exists in relation to God alone ... The reverence I owe to every person is connected with the reverence I owe to God, who brings them into being and keeps them in being.[276]

Our true value does not come from our productivity, success, mental capacity, youth, health, beauty, or conformity to cultural norms, but from God's love. We are called to see each and every person as an object of that love. The fourth-century theologian Gregory of Nyssa, for instance, wrote

> Do not despise those who are stretched out on the ground [that is, the poor and sick] as if they merit no respect. Consider who they are and you will discover their worth. They bear the face of our Saviour. The LORD in his goodness has given them his own face in order that it might cause the hard-hearted, those who hate the poor, to blush with shame ... The poor are the stewards of our hope, doorkeepers of the kingdom, who open the door to the righteous and close it again to the unloving ... [277]

Christians ought, therefore, to be amongst those most strongly committed to protecting people from objectification. If you honour another person as a creature made in God's image, your encounter with them can't be reduced to consumer assumptions. You can never treat another person only as a means to your own ends, or merely a gratification for your own desires. There is always more than that to the person you encounter: they are related to God before ever they relate to you.

This means, among other things, that we should not ignore the consequences of our sexual encounters for the other people involved. We should not think that we can reduce our focus only to what we get from the transaction and ignore what it does to others. In particular, we need to accept responsibility for any children who are conceived as a result. We also need to take care, however, to ensure that taking responsibility does not itself turn (however subtly) into dictating terms, or claiming ownership.

Our intimate relationships, including marriages and civil partnerships, should never be understood to give us ownership of another person. Paul, in 1 Corinthians 7:4, says that in marriage 'The wife does not have authority over her own body but yields it to her husband' – but goes on to say that 'In the same way, the husband does not have authority over his own body but yields it to his wife' (NIV). There is a radical symmetry and equality here, not a relationship of ownership for, in Paul's words,

in the Lord, woman is not independent of man, or man independent of woman. For just as woman came from man, so man comes through woman; but all things come from God. (1 Corinthians 11.11,12)

Our intimate relationships can involve deep commitments to ongoing intimacy, the sharing of material goods and the reshaping of our public roles. They can create all kinds of expectations and obligations between people. They can involve all kinds of compromise and sacrifice. They must always, however, be mutual. They are relationships between creatures of equal value, equal in dignity before God. One person's needs, their integrity, their agency can never simply be disregarded for the sake of their partner's needs.

The starkest forms taken by the rejection of such mutuality are found in abusive relationships. Such relationships are radically asymmetrical. One party takes what they desire from the other but offers only scorn or violence in return, refusing to recognize and respond to the other's dignity. Sometimes, this asymmetry can take hidden forms. The violence might not be physical and the scorn might not be overt, but one person might not allow another person their own voice, their own thoughts. They might seek to write the script for the other person, to undermine the other person's ability to tell their own story or trust any of their own perceptions. They might strip them of independent agency and insight. That is no less abuse, and it is no less an offence against human dignity before God.

Marriage: Questioning the experience of women

Although we have seen that marriage provided financial security and personal safety for women in times and cultures where their rights and social powers were few, liberal and feminist thinking from the second half of the nineteenth century onwards began to criticize marriage for its oppressive effects on women. Harriet Taylor and John Stuart Mill famously charged that marriage turned women into little more than sexual and domestic slaves and, what is worse, schooled them into willing submission to their slavery.

The Victorian case against marriage was based mainly on the laws of the time surrounding marriage. The public identity of the wife was largely submerged into that of her husband, who controlled the marital property even when he may have married into her wealth, thus rendering her economically dependent. Reasonable chastisement was legally permissible, and a man could not be found guilty of raping his wife since they had given consent to the use of each other's bodies. Until divorce became more widely available after 1857, a woman was virtually incapable of permanently escaping an abusive relationship, although formal separation could provide some measure of protection. Even after divorce became a practical possibility, women had to prove a higher threshold of marital wrongdoing than men.

Reform to the marriage laws was part of a wider campaign for the education, emancipation and professionalization of women. But, as many feminists increasingly pointed out, the problem went deeper than a set of inequitable laws. Those laws were merely the expression of wider social assumptions about the subordination of women. The inability to control one's own fertility or to access an independent source of income through paid employment or the pursuit of a profession were also major practical obstacles to equality. Even after the laws were formally changed to reflect a policy of legal equality from the late nineteenth century onwards, marriage remained for some a place of domestic and economic bondage.

Successive revisions to the marriage services of the Church of England have removed language which reinforces such views. Already in 1928, the wife's promise to 'obey' her husband was made optional. *The Alternative Service Book* (1980) adjusted the symbolism of the ring from a one-sided pledge on the part of the husband to provide materially for his wife in return for her fidelity to him to a sign of mutual fidelity and support given by each to each other. The 'Giving Away' was made optional in the Common Worship (2000) liturgy and reframed to avoid any former associations with male proprietorship of women.

At its worst, the Christian tradition has connived in marital oppression and legitimized it with the most powerful of all sanctions: divine authority. At its best it has sought to defend a conception of marriage which is liberating for both husband and wife. The eminent seventeenth-century Puritan Richard Baxter could argue in entirely egalitarian terms that

> The common duty of husband and wife is: Entirely to love each other; ... and avoid all things that tend to quench your love.... To dwell together and enjoy each other and faithfully join as helpers in the education of their children, the government of the family, and the management of their worldly business.... Especially to be helpers of each other's salvation ... to be delightful companions in holy love, and heavenly hopes and duties, when all other outward comforts fail.[278]

For many, conscious of features of Jesus' and Paul's teaching that challenged some of their culture's patriarchal norms of marriage,[279] such mutual, self-sacrificial and indeed liberating love remains the ideal to which marriage aspires in a Christian understanding. It continues to call us to consider carefully whether aspects of our church practice and teaching still reflect inherited and unjustifiable assumptions about the proper roles of men and women in marriage.

The mutual responsibilities of marriage give the church confidence in the ability of marriage to provide legal and financial protection for women who may be vulnerable to male exploitation and to the impact of fathers who neglect their children.

In a true relationship of love, life is shared. The life of the relationship is shaped by the perceptions, the feelings, the agency, of all those involved. Those involved come to understand themselves not simply as subjects, as desiring creatures, but also as the object of another's desire; they learn to know themselves as loveable as well as loving. True love demands mutuality and upholds dignity.

The process by which we discover our identities in Christ should be one in which we discover that each one of us is loved and valued by God as fully, as lavishly, as every other. This is not a denial of the fact that, for each person, the process will involve challenge and transformation, the conviction of sin and repentance. It is, rather, the deep truth that underpins that transformation. God calls us, challenges us and transforms us, because God loves us – and nobody is outside the scope of that love. There is nobody from whom Christ shrinks, nobody whom he is reluctant to touch, to eat with, to share his life with. There is nobody for whom Christ did not die.

One of the areas in which there is disagreement in the Church of England, however, is in the relationship between the two sides of this claim: the call for all to repent and be transformed, and the equal valuing of all people as the objects of God's love. For instance, you may recall from Chapter 7 that the 1991 report *Issues in Human Sexuality* claimed both that 'Homosexual people are in every way as valuable to and as valued by God as heterosexual people' and that 'Homophile orientation and its expression in sexual activity do not constitute a parallel and alternative form of human sexuality as complete within the terms of the created order as the heterosexual'.[280] For some, there is an irreconcilable tension here: homosexual people are told that they are of equal dignity, and yet that there is something incomplete about them compared to heterosexual people, and that they are excluded from a whole realm of intimate relationships that are open to (and highly valued by) others. Many lesbians, gays, bisexuals and others have experienced this as a relegation to second-class status and as a denial that they can belong as fully as others to the body of Christ. Others agree with the report that both of these principles need to be upheld and that they cohere. Any person is as valuable to and as valued by God as any other, no matter what they desire or do, but some patterns of human desire – here sexual orientations – and some forms of human conduct – here patterns of sexual behaviour – are more in tune with God's purposes for human beings than others.

We will be coming back to this in the next section, and in the next chapter, when we talk about welcome and inclusion in the church.

Diversity

God's creation is a dazzling explosion of diversity which speaks of the unutterable beauty, unfathomable grandeur and infinite creativity of the Creator. And so when God made human beings, they too reflected this dazzling diversity. Each one of us displays a unique combination of characteristics, shaped by our genetic inheritance and by our environment – from our environment in the womb before our birth and on through the whole history of our life experiences in the world. We each feel, think and behave differently. We differ in physical constitution, personality, psychological resilience, intelligence and temperament. We each have our own ways of interacting with others in our families, amongst our friends and colleagues and in our wider social contexts. Advances in genetic research have brought increasing understanding of the ways in which human beings are uniquely different from each other. Our diversity is, literally, embedded in our DNA. However, as we saw in Chapter 6, this research has not only been important for understanding the biology and heritability of human traits and characteristics. It has also enabled us to better understand how environmental factors work in combination with genetic factors to explain variation in human characteristics, including sexuality.

The existence of all this variety is not, in Christian thinking, an accident. It is not a tragic fall away from pure spiritual unity into messy physical diversity. God has created materiality, difference, change – night and day, earth and sky, land and water, plants and animals – and called it good. Diversity and distinction among God's creatures is good. It is part of God's gift of life to the world that God has made.

The ideas discussed in the last few pages allow us to say that none of this human diversity reflects a difference in dignity. No human being is worth more than another because of their gender, the colour of their skin, their bodily characteristics, their abilities, their sexuality, their marital status, or even their stance in the church's debates about identity, sexuality, relationships and marriage. The ideas we are discussing now, however, push us to go beyond that. Human diversity is to be welcomed and celebrated. The love of God is displayed in human lives not *despite* their being different, but *in and through* their differences. The infinite glory of God is imaged in and through the intricate pattern of human lives – in all their colours and shapes and sizes – and what we see would be diminished if that variety were to be absent.

Saying this, however, gets us right into the heart of sharp Christian disagreements in this area. On the one hand, this kind of claim about human diversity lies behind some of the critiques of the church's existing teaching on marriage and sexuality. After all, one of the characteristic forms that sin takes is our failure to receive the God-given diversity of creation and of humanity as a gift. We often respond to difference as a threat, and treat others as inferior, or distasteful, or dangerous simply because they are different. We create hierarchies of value based on skin colour, or accent, or birthplace or any number of other forms of unavoidable difference. In doing so, we rope ourselves off from gifts that God is giving us – from people who are created in God's own image and who can show us more of God's glory. Many argue that this is exactly what has happened in the areas of gender and sexuality: that those who are not heterosexual, or who are not cisgender, are being treated as inferior – and that in the process something of the God-given richness and beauty of creation is being denied.

On the other hand, many have wanted to insist that some of the differences that we find in human lives are not matters to celebrate, but are in some sense fractures or distortions. After all, every human life (except Jesus') is a mixture: partly transparent to the glory of God, partly opaque. We are all broken; we are all sinful; we all fall short of the glory of God. None of us is yet as we should be and will be. For all of us, this is reflected in our actions, in our deep habits of mind and feeling, in the patterns of our cultures and societies. Many Christians would want to say that this is also, in various ways, written into our bodies. As we said earlier, the story of salvation told in Scripture depicts the whole world as affected by sin – such that there is a lack of alignment with the purposes of God visible in the very stuff of the world. The world is, as Paul wrote to the Christians in Rome, in 'bondage to decay' (Romans 8.21). We live in a world broken by sin – and many Christians hold that some of the variety of the human body and experience in the areas of sexuality and gender is a result of this breaking.

We have to acknowledge that – in ways that we will be exploring in the next chapter – this is a claim that many will find profoundly upsetting and offensive. It does, nevertheless, have deep roots in Christian thinking, and it plays a central role in the church's disagreements about gender and sexuality. It is therefore vital that we explore it here.

We can and must accept the equal dignity of all human beings, and we can and must celebrate their God-given diversity. We often, nevertheless, make judgements about what is healthy and what is not. We often judge that some of the particular forms taken by human bodies are a result of something not being right.

We do need to proceed with very great caution when saying this. One of the arenas in which people have explored most carefully what it means to say this kind of thing is in the study of disability. The voices of those of us who are disabled have helped us to discover just how complex, how fraught and how dangerous a matter it can be. When do we say that someone has *different* abilities (and acknowledge that the way we run our world constricts and disadvantages people with those particular abilities)? When, if ever, might it be appropriate to say that the person themselves is *dis*abled?[281]

We are learning (sometimes far too slowly) that our identifications of ability and disability have often promoted very narrow pictures of what it is to be 'normal'. They have often, implicitly or explicitly, drawn particular pictures of 'normal' that include being white, or middle class, or educated, or male and that conform to culturally specific models of physical fitness and ability. Our approaches have been shaped by fear of difference and by disregard for the voice and experience of those who are differently able. They have fuelled stigmatization, marginalization and exclusion. They have led to people being treated primarily as problems to be dealt with, not as full members of the community.

As another example, consider someone who has suffered from constant pain since birth – pain that seems to be built in to who they are. That does nothing to undermine that person's inherent and undimmed dignity. It does nothing to diminish the fact that, just as they are, in all the specificity of who they are, they are cherished by God. But this person might well want to say that they are as they are only because something has gone wrong. They might look for healing; and if healing in this life is not forthcoming, they might hope that, when God gathers them into glorious fellowship with Christ, they will finally be freed from their pain. Or they might see themselves quite differently, in ways that those who have never lived with such pain will simply fail to comprehend.

Very similar possibilities, questions and concerns are relevant in the specific areas that we are exploring. When we talked about intersex people in Part Two, for instance, having noted the wide range of bodies that can be classified as intersex, we said that

> **Different intersex people understand, describe, and respond to their bodies in different ways. Some consider their intersex characteristics as elements of a medical condition: something to be diagnosed and, where possible, treated or ameliorated ... Others regard these interventions as a form of violence ... They might regard their intersex characteristics simply as part of the complex variety in which natural human bodies appear.**

For more about intersex (or differences of sexual development), including questions of terminology, see Chapter 6, 'The science of variations in sexual characteristics: intersex' pages 112–113.

For those in the latter category, the very suggestion that they should regard their bodies as suffering from a medical condition, or as a form of disability, might be deeply offensive and hurtful. It can be heard as one more strand in the weave of language that has justified their exclusion and maltreatment. For those in the former category, however, the same language might be liberating.

Related questions come up in discussions of trans experience. As discussed in Part Two Chapter 6, many trans people experience some level of gender dysphoria, and understand that as a medical condition which can be treated by some form of transition. Many insist, however, that being a trans man or woman (rather than a cis man or woman) is not itself a medical condition or a form of disability. It is simply one of the diverse forms that human existence can take, part of God's good gift of human diversity – and transition enables them to inhabit more fully the distinctive identity that God has given them. Transition, in this view, is a medical intervention in their bodies that does justice to the deep patterns of their feeling and experience – deep patterns that are themselves rooted in the trans person's body.

This understanding is sometimes opposed by people who, though they might agree that gender dysphoria is a medical condition, believe that the appropriate medical interventions will be those that reconcile people to the visible sexed differentiation of their bodies – the bodies that God has given them. The celebration of human difference that Christians are called to is a celebration of the different ways in which people inhabit the good order that God has given to creation. Part of this good order is, in this view, the biological distinction between men and women. Those who hold to it argue – in line with the church's traditional teaching in this area – that the story of salvation told in the Bible teaches us that God created human beings to be either male or female. In this view, where people's bodies and the deep patterns of their experience and desire do not align with that good plan, that is a result of the brokenness of the world. Similarly, they might argue that, in God's good design for creation, human beings are intended to be capable of and oriented towards heterosexual relationships (though also free to live without such sexual relationships). Where the deep patterns of people's experience and desire do not align with that design, something has gone wrong.

Identity

We have seen how every human being has a dignity and a uniqueness derived from being created in God's image. And because God is the source of our dignity and uniqueness, we can say that it is only as we look to God that we can truly understand who we are, individually and together. We cannot simply construct, discover or define our identity independently. How, then, are we to understand that uniqueness, that identity that both unites us with all human beings as beloved of God and distinguishes each individual human being as unique and of infinite value?

The Bible has a good deal to say in response to such questions, but 'identity' itself is not a word that it uses. This might alert us to the fact that our approach to those questions may not be the same as the Bible's. Similarly, the Bible's narratives, laws, poetry, prophecy, and teaching embody and convey different ways of imagining what it means to be human, and how human beings can and should relate to others, to God, and to the wider world. These patterns of imagination vary across the different periods covered by the Old Testament, and in the New – and all of those patterns are different from our own. Engaging with Scripture is bound to challenge, surprise and sometimes frustrate us if we are looking for answers to our questions about identity.

The Bible does, however, speak about people's identities – because it gives numerous answers to the question 'Who is this?' or 'Who am I?'. It gives people names, for instance, each one identifying a specific individual. Those names often identify people in ways that say something about their relationships to family, tribe and place (Joshua son of Nun; Bildad the Shuhite; Simon of Cyrene). They often say something about a person's relationship to God (Ishmael means 'God will hear' – Genesis 16.11). Sometimes people's names are changed to reflect a specific encounter with God and God's plans (Abram to Abraham in Genesis 17.5, Jacob to Israel in Genesis 32.28, Simon to Peter in Matthew 16.18). An encounter with God does not leave our identity (or perception of our identity) unchanged, but calls us to transformation. God sometimes helps us discover new aspects of our identity, sometimes calling us to inhabit who we are in different ways and sometimes calling for radical change. This is because identity, in Scripture, is not static, but dynamic and woven into our relationship with God and with one another.

The Bible tells people's stories – Noah, Isaac, Moses, Ruth, David, Samuel, Paul, Barnabas, Mary and Martha, Lazarus and many, many others. People's identities can't be captured simply by static epithets; people have histories. The Bible tells the story of people's actions and interactions over time, what happens to them and how they respond, the choices that they make and that are made about them. As we saw in the previous chapter, these stories are always the stories of bodies, of networks of relationships and communities, and of people whose lives are lived in relation to God.

We find a different kind of expression of identity in the Psalms. They are not autobiographical in any modern sense, but many of them provide a first-person perspective for worshippers to inhabit: 'I know my transgressions, and my sin is ever before me' (Psalm 51.3), 'I will sing to the LORD, because he has dealt bountifully with me' (Psalm 13.6).

In the window onto personal lives that we find in the Bible, a number of consistent factors appear to influence, shape and, at times, define identity.

Identity in time, place and community

The story of Genesis 2 plays on a shortened form of the Hebrew word *adamah* for 'ground' as a name for the first human creature, formed from the ground and the breath of God. Right from the start, there is a link between the human person and place, with bodily existence, with origins, so that the meaning of an individual life is set in a particular place and at a particular time, in a particular culture and with a particular language. This situatedness is a strong influence but not determinative – Ruth is a Moabite, for instance, but chooses to separate herself from an identity rooted in place and tribe in order to follow Naomi; she is shaped by her past but a combination of relationships and personal choice shape her future.

The story of Genesis 1 and the creation of humans, male and female, as part of a wider creation, made in the image of God, immediately sets up the notion of human being as relational. As children grow, they develop their identity not merely through their growing sense of interiority (thinking of who they are and experiencing their own bodies, thoughts and feelings) but by seeing themselves reflected in the eyes and language of others and how others relate to them. It begins with their primary relationship with their parents, then expands into wider circles of relationships. The gaze of others both shapes and reflects identity.

Identity that is shaped by relationships can be both positive and negative: what others reflect to us may be true, may be partial, or may be deeply misguided and destructive. The journey towards understanding ourselves, however, cannot bypass these relationships: it is within them that I learn more fully who I am. Equally, precisely because identity is relational, who I am and how I express my identity has an impact on others, an impact that can be positive and negative in equal measure. To talk of identity is deeply personal, but also deeply communal.

Scripture also draws our attention to the significance of intimate relationships: it is expected, in Scripture, that marriage will change some of the ways in which we think about ourselves and the world around us. This is why the Old Testament has much to say about marriage between people of different tribes and nations. Scripture talks about how what we do with our bodies both reflects and shapes who we are and who we become. Sexuality and identity are intrinsically linked, in ways that can be life-giving, destructive, or an ambiguous mix of good and bad.

This portrayal of identity as relational and situated echoes what we know from social and biological sciences. Identity is a complex mix of what is given, shaped and chosen: a mix of genetics, physicality, relationships, social environment and life experiences.

There is another sense in which human identity is relational. Being made as male and female means – among other implications, which we will return to below – that no one person can comprehend the whole of what it means to be human. Human beings are particular and each is embodied differently. Human identity is something that we hold together, and that we discover together as we come into relationship with one another. In the same way, in Genesis 2, the story of the first human being's loneliness suggests that human beings need to recognize themselves in each other and journey together in understanding who they are and in fulfilling God's mandate in the world.

Individual human beings, however, do not find a sense of self and belonging simply in relation to other individuals but by being integrated into a wider community with its particular culture and language. The story of Israel in the Old Testament is the story of families and lineages. It is a story of the developing identity of a people over time. The link between individual and community is constantly explored in stories of individuals influencing and shaping the nation, and the nation then shaping and making demands on individuals and groups.

In the same way, the New Testament is largely addressed to the Church, with advice, ethical reflections and guidance focusing on the life of the community of faith and, at times, on how this sub-community relates to the wider Israelite community and the life of the Roman Empire. Christian identity is the identity of the Church, worked out in individual lives, yet not individually.

Because human beings are situated and communal, they tell stories of who they are: stories of origins and of ancestors, stories that define the shape and values of their communities and that invite individuals to locate themselves within those stories. People in Scripture are invited to respond personally to the bigger story in ways that shape their sense of self and belonging, in the same way that readers are invited into the Christian story. The identity of the people of God is constantly being reworked, in each generation, to locate it in relation to the past and in its development towards the future.

Identity in Christ

The focus of biblical stories of individuals and communities is often upon calling and character formation. In other words, there is a sense of both a general calling of human beings to conform to the 'good life', to grow in Christ, and a specific calling on individuals, that takes into account their particularity, gifts and flaws. These callings are external or given, as it were, but response to them lies within the realm of human choice and responsibility. Stories of calling and maturation are rarely linear but, rather, take in the complexity of the human character, with persistent flaws and stories of change and transformation. A good example is found in 1 Peter 2.9,10:

But you are a chosen race, a royal priesthood, a holy nation, God's own people, in order that you may proclaim the mighty acts of him who called you out of darkness into his marvellous light. Once you were not a people, but now you are God's people; once you had not received mercy, but now you have received mercy.

This quote from 1 Peter is one of many biblical passages where we find theological descriptions of people's identities. The Bible teaches us that our deepest identity is our identity in Christ – an identity that can unite us with others across any social, political, or cultural distinction (Galatians 3.28). This identity in Christ is, for Christians, an identity that is already ours – an identity that in one sense we already know. In another sense, it is an identity that we are exploring and discovering day by day. It is an identity that we won't know fully until Christ returns.

So if you have been raised with Christ, seek the things that are above, where Christ is, seated at the right hand of God. Set your minds on things that are above, not on things that are on earth, for you have died, and your life is hidden with Christ in God. When Christ who is your life is revealed, then you also will be revealed with him in glory. (Colossians 3.1-4)

Exploring and discovering this identity in Christ means, in part, learning how to tell our own stories in relation to the story of Jesus. We learn to see ourselves more fully as those who have been crucified with Christ and raised with him, as children of God (Galatians 3.26), as temples of the Holy Spirit (1 Corinthians 3.16) and as members of the body of Christ (1 Corinthians 12.27).

We are going to be exploring various aspects of what this means in the remainder of this Part, but for now we want to stress how all-encompassing it is. Christians are called to recognize that this story includes every aspect of their lives. As we learn to retell our stories as the stories of people who are now in Christ, we talk about our *bodies*, our *histories*, and our *relationships*.

We are in Christ as *embodied* beings. 'Do you not know that your bodies are members of Christ?' (1 Corinthians 6.15); 'I appeal to you therefore, brothers and sisters, by the mercies of God, to present your bodies as a living sacrifice, holy and acceptable to God, which is your spiritual worship' (Romans 12.1). We might learn new bodily habits; we might train our bodies in certain ways – but each of us is always negotiating the possibilities and the limits of our specific embodiment. That will include working on and with the patterns of our feeling and desire, the capacities that we attribute to our hearts or guts. These, too, are bodily realities.

We are in Christ as people with particular *histories*. Paul knows that, in Christ, he is a new creation – but he still tells the story of who he was before his conversion (speaking, for example, about being a Pharisee and a persecutor of the church in Philippians 3.4b-6), as well as relating what has happened since. Who he is now is the result of Christ taking up and transforming that whole history.

Similarly, we are in Christ as people caught up in networks of *relationships and communities*. In the same passage in Philippians, Paul talks about being 'a member of the people of Israel, of the tribe of Benjamin, a Hebrew born of Hebrews' (3.5). He now understands and values that inheritance very differently in the light of all that Christ has done for him and in him, but it is still part of who he is – part of the material on which the Spirit is at work in him.

The whole of our identity as Christians is fundamentally given in Christ – and we are in Christ as embodied, storied and social beings. The journey of Christian discipleship is a journey of discovery and of transformation as, by grace, God perfects the whole of one's identity: with the Spirit's help, we discover over time more of what all the stuff of our lives (all that we have inherited and received – our bodies, our histories, our relationships) can become in relationship with Christ, and we take on new relationships and new ways of living. It is therefore no denial of our identity in Christ to say that our identity has deep dimensions that relate to sex and gender.

We become aware while we are still very young children that male and female bodies are different, and that these differences are (in a culture like ours) associated with all kinds of other differences in appearance, sound, behaviour and social role. We internalize that awareness in different ways, and it becomes a very powerful and deeply ingrained part of how we see the world. It also, for most of us, becomes a very powerful and deeply ingrained aspect of how we see ourselves. We see the world and ourselves through gendered lenses, though we might only notice those lenses when for one reason or another they become a problem for us.

Something similar is true in relation to sexual orientation. Most people's experience of sexual attraction to another human being is powerfully shaped by their perceptions of that other person's sex or gender. This is not normally something people experience as being in their own control: it is visceral and automatic. For many, especially when the pattern of their attraction does not match the patterns taken to be normal in the world around them, it can become an important part of their sense of their own identity.

In other words: gender and sexuality run deep. They shape who we think we are, how we think we belong in the world, and how we relate to others. While some LGBTI+ people do not regard their sexual or gender orientation as *defining* their identity, on the grounds that their identity is defined by their new humanity in Christ, some also testify that their sexuality or gender is profoundly *a part of* their identities – and that is true, in differing ways, for all of us.

The question this poses, then, is what it means for us to learn how to make sense of these aspects of our own stories in the light of the story of Jesus. That is not a task that falls uniquely on LGBTI+ people. It is a task for all of us. It is part of what is involved for all of us in negotiating the possibilities and the limits of our specific embodiment, and in working on and with the patterns of our feeling and desire.

Christians are called to bring all that we have been, and all that we are, to Christ – and to learn how, as people formed of all that material, we can glorify God. That is a process that involves deep attentiveness to the gospel – the good news of God's love poured out for us in Jesus. It also involves deep attentiveness to ourselves.

There are three aspects to this attentiveness to ourselves that we should bear in mind. First, each of us will find ourselves working with material that displays a complex mix of stability and flexibility. There are things about ourselves that we can't change and things that we have considerable freedom to change – and all kinds of degrees of flexibility in between. Finding out what kinds of freedom we have, and what kinds of 'given' we're working with, will involve close attention to Scripture, our own experience, engagement with others and learning from other sources – including relevant science, where it can illuminate all that God has given us.

Second, each of us is caught up in a complex mix of recognition and misrecognition. We all have some sense of who we are, what we are capable of, and what our limits might be, of the way we fit into the communities around us. We all also inhabit fantasies and misunderstandings about all that. As we pursue the journey of discipleship, we might need to unlearn some of the mistaken stories we have learnt to tell about ourselves. God as redeemer helps us look at ourselves in truth, and see things we would often prefer not to see about ourselves.

Third, each of us is influenced – in more ways than we will ever unpick – by those around us, in a complex mix of help and hindrance. The process by which any of us learns to tell our own story is profoundly social. From the beginning of our psychological development, we learn our sense of identity in interaction with others, and that continues through our whole lives. For good and ill, we learn all the language in which we tell our stories from others (though we are all also involved in remaking our language, simply by virtue of speaking it). Similarly, learning how to tell our own stories in relation to the story of Jesus is not something we do alone. Christians in part learn what it means to be in Christ from each other – in a process that can be enriching and healing, but which is always also fallible and open to distortion. So the further call for Christians is to learn how to live out our identity in Christ more fully, more generously, more faithfully by living within the community of believers, being formed together.

We might at times need to learn how to break free from the stories that others have told about us or that we have learnt to tell about ourselves – stories that don't do justice to the gospel and that don't do justice to the deep patterns of our own experience and feeling. Think, for instance, of Paul writing to the Gentiles in Ephesus, helping them to break free from a destructive and divisive way in which their identity as Gentiles had been narrated and to learn a new way of narrating that identity – as people 'no longer strangers and aliens' but 'citizens with the saints and also members of the household of God' (Ephesians 2.19).

We might at times need support from others in naming and valuing something about ourselves that we have not known how to speak about or how to navigate. Think, for instance, of Jesus renaming Simon as Peter ('rock') in order to teach him about the role he is being called to play in the life of the Church (Matthew 16.18), or of Moses, learning from his father-in-law Jethro not to see himself as the only one with the capacity to adjudicate the people's disputes (Exodus 18.13-27).

We might at times need to be brought by someone else to a sharp realization of how to tell our story differently. Think, for instance, of the story in 2 Samuel 12 in which the prophet Nathan tells King David a story that triggers David's recognition that he has terribly misused his power. That story gives David a new frame through which to view his own desires and actions – and to recognize the impact that his actions have had upon those with far less power than him.

All of this attentiveness to, and learning about, our own identities is carried out in relation to God. Before we ever are the object of our own gaze, or the gaze of those around us, we are the objects of God's gaze. God's gaze is deeply loving, but it is also perfectly truthful. To know ourselves as God knows us is to know ourselves as deeply loved, but also to face up to our scars and sinfulness. God affirms us, but God also challenges us to discover and inhabit our identity differently. God sometimes challenges us to let go of things we thought were core to who we are, and sometimes to take on things we had not considered before. But those challenges are never an imposition on our true selves; they are always about being freed from the narrow confines of lives turned in on themselves in order to find our true flourishing with others, and pre-eminently with God.

Thinking about identity: An example

Questions about 'who am I?' are present for everyone. Consider someone, for instance, who has always identified as a cisgender heterosexual man (even if those are not the terms he uses). He may not ever have thought about it very carefully, but that identification is likely to be bound up with deep patterns to his feelings, deep ways of seeing the world, deep habits of speech and action – some of which he thinks of as chosen, some as given facets of his particular personality, some simply as part of what it is to be a man. The ways in which he understands himself will have been shaped in subtle and complex ways, day by day, by the stories he hears others telling about what it is to be a man, and by their responses to his ways of performing his masculinity.

Over time, he may (probably with others' help) come to realize that he has learnt deeply problematic stories about what it is to be a man from the culture around him – or perhaps from his church – stories that may have encouraged him to behave badly and have excused his bad behaviour. He may discover that he has misidentified what is 'natural' and what is 'chosen', or what about himself is fixed and what can be changed. He may discover that he needs, with the help of others, to unlearn those stories if he is to respond more fully to the gospel in this area of his life.

There is another way of framing the discussion of identity. In the light of the story told in the previous chapter about God and God's ways with the world, we might say that there are three aspects of our identity as we now perceive it.

- First, there are aspects that are not only important to us now, but that will also belong to us at the resurrection of the dead and in our eternal life with God.

- Second, there are aspects that may be a proper part of our identity now, but that will no longer define us in the new creation.

- Third, there are aspects that we have to judge as broken or sinful, because they are ultimately incompatible with our true identity in Jesus Christ.

How we correlate each of these aspects with gender, sexuality and marriage provides another way in to our conversations and shines a different light on our disagreements about these matters.

See Chapter 5 (pages 88-97) for a discussion about identity in contemporary society and Chapter 6 (pages 103-105) for a discussion of the science of gender identity. For a conversation about gender identity, see Scene 3 (pages 398-404).

Dying and rising

One relationship precedes all others in enabling us to know and develop who we are: the relationship with God as creator and redeemer. As Christians, we believe that however important different dimensions of our identity are to us, our deepest identity is to be found in Christ. The story of God's love for us in Christ, and who we are becoming in relation to that love is the deepest story of our lives. We believe that every aspect of our existence is caught up in that story, including everything that goes into our gender and sexuality, and all our relationships. We believe God desires our fulness, and that God's love is a refining fire, purifying and perfecting us. Ours is a story of dying to sin and rising to new life.

It is not a story in which people have to become pure, righteous or perfect before they can be loved by God. It is a story in which God, in Jesus, comes to meet us as we are and where we are - in the midst of all the mess, brokenness, and destructiveness of our lives. It is a story in which Jesus challenges us to acknowledge our sins, and the harm that they do. And it is a story in which Jesus calls and enables us to change - to turn away from that sin, to have its power over us broken, and to embrace new life with him. In one sense, Christians testify that this has already happened: they have acknowledged their sinfulness, put their trust in Jesus, and been welcomed into his community. We are baptized into Christ's death and resurrection (Romans 6.3-5). In another sense, Christians testify that this is a daily reality: that they need constantly to learn to identify what in their lives is wrong, constantly to turn to Jesus in trust, constantly to discover what it means to forgive and be forgiven and to live new life with him. We live out our baptism in daily life.

Describing the story of salvation - as we did in Chapter 8 - as a love story does not mean downplaying the place of judgement within it. As we said there, the very fact that God is love means that God stands implacably against all that rejects and betrays that love. The same God who is said in Scripture to be love is also said to be judge – and God is judge *because* God is love. God is not indifferent to our distortions, rebellions and betrayals. God's face is set against them; God's wrath burns against them. All of human life takes place against this horizon of God's judgement. Any passion for justice that we experience now, any opposition to the harm that human beings do, any stand against human hatred and enmity, is an anticipation of God's judgement – and our hope for the triumph of God's love is at the same time a hope for the enacting of God's judgement.

What, though, do we mean by 'sin'? There are, in the Bible and in the Christian tradition, numerous ways of understanding the nature of sin.

- God made human beings for love – for loving relationships with God, with each other, with ourselves and with the wider world of creation. Sin is the breakdown of all these relationships. In Genesis 2 and 3 we see all these aspects of breakdown taking place and setting up trajectories going through the rest of Scripture.

- God created and ordered the universe, and God declared this ordered creation good (Genesis 1). Sin is our failure, individually and collectively, to live in accord with the God-given ordering of creation. It is our rejection of, and our falling short of, the good for which we were made.

- God does not leave this broken world to its own devices, but speaks to it, calling it back to the good for which he made it. ('God spoke to our ancestors in many and various ways by the prophets, but in these last days he has spoken to us by a Son' – Hebrews 1.1,2.) Having lost sight of our Creator, and of how to live well with our fellow creatures, we need to hear God's word to set our lives back on course – and we were made to be such hearers and doers of God's word. Sin can be understood as rejection of, or disobedience to, God's address.

- God's word to the world characteristically forbids the making of idols (e.g. Exodus 20.4). Sin can be understood as any way of living that invests ultimate worth in something other than God. If the deepest justification we can give for our decisions, explicitly or implicitly, is that they serve our pleasure, or our power, or our wealth, or our nation or our culture – or even our church – then those things have become our idols and we have fallen into sin.

- God's word to the world offers life in Christ, and invites human beings to receive that life in faith. Sin can be understood as any way of living and acting that does not proceed from such faith (Romans 14.23). It is acting outside of the loving relationship that God has sought to re-establish with us.

- God speaks to the world – the whole world – in love, and commands us to love (Leviticus 19.18; Matthew 22.37-39, etc.). Sin is at work whenever we treat another person simply as a means to our own ends, when we are inattentive to their needs, when we fail to recognize that they, too, are delighted in by their Creator. And sin is at work when we fail to see that we, too, are delighted in by God.

- Sin is not simply a matter of individual wrongdoing. The Bible places strong emphasis on the responsibilities and failings of communities – who, in all the ways listed above, live against the purposes of God. For the individuals who inhabit those communities, therefore, sin is something we participate in at times involuntarily, simply by being part of certain systems and cultures.

- Sin can be understood as the name for all the ways in which our world is arranged to keep the poor poor, to keep the marginalized at the margins, to keep the powerful in power and wealth in the pockets of the rich (e.g. Proverbs 31.8,9). It is a name for the unjust structures of our world, and for all the habits of thought, speech and action that hold them in place.

- Sin is the deep brokenness or disorder within us as communities and as individuals. This brokenness shows itself in specific instances of sinful action, and is in turn reinforced and reproduced by them. Sin in this sense can be pictured as a form of enslavement or captivity, something prior to and holding sway over our conscious thought and action (Romans 7.14-20).

- Finally, sin is an active spiritual power, poisoning and corrupting our world and our hearts (e.g. Ephesians 2.1-3 and Romans 5). It can be experienced as a destructive force, working parasitically within the good creation that God has made, fighting against creation's flourishing – a force opposed to God, though in no way equal to God.

All of these ways of talking about sin are interrelated; all of them (and more) are needed for a full and rich description of the plight in which human beings find themselves and their world.

Different Christian communities, in different times and places – and different traditions or tendencies within the Church of England – can, however, have different emphases. Different elements on the list we have just given can become the key to interpreting the others. Some, for instance, see talk of the 'God-given ordering of creation' as another way of saying that God made human beings for love, and that we become who we were meant to be by the right ordering of our love. For others, it is a way of saying that we need to follow all the instructions of the one who made us and our world, and not just those that focus on love, if we are to flourish, live well, and become the creatures that God intends us to be.

We need to be aware of some dangers that attend our talk about sin.

- We can focus on the sins we see in other people in such a way as to ignore or downplay our own (Matthew 7.3-5).

- We can focus on sexual sin with an intensity that we don't bring to other areas of sin, such as our treatment of the poor or the uses we make of our wealth.

- We can focus so much on the question of whether same-sex sexual relationships are sinful that this becomes the main way in which the contribution of lesbian and gay people to the Church is discussed.

- We can speak about sin in ways that, in effect, tell some people that they are worth less than others in the eyes of God – instead of acknowledging that all are sinners, and all are loved lavishly and valued equally by God.

- We can speak as if the Church were a community in which sinners did not belong – instead of being a community of forgiven sinners, following together the Jesus who habitually feasted with sinners.

- We can, on the other hand, fail to take sin seriously – and fail to realize that all of us who are welcomed to gather around Jesus are called to acknowledge our complicity in injustice, our failures to love and our idolatries, and seek God's help to turn away from them.

- We can be squeamish about what the Bible says about God's wrath and judgement, failing to take seriously the way in which God stands against sin, and God's promise that, ultimately, it will be given no place, no footing, in the new creation.

Natural and unnatural

We said that sin is a 'failure, individually and collectively, to live in accord with the God-given ordering of creation'. A lot of discussion about this area uses the term 'natural' to name what is in accord with this order, and 'unnatural' to name what is not. This is, however, language that can be used in a confusing number of ways – including at least the following.

We can contrast 'nature' and 'nurture' – our biological inheritance versus the experience we gain over the course of our lives.

We can contrast 'nature' and the 'synthetic' – things that arise from the non-human world versus things that arise from human activity.

'Natural' can refer to what is widespread and 'normal' rather than unusual or exceptional.

'Natural' can refer to what seems normal or unremarkable within a particular culture.

'Natural' can refer to something that contributes to physical and mental well-being, as those are currently measured by a variety of medical sciences.

'Natural' can refer to the purpose for which God made something, as opposed to purposes that run against God's plan.[282]

'Natural' can mean 'practically reasonable' as indicating what would appear to be self-evidently true and ethically good.

It is all too easy for discussion to slip from one of these to another. We might start, perhaps, by talking about something that seems normal to members of our culture. We might slip into talking as if that was a biological rather than a cultural fact – an immutable law of nature. And then we might slip further into talking about it as a theological fact, asserting that this is obviously the way God intended creation to work.

It may be that the distinction between 'natural' and 'unnatural' is, in our context, not a very helpful way of naming the real question that we face. These concepts are discussed further in relation to Romans 1 and 1 Corinthians 11 in Chapter 13 of Part Four.

Christians are called to bring all that they are to the journey of discipleship. For each person, and each community, that will involve challenge and transformation, the conviction of sin and repentance. Following Jesus does not leave us as we are. This is as true in the areas of identity, sexuality, relationships and marriage as it is in any other area of our lives – but the question we still have to ask is *how* exactly this drama of sin and salvation plays out in these areas.

At this point in our exploration, we are leaving this disagreement unresolved. We are making no claim at this point about the merits of the arguments involved, or about the role that they should play in the church's deliberations. Our aim here has simply been to explain, as clearly as we can, something of what Christians share and something of what divides them in these areas, in order to clarify, as much as possible, the questions that face the church.

Conclusion

As we seek to understand how identity, sexuality, relationships and marriage fit into the story of love and faith, there are various key claims on which we hope Christians across the Church of England can agree:

- Every human person, regardless of their gender, sexuality, or relationship status, is created in the image of God. Each and every human being comes from God, and is the object of God's care and love.

- God has created human beings to be wonderfully diverse. Their diversity is part of God's gift of life to the world and is to be celebrated and affirmed.

- Our deepest identity is our identity in Christ, and every aspect of our existence is caught up in that story, including everything that goes into our gender and sexuality, and all our relationships.

- For each of us, the discovery of our identity in Christ will involve challenge and transformation, the conviction of sin and repentance, including in relation to our attitudes and behaviour in the areas of gender, sexuality and relationships.

We have seen that some clear answers to questions posed in Part Two flow from these affirmations - such as those we explored in the section on 'Dignity'. We have also seen, however, that these affirmations, by themselves, don't resolve all the church's disagreements.

The church's disagreements about gender and sexuality, in particular, are disagreements between people who can share all these affirmations. They are not disagreements between those who are and those who are not convinced that their deepest identity is in Christ; or between those who take sin and the need for transformation seriously and those who do not; or those who affirm the equal dignity of all human beings and those who do not; or those who celebrate human diversity and those who do not. The disagreements are more specific than that: they are between different understandings of how human dignity can best be affirmed and what Christian discipleship and transformation demand. These disagreements reflect different understandings of how certain aspects of human experience fit within the Christian story. In particular, we have seen that there are deep disagreements about whether certain aspects of human experience, in the areas of gender and sexuality, are to be viewed as reflecting the goodness and God-given diversity of humans as created in God's image, or as marks of the brokenness of that created image which God is working to restore.

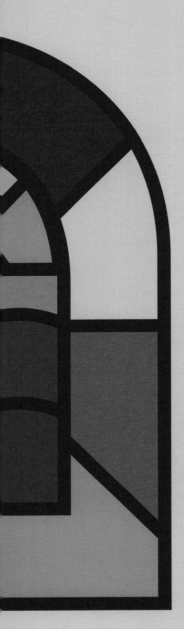

CHAPTER 11

A story about being Church

In this chapter, we continue exploring life within the Christian story of faith, hope and love.

The previous chapter explored some key ideas about human life – ideas that keep on coming up in Christian discussions of human identity, sexuality, relationships and marriage.

In this chapter, the ideas we explore are about the life of the community called to live this story of salvation together: the Church.

As with Chapter 10, this chapter is not an argument leading to one conclusion. It simply sets out some of the ingredients that can go into Christian thinking in this area. We will turn in Part Four to ask where these various ingredients come from, and how judgements can be made about whether they have a place in the Church of England's teaching and practice.

We begin with the idea of the church as a community called to be holy. That is one of the classic descriptions of the Church, and it is often taken to have direct implications for the Church's response to sexual relationships and activity. We then look at the inclusion and exclusion that shape this community's life. Again, these topics have an important place in discussions of the nature of the Church, and they often feature in discussions of the church's response to gender and sexual diversity. We finish with a look at what it means for this community to be marked by serious disagreement – including disagreement about holiness and inclusion.

Holiness

To speak about 'holiness' at this point might seem to some like a step in the wrong direction. It is not a word in wide use outside religious contexts, and to many it can have a rather puritanical feel. The phrase 'holier than thou' might spring to mind – as might images of people who keep themselves aloof from the fun and mess of ordinary life, and who are defined primarily by what they avoid. Yet the idea of holiness has deep roots in the story of salvation, and it is much richer and more positive than these popular associations suggest. It is a word that speaks of life that is dedicated to God and filled with God's love.

The origin and focus of all holiness is God. God is the Holy One – and 'holiness' refers first of all to God's distinctive character, God's life, God's glory. If anyone else is to be holy, it is because they are devoted to God. They embody God's holiness, and communicate it to those around them. A holy life is one that is luminous with God's light, or that echoes God's music. And because God is love, love and holiness are inseparable. A holy life is a life permeated with God's love – a life filled with love for God and love for neighbour.

The Bible displays various ways of understanding and practising holiness. There is, for instance, a priestly tradition in the Old

Testament that focuses on ritual cleanness. There is a wisdom tradition that focuses on inner integrity and individual moral acts. There is a prophetic tradition that focuses on social justice and rightly directed worship. Some of the best known material on holiness in the Old Testament is found in the 'holiness code' of Leviticus 17-26. That code calls for the community of Israel to be organized so that its whole life witnesses to God – in its rituals, its social relationships, its care for the vulnerable, its prevention of economic inequality. The code moves seamlessly between individual and communal behaviour, and between realms that we tend to divide up as religious, political, social and personal.

One strand of this material in Leviticus speaks of separation from impurity. The people are to keep themselves pure, and keep sacred the space within which they can experience God's dangerous presence – dangerous because God blazes against everything that works against God's life, glory and love. By the time of Jesus, some groups in Israel emphasized this strand by requiring ritual purity as a condition of inclusion in the community. They kept themselves separate from those who did not meet those conditions. Jesus, however, was willing to sit and eat with those considered impure. He crossed purity boundaries, bringing the purifying love of God into the lives of those who had been excluded from God's people. Jesus is not contaminated by the impurity that he encounters. He displays a contagious holiness that transforms all that it touches.

This is seen most sharply in the cross and resurrection. On the cross, Jesus is excluded from the community. He is put in a position of impurity. He is numbered amongst the sinners, and cursed. Yet in the resurrection God vindicates him. God declares that it is in Jesus – in all that he did and said, and especially when he was lifted up on the cross – that God's life, God's glory, God's love, God's holiness are displayed. Jesus is the Holy One.

1 Peter is one of the key New Testament texts speaking about the need for the community of Jesus' followers to be holy. It begins (in 1 Peter 1.3-12) by telling its own version of the story of love and faith with hope. It speaks of the gracious mercy of God, of God's gift of life in Jesus, of the faith by which this life is received, of the love for Jesus that animates it, and the hope that accompanies it. Having told this story, it turns to describe the kind of life that the Christian community is to live within it.

Therefore prepare your minds for action; discipline yourselves; set all your hope on the grace that Jesus Christ will bring you when he is revealed. Like obedient children, do not be conformed to the desires that you formerly had in ignorance. Instead, as he who called you is holy, be holy yourselves in all your conduct; for it is written, 'You shall be holy, for I am holy.' (1 Peter 1.13-16)

This community is called to live a life together that has a definite character. That is why it requires discipline. This community is called to live a life that echoes and communicates God's holiness. They are called to shine with God's grace, mercy and love. They are called to be obedient together to the demands of this life. And, if they follow this calling, their life together will be distinctive. They will not live as those around them live.

This new life is a gift. The members of this community have received God's mercy. God has given them new birth. This new life is certainly also a task. Their own action, their own discipline, is needed. Yet if they do live this new life, it is never their own achievement. 'Let yourselves be built into a spiritual house', the epistle says (2.5): it is God, working in them by the Spirit, who makes them holy.

Of course, the Church often fails – sometimes dramatically – to live this distinctive life. All kinds of unholy, unmerciful, unloving life can be found in it. It is not just that its members fail to practise what the church preaches. The Church's teaching, its worship, its processes, its structures and its cultures are all vulnerable to being marred by sin. When we say the creeds and confess belief in the Church as 'holy', we are not claiming that the Church is free from sin. We are declaring our belief that the Church comes from and belongs to a holy God. In its worship and witness – even in the midst of all its failures – it points to God's holiness. It hears God's call to holiness. It stands under God's judgement for its lack of holiness. There should be no element of the Church's life that is immune from questioning in the light of the loving holiness of Jesus Christ. For the Church as a whole as well as for its individual members, the call to holiness often needs to be heard as a call to repentance and to reformation of life. Yet the Church relies upon God's gracious response to its unholiness: God's mercy, God's forgiveness and God's help.

The words 'You shall be holy, for I am holy' in 1 Peter 1.16 are a quote from the holiness code in Leviticus (Leviticus 19.2). 1 Peter

goes on to give a vision of holy living as all-encompassing as
the vision set out in that code. It talks about this community's
relationship to political authorities (1 Peter 2.13-17) and to the
surrounding culture (1 Peter 2.12; 4.3,4), about family life (1 Peter
3.1-7) and about the community members' behaviour towards one
another (1 Peter 4.8-11). It thinks through what holiness can look like
in the cultural and political conditions of the day – and some of the
advice it gives is difficult and controversial.

The heart of it, however, is clear. The holy life which this community
is called to is a life of 'genuine mutual love' in which all the
members of the community 'love one another deeply from the
heart' (1 Peter 1.22).

**Above all, maintain constant love for one another, for love covers a
multitude of sins. Be hospitable to one another without complaining ...
serve one another with whatever gift each of you has received.
(1 Peter 4.8-10)**

It is this, above all, that will make this community distinctive. It is this
that demands transformation of its members' actions, their speech,
and their desires. In order to pursue this life, the community will
have to turn away from 'all malice, and all guile, insincerity, envy, and
all slander' (1 Peter 2.1). Its members will have to put behind them
the rowdiness and sexual dissipation of their former lives (1 Peter
4.3), in order to be devoted to this godly life.

Pursuing this distinctive life will bring this community into conflict
with the world around it. Their calling is not, however, to separate
themselves from the world around them. They are to 'conduct
[themselves] honourably' amongst their neighbours, in a way that
will communicate to those neighbours something of the glory of
God (1 Peter 2.12). There is no fear of contamination here, but a
confidence in Christ's contagious holiness.

For the Church of England today, questions about identity, sexuality,
relationships and marriage are questions about holy living: what
behaviour, what forms of relationship, what patterns of community life
echo to the character of God? What ways of living can embody and
communicate God's life? What ways of living shine with God's love?

Inclusion and exclusion

In February 2017, when – as we saw earlier – the Archbishops of Canterbury and York announced the decision to begin the project that would become Living in Love and Faith, they coined a powerful and controversial phrase. The work that they were proposing on sexuality and marriage would, they said, reflect a

> **radical new Christian inclusion in the Church. This must be founded in Scripture, in reason, in tradition, in theology and the Christian faith as the Church of England has received it; it must be based on good, healthy, flourishing relationships, and in a proper 21st century understanding of being human and of being sexual.**[283]

That proposal, however, raised sharply the question of what 'radical new Christian inclusion' might mean.

In the New Testament, the Church is the community of those who have faith in Jesus. That faith marks out those who are members of this body from those who are not. Faith is not an achievement. It is not something available only to a special class of people, to people who meet some standard of behaviour or status. God calls everyone into this community – regardless of gender, class, ethnicity, sexuality, marital status, age, or ability. The community is meant to extend to 'all nations' (Matthew 28.16-20; cf. Genesis 12.1-3), and to include people 'from all tribes and peoples and languages' (Revelation 7.9). There is a radical welcome here, offered to absolutely everyone, without preconditions. The Church is called to reject the forms of exclusion that mar our world. As Jesus' actions show, this is to be a community that welcomes the poor, the marginalized, the excluded, the deprecated. It is to be a community of radical love and hospitality in which all can find a home. It is to be a community living against the grain of a divided world.

To be welcomed into the Church is to be welcomed into a community devoted to the pursuit of a distinctive pattern of life together. We will be returning in Part Four to discuss the relationship between the Church and the surrounding culture, but it is clear from the New Testament that the Church's devotion to this distinctive way of life – to a life that embodies and communicates God's abundant and holy life – can lead to some forms of exclusion.

Inclusion and exclusion: How should Israel relate to Moab?

A tension between inclusion and exclusion in Israel is a consistent feature of the Old Testament. Israel is commanded to keep separate from its neighbours, yet also to treat the alien and stranger kindly and fairly. In the book of Joshua, Israel goes to war against the Canaanites – yet the very first story tells us of the inclusion of Canaanite Rahab and her household into the people of God, to such a degree that she appears in the ancestry of Jesus. So which texts do we privilege? How do we read together texts that appear contradictory? How do exclusion and inclusion go together?

This tension between inclusion and exclusion is particularly obvious in Israel's relationship with their Moabite neighbours. Should the Moabites, or should they not, be allowed to become part of Israel? The issue aroused all kinds of strong feelings, steeped in fear and history.

The book of Deuteronomy seems clear:

No Ammonite or Moabite shall be admitted to the assembly of the Lord. Even to the tenth generation, none of their descendants shall be admitted to the assembly of the Lord ... because they did not meet you with food and water on your journey out of Egypt.... You shall never promote their welfare or their prosperity as long as you live. (Deuteronomy 23.3-6)

This is hardly ambiguous. Not only are Moabites to be excluded from Israel, but Israel is explicitly under an obligation never to do anything for them.

The book of Ruth, on the other hand, is equally clear. Ruth is from the land of Moab, and is regularly called 'the Moabite'. Yet when she comes with her mother-in-law Naomi from Moab to Bethlehem, the Israelite Boaz not only shows kindness to her but he also eventually marries her. Through their union Ruth becomes the great grandmother of King David. She becomes a key figure in Israel's story.

The presence of two such different voices within Israel's Scriptures suggests that the relationship between Israel and Moab was a divisive issue for some in ancient Israel. This is a tension linked to intense questions of identity, ethnicity, faith, boundaries – and of inclusion and exclusion. So what do we do with these two texts?

Deuteronomy has a strong vision of Israel as the elect and holy covenant people of the Lord, and that vision has shaped both Jewish and Christian faiths. The paragraph about Moabites, however, seems to be about revenge and resentment. It essentially tells Israel to respond to the Moabites in kind: hostility is to be met with hostility. It is a response located in a specific historical context and trauma.

The story of Ruth has a different tenor. Most famous are Ruth's words to Naomi, when she promises the traumatized older woman that she will always be with her, care for her, and share her people and her faith. This self-giving generosity is the very thing that Boaz notices and commends, and it motivates his own generosity towards Ruth. Ruth thereby comes into the heart of Israel's story when Boaz marries her. It is a story about the triumph of loving-kindness, a prime characteristic of the Lord himself (Exodus 34.6,7), which should characterize also those who respond truly to him (see Psalms 111 and 112).

In comparing these two texts, we could argue that the book of Ruth stands closer to the overall moral and spiritual heart of the Old Testament, and of the faith rooted in it, than does the paragraph in Deuteronomy 23.3-6. It lines up, for instance, with the prophecy in Isaiah, in which God promises to bring foreign peoples 'to my holy mountain, and make them joyful in my house of prayer ... for my house shall be called a house of prayer for all peoples' (Isaiah 56.7). The judgement that Christians should privilege Ruth over the paragraph in Deuteronomy looks to be in line with the priorities of the Old Testament itself, quite apart from that of the New Testament.

The question then perhaps arises whether, if the law in Deuteronomy 23 is relativized in the book of Ruth, there might be a similar relativizing or depriviledging of the Levitical prohibition of same-sex intercourse? Or does the absence of any texts commending what Leviticus condemns challenge such relativization?

The Christian community is certainly not a community of the pure and perfect. If members of this community say they have no sin, they deceive themselves. It is a community of people who repeatedly fail in their attempts to live this distinctive life, who repeatedly need to confess, and who repeatedly need to be forgiven (1 John 1.8-10). Exclusion in the New Testament is not about policing the boundary around a community that consistently achieves and maintains some standard of excellence. Rather, exclusion is reserved for those who reject and work against the Church's calling, and who persist in that despite all attempts to win them round (Matthew 18.15-18; 1 Corinthians 5.3-6,11-13; 2 Thessalonians 3.6; Titus 3.9-11).

The Church is a community called to stand against those forces in the wider world that reject and betray the love of God. It is called to recognize those forces and tendencies, to speak out against them, and to call its neighbours away from them. It is called to keep itself from falling into them – and to ask God's forgiveness and help whenever it fails.

Now this I affirm and insist on in the Lord: you must no longer live as the Gentiles live, in the futility of their minds. They are darkened in their understanding, alienated from the life of God because of their ignorance and hardness of heart. They have lost all sensitivity and have abandoned themselves to licentiousness, greedy to practise every kind of impurity. That is not the way you learned Christ! (Ephesians 4.17-20)

There is, therefore, an unavoidable negotiation of inclusion and exclusion in the life of the Church of England which has often handled this negotiation very badly. It has all too often taken to policing its boundaries – refusing people welcome unless they measure up. It has often practised exclusion in ways that line up all too well with the forms of marginalization and oppression that mar the wider world. In relation to the topics we are discussing, the church has sometimes made those whose marriages end in divorce feel unwelcome, and has often made LGBTI+ people feel that they don't and can't belong, simply because of who they are. We have, all too often, defined inclusion and exclusion by some standard other than the holiness, glory and love of God.

Inclusion has become an important value in our society. One reason is the widespread conviction that the way boundaries have been set in the past has often been profoundly wrong. Many people believe that deeply mistaken decisions have been taken in the past about who belongs within our communities and what kinds of behaviour are acceptable. They look at how our communities and institutions have treated women, people from ethnic minorities, people with disabilities, and LGBTI+ people. They believe that these people have been excluded in ways that are morally wrong and that there is a deep obligation to put this right.

Many Christians would agree that the Church has contributed significantly to these wrongs. The Church has sometimes even used the language of holiness in ways that reinforce these failings. Visions of human life have been held up as holy ideals, but those visions have sometimes had more to do with preserving the culture of a particular church, or preserving patterns of privilege within it, than with communicating the holiness of God. The holiness we have proclaimed has sometimes looked very white and middle class, for instance. Failures to address issues of inclusion on the Church's part have had a far-reaching and corrosive effect on the Church's embodiment and communication of God's life. At times – in relation to the Church of England and race, for instance – it seems that we have needed to be dragged along by the surrounding society, rather than being at the forefront in addressing inequality.

This is another area in which we encounter disagreements about sexuality and gender. Some see these as matters of justice. They believe that the Church has failed to live up to its calling to inclusion, that it is being challenged to do much better by voices both from within and from wider society, and that it needs to rethink the images of sin and holiness that it proclaims, recognizing the ways in which they have been used to exclude. They believe that the Church needs to be much more inclusive, to better reflect the loving holiness of God. Others, while agreeing that there are undoubtedly issues of injustice and wrongful discrimination that call for repentance and redress, believe that the Church is called to uphold a distinctive way of life in the areas of sexuality and gender. They believe the Church is called to uphold forms of holy living that cut across many of our society's understandings of what is permissible or desirable – and that might well conflict with understandings of inclusion widespread in our society. They believe that this distinctive way of life is profoundly good for human beings, and that upholding it is itself a way of displaying the love of God.

Christians on all sides of these disagreements can agree that the
Church ought to be a community where everyone is welcome.
No one should be made to feel excluded simply because of who
they are. The Church is meant to be a community that welcomes
the poor, the marginalized, the excluded and the deprecated. We
agree that the Church often fails in this calling and needs to repent
of those failings. The Church is a community of people all of whom
fail to follow God's way consistently. We misunderstand. We harm
ourselves and one another. We don't live up to the standards that
we proclaim. The Church should be a community of mercy. It should
be a place where the weakness of our wills and the failures of our
understanding can be acknowledged. It should be a community
where we can face up to the harm that we have done and are
doing, as well as recognizing the harm that has been done to us.
The Church should be a community of grace. It should enable us to
confess our sins to God, in confidence of forgiveness. It should help
us to repent – to turn, and to keep on turning, towards the life God
has called us into. It should be a community in which every person is
enabled to follow this pattern of acknowledgement, confession and
repentance, and to keep on following it.

In the areas of identity, sexuality, relationships and marriage,
however, we disagree about the patterns of behaviour that are
consistent with this community's calling. We disagree, therefore,
about the kinds of change called for from the people who are
welcomed into this community. We disagree about what it would
look like for someone to work persistently against the life to which
this community is called.

The questions about identity discussed in the previous chapter
make these questions more difficult. Suppose I am a trans man, and
that understanding myself in those terms is a deeply rooted aspect
of my identity. I might hear a church say, 'You are welcome here, but
you need to know that we think that the way you describe yourself
is seriously mistaken.' To say the least, that risks me receiving the
message: 'You are not really welcome as the person you actually
are.' If I have transitioned, and have experienced that as a deep
liberation, and a church says, 'You are welcome here, but your
involvement will be limited while you still live as a man', I am very
unlikely to agree that the Church is actually willing to welcome me
as the person I believe myself to be. Or suppose I am a lesbian in
a long-term relationship, and a church says, 'You are welcome, but
you won't be eligible for a role in leadership while you are still in

that relationship – or at least whilst it is sexually active.' I am very likely to experience this as another form of rejection and exclusion, especially if I notice that no such questions about sexual activity are asked of my straight friends, and that nobody criticizes those friends when they say how central those relationships are to their identity and their well-being.

Yet for those of us who do believe sexual relationships between people of the same sex are sinful, or that transitioning gender is a rejection of God's good intention for us, the making of distinctions like this is unavoidable. It is a normal and necessary feature of the welcome that the Church extends to all. If the Church is understood as the community of those who follow the way of Christ, and if that way truly is incompatible with these behaviours, then it is necessary at some point to communicate that such ways of life are sinful and subject to God's judgement. That means communicating God's call to repentance as the means of being fully included in the life and ministry of the Church.

Others of us disagree. We believe that there is nothing about same-sex sexual relationships, or about transitioning, that is incompatible with the life of Christ's body. We therefore believe that placing limits on people's full involvement in the life of the Church because of these things is a betrayal of the Church's calling and identity. If the Church is the community of those who follow the way of Christ, and if that way truly is incompatible with this kind of exclusion, then people need to be challenged to leave behind behaviour that perpetuates these exclusions.

The question we are left with is not so much a question about welcome or inclusion. It is another version of the question raised at the end of the previous section. How are Christians to discern what is compatible, and what is incompatible, with the life of Christ's body? How are we to discern what is holy – what embodies and communicates the loving kindness of God?

We are also, however, left with another question: How is the Church of England to handle deep disagreements about these matters – disagreements about which forms of life are to be commended as holy and fitting for those in Christ, and which named as sins from which one needs to seek God's grace and power to turn away?

Inclusion and the transformation of community

'Inclusion' can be a problematic word if it is taken to suggest that the community is simply being asked to do a favour to those currently excluded from its life. The inclusion of those who are currently excluded, or the fuller inclusion of those who are marginalized, does far more than this. It can heal, enrich, and even transform the life of the community itself. Those who are included bring gifts with them, as much as they receive a gift from the community. Inclusion is about more than opening a community's doors more widely, or expanding the range of people welcomed into it. It is about the transformation of the community itself.

Disagreement and communion

Disagreement has always been a feature of the life of the Church, as the pages of the New Testament demonstrate.[284] However painful it is, it seems to be unavoidable. It can emerge even when all concerned are prayerfully and diligently seeking to be faithful to Christ. After all, faithfulness in mission will continually draw the church into new situations where it will face new questions to which there will not be ready-to-hand answers. Different people will make differing responses. A constant process of sifting and discernment is therefore essential for the Church, as the Spirit leads it into new situations, new understandings and new ways of being.

Disagreements within the church are often messy. People on all sides have (acknowledged and unacknowledged) emotional investments in the matters they argue about. They occupy uneven distributions of power and responsibility (again, acknowledged and unacknowledged). The history of any disagreement in the church is filled with complex biographies and messy politics, as well as with ideas and arguments. And although there can be a tendency for people involved in a debate to think that it is only their opponents who are driven by emotion, or whose motives are political, these complexities affect everyone.

See Scene 4 (pages 406–412) for a conversation about church and questions of identity, sexuality, relationships and marriage.

Some disagreements create more difficulties than others in the life of the Church. It can be helpful to think in terms of there being three broad types of disagreement.

- First, there are disagreements in which each group believes the other to be advocating something simply incompatible with the good news of Jesus. They think the other group is teaching something that amounts to a rejection of Jesus' call on one's life. Some will say that the people involved are no longer serious about living as Jesus' disciples, and that they cannot be considered Christians in any meaningful sense. Others will say that the people involved might still be Christians, but that their teaching is not – and perhaps that they are putting their own and others' eternal salvation at risk.

- Second, there are disagreements that don't cut right to the heart of our understanding of the gospel in this way, but that do undermine our ability to live and work together as one church. They make it hard to worship together, to share sacraments, to have a single structure of ministry, oversight and governance. A lot of ecumenical disagreements take this form. We recognize one another's communities as Christian churches, teaching the gospel, but we disagree about matters that impair our ability to live and work together as one church.

- Third, there are disagreements that don't make us think that those who disagree with us are rejecting the gospel, and that don't prevent us working together as one church, even though we do think them wrong about something that matters.

Disagreements are especially dangerous for the life of the Church when they get stuck. That is, they are especially dangerous when the people involved lose any sense of how they might ultimately move through the disagreement to fuller agreement in the truth of the gospel. One factor in them getting stuck is sometimes that people disagree not only about the issue at hand, but also about the category of disagreement that they are having. The combination of these two levels of disagreement can make it very difficult for those involved to hear and respond to one another.

I might believe that our disagreement jeopardizes my ability to recognize you as sharing the same faith – the faith handed down from the apostles onward. You might believe that it does not extend that far but that it does make it difficult for us to continue to be members of the same church. A third person might take it for granted that we should be able to respect one another's opinions on the matter and carry on within the same church. In such a situation, it will be hard to find the right 'register' for our conversation. All that is likely to be made much worse if the difference in perception is not acknowledged or reflected upon.

This kind of disagreement – where we can't even agree on how deeply our disagreement cuts into our ability to be church together – is likely when we are facing the kind of disagreements described in this and the previous chapter. We have noted disagreements about how the boundaries of the Church's life are drawn, or about the nature of inclusion in the Church. Those are, in effect, disagreements about how we decide which matters are crucial to the life of faith, or to the life of the Church, and which ones are in some way secondary. They are often, in other words, about where to draw the lines between the categories of disagreement listed above.

That might help us to make sense of what is happening in the Church of England and in other churches regarding questions of sexuality, gender identity, relationships and marriage. Different participants in these debates see them corresponding to each of the three types of disagreement set out above.

For some of us, the Church of England's received teaching that the only proper place for intimate sexual activity is marriage between a man and woman is an integral part of Christian discipleship. Those who not only doubt that teaching but encourage other people in the name of the church to disregard it are advocating a path that leads away from following Christ. They are leading people away from communion with Christ and making them subject to Christ's judgement. While they persist in that teaching and behaviour, they have separated themselves from the body of Christ.

For others of us, a refusal to include LGBTI+ people in the life and ministry of a church because of their sexual activity is itself incompatible with the way of Jesus Christ. Those who not only persist in thinking this way themselves, but who are determined to perpetuate this exclusion in the authoritative actions of a church, cannot be recognized any longer as teachers of Christ's gospel. They have betrayed the bonds of love and put themselves out of Christ's company.

Still others of us see these disagreements as falling into the second category above. The issues are serious. We believe that those who disagree with us are seriously mistaken. And though we think that those mistakes don't amount to a rejection of the gospel, we believe that a church such as the Church of England needs to be consistent, and needs to be able to communicate its teaching on these matters clearly and coherently. We might therefore think that, if people continue to disagree about these matters, we won't for long be able to remain in a single ecclesial communion together, at least not without some significant differentiation within it.

Finally, of course there are others of us who struggle to understand why this disagreement should be in any category other than the third. After all, learned and devout Christians have come to different conclusions. Bishops and archbishops have come to different conclusions. Is it not possible, we ask, for everyone to accept that it is going to take some time for truth to emerge in a definitive and compelling form, and that in the meantime, while the debate continues, provision should be made for a variety of opinion and of practice?

Many Christians will want to say that unity is crucial here. Christians stand together in union with Christ. We are bound not to abandon one another or accept separation from one another. We should work at finding the greatest degree of unity we can, as brothers and sisters in him. The challenge, however, is that all Christians would probably agree that there are some disagreements that do impair our ability to live and work together – disagreements that require some kind of practical differentiation even if we remain in a single church together. And most Christians would probably agree that there are some disagreements that push such impairment to breaking point. There are disagreements that cannot be held within the bond we share through faith in Christ, and that will require us to walk apart for the foreseeable future. In the twentieth century, for instance, in South Africa, some in the churches supported apartheid, arguing that black people were inferior to others because of their ethnicity and therefore deserving of inferior treatment. Such views were in the end judged unfaithful to Christian doctrine and incompatible with Christian discipleship.

Some disagreements impair the possibilities for communion. Some do so drastically; some make communion with one another impossible, within the one, holy, catholic and apostolic Church or within *this* particular church serving this particular society. Within the Church of England, we do not agree whether we are having that kind of communion-threatening disagreement on sexuality and marriage or not.

What then does it mean for Christians to disagree in such a context? How should our disagreements be pursued? How should we behave towards those with whom we disagree? How do we live out our claim that 'though we are many we are one body, because we all share in the one bread'?[285] These are urgent questions, not least because there are many who are yet to come to a settled judgement on the questions that divide us. Many wish to keep talking across the breadth of perspective within the Church of England, including with those who have already made up their minds.

Conclusion

The Church is called to be holy. It is called to be a community that expresses God's lavish love to the world. It is called to be a community where everyone is welcome, and from which no one is made to feel excluded simply because of who they are. It is called to be a community that welcomes the poor, the marginalized, the excluded and the deprecated. It is called to be a community in which all people are welcomed into a distinctive form of life, which embodies and communicates God's distinctive character, God's life, God's glory. And so it is called to be a community in which people are enabled to recognize their sin, repent, and receive forgiveness.

The question still remains, however, in our discussion of identity, sexuality, relationships and marriage: Which patterns of life are consistent, and which inconsistent, with God's holiness?

CHAPTER 12

A story about ways of human loving

In Chapter 10, we asked how people's own stories can fit within the overarching story of love and faith. In Chapter 11, we asked how the Christian community can inhabit that story together.

In this chapter, we continue this exploration, focusing on specific patterns of living that Christians have understood to be ways of living in this story.

We will begin with the general idea of holy living as involving self-denial or discipline. We will then look at two specific forms of life that Christians believe can exemplify this: celibacy and marriage. We finish by asking what sex is for, and what kinds of self-discipline or self-denial are called for in sexual relationships.

As in the previous two chapters, this chapter will describe various disagreements that Christians have about these matters, and will set out some associated questions. It won't provide definitive answers to those questions. Its focus is, instead, on helping us to frame those questions well, and to understand what is at stake in the different answers that Christians give to them.

Loving to the end: self-denial and abundant life

Then Jesus told his disciples, 'If any want to become my followers, let them deny themselves and take up their cross and follow me. For those who want to save their life will lose it, and those who lose their life for my sake will find it. For what will it profit them if they gain the whole world but forfeit their life? Or what will they give in return for their life? (Matthew 16.24-26)

Following Jesus involves denying ourselves and taking up our cross (Matthew 16.24; Luke 9.23). Jesus' followers are called to live lives that, left to our own devices, we would not automatically live. To follow Jesus means learning new patterns of action, speech, thought, imagination and feeling. It involves a new ordering of our desires – as we learn to love ourselves, our neighbours and God as we should.

We were made for this ordering of our loves. It is proper to us, and entering into it is a homecoming, a restoration. Jesus did not come to destroy us, but so that we might have life, and have it abundantly (John 10.10). Yet because we have grown up in a world marred by sin, we are shaped by selfishness, greed, fear, despair and self-loathing. The journey to find or save our lives therefore involves losing them – denying these destructive impulses, dying to our old ways, in order to learn the fulness of life that comes from following Jesus.

The language of self-denial, discipline and renunciation is not popular. Yet our world faces an ecological crisis bound up with a relentless addiction to consumption on the part of the privileged few. We are facing up to the prevalence of sexual harassment and of everyday racism and sexism. It is becoming clearer to many in and far beyond the Church how important it is for us collectively to discover new habits, to practise restraint, and to learn a new ordering of our desires.

It is, however, difficult to speak well about self-denial. Part of the challenge is to show how such self-denial can be accompanied by a deep appreciation of the beauty and goodness of bodily life, and the delight that is possible in the beauty, touch and movement of another. These have not always been the hallmarks of teaching about self-denial in the Christian tradition. Yet we were made for delight in God, in others, and in ourselves. Self-denial is needed not to overcome delight, but to discover a truer and fuller delight.

Self-denial is a matter for communities as much as for individuals. As followers of Jesus we are called to learn how to order our lives and desires together, and how to support one another in this learning. Yet demands for discipline and self-denial have too often been used to reinforce uneven distributions of power within communities. They have been used to police people who don't meet a particular community's standards of decency. They have been used to keep people in the place assigned to them in a culture's hierarchies. They have been used to silence people who speak and act in ways that disrupt a culture's power dynamics. They have been used to control and to shame. And yet the desire for domination, the desire to preserve privilege, the desire to exclude those who differ, are exactly the kind of disordered desires from which we need to be rescued.

Self-denial, discipline, restraint, renunciation – they are all, in Christian theology, important not for their own sake, but for the sake of what they enable. They are tools for training wayward human beings. They can orient us towards, and enable us to enjoy, abundant, fairer life together. They are there to lead us toward a proper love of self, neighbour and God, to enjoy in full the goodness of God's creation, and to live at peace with one another.

The pursuit of discipleship, and of the discipline and self-denial that it involves, can sometimes take the form of a 'rule of life'. A 'rule of life' is a specific, long-term, life-shaping commitment, held in place by explicit promises both to avoid certain behaviours and to pursue certain positive habits.

The idea of a 'rule of life' has its origins in monasticism. Life in a religious order involves commitment to a specific form of community life defined by a rule – such as the Rule of St Benedict. It normally involves giving some things up – such as personal property or sexual activity – but that is undertaken for the sake of the positive form of life which it helps to make possible: a life devoted to prayer, friendship and service lived out with others.

In recent years, the idea of developing and pursuing rules of life in many other contexts has become increasingly popular. In the diocese of Winchester, to give just one example, church communities and individuals are being encouraged to develop rules as a way of putting their relationship with God into practice, a way of balancing action and reflection. It isn't about 'keeping the rules'; it is about discovering how they can grow as Christ's disciples in the rhythms and relationships that make up our everyday lives.[286]

This idea provides one way of thinking about some of the topics covered in this book. In the remainder of this chapter, we explore some of the ways in which Christians understand our relationships and sexual lives to be arenas for discipline and self-denial, and more specifically for the following of rules of life.

Celibacy

One pattern of discipline that many Christians have pursued is celibacy. That is, Christians have found themselves called to various forms of discipleship – and some of those forms have required sexual abstinence. They have valued celibacy because it enables intensive dedication to prayer and to the work of Christ's kingdom.

Celibacy might, at first glance, seem not to have an obvious place in the story of salvation. We have already talked about Genesis 2, where we are told that it was not good for Adam to be alone. We have acknowledged that Adam's need for intimacy could not be satisfied by God alone. But those who embrace celibacy as part of their discipleship are not turning away from intimacy. They are turning away from one kind of intimacy for the sake of others.

As we explored in Chapter 2, the prime example of this way of life is Jesus. There is no mention in the Bible of Jesus having a wife or children. When his family interrupts his teaching, it is not a wife or children but his mother and brothers who appear (Matthew 12.46,7). Yet Jesus did not lack anything proper to a fully human life. He lived, in the midst of the community of his followers, a life utterly in tune with God's intentions for humanity. However good and important they might be for many, marrying and having children cannot be regarded as necessary to abundant life for everyone.

Paul, in his advice to the Corinthian church, makes it clear that different people are given different gifts (1 Corinthians 7.7). They are called to different patterns of life (1 Corinthians 7.17), and these include married life and the life of celibacy. As gifts from God, each of these patterns of life can be lived to God's glory, as a form of abundant life. In fact, Paul gives a certain primacy to celibacy over marriage as a context for the pursuit of discipleship. In contrast to those who are married, he says, 'An unmarried man is concerned about the Lord's affairs – how he can please the Lord…. An unmarried woman or virgin is concerned about the Lord's affairs: her aim is to be devoted to the Lord in both body and spirit' (1 Corinthians 7.32, 34 (NIV)). Nevertheless, in a different context, and for different reasons, Paul advised younger widows to remarry (1 Timothy 5.11-15).

Celibacy and eschatology

There are two main senses in which celibacy has been understood to be 'eschatological' – that is, related to the end times.

First, the valuing of celibacy in the Early Church was associated with the expectation that Christ would soon return, and the present order of life would pass away. If the end is coming soon, there is little sense in making arrangements for the stable succession of generations.

Second, celibacy was seen as an anticipation – a sign or foretaste – of the new order of things that Christ's return would usher in: an order in which, Jesus says, people 'neither marry nor are given in marriage, but are like angels in heaven' (Matthew 22.30).

This was no less countercultural at the time than it is today. It meant that – in contrast to the views circulating in much of the surrounding society – marriage and family life were no longer seen in the Early Church as a duty that all responsible citizens were supposed to undertake. In particular, in a society in which women were under the rule of their father or the rule of their husband, the Christian valuing of celibacy could sometimes give women an unusual degree of freedom.

A religious order is a community bound by vows and abiding by a shared rule of life. Such orders have been one of the main contexts, historically and today, in which Christians have pursued vocations that involve celibacy, though not all religious orders require it. Today, these orders can take many forms (including in the Church of England): there are gathered communities of monks or nuns, dispersed networks of people who share a common vow, and various other forms.

In recent years, a network has developed of people dedicated to the 'Single Consecrated Life' (SCL). Its members make a vow,

> in a way similar to that which others choose when they make a vow of marriage. It is a loving response to a God who invites someone to consecrate his or her sexuality in this way. It is a distinctive charism and is incarnational; it is a counter-cultural witness in a world obsessed with sex and binds the vowed person to Christ to serve him with a new freedom. Those who respond to this invitation discover that God does indeed bless them. They are more available to others and they have an inner solitude that can foster prayer, but they also learn that like their married friends, they need to renew their vow every day.[287]

It is important to distinguish this, however, from involuntary singleness. Those in the SCL network feel themselves positively called to singleness, able to affirm it as a gift of God, and as something that they desire and – in some sense – choose. For others, singleness might be experienced more as something unchosen or involuntary.

For some, it is simply the circumstance in which they currently find themselves. It might bring with it distinctive possibilities but also distinctive temptations. It might demand some distinctive forms of discipline, and distinctive forms of support from the wider Christian community – but it may well not make sense to them to think of it as a gift or calling, or as a 'rule of life', still less as a state in which they vow to remain. According to the Church of England's teaching, this kind of discipline – and the kinds of support that should accompany it – are relevant to a very wide range of people. The church teaches that the only proper context for sexual relationships is within marriage, and therefore asks for sexual abstinence from all those who are not married.

Given this teaching and the teaching that marriage is between a man and a woman, particular questions arise about celibacy, discipline and rules of life for gay and lesbian people.

Some lesbian and gay people understand the church's teaching on these matters as an expression of what following Jesus demands. They understand their calling to follow Jesus as bringing with it a demand for celibacy – and they experience this as a costly but important discipline. Some think of it as involving something like a rule of life: a promise, made with others, and supported by the wider community, which enables a pattern of discipleship and flourishing.

Others do not understand that the church's teaching on these matters is an expression of what following Jesus demands. The talk in this context of 'discipline' or 'self-denial', and still more of 'rule of life', can be heard as a way of dressing up something that is being imposed by the church as if it were a gift or a freely chosen commitment. They recognize that celibacy can be for some a gift and calling from God, but they deny that this gift and calling are automatically given to lesbian and gay people. And some argue that to impose such a pathway on people while calling it a gift or celebrating it as a calling makes it harder for those affected to be honest about their experience and about the cost and pain of what is demanded from them. They also sometimes find that their criticisms are treated as if they were rejecting the whole idea of self-denial, or the whole idea that discipleship demands discipline and transformation. The argument, however, is not about whether discipline and self-denial are called for from Jesus' disciples, nor whether celibacy is a discipline that is required in some circumstances and that, for some, might be a valued element of a particular vocation. The argument is about whether celibacy is the only appropriate expression of discipleship for lesbian and gay people – and these Christians answer that it is no more and no less of a possibility than it is for heterosexual people.

Covenant

The Hebrew term *berith* describes a variety of relationships between people, and between people and God, in which strong commitments were made on both sides, often ratified by swearing an oath and sacrificial rituals. It is usually translated as 'covenant', though 'treaty' or 'peace-treaty' would fit some contexts.

At an international level, there are examples of treaties between nations in the Ancient Near East. These could be between equals – such as the agreement Hiram, king of Tyre, made with David and later with Solomon, to foster a trading relationship (1 Kings 5.1, 9.10-14). Or they could be between a superior power and vassal peoples – such as Joshua's treaty with the Gibeonites (Joshua 9.15).

Israel came to envisage their relationship with God somewhat along the lines of the latter kind of treaty. God was the Great King who had initiated a massively beneficial relationship with Israel (releasing them from vassalage to an alien power in the exodus) and called for their exclusive loyalty, worship, and obedience in return. The covenant portrayed as mediated by Moses at Mount Sinai was the consolidation of this bonded relationship, based on God's redemption (Exodus 19.3-6), ratified by sacrifice (Exodus 24), and affirmed in strong reciprocal commitments (Deuteronomy 26.17-19).

The idea of a covenant relationship was applied to much earlier events in biblical history as well. After the flood, God tells Noah that he has made a covenant with all life on earth, in language that echoes and renews the blessing of creation itself. In response, humans (and animals) will be held accountable for the shedding of human blood (Genesis 8.20 – 9.17). Then later, God initiates a covenant with Abraham and Sarah, promising four things: that they will become a great nation, that there will be a relationship of blessing between God and this people, that they will possess the land God sends them to, and that the impact of God's blessing on Abraham will ultimately be felt and invoked among all nations on earth (Genesis 12.1-3; 15; 17). Abraham's response of faith, demonstrated in obedience (Genesis 15.6; 22.15-18; 26.2-5), becomes the model for Israel and for God's people in all nations ever after (Romans 1.5, 16.26). Later still, God initiates his covenant with

David, that a descendant of his will forever reign over Israel (2 Samuel 7). And again, the required response is obedient walking in God's ways (Jeremiah 22.1-9).

Three elements seem fundamental to the biblical covenants. First, there is a relationship and a history. God initiates the covenant on the basis of something God has done or said and the covenant is then built into an ongoing story of that relationship. Covenants speak of the sovereign grace of God, choosing, redeeming and calling people into responsive relationship with God and one another.

Secondly, there are reciprocal promises and commitments. The definitive covenant affirmation, 'I will be your God and you will be my people' embodies both God's faithful commitment to his people and their obedient commitment to God.

Thirdly, there are sanctions. Broken treaties incurred severe penalties. The broken covenant between Israel and God brought upon them the curses that had been explicit within it, as the prophets warned. Nevertheless, beyond judgement lay the prospect of restoring grace, as the prophets also foretold.

At a personal level, covenants could be made between individuals, to ratify reconciliation after a conflict (e.g. Laban and Jacob, Genesis 31.43-54), or to consolidate a relationship of love and strong reciprocal commitment (e.g. David and Jonathan, 1 Samuel 20.11-17,23,42). Again, we observe a historical relationship, mutual commitment, and sanctions embedded in the act of calling God to witness the promises made and so to monitor whether they were kept or not.

In prophetic texts, the metaphor of covenant-breaking was one of the ways that Israel and Judah's rejection of God and disobedience of his laws could be described. Another vivid metaphor was to compare Israel to an adulterous woman (Ezekiel 16.15), and to portray adultery and divorce as forms of covenant-breaking (Proverbs 2.17; Malachi 2.14). Unfaithfulness to religious practice was comparable to marital unfaithfulness. The juxtaposition of these two metaphors has led some scholars to hold that marriage could sometimes be characterized as a covenant. Marriage, then, was seen as a commitment made before God that called for a faithfulness analogous to God's demand on Israel, with comparable sanctions. Other scholars, however, would argue that, while Israel's covenant could be metaphorically compared to a marriage, marriage itself is never explicitly described as a covenant in the Old Testament.

Paul does not actually use the term covenant in the context of marriage, though he does build richly scriptural imagery into his affirmation that the marital union of husband and wife, quoting Genesis 2.24, is a mystery that speaks of the relationship of Christ and his church (Ephesians 5.31,32). Similarly, the closing chapters of the Bible juxtapose the ultimate covenantal fulfilment ('they will be his people and God will be...their God') with the union of the heavenly bridegroom with his earthly bride (Revelation 21.1-3).

Marriage

Married life can be thought of as a 'rule of life'. It, too, is a gift from God. It is one distinctive way of life amongst others. It demands of those who pursue it particular kinds of attentiveness, care and self-restraint. It is sealed by vows. It is, or should be, recognized and supported by the wider community.

At the heart of this rule of life is the rule of fidelity: the commitment of each partner to be faithful to the other. This involves, of course, a refusal to have sex with other people, but it includes much more than that, too. It involves a promise of loyalty, and a promise of mutual care 'for better, for worse, for richer, for poorer, in sickness and in health'.

Faithfulness is central to Christian accounts of marriage, but the emphasis on it can be misused. In particular, an insistence on faithfulness has been used to pressure women and their children to stay in abusive relationships. While the faithful, self-giving love of God provides a pattern for human love, we still need to take into account questions of power, justice and dignity as we work that love out in the context of human relationships.

This way of life can be undertaken for many reasons. At the heart of a Christian understanding, however, is the idea that marriage provides one compelling way of reflecting and embodying the love of God – the love for which human beings were made, the love that brings us life. The disciplines and self-denial that marriage involves are there to enable it to realize this possibility.

Marriage as lived by fallible human beings can, of course, betray this purpose. They can lack intimacy. They can be faithless. They can be harmful. They can be abusive. They can damage the partners, children, wider family and surrounding community. They can go wrong and break down in endless ways. They can end up hiding rather than displaying God's love. Those betrayals and failures, however, can be understood in Christian thinking not as demonstrations that the whole idea of marriage is mistaken, but as corruptions of something good – something with the capacity to be quite different.

Marriage is very rarely referred to as a sacrament in the historic formularies of the Church of England.[288] As we saw in Chapter 3, however, much Anglican teaching has therefore tended to regard it as *sacramental* – as having some of the characteristics of a sacrament. Sacramental actions don't simply point to, or tell us about, the mystery of salvation. They aren't simply parables. They are a means by which God invites us into that mystery and helps us to inhabit it – and so, in the Common Worship marriage service, marriages are described as 'a means of grace'. They are gifts from God, given to help us know more of God's redeeming and healing love in the fractured reality of our lives. The love that a couple experiences in marriage, and that they work at embodying and displaying, isn't simply something that resembles God's love. God is directly at work in it, drawing the couple into love and helping them to love better, and to love and be loved more fully.

Marriage is a God-given context for learning about love and faithfulness. It is a context in which we can learn about finding ourselves by losing ourselves. At its best, it doesn't just do this for the couple themselves, but for their community and the society in which they live. It can do it in a specific way for those who share their household, especially any children born to them or entrusted to their care. At the same time that it binds two people together so closely that they become one flesh, marriage turns them outwards to serve and bless others – just as the union between Christ and the Church should overflow into blessing for the world. A sign and instrument of God's purposes for creation, marriage is also a foretaste of their fulfilment. No wonder the Bible regularly uses imagery of the wedding banquet for the life of the world to come.

Jesus' teaching on marriage

Discussions of Christian marriage, as we saw in Chapter 3, are rooted deeply in Scripture. In particular, they often refer to the teaching of Jesus on relationships in the Gospels. This is not to say that Jesus taught extensively and systematically on marriage and sexuality – he did not. But the Gospels open a window onto the world of relationships in Jesus' day, and his interaction with the lives, questions and struggles of those around him. They also tell us that Jesus was loved and nurtured within the marriage of Mary and Joseph.

Jesus uses the imagery of marriage as a way of conveying deeper stories about God. His parables regularly use wedding imagery to describe the good news of life and joy that he brought as well as the demands that God's way of life makes upon us (Luke 14.15-24; Matthew 22.1-14; Matthew 25.1-13). They also depict Jesus as the bridegroom (Mark 2.19,20; John 3.29). Together with stories such as the wedding at Cana, the parables show how weddings were occasions of joy and community bonding, and an important and normal part of daily life.

In the background of stories and teaching we catch glimpses – though only glimpses – of how marriage worked in Jesus' context. Those glimpses can help us understand the cultural backdrop to Jesus' more overt teaching. Marriage was dominated by agreements between men, transferring responsibility and support of a girl from her father to her husband. There were dowries, gifts, a wedding feast and, at times, legal documents (though these would usually have been the preserve of those educated and rich enough to be able to read). There is very little indication that they contained an explicitly religious ceremony. They seem instead to have focused on community celebrations. Virginity is regularly emphasized, particularly for women, as we see in the story of Mary, the mother of Jesus. The vulnerability of women who have lost their husbands also comes through repeatedly, with stories such as the parable of the widow's mite (Luke 21.1-4), or the raising of the son of the widow of Nain (Luke 7.11-17). In the world of the first century, women would face hardship and poverty if they did not remarry after being widowed or after divorce, and this forms part of the background to Jesus' sayings.

Jesus' teachings on matters of sexuality are relatively few – under forty verses in all (Matthew 5.27-30, 31,32 [Luke 16.18]; 15.19 [Mark 7.22]; 19.2-9 [Mark 10.2-12]; 19.18 [Mark 10.19]; 22.30 [Mark 12.25; Luke 20.35,36]; and Luke 15.13,30). His teaching on sexuality centers mainly on adultery (Matthew 5.27-30; 15.19 [Mark 7.22]; 19.18 [Mark 10.19]) and divorce (Matthew 5.31,32 [Luke 16.18]; 19.2-9 [Mark 10.2-12]). However, he does also condemn sexual immorality (*porneia*) in general. We find this in a list of sins that he says come from the heart (Matthew 15.19 [Mark 7.22]). The term *porneia* covers a range of sexually immoral practices but can refer more specifically to prostitution, fornication, unchastity, forbidden marriages and, metaphorically, to worshipping any but the one true God.

Although Jesus does not offer a comprehensive account of what marriage is, who should marry, or what a good, positive marriage looks like, we can still glean important insights through his answers to specific questions, such as on divorce or his teaching on adultery.

Mark 10.2-12 and Matthew 19.3-12

Two of the main texts that open a window onto Jesus' view of marriage are the parallel accounts of Mark 10.2-12 and Matthew 19.3-12. In both of these, Jesus is asked about the legitimacy of divorce.

Jesus' teachings on divorce are quite stark. The law assumed that divorce happened and gave instructions as to how divorce should be conducted (Deuteronomy 24.1-4). It gave very little specific indication of what circumstances or grievances would justify divorce. By the time of Jesus, there was considerable discussion of what kinds of behaviour might justify divorce and how divorce ought to be conducted. Famously, the eminent Jewish teachers Hillel and Shammai disagreed over grounds for divorce. Hillel permitted divorce even if a woman cooked her husband a bad meal, whereas Rabbi Shammai only permitted it in the case of adultery (Mishnah, Gittin 9.10). No Jewish teacher that we know of ever questioned whether divorce ought to be permitted at all – except Jesus.

Some Pharisees came, and to test him they asked, 'Is it lawful for a man to divorce his wife?' He answered them, 'What did Moses command you?' They said, 'Moses allowed a man to write a certificate of dismissal and to divorce her.' But Jesus said to them,

'Because of your hardness of heart he wrote this commandment for you. But from the beginning of creation, "God made them male and female." "For this reason a man shall leave his father and mother and be joined to his wife, and the two shall become one flesh." So they are no longer two, but one flesh. Therefore what God has joined together, let no one separate.'

Then in the house the disciples asked him again about this matter. He said to them, 'Whoever divorces his wife and marries another commits adultery against her; and if she divorces her husband and marries another, she commits adultery' (Mark 10.2-12).

Given that every other rabbi taught that God's Law permitted men to divorce their wives, Jesus' teaching here in Mark 10 seems remarkably restrictive, though we should note that in Matthew 19 he is closer to Rabbi Shammai's position in cases of adultery.

The question about divorce posed to Jesus refers to what men could do to women – the woman being comparatively powerless in the relationship. It is a negative question, meant as a test – and Jesus does not simply provide an answer in the terms set. Instead, he roots his answer in a positive account of marriage, linked to the creation stories, with the words 'in the beginning'. The creation accounts themselves do not mention marriage as such, but Jesus clearly associates them with the practice – and reads them in a way that affirms the mutuality between the couple rather than reinforcing uneven power dynamics.

As we saw in Chapter 3, the link between creation and marriage that has formed the basis of Christian understandings of marriage is legitimized and underlined by Jesus' teaching. Whilst the stories of Genesis portray God as blessing the couple so they are fruitful and produce children (1.28) and bringing the woman to the man (2.23), there is no explicit mention in those stories of God joining them together in an indissoluble bond. So here we see Jesus extending the meaning of the creation story, and introducing the idea that God is actively taking part in the 'joining together' of a couple.

Jesus talks about a couple becoming 'one flesh'. In Hebrew, in the creation story, this most likely refers to the two becoming one kin, one people (see Genesis 29.14 and 2 Samuel 5.1) rather than just sexual union. The saying therefore alludes to the wider setting for marriage, that of families and communities. Quoting this verse in the context of a discussion on divorce points to the wider social consequences and effects of marriage breakdown too. The phrase 'one flesh' in Greek more readily points to sexual union, but the connotations of the Hebrew are still present.

Jesus' answer also refers back to the creation of 'male and female', taken as the presupposition for his next quote; in other words, God created human beings male and female, and, on this basis, a man will leave his father and mother and be joined to his wife. This is often read as an affirmation that marriage is by nature the union of a man and a woman, because it is rooted in the biological differentiation between men and women in creation, and in the possibility of procreation (the result of God's blessing in Genesis 2). It is also the case that Jesus is answering a specific question about whether it is lawful for a man to divorce his wife, and he is therefore giving a specific answer to a specific question about men and women. Some would argue that just because Jesus affirms one type of relationship it does not necessarily invalidate other shapes of relationship as long as they are consistent with what Scripture affirms as good and holy. In Jesus' cultural context marriage would only have applied to a man and a woman, which means, some suggest, that both the question and the answer take that for granted.

Several other features of Jesus' answer are worth noting. First, he redirects his questioners' attention to the principles underlying the law of Moses. In this case, the principle underlying the permission for divorce was not the gift of God in creation, but the reality of sin and brokenness: 'hardness of hearts'. In a context where divorce was particularly hard on women, and left them vulnerable and needing to remarry quickly to ensure their survival and that of their children, a certificate of divorce was needed for them to prove they were free to marry and not committing adultery. Jesus, however, makes a move that breaks with tradition. He does not focus on women alone being at risk of committing adultery, but argues that men who remarry are also committing adultery. He introduces a mutuality that was absent in the law of Moses, and goes some way towards redressing the power imbalance of ancient marriages. Bringing in the Genesis passage about being 'one flesh' was also a way to redirect attention from legal to moral questions, and challenge the men who had sought to test him.

The strength of Jesus' comments against divorce need to be read against the specific setting of those testing him with their questions, as well as their focus on a man's rights. Jesus does not dismiss the possibility of divorce, but rather reaffirms God's intention for marriage and sets divorce in the context of human brokenness.

Second, it is worth noting that Jesus says nothing about procreation. Marriage here, just as in Genesis, is not seen as solely linked to the possibility of children, but as a good and valuable part of God's design for humanity in and of itself, though of course the arrival of children would have been a normal expectation in a culture without modern means of contraception.

This passage therefore opens up a window onto Jesus' view of marriage, a view both steeped in the culture and expectations of his time, yet challenging to his hearers, and using the biblical tradition in unexpected ways.

Matthew 5.27-30
The first set of teaching we looked at was limited by its setting as an answer to a question on divorce. The other major set of teaching of Jesus in relation to marriage concerns adultery. Once again therefore we will gather clues about his view of marriage obliquely, as a by-product of a discussion of what is going wrong in the world around him.

Jesus mentions adultery in a list of vices (Matthew 15.19; Mark 7.22) and he affirms the commandment given in Exodus 20.14, 'you shall not commit adultery' (Matthew 19.18; Mark 10.19). However, he only explores what he means by this command in one place, Matthew 5.27-30:

You have heard that it was said, 'You shall not commit adultery.' But I say to you that everyone who looks at a woman with lust has already committed adultery with her in his heart. If your right eye causes you to sin, tear it out and throw it away; it is better for you to lose one of your members than for your whole body to be thrown into hell. And if your right hand causes you to sin, cut it off and throw it away; it is better for you to lose one of your members than for your whole body to go into hell.

Here Jesus expands on the commandment not to commit adultery. In the law of Moses, it was addressed to Jewish men, and applied specifically to a man sleeping with a woman already married to someone else. Technically, sexual relations by a married man with an unmarried woman or a prostitute would not be adultery, whereas any sexual relationship outside marriage would be considered adultery for a married woman. Once again, Jesus confounds expectations and extends the reach of the Mosaic laws. He extends the prohibition to include not only sexual intercourse with another woman (assuming the man is married) or with a married woman (if the man is not married) but to nurturing sexual desire for another woman (whether married or not). The language used ('in order to desire') makes it clear that Jesus is talking of feeding desire here rather than sexual attraction in and of itself. The context of marriage and adultery makes it equally clear that Jesus is not prohibiting sexual attraction between an unmarried man and an unmarried woman.

Jesus' language is deliberately strong and provocative. He is making his point forcefully and graphically, and with some hyperbole to underline its importance. The focus is not only on faithfulness and the prohibition of adultery, but widens to encompass questions of attitudes and responsibility (as with the other examples this text is set alongside). The issue here is about intent, rather than just actions. Jesus made a shift from what can be prosecuted in a court of law – murder and adultery – to how we relate to one another and think of each other. In particular, he stresses, (together with other Jewish teachers of the time) that men should take responsibility for their sexuality. Women are not a danger or threat, and cannot be blamed for men's own attitudes and excesses. Just as with the example above, Jesus is implicitly addressing some of the power dynamics inherent in marriage at the time, as well as reaffirming the importance of fidelity and commitment.

The teaching of Jesus therefore indirectly provides us with specific statements on marriage. The focus on adultery and divorce reinforces the importance of faithfulness and commitment, whilst introducing a stronger notion of mutuality and reciprocity than were present in the mosaic laws, in line with the evolution of rabbinic teaching at the time. Yet this focus on problematic sexual activity is set within a wider context of taking marriage and weddings as a positive aspect of life, one that is suited to help illustrate the nature of God, of God's kingdom, and God's relationship with humanity. This is imagery that will be extended in the rest of the New Testament, particularly in the letters of Paul. Perhaps most important for our purpose here is Jesus' use of Old Testament texts to root faithful committed relationships into the order of creation, and his description of God being active in the joining together of two people in marriage.

Sex

Finally, in this chapter on holy living, and on the disciplines and rules of life that are part of discipleship, we need to talk about sex. Sexual relationships are one particular area (amongst many others) in which self-denial matters. Think, for instance, of some of the constraints upon sexual activity that we have already explored in this book. We have spoken about the need

- to pay proper attention to consent, and to be aware of the power dynamics that can skew it (in marriage, no less than in other contexts);

- to refuse to treat a sexual partner as nothing more than a means to our own gratification;

- to take responsibility for the consequences our sexual behaviours have on others; and

- to hold to the promises of faithfulness that we make.

Abiding by constraints like these is not automatic. At times, they run against our inclinations – and, in the area of sexual desire, our inclinations can be very strong indeed. They demand discipline, not just in the sense that they demand the sometimes stern exercise of our wills, denying ourselves something that we want – but in the sense that they are habits we have to learn, to practise, to get better at over time. We need support from those around us, and ways of being held accountable for our actions.

See Chapter 3 (pages 32-34) for a discussion about the gift of sex in marriage. See Chapter 5 (pages 78-85) for a discussion about sex in contemporary society and Chapter 6 (pages 114-115) about the relationship between sex and well-being. Go to Scene 2 (pages 389-396) for a conversation about Christian perspectives on sex and relationships.

Chastity

Today, the word 'chastity' simply means 'sexual abstinence'. In earlier discussions, it was often used for all forms of 'appropriate restraint and moderation in sexual matters'.[289] It may be a word that is now impossible to retrieve, given the connotations it has acquired – but a chaste sexual life is not necessarily, in traditional discussions, one in which there is an absence of sex or an absence of pleasure in sex. A chaste life is one in which sexual activity is rightly ordered, and serves the true flourishing of those involved.

To understand what this means more deeply, we need to understand what sex is for, within the story of faith, hope and love. There are, in the Christian tradition, two main answers – and they are suggested by the first two chapters of Genesis.

The first answer is suggested in Genesis 1.28. Immediately after hearing that God created human beings 'male and female', we are told that 'God blessed them, and God said to them, "Be fruitful and multiply."' Sex is not directly referred to, but it is implied: these human beings are meant to reproduce – and to fill the earth. Sex exists, in part, for the sake of reproduction – for the continuation of the human race. It is, as we saw in Part One, a way in which life is given to others, to the world. But fruitfulness here is not simply about biological descent, but about human beings, together, caring for the earth and for one another, imaging the God who cares for all of creation.

The other answer is suggested in the next chapter:

The LORD God said, 'It is not good that the man should be alone; I will make him a helper as his partner.' ... So the LORD God caused a deep sleep to fall upon the man, and he slept; then he took one of his ribs and closed up its place with flesh. And the rib that the LORD God had taken from the man he made into a woman and brought her to the man. Then the man said,

'This at last is bone of my bones
and flesh of my flesh;
this one shall be called Woman,
for out of Man this one was taken.'

Therefore a man leaves his father and his mother and clings to his wife, and they become one flesh. And the man and his wife were both naked, and were not ashamed. (Genesis 2.18, 21-25)

Here, the couple's sexual relationship seems to come more directly into view. It finds its meaning in the context of the partnership between them – and in their mutual support in the task of tending the garden. Sex, here, has to do with mutuality, companionship and shared endeavour, and with the joining into one of two people, and their helping each other, being partners together in God's work in creation.

In the light of the poetry of the Song of Solomon (discussed in Chapter 3 and again below), we might go further. Sex serves the mutuality, companionship and unity of a couple by enabling them to delight in one another. Nothing we have said about the need to avoid a one-sided gratification means that sex can't be about mutual delight – and a delight that is overwhelming, passionate and physical.

Former Archbishop of Canterbury Rowan Williams has written about the way that sex can be a context for learning. If it is to be more than one-sided gratification – if, that is, it is to be an experience of mutual delight – then each partner's seeking of their own delight is wrapped up with their seeking of the other's delight, and with their delight in the other's delight in them.

> For my body to be the cause of joy, the end of homecoming, for me, it must be there for someone else, be perceived, accepted, nurtured; and that means being given over to the creation of joy in that other, because only as directed to the enjoyment, the happiness, of the other does it become unreservedly lovable. To desire my joy is to desire the joy of the one I desire: my search for enjoyment through the bodily presence of another is a longing to be enjoyed in my body.[290]

A sexual relationship in which there is genuine mutuality can be one way in which we learn to recognize ourselves as lovable and as loved. We can learn not just to think that, but to feel it, to experience it. And this can, Williams suggests, help us to recognize ourselves as 'being the object of the causeless loving delight of God'.[291] It is not the only route to such knowledge, or an infallible route – but for a Christian who is learning the intertwined love of self, neighbour and God, a sexual relationship can be one more context for that journey.

The role that sex can play is connected, however, to the quality of the relationship that is its context. Most obviously, it assumes that sex takes place in a relationship that is loving – one in which each partner cares for and delights in the other. It assumes that each partner has the good of the other at heart. It also assumes that sex takes place in a relationship that is faithful – one in which each partner has committed to being there for the other, and taking this journey of learning together. It assumes that each partner can rest in the knowledge that they are safe with the other – that they are held together by their vows, and not by their appearance or by their sexual performance. Williams therefore says

> I believe that the promise of faithfulness, the giving of unlimited time to each other, remains central for understanding the full 'resourcefulness' and grace of sexual union. I simply don't think we'd grasp all that was involved in the mutual transformation of sexually linked persons without the reality of unconditional public commitments: more perilous, more demanding, more promising.[292]

This picture – of two people taking a lifelong journey on which they learn to love and be loved, and in the process learn more of God's love – can become idealized in a way that does not take account of the actual conditions of human life. All people involved in sexual relationships fall short of it in numerous ways. We fail in the care, consideration and commitment involved – sometimes disastrously so. Marriages can become contexts for exploitation, degradation and danger. They can become unrecognizable in comparison to God's intention for them. Here, as in every other area of our lives, we stand in need of God's challenge to our selfishness and our distorted desires, and of God's mercy and forgiveness, God's help and, in some cases, liberation.

In the Church of England, we agree on condemning sexual relationships that are exploitative, in all the kinds of ways discussed earlier. We also agree on promoting the kind of faithfulness and loving commitment described above. We disagree, however, in other respects.

Some of us maintain – in line with the Church of England's teaching in this area – that marriage between a man and a woman, held together by promises before God and the wider community, is the only proper context for a sexual relationship. Those living in sexual relationships other than marriage are to be welcomed into the life of the church and should not be shamed or condemned – but growing in Christ and walking the path of holiness will involve recognizing the need to live differently in this area, as in other areas, of their life.

Some of us say that the critical point in a relationship is where the couple have committed themselves to the lifelong relationship of marriage, and that this promise to be with and for each other and for whatever children come from their union, is the point at which sexual intercourse becomes a fully responsible action of love.

The Song of Solomon

'I am my beloved's and my beloved is mine' (Song of Solomon 6.3, cf. 2.16). These simple and expressive words stand at the heart of the Song. They imply trust and mutual delight. They also imply a transformed identity, whereby one person now recognizes that they are constituted by their relationship to another. They are not isolated or autonomous, but are discovering self and life in mutual self-giving with one another.

It is because such a portrayal of love is central to the Song that it becomes natural to read this language about two human lovers as also depicting a relationship of love between humans and God. The relational dynamics, if not identical, are similar. The notion that love is a relationship of mutual trust and delight, and that this is transformative of life as a whole, is central to the biblical portrayal of God and humanity.

The Song presents the lovers as now united, now divided, now finding each other, now being separated. This is a dynamic that resonates readily with the spiritual life, where moments of intimacy with God are often fleeting. It also resonates with the ebb and flow of human intimate relationships, in which the quest for intimacy must be ever renewed. The note on which the book ends is that of continued longing: 'Make haste, my beloved...' (8.14). One of the effects of this is to see the lovers' desire as dynamic, never able to rest, never able to think that 'they have made it'. Complacency has no place in the love of this Song.

The woman speaks extensively, and she speaks first at the outset of the poem. There is no sense of hierarchy or subordination, in which the woman is inferior or must wait to speak. The Song is radical and unusual in the way that the woman is entirely free to express and celebrate her female sexual desire and pleasure, and she sets the tone for the Song as a whole.

The Song in itself is not concerned with the social dimensions of marriage, the union of families or the raising of children. Even the woman's precise status in relation to the man is unclear. Its interest is solely with the relationship between the man and the woman who call each other, 'my love', 'my beloved'. The focus is on desire and delight in the other person and of themselves. Again, analogies with relationship with God readily come to the fore.

The Song's focus on the relationship between the woman and the man as desirable and precious in and of itself has real resonance with some contemporary concerns that focus on a relationship of love as a good in itself, irrespective of children or family ties. This is hardly to suggest that the Song could underwrite free sexual relationships between the unmarried in a certain contemporary mode. There are numerous reasons for this: the Song focuses on one, and one only, as the object of love; the ready analogy with relationship with God puts interpretative priority on trust, commitment, persistence and faithfulness; and the Song should not be used in isolation from other voices in Scripture. Nonetheless, the distinctive note that the Song sounds should be heard, in its celebration of physical, even erotic, love, and its pure delight in a relationship of intimacy.

Some of us hold that faithful commitment can take other forms than marriage, and that there are many people who in other ways have made a commitment to live together as a couple that the church can recognize as good, while at the same time also inviting them to take a further step to confirm that commitment before God and the community.

Some of us say that sexual activity belongs as appropriately to same-sex as it does to opposite-sex relationships – whether we think that means within a same-sex marriage, or within the relationships of those who have committed themselves to marriage, or within other patterns of faithful commitment.

Conclusion

The journey of discipleship is costly. For the sake of the abundant life which God invites us into, various kinds of self-denial, discipline and restraint are called for. We need to unlearn old habits, and learn new ones. We need to practise relating to one another in ways that can produce mutual love, joy and peace. Although we were made for these things, they don't come naturally to us.

This pattern of self-denial for the sake of abundant life is a characteristic shape of life lived within the story of love and faith. We have seen something of how it can play out in the celibate vocations that some Christians experience. We have seen it in the vows of faithfulness that are made in marriage. We have seen it in the mutuality, consent and faithfulness called for in sexual relationships.

We have also, once again, encountered Christian disagreements, especially in relation to the patterns of discipline appropriate for lesbian and gay people. Those are not disagreements about whether discipleship is costly, or whether it calls for the sometimes difficult reordering of our desires. They are not disagreements about whether Christians are called to self-denial and restraint. They are disagreements about the specific disciplines we are called to and about the ways in which those disciplines work for people in different situations.

How can Christians discern what in our lives corresponds to God's good intentions, and what does not? How do we learn what is good, right and holy – and what is sinful? It is clear that different Christians are answering this question of discernment differently.

In the course of this book so far, however, we have seen some of the factors that can feed in to that process of discernment:

- Investigation of what the Bible says, and whether it tells us that something in our lives runs counter to God's intentions.

- Exploration of what the Church has said over time, including the ways in which it has articulated its understanding of God and God's ways with the world, but also the ways in which it has categorized and treated people.

- Scientific discussions about how different facets of our experience have arisen, and about their wider effects, including their impact on our physical and mental well-being.

- Reports of people's own experience, and of whether we experience something as a problem, a form of brokenness or as a gift that brings our healing and restores our wholeness.

- Discussions of the culture in which we are involved, and which we have all to some extent internalized – and which might have shaped very deeply how we experience ourselves.

The problem is that we disagree – and disagree deeply – about how these factors (and others) go together, and about how they should inform our judgements. The nature and sources of these disagreements are the subject of **Part Four**.

Encounters

Meet WILL

Will grew up in a Christian home and has always found his faith to be 'a source of strength and warmth and comfort'. He lives in the north, on the outskirts of the large city where he is a software developer and lives down the road from the church he belongs to. It's a close-knit community of people who are in and out of each other's homes, committed to seeing God at work in this visibly tough area.

It wasn't until he was 18 that Will realized he was gay. 'For a year I prayed, "God, I don't really want to be gay. And if you can change that, it would give me some comfort and peace. But your will be done." After a year I stopped praying that "change me" prayer, and tried to say, "God let me just accept what you want for my life", and that for me means celibacy until God makes a change which he may or may not do, and I'm not counting on it. So I'm a 25-year-old who is expecting to be celibate for my whole life.'

'Suffering is really fruitful in the church, but we're scared of it.'

Will talks about how the prevailing culture makes this difficult. 'There's no music that's for me, because music is about love and sex. And it's not uncommon that you hear stuff on the radio being very kind and loving towards Christians who've chosen to embrace their sexuality and enter relationships. But it seems like it's too scary for them to publicly defend people in my situation. But that just means that we're abandoned. [...] I guess part of the problem with this issue is that people don't want to inflict suffering on each other, so they try to find a shortcut out of it. Suffering is really fruitful in the church, but we're scared of it.'

Will has built up many strong friendships in his church, but, he says, 'friendships don't meet all the loneliness needs that a relationship does. I'm not even just talking about sex, because I think living without sex is hard, but living without someone who you always know is going to be with you in whatever frame of mind you're in, always there [...] next to you, and physically touching skin. You can't get that from a friendship. Male friendships, or at least my male friendships, are kind of non-touchy. Definitely lacking physical touch.

'The Bible is quite positive about singleness – making you more available and useful for doing God's work. So, I thought, it means that I'm going to have a more intimate close relationship with God. My prayer life is probably more intense than other people's. But I've been realizing that it's not the same thing. I thought that God would be there sort of personally. And I'm not really sure that's the way I see things anymore because it hasn't come to fruition in that way. I can't say, "Well, I'm not lonely, because I've got God."'

Will goes on to talk about his mental health. 'I've had really quite bad mental health. So from the age of 19 I've just had a building feeling of sadness, loneliness, anxiety. For the last five years, I've struggled with suicidal thoughts every day. And I made three attempts on my life. And it's not because I believe that I'm condemned or that life isn't valuable as a single person, it's just that it's really hard.

'I'd like to feel supported in my decision to follow my understanding of the Bible. I experience a lot of pressure on me and my local church from other Christians and non-Christians to change to a different reading of the Bible. I'm fine living in a wider church that contains churches that affirm same-sex relationships. As long as we can have the conversation about it. I'd just like to feel safe *inside* the church – so that we're encouraging each other to be bold and different *outside* the church.'

Meet SOPHIE

Sophie describes herself as a gay, cisgendered woman in her forties. She and her partner, Rosie, have lived together for twelve years and been in a civil partnership for eleven years. They have two children, aged ten and nine. 'So we are a good, strong family unit. Their father is a very good friend of ours, who's a gay man who agreed to be a donor for us. So, both of us gave birth to one child each, but they've got the same biological father, who's very involved in their lives. He wears

'I think that sometimes within the church culture, we don't notice how odd we Christians seem to others.'

a big pink handbag over his shoulder and he's fantastic. So, our son's christening was in our Anglican church. Adrian and his partner were there, my partner and I were there. And all our extended relatives; it was just beautiful.

'At the school my children go to, there are more families who have same-sex parents than there are families who go to church regularly. So, for my daughter, having lesbian mothers is not even something she notices. But saying that she's a Christian is weird and strange. I think that sometimes within the church culture, we don't notice how odd we Christians seem to others.'

Sophie – and eventually the family – found their spiritual home in the Metropolitan Community Church. Sophie was actively involved in leading the church for a number of years. She often found it to be a place of refuge for LGBTI+ people from other churches. She remembers 'in my 20s looking at what was going on in the Church of England and mostly feeling pity for those poor gay people who were trapped in what was quite an unhealthy and prejudiced and unpleasant hierarchical organization. And the people who fell out of those churches came to MCC and we welcomed them. We told them that they were loved. And you saw people change from frightened, closed in people whose self-worth was so low coming to know the God who made them and loved them, and opening up, and just growing and changing and transforming. People having been hurt by mainstream churches transforming into people who knew themselves to be loved.'

Prayer has been a vital part of Sophie's life: 'I suppose I prayed a lot more than most 16- or 17-year-olds do when I first knew I was gay.' When the family decided to start worshipping at their local parish, Sophie sensed a call to ordained ministry in the Church of England. This was a decision that she had to wrestle with in prayer, especially as Rosie found it hard to support Sophie being ordained in a church that does not allow clergy to be in same-sex sexual relationships.

The Gospel text about Jesus and his disciples eating grains of corn on a Sabbath proved to be decisive in enabling Sophie to continue to pursue the path to ordination: 'It was almost like Jesus was saying, "Well, I'm Lord of the church. Some people might have done some bad stuff to it, but I made it, and that makes it good. And if I want you in that field eating that grain, then that's where you're going."'

Meet AUSTIN

Austin knew he was different when he was about four years old, when he told his preschool teacher how beautiful a young lad dressed as a soldier was. He was roundly told off by his teacher – a memory that has haunted him ever since. He joined an evangelical youth group. Same-sex relationships weren't talked about and so Austin just prayed that his sexual feelings – which he thought were sinful – would go away.

'The more you pretend, I think the less you are as a human being.'

Eventually he plucked up the courage to talk to a GP in his congregation whose advice was to 'find a good woman and get married'. So that's what he did – but the feelings didn't go away. The marriage lasted 14 years. He had a good job, they had a big house, two cars and two sons.

It was when he started training for ordination that things began to intensify – to such a degree that one day, when waiting for the train, 'all of a sudden everything went into slow motion, like the train and the tracks and the train and tracks…' Austin recounts that it was a vision of one of his sons holding a teddy that saved him from doing anything at that moment. But it was then, also, that he knew he 'had to do something. We couldn't live like that.'

At this point in the story, Austin breaks off to talk about people who call themselves same-sex attracted and remain celibate. 'They say they acknowledge their feelings but won't do anything about them. Well, I did that for 14 years, but you can't do it forever. Well, you can, but I think you then look back on your life and think, oh gosh, I didn't live. I wasn't real, I wasn't… The more you pretend, I think the less you are as a human being. I remember when I was married and I couldn't touch Caroline easily or hold hands, but then neither could I have warm embraces or friendships with other people because I wasn't who I was.'

He also reflects at length on trans people, empathizing with the difficulties they face when deciding to transition: 'It's painful but it's releasing. It's painful for people around, of course, because a lot of people can't understand it; I understand that. But what about the person themselves who has had to endure bullying and self-harm and feelings of suicide – what about that person? They haven't just woken up one day and said, "I think I'll be trans tomorrow because it's an ideology I think I'll follow." […] I just think we need to understand that people do feel like that and there's nothing wrong with them and God hasn't made a mistake because if you go down the line of God making mistakes then, well, you go down the line of disabled; it's crazy isn't it?'

Austin is now a vicar and happily partnered with Simon, who also plays an active part in the life of the church. Austin has excellent relationships with his adult sons and his former wife. He describes his story as 'a happy story'.

Meet MIA AND HER FAMILY

Mia grew up in the Far East in a non-religious family. Her family moved to the UK where she was invited to a Baptist church at around the age of 13 by her next-door neighbour. She became a Christian. For Mia finding faith also meant finding somewhere to belong in an otherwise new culture. 'I found my safety and security within that environment, but it was quite a strict environment. The men were the leaders of the church and views of the moral code, I would say, were very, very strong in that church... The teaching was that you didn't sleep around before you got married and all that business. In terms of sexuality, homosexuality was not really God's will for you. That was the sort of teaching about that.'

> 'everyone else was sleeping around and living together, but we weren't, and it was very hard to explain that.'

Mia went to a college in London where she found a very different culture than the one she had been a part of at her church and also in her Asian background. 'The biggest society was the LGBT one. I met people that I'd never met in my cosy church. I began to sort of wonder how I would marry up my faith and what I thought God was telling me about holy human behaviour with the actual people that were becoming my really, really good friends.

'I got married to my husband and he was the same as me. We followed the very traditional route, as you would; we sort of followed all the rules. But there were lots of our friends that didn't and it was always kind of difficult really – when you make that choice that you think comes out of what you're taught in the church. Yes, everyone else was sleeping around and living together, but we weren't, and it was very hard to explain that. The only way that we were taught to explain that was that this is what holy life looks like. But that's just not very friendly; it's not very realistic.'

Her own daughters have found her adherence puzzling. 'They'll say to me, "Did you not live with other people before you met dad?" "No." "Why not?" Try to translate what we'd felt was the teaching of the church to them, and it seems like we're talking a different language completely.'

Mia reflects on the attitude of her eldest daughter. 'She is heterosexual but she's got lots of gay friends. She says the thing that puts her off church most is when people don't accept gay people. This generation has grown up with different sexualities and the idea that people are fluid. If people in church can't get their head around it, it puts them off church. It's so fundamental to who they are, you know?'

Almighty God, Father of all mercies, we your unworthy servants give you most humble and hearty thanks for all your goodness and loving kindness.

We bless you for our creation, preservation, and all the blessings of this life; but above all for your immeasurable love in the redemption of the world by our Lord Jesus Christ, for the means of grace, and for the hope of glory.

And give us, we pray, such a sense of all your mercies that our hearts may be unfeignedly thankful, and that we show forth your praise, not only with our lips, but in our lives, by giving up ourselves to your service, and by walking before you in holiness and righteousness all our days;

through Jesus Christ our Lord, to whom, with you and the Holy Spirit, be all honour and glory, for ever and ever. Amen.

Common Worship: adapted from
The Book of Common Prayer

PART FOUR

Seeking
answers:
how do we
hear God?

The purpose of Part Four is to consider how we go about seeking and finding answers to the question, what does it mean for us as individuals and as a church to be Christlike when it comes to matters of identity, sexuality, relationships and marriage? And how is it that we reach different conclusions from one another about these things when we are all seeking to follow Jesus?

In **Chapter 13** we begin, once again, with the Bible, affirming its revelatory purpose and transforming power as we explore what is involved in reading and interpreting it. How do followers of Christ come to different conclusions, especially about the texts that are often used in discussions about identity, sexuality, relationships and marriage?

Chapter 14 reminds us that God forms us through our life together as the Church. How are we – or should we be – formed by the Church's history and tradition, its global character, its universal calling, its great diversity?

Chapter 15 explores how we are shaped by God's creation. What insights does our understanding of the natural world offer about human identity, sexuality, relationships and marriage?

In **Chapter 16** we think about the question of culture and its relationship to the gospel. How do we discern God's presence in our culture? What aspects of culture resonate with the gospel? And how and when are we called to challenge culture – perhaps both within and outside the Church?

Chapter 17 invites us to consider the place of individual conviction and conscience in our Christian life. How do we discern what is of God and what is of us? How do we respond to Christians whose convictions are different from our own?

In **Chapter 18** we turn to prayer in the confidence that God is a God who loves to communicate with us and to guide us into all truth.

How are we to 'discern what is the will of God – what is good and acceptable and perfect' (Romans 12.2)?

Part One began with God and God's gift of life, life together, experienced in relationships with God and with each other in families, friendship and marriage.

Part Two explored questions that we face, as a society and as a church, in the midst of changing attitudes and practices in these areas.

Part Three asked how those questions relate to the story Christians tell about God and God's ways with the world – the story of faith, hope and love. It showed that there are, in that story, rich resources for a response: there is good news for the world about identity, sexuality, relationships and marriage. Part Three also showed, however, that Christians have different ways of drawing on those resources, and at times have different understandings of what that good news might be.

Part Four asks how Christians learn to tell this story, and why they sometimes tell it differently. It asks how God seeks to communicate with the world in order to transform it, and it asks how we in turn discern what God is saying and doing among us. What sources should we turn to? What kind of thinking should we be doing? What is really at stake in the differences between us?

Part Four is the 'Method' section of this book.

When we know the way to our destination we don't need to consult a map. We don't normally need to talk about method. Much of the time, we know what route to take, how to go on with our lives. Our muscle memory, our habits, our patterns of imagination and understanding, our structures and institutions – much of the time, they seem to work, and they carry us through.

Even when questions and difficulties arise, we don't normally need to talk about method. We find our bearings by using familiar landmarks. We turn to familiar resources to find answers. In the church, we look to our habitual ways of telling the Christian story. We draw on familiar Scriptures in familiar ways. We listen to the same people we have listened to before. We apply well-trusted patterns of thinking to new topics.

However, we do need to get the map out when we are confused, either about the destination or about how to get there. Similarly we only need to talk about method when something has gone wrong, or seems to be going wrong – when these familiar habits aren't enough. These habits might have left us with disagreements that we don't seem able to resolve. They might have left us not knowing what to make of particular people's experience, or how to respond to their pain. They might have left us unsure what sense to make of new discoveries. They might have left us talking past one another, frustrated that communication seems to have broken down. Talking about method is a way of checking the workings of our normal ways of thinking, to see why we're not making the progress we had hoped for. Taking the map out and looking at it together might help us to understand how the different trajectories we have followed take us to different destinations.

That's why this discussion comes now, in Part Four. It is an attempt to diagnose the difficulties that we ran into in Part Three – the apparently incompatible answers that Christians have produced, and keep on producing, to the questions raised in Part Two.

A shared foundation

When we do check the workings of our ways of thinking, the first thing we find is that there is much that Christians share. In particular, there is a deep common shape to all our responses.

We are all seeking answers as people who worship the triune God: Father, Son, and Holy Spirit. We believe in a God who made the whole world for love, and who made human beings in God's own image. We believe in a God whose love for the world never dims, even when the world turns away (Romans 5.8; John 3.16). We believe in a God who calls the world back into love – into a life so filled with love that there is no room left for fear, hatred, or despair (1 John 4.18). And we believe that it is good and right to turn to God as we seek answers to the questions that face us. 'For he is our God, and we are the people of his pasture, and the sheep of his hand. O that today you would listen to his voice!' (Psalm 95.7).

We are seeking answers as followers of Jesus. We believe that Jesus, crucified and risen, is God's Word spoken to the world, calling all people out of brokenness and sin and into flourishing life (1 Peter 2.9). We believe that Jesus is God's gift of love to the world, that he shows us what God's love truly is, and that he calls us to embody that love ourselves (John 3.16; 1 John 4.10-12). And we believe that Jesus is not dead but alive, that we have been welcomed into his family, and that he continues to speak to guide us (Acts 9.4,5; 23.11). We believe that, as we seek answers, we need to hear again and again this Word spoken to the world in Jesus, and to be obedient to that Word.

We are seeking answers as people who depend upon the Holy Spirit. We believe that God's Holy Spirit guides and teaches us, taking us deeper into knowledge of Jesus and of what following Jesus demands (John 14.26; 16.13). We believe the Spirit gives us the Bible to tell us of all that God has done for us, and supremely to witness to Jesus. We believe that, in all kinds of ways, it is possible for us to listen to the prompting of the Spirit – to have our eyes opened, our minds shaped, our lives given direction, by the Spirit's guidance. We believe that the Spirit calls us to the recognition of our failings, to penitence, and to new life. We believe that, as we seek answers to our questions, we need to listen to what the Spirit has said in the past and to how the Spirit is working and speaking in our world today.

We also agree that our quest for answers needs to be rooted in prayer. We need God's help to hear God's voice. We need the Spirit's guidance and inspiration to set our feet on the right path. There is a lot that we can do to seek out answers, but ultimately we have to offer all our work up to God, in frank acknowledgement that it cannot be enough. At every step of the way, we need God's help. In prayer, we focus our thoughts, our imaginations and our affections on God, and we ask God to unmake and remake them in ways that go beyond anything that our own efforts could achieve.

We make that prayer in trust. We can't trust in our own abilities. There is no method that will guarantee that we will follow Christ faithfully and know how to speak the good news of Christ to the world. Instead, we place our trust in God (Psalm 146; 1 Peter 1.21). We believe that God speaks, not to issue arbitrary instructions, nor to pass on information in the abstract, but to call all God's creatures into fellowship with God and with one another. We believe that God's speech is richly effective, bringing new life into being (Isaiah 55.10,11). In seeking to hear what God is saying to us and to the world, we trust that God can speak, has spoken, and will speak.

The road ahead

In Part Four, we will ask

- How does God speak in Scripture – through all the words gathered together in the pages of the Bible?

- How does God speak through the Church – through its present life and through the whole history of its existence?

- How does God speak through creation – through the whole world that God has made, which we are a part of?

- How does God speak through voices from beyond the Church – through the questions and discoveries and challenges of our wider culture, which God sends us into with good news?

- How does God speak through the shaping of people's consciences and convictions – the deep patterns of their belief and imagination, formed by their faith and their experience?

We believe that God graciously speaks to us in all these ways, and that we can all learn to hear and recognize God's voice (John 10.3-5). God doesn't speak through all of them in the same way, and they don't all have the same priority for us – we will, for instance, be talking about the Bible's unique authority – but in all of them we are listening for the one voice of God: the voice that has its fullest and richest expression in Jesus. We are seeking to root our thought, speech and action in Jesus, so as to take captive every thought in service to him (2 Corinthians 10.5).

> **O Lord, from whom all good things do come:**
> **Grant to us thy humble servants,**
> **that by thy holy inspiration,**
> **we may think those things that be good,**
> **and by thy merciful guiding may perform the same,**
> **through our Lord Jesus Christ.**[293]

CHAPTER 13

The Bible

The life of the Church is soaked in the Bible. Go to any Anglican church and you will drink the Bible in week by week or even day by day in worship.

It will pour over you in the prayers you say, the songs you sing, the sermons you hear, and probably from the windows and the walls of the building that surrounds you. And you will constantly hear it bubble up in our conversations about identity, sexuality, relationships and marriage.

As Christians seek to discern God's will in those areas, we constantly quote, analyse and argue about the Bible.

The Bible holds the central place in our accounts of how we hear the voice of God. In the words of a sermon published in the Church of England's *First Book of Homilies* (1547),

> there can be nothing either more necessary or profitable than the knowledge of Holy Scripture; ... in it is contained God's true word, setting forth his glory, and also man's duty. And there is no truth nor doctrine necessary for our justification and everlasting salvation, but that is, or may be, drawn out of that fountain and well of truth... And as drink is pleasant to them that be dry, and meat to them that be hungry; so is the reading, hearing, searching, and studying of Holy Scripture to them that be desirous to know God, or themselves, and to do his will.[294]

Familiarity with the Bible may be uneven around the Church of England, and rapidly vanishing in wider society, but it remains the bedrock of our faith. If we are trying to discern God's will for our relationships and for the forms of intimacy that we enjoy, it is natural and necessary for us to turn to its pages.

In this chapter, we first look more closely at what the Bible is, and at our shared reasons for turning to it. We then turn to some of the disagreements about the Bible's nature and purpose that shape our arguments about relationships, sex and identity – and how we might respond to those disagreements.

Human and divine

The Bible is a collection of books gathered together over many centuries. It contains laws, poems, stories, letters, wisdom sayings, and prophetic pronouncements. Whenever you read it, every word you read has a human history. Every one of them was written by a human hand, in a particular place and time. Every one was touched by many other hands before it ended up in this collection we call the Bible. The Bible therefore rings with the voices of all kinds of people. It is shaped by their differing backgrounds, their cultures, their assumptions and their experiences – including their affections and desires, their intimate relationships, and their sense of their own identity.

Our own reading of the Bible is no less shaped by history. Our backgrounds, our experience and our assumptions influence how we read – and so do the background, experience and assumptions of all the people who taught us how to read it. When we read, we are as entangled in the tapestry of history as is the Bible.

At the same time, Anglicans believe that the Bible is, in a classic phrase, 'God's Word written',[295] and that God works through our reading of it. We believe these humans' words are words inspired by God (2 Timothy 3.16) and that we can hear God speak to us through them.

On the whole, Anglicans have tried to hold all these claims together. We do not think that the Bible would somehow be *more* the product of God's guiding hand if it were *less* the product of human hands. Our reading of it in the present would not be *more* capable of serving God's purposes for our lives if it could somehow be *less* our own activity.

> **Anglicans affirm the sovereign authority of the Holy Scriptures as the medium through which God by the Spirit communicates his word in the Church and thus enables people to respond with understanding and faith. The Scriptures are 'uniquely inspired witness to divine revelation', and 'the primary norm for Christian faith and life'.**
>
> *The Virginia Report* (1997) [296]

God's purposes

The human authors of the Bible wrote for multiple reasons, and we read their words for many reasons. What, though, can we say about *God's* purposes, and how *God* uses the Bible?

Across our differences, Anglicans affirm that God gives us the Bible for two central and inseparable purposes. The first is to tell us the good news of God's saving love, and the second is to call the whole world into holiness.[297]

Witness to the loving and redeeming purposes of God fulfilled in Jesus is the deep melody around which all the Bible's voices are orchestrated. We read all of its parts gathered into a 'canon' (which means both 'an authoritative list' and 'a standard or norm'), and that canon has Jesus at its centre. We read it in the midst of worship that turns our minds and hearts to that centre.

In the words of the great Elizabethan theologian Richard Hooker,

> The main drift of the whole New Testament is that which St John sets down as the purpose of his own history: *These things are written, that ye might believe that Jesus is Christ the Son of God, and that in believing ye might have life through His Name.* The drift of the Old, that which the Apostle mentions to Timothy: *The Holy Scriptures are able to make thee wise unto salvation.* So that the general end both of Old and New is one.[298]

God speaks to the world through the Bible, guiding, challenging, correcting and encouraging us (Proverbs 3.12; Hebrews 4.12; Jeremiah 15.16). All people are called to turn away from everything in their lives that rejects God, to turn to God in faith, and to grow into loving relationship with one another and with God. God's great purpose is that we 'may share [in] his holiness' (Hebrews 12.10), 'the holiness without which no one will see the Lord' (Hebrews 12.14).

God uses the words of the Bible as a school of righteousness, of justice, and of love. In this school, the deepest learning we undergo is the shaping of our love: our love for God and our love for all our neighbours (Mark 12.29-31). Our reading shapes our desires, our imaginations, our emotions, our habits, our ideas, our relationships, our institutions, the structures of our society, and our cultures. It shapes all the physical stuff of the lives we live as bodily creatures together in the world. All of life is caught up in the curriculum of this school.

Christians make and debate all sorts of other claims about the Bible: claims about how historically factual it is, about its unity and its clarity, about its authority, and about its relationship to all the other ways we hear God. However important these other claims are, the central claim we make together about the Bible is that by the grace of God it is fit for these two purposes. God uses the Bible to witness to the saving work that reaches its fulfilment in Jesus, and God uses the Bible to draw us into holiness, 'that through believing [we] may have life in his name' (John 20.31).

> Holy Scripture containeth all things necessary to salvation: so that whatsoever is not read therein, nor may be proved thereby, is not to be required of any man, that it should be believed as an article of the Faith, or be thought requisite or necessary to salvation.

The Thirty-nine Articles[299]

Different approaches

In November 2010, the then Archbishop of Canterbury, Rowan Williams, asked the Church of England's General Synod how people who read the same Bible, and share the same baptism, could come to such diverse conclusions about human sexuality.[300] John Sentamu, Archbishop of York, returned to this question in his final Presidential address to Synod in July 2019, saying that 'Nine years later there has been little, if any, progress in answering it.'[301]

People may agree on the points made so far in this chapter, but that still seems to leave many unanswered questions and disagreements. In this section and the next, we are going to set out some of the different approaches to Scripture that have been visible in Church of England debates about identity, sexuality, relationships and marriage. Our aim in this part of the chapter is to *describe* those different approaches – and, we hope, to do so clearly, in terms that those who pursue them will recognize as fair.

It is only later in the chapter that we will turn to the distinct task of *evaluation*. We will ask, first, whether these different approaches do justice to the claims discussed above: that the Bible comes to us from God's hand as well as from human hands, and that it witnesses to God's saving work and calls all people to holiness. We will also ask whether these different approaches are in line with the Church of England's commitment to the Bible's authority – including its commitment 'not … to ordain any thing that is contrary to God's Word written'.[302]

Context matters

Some of our disagreements relate to the outworking of one of the central principles of responsible biblical interpretation: 'Don't take texts out of context!' If we are to read any part of the Bible well, we need to consider three kinds of context:

- *textual context* – because individual verses or phrases are set in larger texts that have particular literary genres, that have various kinds of flow, structure, purpose or argument, that make a difference to how we read them;

- *historical context* – because every word of the Bible has a human history, and we can investigate the meanings that a text had in the contexts in which it was first produced and received; and

- *canonical context* – because all of these texts have been gathered together into a canon, and we can ask what difference it makes to read any text in the context of this whole canon.

Some of the differences in approach to the Bible that we find around the Church of England have to do with historical and canonical context.

Historical context

Every word of the Bible has an original context in human history. When we study a particular text, we normally need to investigate and understand its meanings in that context if we are to read it well. We can therefore investigate the meanings that any given biblical text had for the people who first wrote it and for their first audiences.

There are two aspects to this principle.

- It involves reconstructing, as best we can, the contexts in which the text appeared, the concerns and assumptions that might have shaped it, and the purposes for which it was written.

- It means being alert to the differences between those contexts, concerns, and assumptions and our own. There might be times when our own contexts and expectations, and the contexts and expectations that have shaped our traditions of interpretation, lead us to make assumptions and claims about the text that don't fit well with its historical meanings.

This is one source of disagreements in the church about matters of identity, sexuality, relationships and marriage.

We have already seen in Chapter 12 that such questions come up, for instance, when we are trying to make sense of Jesus' prohibitions against marriage after divorce, and his equating of it with adultery (Mark 10.1-12; Luke 16.18; and Matthew 5.32; 19.9). We asked whether Jesus was responding to the specific form of divorce in his own historical context – where Jewish men could simply divorce their wives for any cause at all and then marry again – or whether he was issuing a prohibition that applies in any and every context. Rather different applications of Jesus' teaching to present-day divorce might flow from these two different understandings of the relevant texts.

Similar disagreements crop up regularly in debates about same-sex relationships. There is no dispute that a number of biblical texts contain condemnations of same-sex sexual behaviours or relationships. But what were the behaviours or relationships imagined and addressed by the authors of these texts, and why did they reject them? How similar are the forms that we encounter and experience today? Did the biblical writers, for example, view same-sex sexual relationships negatively because they violated God's purposes for men and women in creation? Or were their targets very different from the committed, loving same-sex sexual relationships that we encounter today, perhaps because they refer to abusive relations, promiscuity, or sex in the context of pagan religious practices? And what if we are not in a position to give a firm answer to these questions, because we simply don't know enough about the historical context or about the meanings of the words used? Again, rather different applications of the Bible's teaching to present-day situations flow from different answers to these questions. Some of the disagreements explored in Part Three focused on just these kinds of question, and we will be looking in more detail at the relevant texts below.

See, for example, the discussion of Romans 1.26,27 on pages 289–291 in this chapter.

Canonical context

When we think about reading the Bible, we often think of focusing on one particular verse or chapter at a time, or on a selection of verses that we see as having a common theme (such as the passages on divorce referred to above). But to hear God's voice we need to listen for it in and through all the human voices gathered within the pages of the Bible. We treat each of these texts as 'biblical' because they have been brought together into a single canon. We need, therefore, to ask what difference it makes to read any text not just in its original context but also in this *canonical* context.

Here we find some further different sources of disagreement in the church about matters of identity, sexuality, relationships and marriage.

Sometimes, as with the divorce example, the challenge is that we have different texts to consider. Different texts can be in conversation with one another. Jesus' teaching on divorce, for instance, is in conversation with earlier teaching in Deuteronomy 24, and with Genesis 1 and 2. Different texts can also sometimes be in tension or apparent contradiction. As we saw in Chapter 12, for instance, Jesus' teaching on divorce as recorded in Mark and also in Luke is more restrictive than it is in Matthew. In Matthew, Jesus gives an explicit exception to teaching that in the other Gospels seems to be presented as absolute (Matthew 5.32, 19.9). And then there is Paul's later teaching in 1 Corinthians 7, which refers to Jesus but also adds to his teaching (1 Corinthians 7.10-13). On hearing these various voices in the canon, how can we discern the voice of God? Is there a coherent 'biblical' perspective that gives unity to all this canonical diversity and complexity? Can we see a pattern of 'progressive revelation' as God's will is revealed through time? Or is such unity lacking – and, if so, what does that mean for our response?

At other times, there may not be so stark a diversity amongst texts addressing the same theme. Nevertheless, some may think the teaching of these texts together is in tension, or is even incompatible, with the canonical witness as a whole. This is a point we will return to in the next section, 'Unity and authority'.

Marriage and the Bible

Scripture gives both rich, textured stories of many marriages and prescriptive teaching about intimate and sexual relationships. As we saw in Chapter 9, many of the people we meet in Scripture struggle with life and with relationships, and sexuality and marriage are deeply marked by brokenness. One of our tasks in reading Scripture is to consider this varied picture, to see how the more prescriptive texts fit with the stories, and to consider how we understand and use the stories.

When we try to offer a 'biblical view of marriage' we are engaging in biblical interpretation. We are looking at how things fit together across the canon. We seek to interpret different parts of Scripture and try to discern the direction of the stories (which is not always obvious, especially if a story mentions marriage but marriage is not the specific focus) and the purpose of the various laws. In addition, we also need to read each text in context, considering its historical nature and how far its message relates to a particular culture, and how far it may be universal.

There are therefore several questions before us: How do we do justice to the textual and historical context of specific texts? Is it right to look for a unified account within the canon? Is it possible? If we do, what kind of questions are we asking, and how do we weigh up different material? And if we think there is no unified account, is it still possible to derive ethical teaching on relationships from Scripture? And what questions, presuppositions and hopes do we bring to the text as we seek to engage with it?

As set out in Part One, a broad consensus developed in the teaching of the Church that a clear biblical picture of marriage emerges when you consider Scripture as a whole, and in particular when you read it in the light of the teaching of Jesus on marriage (see pages 246–252). Because Jesus specifically teaches on marriage, linking it back to the creation of men and women, in Matthew 19 and Mark 10, these specific texts, interpreting marriage as a lifelong union between a man and a woman, became a lens through which to interpret all other texts, a reading reinforced by the narratives of Scripture which describe marriages of people of the opposite sex. Although having children is not always possible (as various stories demonstrate), both male and female biology are essential to marriage, because they are necessary for procreation. Faithfulness and monogamy are also central in this account. It looks to the Genesis texts where the man and woman become 'one flesh', and to the nuptial imagery used for God's covenant with Israel. As a by-product of seeing faithfulness and exclusivity as central to marriage, the Church also taught that intimate sexual activity has its proper place only within a committed, faithful, permanent relationship – and this type of relationship is described in Scripture and tradition as 'marriage'.

From this perspective, relationships that deviate from this ideal (including same-sex relationships) tend to be portrayed negatively in biblical stories and condemned in legal and ethical teaching because they depart from these creational and covenantal norms for marriage. This is taken as a normative account, which can be held up as an ideal or template, though there are differences in how different groups respond to relationships that depart from these norms.

The Church has had to respond to the complex realities of life, and therefore accounts have developed that still honour the norm or ideal, yet make space for variance. Here it has recognized that Scripture also makes provision for and describes patterns of relationship other than marriage as described above: divorce is mentioned and permitted in the law of Moses; imperfect marriages such as David's and those of many other people of faith do not prevent God's grace being at work in their lives.

This, then, opens up another question about how human beings live faithfully in relation to marriage in a broken world. Here, grace and mercy become central principles. The difficult question then becomes, what kind of accommodations can be made? How do we decide when to accommodate, and when to reject, certain configurations of life? How can this change across times and cultures? And does this create a sense of some relationships only being 'second best'?

In recent years, some Christians have argued that the Bible's view of marriage can legitimately include same-sex couples. They agree that the overall picture of marriage in Scripture tends towards loving faithfulness and covenant loyalty as in the imagery of God and Israel and Christ and the Church. They view the male-female structure in the Genesis narrative as illustrative (perhaps seeing it as referring to the most common kind of pair that people form) rather than morally normative, and highlight the New Testament's apparent lack of interest in procreation. The absence of same-sex relationships in Scripture is seen as arising simply because the historical context of the time did not envisage such relationships as being able to embody these qualities of marriage. This may be due to different cultural norms, to embedded cultural prejudice or because same-sex behaviour that was visible was transient and exploitative.

Those who take this approach may also argue that the deepest principle that Scripture gives us for our ethical thinking is love

– or liberation (because Scripture consistently sides with those who are oppressed or invisible). If this is the case, then would not that arc of liberation and the central message of love move us to accept today same-sex relationships that display the fruit of the Spirit – love, patience, kindness, generosity, faithfulness, gentleness and self-control – while rejecting forms of relationship that are damaging? Here, a biblical view of marriage and relationships is not derived primarily from the Bible's stories of marriage or from specific teaching on marriage, but from deeper underlying principles that Scripture gives us for the whole of life. Yet advocates of the Church's traditional reading would ask, if your understanding of those underlying principles brings you into conflict with the explicit teaching of Jesus about marriage, then is your understanding wrong?

Advocates of each of these approaches appeal to the Bible and try to read it carefully. They emerge, however, with different understandings of what the Bible requires of us – different understandings of what might be meant by a 'biblical view of marriage'.

Reading some relevant texts

As we have seen, Scripture as a whole, and every part of it, presents us with challenge, comfort and wisdom. However, some texts in Scripture have been identified as particularly relevant to debates on sexuality and gender issues and have therefore been prominent in church debates. Although small in number, these texts are all negative towards the sexual behaviour they describe and they have traditionally been seen as demonstrating a straightforward, consistent biblical witness against all same-sex sexual activity.

Their prominence in debates means that we now need to turn to them, while, at the same time, acknowledging that there are questions about whether these passages should be used as a starting point and the weight that should be given to them. We need to be alert to the fact that narrowing our interest to a few texts is likely to give a distorted picture of how Scripture as a whole speaks to us. We also need to recognize that these texts have sometimes been used to silence the voices and questions of LGBTI+ people, or to exclude them from fellowship – which has led to these texts being experienced and described as 'clobber texts'.

These texts should not be read in isolation from their wider textual and cultural contexts. Questions have been raised, for instance, about what acts they described and condemned in their original historical contexts, and how they relate to today's faithful, committed same-sex unions (with some arguing they have nothing to say concerning them).

We also need to think about how we put these texts together with all the other relevant biblical texts before we make wider claims about what Scripture says. That will shape our decisions about which interpretation is right, especially when individual passages appear to be either ambiguous or conflicting.

It is therefore necessary to turn to these texts, to wrestle with their complexities, and to explore how different groups and scholars understand them in their own right and as they fit into the wider themes of Scripture.

We will explore them in the order in which they appear in the canon.

Genesis 19 (with reference to Judges 19)

The disturbing story of Sodom and Gomorrah in Genesis 19 is one of abuse and violence, leading to the destruction of an entire town, and (like the similar story in Judges 19) it is often described as a 'text of terror'. Two angels are travelling, and arrive in Sodom, on a mission of judgement. Sodom is said to be wicked – in direct contrast to Abraham's 'righteousness and justice' in 18.19. Its wickedness is described in non-specific terms that connote general injustice and evil. As the angels arrive in Sodom, Lot offers them hospitality, as did his uncle Abraham in Genesis 18. Late in the evening, the men of the city surround the house, threatening to rape the strangers, a threat they are never able to implement due to being blinded by the angels after Lot offers them his virgin daughters instead.

The 'sin of Sodom' became associated with the sexual demand of the men of the town, and from there, with homosexuality. The association however is questionable, and not a move made in the text itself. The context is one of violence and xenophobia, of a mob seeking to hurt and humiliate those who do not belong to the city. Their actions are an exercise of power. Just as we would not take a text about heterosexual rape as a text speaking of heterosexual consenting relationships, there is no reason to take this text as speaking about consensual same-sex relationships. It is a text about violence, power, and the distortion of sex for evil ends.

Reading the text in canonical context, Sodom becomes an axiomatic reference to an evil city, as for instance in Ezekiel 16.49,50: 'This was the guilt of your sister Sodom: she and her daughters had pride, excess of food, and prosperous ease, but did not aid the poor and needy. They were haughty, and did abominable things before me; therefore I removed them when I saw it.' This verse sets the sins of Sodom in the wider, common context of pervasive injustice. Jude verse 7 mentions sexual immorality and 'lust for strange flesh' (KJV). It is not difficult to see how the first of these phrases applies to a story of sexual violence. This second phrase – with its reference to 'strange flesh' or 'other flesh' – would be an odd way to speak about same-sex relationships (which would be desire for the 'same', not the 'other') and more likely refers to the men demanding to have sex with angels. Jesus himself mentions Sodom and Gomorrah, in Matthew 10.14,15, as an example of typically wicked cities that came under judgement, this time in the context of the refusal of hospitality.

Extra-biblical writings show that by the time of the New Testament, the story of Sodom was often associated with sexual sin, and with same-sex behaviour more specifically. However, in terms of the text of Scripture itself, we can only say that Sodom is a city that displayed many features of injustice and oppression; whether same-sex relations *in themselves* are here considered always sinful is not explicit in the text itself.

The story of Sodom however is not unique in the canon. A companion text appears in Judges 19, telling a very similar story: a man, a Levite, whose concubine has left him, goes to try and bring her back to him. On their journey home, they stop in Gibeah. They are offered hospitality by an old man. At night, men of the town surround the house and demand that the Levite be brought out for them to have sex with. Just as in the Sodom story, the host offers the women in exchange. Unlike in the Sodom story, however, angels do not intervene, and the Levite throws his concubine to the crowd, who rape her and leave her unconscious, possibly dead. The next morning, the Levite takes her home, dismembers her, and sends her body parts as a summons to war. The war will wipe out the tribe whose men are responsible for the rape.

The two stories use the same plot and the same words. Yet the story of Sodom is famous, and associated with same-sex questions, whereas Judges 19 is not, despite the threat of homosexual rape being present in both. Reading both stories together helps us see a pattern of the abuse of sexuality in conflict between men. In both texts, the initial intended male victims are strangers. The threat of rape is a threat of othering, of turning them into less than what they are. In patriarchal cultures where women are considered of less value than men, to treat a man as you would a woman is a serious insult, and a deep threat to personal identity.

The homosexual element of the story therefore would have provoked horror in readers – but primarily horror at the violation of masculinity and ideas of what men should be. That men could be penetrated, be passive, be abused, as women are, is an existential threat to their concept of what it means to be male. Sex here is used as a weapon: if the Levite himself is not raped, then he is humiliated through the rape of his concubine, whom he is unable (or unwilling) to protect. His masculinity is diminished either way. The exchange shows that sexual orientation is not a primary concern of the narrative. And behind both texts, the spectre of male-on-male sexual violence is raised as a possibility so taboo that it is never actualised in the text itself, yet remains as a testimony to the danger of power struggles. Reading Genesis 19 and Judges 19 together begs us to consider questions of power and violence as central to both texts.

Leviticus 18.22 and 20.13

Two verses from Leviticus are often the focus of attention in debates about sexuality, often quoted as if their meaning is straightforwardly clear and can be applied straightforwardly to today, unlike most of the rest of the book.

'You shall not lie with a male as with a woman; it is an abomination.' (Leviticus 18.22)

'If a man lies with a male as with a woman, both of them have committed an abomination; they shall be put to death; their blood is upon them.' (Leviticus 20.13)

Both verses stress the seriousness of the practice described with the word 'abomination' and, in the second, by requiring the death penalty. The question is, what exactly do these verses describe?

Traditionally, the wording has been read as straightforward, addressed to any reader, and applied to all male same-sex relations. It has, for example, been argued that in its literary context, Leviticus 20.10-16 names different ways of contravening the commandment against adultery and departures from the norm of sex between a man and a woman within marriage. This argument however is somewhat difficult to sustain if one considers that adultery in Leviticus and Deuteronomy applies specifically to a man sleeping with an already married woman, or a married woman sleeping with any other man, rather than departures from monogamy as a whole – men straying from their (main) wife are not considered to be committing adultery against their wives.[303]

Some have argued that some form of coercion or violence must lie behind the prohibition but this is not immediately apparent in the text. The context of both chapters looks at a range of prohibited relationships, which are more likely to be consensual. Laws governing rape and prostitution are found elsewhere (Deuteronomy 22.25-29 and Deuteronomy 23.17,18), but do not seem to form part of the context here.

The primary cultural and theological driving force behind the list of prohibited relationships seems to be the protection of the integrity of marriage within the framework of the extended family structure in Israel, the house of the father. The laws establishing sexual boundaries and prohibited zones would prevent such an extended community of kinship living together in close proximity from becoming a commune in which any woman was available to any man. The laws were meant to create a safe space that protected the more vulnerable, and enabled the household to flourish as a whole. Any action that threatened the well-being or survival of the household is treated severely, hence the use of the word 'abomination'.

The cultural context of the household however makes interpreting this verse more difficult. The household laws are usually understood to be addressed primarily to the head of the household – who has the power to enforce them – or potential heads of household. It can thereforebe argued that its underlying intent is to restrict the sexual access of the most powerful member of the household to those who are more vulnerable, which reintroduces the possibility that the text has coercive or abusive relationships in mind. Some have also suggested the prohibition may concern specifically two heads of different households coming into a relationship – which would threaten the stability of both extended families. In any case, the majority of these laws seem to apply to men with a degree of power. This does not mean that none of Leviticus then applies to anyone else – Leviticus still regulates and shapes the life of the entire community, but it is seen and shaped through the primary regulator of household life.

One initial question about these verses is therefore the scope of the prohibition: is it a prohibition for all people, at all times, or restricted to (already married) men with dependents? Even if the prohibition seems to apply fairly indiscriminately, this does not tell us how it should transfer to a different context or be understood in canonical context. After all, there are many laws from Leviticus that Christians feel under no compulsion to follow, some of them because they are considered to be culture- and time-bound and others because the Bible itself gives us clear theological reasons why they no longer apply in the light of Christ. Chapter 18's introduction and conclusion both emphasize that the practices forbidden to Israel are characteristic of non-Israelite inhabitants of Canaan. So it is possible that the prime force of the prohibition is against a specifically Canaanite practice, against which Israel's identity is demarcated, rather than a universal directive – though it is unclear why something displeasing to God in the Canaanite world would be solely culturally-bound. Levitical laws, however, are sometimes reflected in New Testament teaching, and these verses are generally agreed to be the source of comments on same-sex activity in 1 Corinthians 6 and 1 Timothy 1, which indicates that they were seen as scripturally authoritative for Christian ethical discipleship.

It is also worth noting that this law has nothing to say about women in same-sex relationships.

Leviticus therefore raises what will prove a recurring issue of interpretation: how we read it and what force we ascribe to it depends not simply on these two verses read in their textual and cultural context. It also depends on the wider theology that we construct from the biblical canon on gender, sex, relationships and marriage, on how far we think the text of Scripture speaks with one voice on these matters, and on what we think about the nature of its authority, and on how we understand the move from the text's historical setting to today's context.

Romans 1.26,27

**For this reason God gave them up to degrading passions.
Their women exchanged natural intercourse for unnatural, and
in the same way also the men, giving up natural intercourse with
women, were consumed with passion for one another. Men committed
shameless acts with men and received in their own persons the due
penalty for their error.**

These verses need to be placed within their wider textual and
rhetorical context in Romans. Paul is primarily making the argument
that all human beings, Jews and Gentiles alike, are fundamentally
in the same position before God and cannot pass condemnatory
judgement on others while exempting themselves. (The punchline
to this passage comes in 2:1ff, though that is often lost because of
the later insertion of a chapter division). Everyone has sinned and
needs to receive God's grace and transformation.

Paul's overall argument in Romans 1 – 3 starts with creation. The key
idea is that human suppression of the truth about God as creator
(refusing to give glory or thanks to him as such) has led to idolatry,
the exchange of the living and immortal God for objects within
creation, the exchange of the truth of God for a lie. This catastrophic
exchange results in God 'giving them over', leading to disorder and
confusion within human life, in manifold ways – most of which are
not to do with sexuality (1.29,30). There is no sense of a hierarchy
among the sins mentioned, of any of them being more important
or severe than others, but Paul does make an explicit and longer
reference to sexual immorality in verses 26-27. These verses are now
hotly disputed between proponents of different interpretations.

On the one hand, traditional interpretations argue that one
manifestation of humanity's exchange of God for idols is the
exchange of male-female sexual intercourse for same-sex relations,
both between men and (only here in Scripture) between women.
This is understood to be a reference to humanity rejecting God's
design in creation (and Paul's language here has several echoes
of Genesis 1), which would make Paul's disapproval of same-sex
intercourse absolute.

Some have argued, however, that Paul may have had same-sex
prostitution or pederasty (older men having sex with male youths)
in mind, or pagan worship, though this is not explicit in the text.

Paul does not seem to be referring to coercive, power-abusing or violent same-sex intercourse, since he appears to be speaking of freely chosen, consensual behaviour of men with men and women with women (which were known in the Greek world, although some scholars argue Paul is referring to non-vaginal male-female intercourse here). Therefore these verses have been seen as applying straightforwardly to same-sex relationships.

Others have pointed out that these verses are more complex and problematic than this. So, for instance, Paul's presentation of 'exchanging natural intercourse for unnatural' seems to be presented as fundamentally a free choice to depart from 'natural intercourse' on the part of those involved. An understanding of sexuality simply in terms of choice does not tie in with either the experience of LGBTI+ people or with contemporary understanding of sexual orientation informed by science. This raises questions of how we approach texts from specific cultural contexts, reflecting their understanding, and relate them to our own. Part of our problem is juxtaposing a text from a culture that spoke of sexual *actions* (as discrete acts) together with our own culture and its understanding of sexual *orientation* as a key component of identity, rather than a freely chosen action. Paul is not speaking of communities of people and their identities here but about specific actions and behaviours. If, however, Paul is not addressing those with specific orientation, he could be making an argument about how some choose specific means of sexual gratification at the expense of others, exercise power within sexual relationships, or use sex as some form of weapon.

Alongside this element of choice, the other way in which Paul depicts same-sex sexual practices in 1.26,27 is that they are 'unnatural' (literally 'against (or beyond) nature'). This language gives rise to many questions – What is 'natural', and why? What constitutes 'natural law', and why? Who should determine such questions, and why? Paul makes two other appeals to nature. The first, in Romans 11.24, is metaphorical: the action of God in bringing the Gentiles into the promise is as unexpected as if a gardener were to graft a wild olive, against nature, into a cultivated olive tree. The second, in 1 Corinthians 11.13-16, is when Paul argues that it is 'natural' for men to cut their hair and women to have long hair. This would seem to be a culture-based, rather than an immutable, judgement. This cultural convention is, however, one that in the Ancient World, and perhaps in Paul's argument, was linked to signals of sexual availability. It can therefore be argued that what is at stake in Paul's mind is not the length of hair, but sexual morality. Discerning the meaning of 'natural', and the applicability of the argument is therefore more complex than it first appears, and rests on factors beyond these few verses (which is why we gave some attention to the meaning of natural in Chapter 10). It depends again on wider theological ideas about marriage and the significance of gender, on our beliefs about the place of science and experience, and the ways in which we read Scripture, as well as an understanding of the culture of the time.

> See the discussion about 'Natural and Unnatural' in Chapter 10 pages 215–216 and 'Natural knowledge' in Chapter 15 pages 335–338.

1 Corinthians 6.9-11

Do you not know that wrongdoers will not inherit the kingdom of God? Do not be deceived! Fornicators, idolaters, adulterers, male prostitutes, sodomites, thieves, the greedy, drunkards, revilers, robbers—none of these will inherit the kingdom of God. And this is what some of you used to be. But you were washed, you were sanctified, you were justified in the name of the Lord Jesus Christ and in the Spirit of our God.

Here in 1 Corinthians Paul is speaking directly to a church whose life together failed to display the love of Christ. He addresses the shortcomings of the church and its members in some detail in Chapters 5 and 6, beginning with a startling example of sexual immorality – a man living with his father's wife. Chapter 5 then has two successive lists of sins ('vice lists', as they are sometimes known) in verses 10 and 11, the second longer than the first. Just as in Romans, they include a whole list of different types of sin, not solely sexual ones. 1 Corinthians 6.9,10 continues in the same vein, with an even longer list and two warnings that those who do these things will not inherit God's kingdom. Paul's main point is: look at what you used to be! But even for people like this, there is hope. You have been welcomed into the family of God.

Whilst Paul includes many different types of sin, he does provide a longer explanation of the specific impact of sexual sin (in heterosexual contexts) in 6.15-20, referring to it as sinning against 'your own body'. This chimes with what we know today of the importance of sexuality for well-being, and the impact of sexual experiences (particularly negative ones) on questions of self-esteem, shame and the ability to form wider relationships. Paul relates the importance of looking after our own body and honouring (or glorifying) God with our bodies to the significance of the embodied human person as the 'temple of the Spirit'. The fundamental dignity of human beings dictates that we should treat our bodies and those of others with respect.

The question is then, what does this look like in practice? If we now go back to Paul's list, we find two words, translated in the NRSV as 'male prostitutes' and 'sodomites'. These appear in the final list only. The exact meaning of these words is contested. The first is a Greek word for 'soft' and may be best understood to mean 'appearing effeminate'. The second is a word apparently invented by Paul, meaning 'males who bed together', deliberately echoing Leviticus.

Scholars disagree on where we go next. Reading the vice list as a whole, there is a recurrent sense of the problematic nature of self-seeking and grasping at other people's expense, or even at one's own expense. For example, the adulterer takes away the reputation or self-worth of others; drunkards diminish themselves through overruling their faculties and self-control and risk hurting others. Some therefore argue that the kind of same-sex sexual practices Paul has in mind are abusive in some way, such as the bodies of the strong and socially powerful taking advantage of the bodies of the weak.

Some argue that the words Paul uses refer specifically to such abusive practices. The first word could refer to a male prostitute becoming a soft, passive partner, abused by the other. Both words together could refer to the Greek practice of older men (the aggressor) taking young boys (the soft ones) as lovers. If this is what these texts refer to, would Paul's opposition be relevant to committed, loving relationships?

Whilst this interpretation is possible there were common Greek terms used to describe these practices, not used here by Paul. Others therefore disagree with this interpretation and argue that the first word, 'soft', refers to any male partner becoming passive by allowing himself to be penetrated (i.e. becoming like a woman, in a patriarchal context that defined women as passive), whilst the second has no explicit connotations of coercion. In this reading,

Paul straightforwardly lists same-sex intercourse along with other behaviours of those who are not obedient to God.

A further difficulty we face is that vice lists offer no explanation as to why what they reject is sinful. This is not a problem when – as with the other terms on the vice list – it is fairly obvious to us. However, in a context such as ours, justification is increasingly sought as to why a loving, same-sex relationship would necessarily be sinful, or against the dignity of the body. Such justification is not offered here and so once more we have to go to other scriptural texts, arguments about gender complementarity or concepts of the natural, which put this verse into a wider arc of the canonical context and biblical and theological interpretation.

1 Timothy 1.8-11

Now we know that the law is good, if one uses it legitimately. This means understanding that the law is laid down not for the innocent but for the lawless and disobedient, for the godless and sinful, for the unholy and profane, for those who kill their father or mother, for murderers, fornicators, sodomites, slave-traders, liars, perjurers, and whatever else is contrary to the sound teaching that conforms to the glorious gospel of the blessed God, which he entrusted to me.

Here in 1 Timothy we find another wide-ranging list of vices which are described as contrary to both the law and the gospel. The term found in 1 Corinthians 6 and apparently coined by Paul based on Leviticus reappears here. Accordingly, the arguments on the meaning of the term there would apply here also, and with the same scriptural undergirding.

Once again there are debates as to what is being referred to and the rationale for the list. Some have argued that the list follows the order of the Ten Commandments and that the term translated here as 'sodomites' refers to same-sex sexual behaviour as violation of the seventh commandment against adultery. (As we noted earlier, this is arguably also the significance of the list of sexual offences that follow the primary one of adultery in Leviticus 20.10). Others, however, tie the term to the phrase that follows, which refers to slave traders. It could then be understood to refer to same-sex prostitution and to what we could call sex trafficking of male slaves – though that would be an unusual and debatable extension of the single word Paul uses.

Conclusion

With each text here, we have met different interpretations. Each involves different claims about how to read the texts properly in their textual, historical and canonical contexts, and how to understand what they say to us today. Until relatively recently they were universally and uncontroversially read as consistently rejecting all same-sex sexual behaviour. We have seen, however, that some now question this and interpret them as more narrowly focused, so leaving open the possibility of approving faithful, committed same-sex relationships.[304]

How we interpret each of these texts depends on what else we take into account in our interpretation. What do we believe Scripture as a whole says about gender, about sexuality, about relationships, about marriage? How do our beliefs about these things shape the way in which we read these particular texts? How do we enable different parts of Scripture to shape how we read these texts, and does reading these texts shape our overall theology of relationships?

How we understand the authority of these texts in relation to today also depends on our understanding of the Bible's authority, unity and purpose. These are topics that we will explore in a moment. It also, however, depends on how we answer further questions, which later chapters will help us to consider. What is the weight of the received wisdom of the Church around the world, in our discerning how to read these texts? If we dismiss what seems to be obvious on first reading, are we saying there is no 'plain meaning' to Scripture and that only experts can read Scripture well? How do we give particular attention to the experience and understanding of those whose own lives are most directly affected by how these texts are interpreted?

Unity and authority

The questions about canonical context that we raised above are entangled with others – especially questions about how directly, and by what means, people expect the Bible to provide God's authoritative answers to the questions that concern us. Disagreements about the nature and form of the Bible's authority form a second axis along which the variety of opinion in the Church of England can be arranged – distinct from the disagreements about context described earlier.

In the interests of describing the range of possible answers to these questions, we have imagined convening a panel illustrating the wide spectrum of opinion that you might find around the Church of England (though we will be asking below the question of how well the opinions expressed align with its formal teaching). We have imagined asking each of our seven panellists to tell us something about how they listen to God in the Bible, and we think that each of their voices represents an approach that you might hear from pews and pulpits around the country. Their opening statements might run something like this:

Speaker 1: I believe that God loves us enough to have given us a manual for living. By the grace of God, the Bible is truthful, withour error, and clear. Everything we need to know for our salvation, and to live holy lives pleasing to God, is right there on the page. We simply need to read it, and obey it – and that includes all that it says about identity, sexuality, relationships and marriage. Most of what people mean when they talk about 'interpreting' the Bible is one attempt or another to avoid listening to its plain teaching.

Speaker 2: I agree that the Bible tells us what we need to know in order to understand God's loving purposes for us. It is given to us by our Creator, who knows all about what is good for us, and who wants to communicate that to us. We can trust such a God to have spoken to us clearly and coherently – and I think that the answers the Bible provides to our questions, including our questions about identity, sexuality, relationships and marriage, are indeed clear and coherent. I do want to stress, however, that we need to read *everything* that the Bible says about marriage and sexual relationships, that we need to pay attention to each text's historical context, and that we need to read them in the context of the Bible's wider message, in order to find a trustworthy framework or blueprint for our thought and practice.

Speaker 3: I broadly agree, but I want to stress the care we need to take in putting the pieces of biblical teaching together – and the danger of taking any part on its own. God has given us the Bible as a whole, expecting us to learn from the interaction of all its parts. Sometimes one text qualifies another, or shows that another was giving guidance only for a specific context, or helps us see that another was revealing only part of the truth. God invites us to the labour of reading all the relevant texts together. It is only when we do so – and especially when we read all of the Bible in the light of Christ's work and teaching – that we will find the answers we are looking for.

Speaker 4: I like your stress on taking care as we put the different parts of the Bible together, but I want to say more about it. I don't see that task as simply one of resolving difficulties, or finding ways to smooth out the Bible's rough edges. I think there are deep and pervasive tensions in the Bible, and that they are there for good reason. It is an inherently complex conversation between multiple voices. I think that we need to acknowledge those tensions, explore them, go on learning from them, and dwell with them, as we think through our questions about identity, sexuality, relationships and marriage. In fact, I think God invites us to this kind of dwelling with the text. I think the Bible is too complex, too mobile, and too lively to be called a blueprint or a framework.

Speaker 5: I agree that God has given us the Bible as a whole, expecting us to learn from and dwell with the interaction of all its parts, but I want to push what you say a bit further. I think that when we read all the relevant biblical texts together, we do discover that some of them, taken by themselves, are misleading. Listening to the Bible as a whole means learning to discern what is more central to it, and what is less central – and I think God expects us to make that discernment. For example, when we do that, I think we find that some of what we read in the Bible about identity, sexuality, relationships and marriage just doesn't line up with the most central things the Bible says about love. So I think the Bible itself teaches us not to take those passages as instructions for our lives now, and to find some creative new way of reading them.

Speaker 6: I would want to push that even further. I believe the Bible is given to us for the one purpose of teaching us about God's love for the world – especially its fulfilment in Jesus. I want to say that the Bible is a collection of human words brought together by God to witness to that love, and ultimately to Christ. Everything in it is given to us for that one purpose. I do trust that God has provided us with witnesses whose testimony is sufficient to teach us this love. But I also think that the testimony is provided by fallible human voices, all of which need testing against that central message. I believe the Bible calls us to work out our own answers to our questions about identity, sexuality, relationships and marriage, in the light of this central message. And I expect that the answers we give to specific questions will sometimes be quite different from the answers that the biblical authors gave, because we no longer agree with some of the other assumptions they brought to the process – and that we will therefore have to say 'no' to some of their answers.

Speaker 7: I agree that the Bible is a collection of fallible human voices, but I'm wary of what you say about God bringing these texts together, and giving them to us for some central purpose. I do think that it is a book produced by people who were caught up in movements of God's Spirit in history – but their words only do uneven and partial justice to what they glimpsed. You can certainly find some important truths in Scripture, sometimes powerfully and beautifully expressed, but they are mixed in with all kinds of other material, some of it horrific.

These are only very brief and simplified sketches of some of the different voices you might hear around the church.

Evaluating the voices

Having set out these seven voices, we need to ask some evaluative questions. In this section, we'll ask some general questions about how these seven voices relate to the description of the Bible that we gave earlier in the chapter. In the next section, we'll ask more specifically about their compatibility with the teaching of the Church of England.

Human and divine?

In the first section above, we said that the Bible comes to us from God's hand as well as from human hands. The first speaker above appears to deny one side of this claim, and the seventh to deny the other. That is, the first speaker seems to deny – or at least to give very little attention to – the humanity of the text. The rich and varied lives and contexts of the Bible's human authors, and the rough texture that their voices give to the text, seem to be washed out in the glare of this speaker's claims about God's authorship of these words. The seventh speaker seems to deny that the text is given to us by God, for God's purposes. The complex humanity of the Bible's authors fills the screen, and there is little space left for God.

There may be things to learn from those who identify with these two voices. They may bring challenges that the church needs to hear. They may see things in the text that others miss. Their approaches nevertheless take them beyond the mainstream of the church's conversation about the Bible's authority and purpose, as we described it above. We will be asking below whether some of the other voices advocate approaches that similarly place them beyond this mainstream, as it is identified in the Church of England.

Disagreeing about authority

To begin evaluating the claims of speakers 2 to 6, we can refer back to the claim we made in the first section of this chapter ('God's purposes', pages 275–276): that the Bible is God's instrument, telling us of God's love and calling us into holiness. These remaining five speakers share

- a commitment to growth in holiness and love;

- a commitment to the diligent reading of the Bible as God's instrument for training in holiness and love, and instructing us for salvation;

- a determination to attend to the way the words of the Bible run;

- a desire to have their consciences formed by the dynamics of those words;

- a conviction that Christ stands at the centre of the Bible; and

- a belief that the Bible's deep purpose is to unite us with Christ and to draw us into Christlike love for God and neighbour.

All of these speakers believe themselves to be taking the Bible seriously – in fact, each may think that they are taking it *more* seriously than the others. All of them are determined to be obedient to God's purposes in giving us the Bible, as they understand those purposes. They can't simply be divided up into those who are trying to be obedient to God's voice and those who are not. Nevertheless, the disagreements between them are serious. Each may think that one or more of the others is in serious error: that they have mistaken what the Bible is, misunderstood what it says about itself, and failed to recognize in it God's true purpose.

These speakers each believe that the Bible is God's means for telling us truth that we can rely on – truth that we can and should build our lives on. For all of them, then, the Bible has divine *authority*. They disagree, however, about the nature of that authority. One of the sharpest disagreements will be prompted by Speaker 5 and especially Speaker 6 saying that there are teachings in the Bible that are not authoritative for us. Can they really be said to be committed to the 'sovereign authority of the Holy Scriptures' if they say this? Are they not picking and choosing which bits of the Bible to follow? Aren't they therefore (in effect, if not in intent) setting themselves up in authority over the Bible?

Speakers 5 and 6 might respond in this way. In their view, the Bible appears to be repeatedly commenting on, questioning, critiquing and even correcting itself. As we have seen, Deuteronomy is clear, for instance, that Moabites cannot become part of Israel (Deuteronomy 23.3-6), but the book of Ruth makes it clear that Moabites can – and that it is part of God's great plan of salvation that they should. Deuteronomy sets out clearly a covenant in which obedience will bring blessing, disobedience will bring suffering (Deuteronomy 7 – 9), but the book of Job refuses that understanding of covenant. Leviticus sets out dietary laws distinguishing clean from unclean animals (Leviticus 11), but the book of Acts shows us God setting aside that distinction (Acts 10.9-16). And, as we have already seen, Mark and Luke have Jesus prohibiting all divorce; Matthew introduces an exception. If we attend to how the Bible reads itself – how one part responds to another – we will find (Speaker 5 and 6 might say) that we are repeatedly taught – by the Bible – not to follow what had looked elsewhere – in the Bible – like a clear teaching. And they might note that this is not simply a matter of the relationship between the New Testament and the Old; it is a dynamic that we find already *within* the Old Testament, and see again *within* the New.

Speaker 5 believes that the Bible's teaching about identity, sexuality, relationships and marriage is one more area in which the Bible teaches us to question, critique and correct the Bible – and that being faithful to the Bible's teaching as a whole means following through on that process. Speaker 6 believes that we need to go beyond simply noticing specific instances in which the Bible questions, critiques and corrects the Bible. We need to allow ourselves to be taught by this kind of material what kind of book the Bible is, what the nature of its authority is, and what kind of discernment we need to use in reading it. Otherwise, we risk imposing on it our own understanding of what a coherent and authoritative text ought to look like.

Speakers 2 and 3 might respond that, while it is important to recognize diversity, dialogue and development within the canon, Speakers 5 and 6 are, in their opinion, exaggerating the extent, depth and significance of these features. These features are better understood as the result of different emphases expressed in different contexts, within the one unfolding story of God's progressive revelation until Christ. Speakers 2 and 3 might insist that we remain committed to the quest to synthesize the varied human voices and find coherence and unity in the biblical witness as a whole on specific issues. The Bible is 'God-breathed' (2 Timothy 3.16 (NIV)), the reliable and authoritative speech of a truthful and faithful God whose voice we hear speaking to us 'as if by one mouth' (Augustine, *Contra Faustum*) in and through these human words. The Bible itself witnesses to its authority and dependability as a guide for life ('The law of the LORD is perfect...The precepts of the LORD are right' (Psalm 19.7,8)). Jesus' own attitude to the Scriptures seems to reflect this. How, they might ask Speakers 5 and 6, is that compatible with the idea of our correcting what Scripture teaches?

Speakers 2 and 3 might go on to say that the Church, from the early centuries, has resisted accepting incoherence and irreconcilable disagreement in the Bible's teaching. Its teachers believed there to be, and therefore sought to discern, internal consistency within Scripture – with theologians like Tertullian warning 'there is nothing to be more sedulously avoided than inconsistency'.[305]

We have only given very brief versions of the claims that the participants in this argument might make. There is much more to say. This is not, however, an argument between one group that sits light to the authority of Scripture and another that takes it seriously.

It is one where there are different understandings of what the Bible itself bears witness to as to its nature and what it means for it to have authority. It is an argument in which each participant might try to convince the others by drawing their attention to features of the text and urging them to take those features more seriously. Each is determined to do justice to the way the words of the Bible run.

Disagreeing about the Bible's message

Another disagreement might surround speaker 6's claim that 'the Bible is given to us for the one purpose of teaching us about God's love for the world'.

Speaker 6 might say that this approach takes its cue from Jesus, who says, 'In everything do to others as you would have them do to you; for this is the law and the prophets' (Matthew 7.12) and that 'all the law and the prophets' hang on the two love commandments: loving God, and loving neighbour (Matthew 22.37-40). Teaching us to love is the purpose for which God has given us the Bible, and therefore – in the words of Augustine – 'anyone who thinks that he has understood the divine Scriptures or any part of them, but cannot by his understanding build up this double love of God and neighbour, has not yet succeeded in understanding them.'[306] And because Christ is the one in whom God's love for the world is most fully expressed, Christ is the heart of the Bible – the one who lives and teaches the love that is the key to every other part. To say that the Bible is given for this one purpose, Speaker 6 might say, is not to curtail its authority but to acknowledge and be obedient to its place in God's work.

The other speakers might respond that while love is indeed central, what Speaker 6 has said is too reductive an account of what Scripture both speaks about and claims as its purpose. It rebukes and trains us in righteousness and equips us for every good work (2 Timothy 3.16,17). It does much more than simply appeal to love, and it does not leave us to fill out for ourselves what love requires. It shows us how to live and love well. Through laws, stories, wisdom sayings, prophetic voices and apostolic directions, and supremely in its witness to Jesus, it speaks to us of God's justice, goodness and holiness as well as love, and to God's specific good, loving purposes for us in creation and redemption. Although summed up in the Golden Rule and double love command, Jesus' vision of the life of love God calls us to is much broader and richer. Augustine's own work shows that it is by careful reading and understanding of the Bible as a whole, and by trusting obedience in response to its teaching, that true love takes shape for us and in us. We need to cover the Bible's curriculum fully in order to learn what love truly is, hear what the God who is love demands of us, and be led and transformed by the saving and purifying love of God poured into our hearts.

Deep disagreements

We have only had space here to give very brief sketches of the arguments that arise. To pursue them properly would require many books, the detailed discussion of all kinds of biblical passages, not to mention proper engagement with figures from the theological tradition.

It is worth recognizing, however, that the kinds of differences that we have been exploring have proven – over decades of intense debate – resistant to being overcome by argument.

In part that is because multiple kinds of disagreement are tangled together. What someone believes about the unity of the Bible will affect what they believe about God's purpose in giving us a Bible like that – and vice versa. What someone believes about the appropriate response to the Bible will be affected by what they believe about its unity and purpose – and vice versa. For each speaker, these beliefs about authority, purpose, unity and appropriate response are interwoven – and they are likely to have grown up together. In other words, each speaker inhabits a different vision of the Bible's nature, made up of complex, mutually supporting convictions.

In part, the challenge is that the convictions that underlie these approaches go deeper than argument. The different speakers are likely to inhabit different patterns of imagination about what the Bible is, and to have different emotional reactions to it. They are likely to have different interpretative instincts, that colour (in more ways than they can detect) all their engagements with Scripture. They are likely to have somewhat different visions of how exactly the reading of the Bible informs Christian life – and those visions will be held in place by a weave of different practices and conversations.

And yet recognizing how intractable these disagreements are does not mean that they are not serious, or that we can simply give up on the task of evaluation. In the next section we move to the question of how these different voices relate to the Church of England's doctrinal commitments.

Living with disagreements: The teaching of Paul in Romans

The Early Church struggled with heated disagreements. Many of these concerned the relationship between Jewish Christians and new converts. Should they observe the same disciplines and practices? What belonged to culture, and what was essential to life in Christ? This wasn't just a question of ethics, but a question of deeply-felt identity on all sides. We see these struggles in the story of Peter and Cornelius in Acts, in the events that lead to the Council of Jerusalem, in the letters of Paul (Galatians in particular). The end of Paul's letter to the Romans helps us get a glimpse of Paul's approach to deep disagreement in the new Christian community over observance of food practices and festivals.

Paul writes:

Welcome those who are weak in faith, but not for the purpose of quarrelling over opinions. Some believe in eating anything, while the weak eat only vegetables. Those who eat must not despise those who abstain, and those who abstain must not pass judgement on those who eat; for God has welcomed them. Who are you to pass judgement on servants of another? It is before their own lord that they stand or fall. And they will be upheld, for the Lord is able to make them stand.

Some judge one day to be better than another, while others judge all days to be alike. Let all be fully convinced in their own minds. Those who observe the day, observe it in honour of the Lord. Also those who eat, eat in honour of the Lord, since they give thanks to God; while those who abstain, abstain in honour of the Lord and give thanks to God. (Romans 14.1-6)

There are divisions, and some believers call each other 'weak' and others 'strong'. Those who feel free to eat anything are tempted to despise (i.e. look down on) those who do not, while those who eat restrictively are tempted to judge (i.e. find moral fault in) those who do not. It isn't difficult to recognize these attitudes in debates throughout history.

The striking thing is that Paul makes no attempt to resolve the difference between these groups, as though one position were right and the other wrong. Rather, he appears to recognize that certain differences among Christians may be intractable, incommensurable, irresolvable. Therefore his concern is how Christians should live with differences of principle and practice. On the one hand, he is clear that they must continue to recognize each other: they are to welcome each other, and they each belong to the same Lord. On the other hand, they must resist the strong urge, when in each other's presence, to focus on their points of disagreement, with each trying to point out why they are right and the other is wrong ('quarrelling over opinions'). Paul sees such behaviour as representing a fundamentally self-oriented, self-serving outlook that is incompatible with what Jesus has come for, which is to bring about a new creation in which people are fundamentally reoriented towards God and, through God, towards each other.

If believers in Christ are reoriented through Christ's death and resurrection, they must see that certain attitudes and practices become inconsistent with their new identity. So Paul turns from the particular issue at hand to the basic attitudes of despising and judging one another. He directs believers to their accountability to their Lord and Master, which must shape their attitude towards one another.

Heated debates between Christians are not new, but Scripture gives us models for handling these disagreements and realizing that hotly contested issues today may become much less central tomorrow.

One way of trying to summarize the argument is that, for Christians, questions of truth have inescapable moral and spiritual dimensions. It is not just a matter of what we believe and do, but also a matter of how we believe it and do it: 'If I... understand all mysteries and knowledge... but do not have love, I am nothing' (1 Corinthians 13.2).

But does this mean that, in effect, 'All you need is love'? These words represent a principle which it can be hard to hear without overtones of the 1960s, and a sense of 'anything goes'. Yet the new community certainly did have boundaries. The issue is one of discernment. How do we, as Christians, learn to discern the ways and will of God? How do we do this through a constant, dynamic engagement with Scripture, open to being transformed by the Spirit? How do we hold these debates in a way that keeps the right focus, on what matters most?

And how do we discern 'what matters most'? Are the debates we face today of the same nature, or order, as the ones the Early Church was facing? The bringing together of Jews and Gentiles into the nascent Church was a historic, unique event, triggered by the complete transformation of history in the incarnation. God was doing a new thing, and God's people had to re-evaluate the story so far in light of the coming of Jesus, his teaching, death and resurrection. The question for us, therefore, is whether we can use these early disagreements as a paradigm for today, or whether the nature of our disagreements is different; and we should note that the value of Romans 14 for how we handle disagreements about homosexual practice will turn on interpretations of Romans 1 that we looked at earlier in this chapter.

It would be misleading to suggest that the pattern that Paul is pursuing in Romans is the only pattern in the New Testament. In fact, there are other types of disagreement whose outcome seems to be exclusion of some kind, rather than agreeing to disagree. These centre around believers persisting in behaviours that the community of faith judges to be sinful or promoting false teaching (e.g. Matthew 18.15-18; 1 Corinthians 5.4,5; 1 Corinthians 5.11-13; 1 Corinthians 6; 2 Thessalonians 3.6; Titus 3.9-11). The reasons for exclusion vary: from trying to encourage a believer back into the fellowship, to avoiding contamination, to preserving unity. These texts are in tension with texts such as Romans 14, and illustrate the dynamic nature of holiness or righteousness both as given and as something Christians are encouraged to work towards (see, for example, Hebrews 12.14). What seems to be at stake here is persistence in certain behaviours, or a wilful disregard for what is right or the way of Christ. It is the spiritual attitude of moving away from God rather than seeking God that is at stake. Discerning what type of question we are considering, then, becomes key – though Paul's warning about attitudes within disagreement are still deeply relevant.

Scripture presents a God who gives fully and unreservedly of himself in Jesus. But Scripture makes clear that God does not instantly or simply spell out all that follows from that self-giving. We see demanding processes of discernment at work already within the biblical canon, and these continue in the historic life of the Christian Church in its many forms.

The Church of England's position

The positions that we have sketched in these pages are a complex mix of agreement and disagreement. The agreements are important, but so are the disagreements, and we need to ask whether there are limits to the approaches to the Bible that should be allowed to shape the teaching and practice of the Church of England.

The church is governed by canon law, and that law tells us what the church's sources of authority are – pointing primarily to the Bible, and then to the Thirty-nine Articles of Religion, *The Book of Common Prayer*, and the Ordinal (the liturgy of ordination, 1550). We will be coming back to this in the next chapter, to ask what kind of authority the Articles and other texts mentioned have in the church today. For now, we are simply asking whether the canons and articles determine which of the voices set out above can be affirmed as consonant with the formal teaching of the church.

Canon A5 states that 'The doctrine of the Church of England is grounded in the Holy Scriptures...'[307] This in itself does not help us decide, as we have seen that all of the speakers (except perhaps the seventh) could affirm this. There is more detail, however, in the Articles. Article 20 states that 'it is not lawful for the Church to ordain any thing that is contrary to God's Word written', and that we should not 'so expound one place of Scripture that it be repugnant to another'.[308]

Speaker 5, and more clearly speaker 6, argue that the Bible can teach us *not* to follow something that looks like a clear biblical teaching. The case against them would say that they are clearly asking the church to expound one part of the Bible as being in conflict or incompatible with (or 'repugnant to') another. And on that basis they ask the church to adopt teachings or practices 'contrary to God's Word written'. Does the official teaching of the church rule out the approaches advocated by these speakers –speaker 6, possibly speaker 5, and maybe even speaker 4, in addition to speakers 1 and 7?

Speaker 6 (for instance) might respond that Christ is the Word witnessed to by the whole of Scripture, and that Christ shows us that teaching love is Scripture's one purpose. They insist on allowing that central message to govern their reading of the whole Bible – and they might say that this is precisely how to avoid expounding 'one place of Scripture that it be repugnant to another', and precisely how to do justice to the Bible as 'God's Word written'.

Again, we have only sketched complex arguments here, with frustrating brevity. To resolve them – if resolution is possible – would take much lengthier discussion. We can ask, however, whether the Church of England has already discussed these matters, and come to conclusions that can guide our present discussion. And we are certainly not the first generation to face these questions. Versions of them have been posed throughout the past century in various Church of England discussions. There has been a complex ebb and flow in the answers given.

Sometimes, more conservative answers have been given with confidence. The 1930 Lambeth Conference, for instance, declared that

> **We affirm the supreme and unshaken authority of the Holy Scriptures as presenting the truth concerning God and the spiritual life in its historical setting and in its progressive revelation, both throughout the Old Testament and the New.**[309]

Sometimes more liberal answers have been given, as in the 1938 report on *Doctrine in the Church of England*, which argued that

> **The tradition of the inerrancy of the Bible commonly held in the Church until the beginning of the nineteenth century ... cannot be maintained in the light of the knowledge now at our disposal. It**

will already have become apparent that this belief in its inerrancy is in our judgement in no way necessary to a full acceptance of the Bible as conveying to us God's revelation of Himself.[310]

> See also the discussion on pages 317–318 in the next chapter about the 1968 Report on *Subscription and Assent to the 39 Articles*, and the changes to the 'Declaration of Assent'.

The more normal pattern has been, however – in such contexts as the 1958 and 1988 Lambeth Conferences, or the 1998 Virginia Report from the Anglican Communion's Inter-Anglican Theological and Doctrinal Commission – an affirmation of the unique authority of Scripture, without any clear ruling on what kinds of approach to Scripture this affirmation rules out. At the 1958 Lambeth Conference, for instance, it was resolved that

> The Conference affirms its belief that the Bible discloses the truths about the relation of God and Man which are the key to the world's predicament and is therefore deeply relevant to the modern world.[311]

Conclusion

This chapter has tried to *describe* the different approaches to the Bible that shape the Church of England's debates about identity, sexuality, relationships and marriage. We have begun to see how they might be evaluated but have not reached the point where we are able to *resolve* them.

We have seen that there are multiple forms of disagreement. On the one hand, there are disagreements that focus on the historical context of key biblical passages and the difference that this context makes to the lessons we should draw from them. That is one axis of the church's disagreements about the Bible. It is often a disagreement among people who share the visions of the Bible and its authority set out in the first three or four voices, but who differ on the interpretation of specific texts and so come to different conclusions about what those texts demand from us in the present, in relation to questions about identity, sexuality, relationships and marriage.

On the other hand, we have seen that there are debates that focus on the nature of biblical authority – the material we have covered in the last three sections of the chapter. This is the debate between the seven voices set out above. Someone who took a position on the authority and purpose of Scripture set out in the fifth, sixth, or seventh voice might agree with either side in the debate about historical context described in the previous paragraph. These two debates are at least partly independent of one another.

In all of our reading, and across our differences, however, our governing conviction remains the same as that expressed in the 1958 Lambeth Conference's report on the Bible:

> **The Bible and the modern world seem at first sight to be very far apart, and even among those who wish to see the bearing of the one upon the other, there are many who are perplexed as to how to do so. This book is written in sensitiveness to this perplexity, but in the conviction that it is through the Bible that the modern world can come to understand itself.**

In the remaining chapters of Part Four we explore other aspects of what it means to listen to God as we read these words of the Bible together. God doesn't only speak to us through the Bible, and our reading of the Bible never takes place in a vacuum. Our reading of the Bible is shaped and supplemented

- by reading it together, especially in the context of our worship;

- by our belief that the same God who speaks through the Bible also spoke the whole of creation into being;

- by our conversations with the diversity of human cultures;

- by our listening to our own and to others' distinctive experiences of and convictions about God speaking to them; and

- by prayer for God's help and guidance.

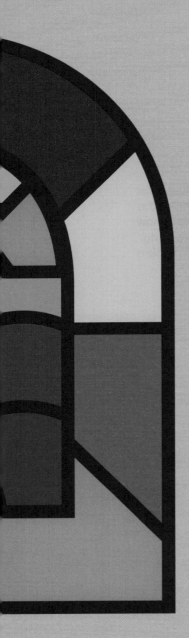

CHAPTER 14

Church

God creates people to be together, and works in and through communities.

In the Old Testament, we read that God responded to the brokenness and sin of the world, their fracturing of togetherness, by bringing into being a people – the people of Israel, called to be a light to the world.

In the New, we read that God, without breaking faith with Israel, brought into being the Church to reach out to the whole world with the message of Jesus.

The God who has spoken and still speaks to us through the Bible has also spoken and still speaks to us in the life of the Church.

Jesus gathered a community of disciples around himself. By word and by deed, by interpreting Israel's Scriptures and by telling new stories, by what he suffered and by his resurrection, he taught them. He gave them the Holy Spirit to remain with them, to lead them into the riches of his teaching, and to enable them to carry that teaching into every part of their lives and every part of the world. The Church is the community that holds onto and explores this teaching together. It is the community that reads and rereads that teaching in every context that the Spirit takes it into – constantly discovering, by the Spirit's guidance, more of this teaching's abundance. Given the divisions in the Church's life, the failings, and the sometimes damaging patterns of what it says and does, this is a claim that requires careful handling – but we believe that the gift of God's voice can be heard in the Church.

In the introduction to Part Four of the book, we identified the central question for the current chapter as: how does God speak through the Church? Yet it is of course also the Church that is listening in order to hear God speak – through Scripture, creation, culture, experience, conscience and prayer, as discussed in other chapters here. So what does it mean for the Church to listen to hear God speak through itself? We believe that Christ has entrusted the gospel to the Church and sends the Holy Spirit to lead the Church into all truth (John 16.13). We also know that Christians disagree in ways that can be serious and long-lasting, as was explored in Chapter 11. When that happens, we need to remember that the truth of the gospel is given to the Church that is One, Holy, Catholic and Apostolic, and to seek to measure our own understanding against that of the Church in its fulness, across time as well as space. Hence the two main parts of this chapter – beginning with 'Listening to the tradition', the Church through history, we then turn to 'Listening to and as the whole Body', the Church around the world. In both contexts, critical questions arise about authority: who speaks *for* the Church? How do we distinguish 'what the Church is saying' from 'what some Christians happen to be thinking'?

Listening to the tradition

The Church is the community that follows Christ, holding on to his teaching and living by it. Each generation receives that teaching from previous generations, and passes it on to the next – just as Paul, back in the first century, said that 'what I received I passed on to you as of first importance...' (1 Corinthians 15.3ff (NIV) and 2 Thessalonians 2.15). This 'passing on' is at the heart of what we mean by 'tradition': the word comes from the Latin *tradere*, meaning 'to hand over, deliver, or bequeath'.

In all our deliberations as Christians, we are always part of this long history of receiving and passing on. We are the latest generation in a very long line of transmission. Previous generations' understanding of the faith is passed on to us in all sorts of ways: in our creeds and liturgies, our hymns and worship songs, in sermons, in Sunday School classes, in Bible study notes and groups, conversations and books – and we pass it on in turn.

We have eyes and ears shaped by what we have inherited from earlier generations. It affects what we see when we look at the Church, at the world, at the Bible, and at each other. It colours the whole process of our listening to the voice of God. It gives our deliberations a distinctive flavour, in relation to the deliberations of other groups – and it can give us a vantage point from which to recognize that other groups' deliberations are also shaped by particular traditions of thought and practice, in ways that might not always be visible to them.

We can of course ignore this history that we inhabit. We can try to convince ourselves that it has not shaped the ways we think, feel, and practise our faith, and all the ways in which we listen to God – but we will be deceiving ourselves. It is better to acknowledge the influence, to listen closely to the voices of the tradition of which we are part, and to become respectful but critical participants in an ongoing conversation. All the other ways we have of listening to God (all the various forms discussed across Part Four) have the capacity to question the tradition we have inherited, and to set off processes of re-evaluation – but even those processes of questioning and re-evaluation will themselves be shaped by what we have inherited.

Think, for instance, about the ways in which this tradition relates to our reading of the Bible.

Tradition and the Bible

We do not read the Bible alone, but in the whole community of the Church. We read with Jesus, with the apostles, with the Early

Church, and with every generation of Christians down to our own time. We may not realize that this history of reading has shaped what we see when we open the Bible – but it certainly has. It has shaped what we see in particular passages. It has shaped our understanding of what Scripture is for, and of how we are supposed to relate to it, by making us part of a vast, centuries-long conversation about the nature and limits of scriptural authority and interpretation. And, more deeply still, it has shaped our imaginative grasp of the whole plot or scope of the Bible, and our sense of what are its central claims.

The Bible and the Church

Jesus' own Bible was what we call the Old Testament: the Hebrew Scriptures. They were laws, prophetic oracles, historical narratives, and psalms of worship that had arisen over the centuries as God spoke within the life of God's people. When Jesus formed a community of disciples around him, they learnt to read these Jewish Scriptures in new ways. His community was shaped by, and learnt to inhabit and pass on, this new reading.

Over time, as the Spirit worked in their midst, this community in turn produced writings witnessing to Jesus and to what it had learnt from him. As more time went by, the community recognized that some of these texts had special authority, because of the directness of their witness. These writings became the New Testament canon – and Old and New together became the book of this people. Book and people therefore belong together, and there is no simple answer to the question 'Which came first?'

The rule of faith

In the centuries when the canon was still being formed, some of the leaders and teachers of the Church taught a 'rule of faith'. That is, they taught that there was a consistent plot to the Christian story, which could be captured in simple summaries. They claimed that, in outline, this rule went back to the apostles, even to Christ himself. They justified their presentations of it by referring to texts that they believed went back to the apostles, and to the texts of Israel's Scriptures that the apostles interpreted. The rule was, in a sense, a summary or outline of all those texts – though it is also true that texts were recognized as apostolic in part because they corresponded to this rule.

Drawn from the Scriptures, the rule could guide the faithful reading of those Scriptures. It was not an independent source standing alongside the Bible, but neither was it simply a redundant summary: it helped Christians learn how they could read the whole Bible together as one story.

Creeds

The rule could be used to guide the Church's discernment when disagreements broke out, and rival teachings vied for acceptance. In turn, those disagreements pushed Christian teachers to elaborate and refine their statements of the rule. Eventually, this process of dispute, elaboration and refinement led to the calling of councils, and to the production of formal statements of belief – the creeds.

In the Church of England, we have tended to give particular weight to a series of early 'ecumenical' councils (that is, councils supposed to be of the whole Church rather than of some local part). Most notably, we look back to the creeds produced at those councils, particularly the Nicene Creed. The Apostles' Creed, although it does not derive from a council, has similarities in structure, content and function to those early articulations of the 'rule of faith'. The Athanasian Creed is a more technical summary of the Church's teaching about the Trinity and incarnation, but it too includes the same basic plot.

You get some indication of how important these creeds are in the Church of England by seeing that they have found a place in our liturgies – most obviously the Nicene and Apostles' Creeds. They are not just vision statements tucked away on the 'About Us' page of our websites: we say them together week by week, as part of our worship.

The creeds are not an authority set over the Bible. The Church of England is governed by canon law, and Canon A5 states that 'The doctrine of the Church of England is grounded in the Holy Scriptures, and in such teachings of the ancient Fathers and Councils of the Church *as are agreeable to the said Scriptures*.' The Thirty-nine Articles do say that the Church has 'authority in Controversies of Faith' but they also state that councils 'may err, and sometimes have erred, even in things pertaining unto God. Wherefore things ordained by them as necessary to salvation have neither strength nor authority, unless it may be declared that they be taken out of Holy Scripture.'[312]

How does the tradition shape our reading?

Simple statements about the relative authority of the Bible and the creeds – or the Bible and tradition more broadly – often fail to capture the lively complexity of the relationship. We insist that the Bible is the final authority against which we must test the claims of tradition (including the claims of the creeds) – but to engage in that testing we must actually read the Bible. And, because we can only read as the readers we have become, we unavoidably read with imaginations shaped by the tradition of which we are a part – the very tradition that we are trying to test.

That does not mean that the tradition we have inherited can't be tested against the Bible. Reading the Bible, even through tradition-coloured spectacles, can and does lead to challenges and questions to the tradition. That possibility is even stronger when we read alongside others who don't wear exactly the same spectacles as us. That is why reading alongside others who have been formed by different traditions across the world and down the centuries – including by different theological traditions within our own church – is so important. In the words of the Inter-Anglican Theological and Doctrinal Commission,

> [T]he Scriptures and the creeds speak in many contexts, both in the history of the church itself and in the various cultures and societies of the contemporary world; and it is this fact which, in the end, can set them free from the narrowing or distorting effects of any particular way of reading them. [313]

The Church of England's tradition

The process of receiving and passing on the faith takes place in the whole Christian Church – but it has also taken place specifically within the Church of England. The Church of England's processes of learning, debating, and teaching have not been sealed off from the life of the wider Church, but they have left their mark in a distinctively Anglican inheritance. That inheritance properly shapes our church's deliberations today.

The Church of England gives a privileged place to what are called its 'historic formularies' from the Reformation period. Canon A5 states that the doctrine of the Church of England 'is to be found in the Thirty-nine Articles of Religion, The Book of Common Prayer, and the Ordinal', and Canons A2, A3 and A4 that 'The Thirty-nine Articles are agreeable to the Word of God and may be assented unto with a good conscience by all members of the Church of England', that 'The doctrine contained in The Book of Common Prayer … is agreeable to the Word of God', and that 'The … Ordinal is not repugnant to the Word of God'. These canons point members of the Church of England who are seeking to listen to the voice of God to these particular sources as authoritative guides, under the authority of Scripture.

The Book of Common Prayer

It is probably best to begin with *The Book of Common Prayer*. Over the centuries, it has done more to shape the Church of England than any other source except the Bible. It has shaped our imaginations, our vocabulary, and the rhythms of our lives in more ways than we can know. It remains one of the standards of Anglican faith and practice, even though the development of new liturgies over the past century means than many in the Church of England and other parts of the Anglican Communion don't now experience it directly.

Many in the church, when discussing the questions raised in Parts Two and Three, will point to the marriage service in *The Book of Common Prayer* which was drawn upon in Part One. That service provides the anchor for the Church of England's doctrine of marriage, although, as we already noted, the Common Worship Marriage Service contains distinctive elements which are different in some respects from the Prayer Book's Order for the Solemnization of Marriage.

There is a broader point to make here, too. Our listening to God takes place – or *should* take place – in the context of our common life of worship and prayer. In ways that go deeper than we can detect we are shaped by, and trained to hear God in and through, our worship together.

We see this, again, in relation to our reading of the Bible. For many Anglicans our liturgies provide the central context in which we encounter the Bible – as it is read and preached on, and as it flows through the liturgies themselves. The shape of our liturgies affects our understanding of this encounter with the Bible, and also affects our sense of the whole Bible within which are found the fragments that we read on any one occasion. We are part of what the 1988 Lambeth Conference called 'a continuing process of interpretation, at the centre of which is the exposition of the Scriptures in the setting of the liturgy itself'.[314]

For many Anglicans, the words of Scripture are particularly connected to the sacraments, which are, in the words of Article 25, 'certain sure witnesses, and effectual signs of grace, and God's good will towards us, by the which he doth work invisibly in us, and doth not only quicken, but also strengthen and confirm our faith in him.' In the words of a much more recent Anglican document,

> **The Scriptures are read and interpreted in the round of common daily prayer and in the celebration of the sacraments. In worship the faith is encountered in the hearing of the word and the experience of the sacrament. In the sacrament of baptism Christians die and rise again with Christ through the waters of baptism to new life in him. In the eucharist they encounter the central mysteries of the faith ..., the making present of those past events and the experience of future glory, through the power of the Holy Spirit.**

The Virginia Report (1997)[315]

The Articles of Religion

The Thirty-nine Articles provide an authoritative statement of the Church of England's doctrine, including such matters as its doctrines of Scripture and of tradition. All deacons, priests and bishops of the Church of England have to make a 'Declaration of Assent' to the Articles and other historic formularies when they are first ordained, and on each occasion when they take up a new appointment. Licensed lay ministers also have to subscribe to it. You will have found various of the Articles quoted throughout the pages of this book.

In 1968, a report on *Subscription and Assent to the 39 Articles* was produced by the Archbishops' Commission on Christian Doctrine. Focusing in particular on the approach to Scripture set out in the Articles, it called for the then current Declaration of Assent to be changed, so that it would 'not tie down the person using it to acceptance of every one of the Articles', and would leave open 'The possibility of fresh understandings of Christian truth', while also leaving room 'for an appeal to the Articles as a norm within Anglican theology'.[316]

In response, in 1975, a new form of Declaration of Assent came into force in the Church of England.[317] The preface states of the Church of England that

> It professes the faith uniquely revealed in the Holy Scriptures and set forth in the catholic creeds, which faith the Church is called upon to proclaim afresh in each generation. Led by the Holy Spirit, it has borne witness *to* Christian truth in its historic formularies, the Thirty-nine Articles of Religion, the Book of Common Prayer and the Ordering of Bishops, Priests and Deacons.

In response, the person being ordained or licensed affirms their loyalty to 'this inheritance of faith as your inspiration and guidance under God in bringing the grace and truth of Christ to this generation and making Him known to those in your care, and declares their belief in, this inheritance of faith.'

Opinions around the Church of England differ about the implications of this form of the Declaration for appeal to the Articles in disagreements like ours. Similarly, although the church's canon law says that the doctrine of the Church of England is 'found in' the Articles and the other historic formularies, recent legal cases have raised similar questions about the implication of that wording for the Articles' status in the church's disputes.[318]

The role of bishops

The historic formularies give a particular role to bishops in maintaining the tradition of the Church of England. In the 1662 Ordinal, the Archbishop asks the bishop-elect,

> Be you ready, with all faithful diligence, to banish and drive away all erroneous and strange doctrine contrary to God's Word; and both privately and openly to call upon and encourage others to the same?

to which the answer is 'I am ready, the Lord being my helper'.[319] This both reflects the church's traditional understanding of the calling of a bishop and is rooted in biblical exhortations such as Acts 20.28-31 and Titus 1.9.

One way the bishops fulfil this calling is in their teaching. They teach alongside all kinds of people whose teaching shapes people's faith around the church: parents, Sunday School teachers, friends, popular Christian teachers, clergy, and many others. Bishops preach and give guidance and exercise their own ministry of teaching in a variety of ways, but they also have a deeper role – to oversee the teaching going on in the church, guard its truth and guide its understanding. That means that bishops are called to attend to the various flows of teaching that shape the life of the church, and to concern themselves with the health (and the sicknesses) of that whole ecosystem in which the faith is taught and learnt.

This will involve them attending closely to all the dimensions of healthy teaching that we are exploring in this part of the book. Bishops will, collectively, look at how deeply the pattern of teaching in the church as a whole is sending down roots into the Bible, how richly it is informed by the Christian tradition, how attentive it is to what we know of the natural world, and how seriously participants in it are engaging with their mission context and with one another's deep convictions. They will look at how well the church is encouraging, resourcing, and making use of those who do have formal and informal teaching roles. They will make judgements about how present teaching relates to the limits that earlier generations of the church have identified as necessary to protect the overall health of the Christian faith. This is how they 'govern Christ's people in truth [and] lead them out to proclaim the good news of the kingdom'.[320]

In doing these things, the bishops' most important teaching role may often be indirect, expressed through those acts in which they recognize, bless, commission, encourage and challenge the teaching of others.

Perhaps one of the most significant teaching roles that bishops play in Anglicanism is in relation to the liturgy that is so crucial in shaping the hearts and minds of worshippers. This is why bishops have a particular role in determining the liturgies that can be used in the Church of England.

From time to time, however, their teaching and oversight role may involve the bishops in more direct intervention, especially when the church is marked by deep disagreement. Such interventions can't simply be a matter of the bishops placing themselves at the centre of the picture, becoming those through whom right teaching flows securely outward. But it can take the form of diagnosis and repair: a diagnosis of how the whole ecosystem of teaching within the church has become unhealthy, and an identification of what is needed for it to regain health.

Sometimes, that contribution has taken the form of a report or other pronouncement such as pastoral guidance.[321] Living in Love and Faith does not look much like any of these earlier documents. It is a much bigger exercise involving not only this book but a range of other resources. Although a number of bishops have been directly involved in producing these materials, the main role of bishops has been to oversee them, inviting others to help create them, shaping an educational endeavour through which the whole church – bishops included – learns together.

Nevertheless, as described in Chapter 7, Living in Love and Faith stands in a long line of reports and statements on identity, sexuality, relationships and marriage within the Church of England and wider Anglican Communion. Taken together these represent an extended and complex effort of corporate discernment which has sought to listen obediently to God's voice in all the ways we are discussing in Part Four.

Listening to and as the whole body

'Discerning the mind of Christ for the Church is the task of the whole people of God.'[322] In Acts 15, the apostles and elders gather in Jerusalem to resolve a serious controversy facing the Early Church. Much of the business of this meeting was taken up by testimonies from Peter and from Paul and Barnabas. They spoke about what they had heard from the Spirit, and of the surprising work that they had seen the Spirit doing amongst the Gentiles.

That report was not in itself conclusive. It met with a process of discernment: the apostles and the elders met for discussion and prayer, and to test what they had heard by reading Scripture together – but listening to the stories that Paul and Barnabas told triggered that process of discernment and reading.

We are also told that, when they did reach a decision, the apostles and elders did so 'with the consent of the whole church' (Acts 15.22). They did not, in other words, conduct their discussion in isolation from the wider life and conversation of the Church. This is the outworking of the Pentecost principle that, as Joel prophesied, God can speak through any believer, whatever their gender or social status (Acts 2.16-18).

Listening to what God is saying to God's Church, discussing it critically together and testing it against Scripture, is something that we do *together*. We listen to God in part by listening to one another; by allowing ourselves to be challenged, questioned, informed and enriched by one another. That is especially true when the topics we are exploring have to do with the deep patterns of one another's experience, or with some of the most intimate relationships which we are involved in. This can't be an abstract discussion between anonymous points of view. Our deliberations need to be shaped by wide engagement with all kinds of people, who can bring a wealth of experience to bear.

Decision-making in the Early Church: Does Acts 15 help us?

In recent years the stories in Acts 10 –15 about how the Jewish followers of Jesus came to include Gentiles in the Church have often been appealed to in relation to our current disagreements over sexuality. Whether, and in what ways, this development in early Christian belief and practice can shed light on our different questions around identity, sexuality, relationships and marriage is contentious.

Some have argued that there are important parallels between their disagreements and ours. In the Early Church we are seeing God's people having to recognize that those they had made outsiders (because they were not Jews), and viewed as immoral, were being given God's Spirit and included in God's people. The people of God were therefore being led, through painful tensions, to become more inclusive and to accept people and patterns of life they had historically rejected. The story of Peter's vision in Acts 10 makes clear that this challenged long-held traditions based on the plain reading of Scripture concerning food laws. Those who reached out to Gentiles and welcomed them and advocated that they could be included without accepting the requirements of the Law therefore faced major opposition. Nevertheless, the Church learnt not to place on people 'a yoke that neither our ancestors nor we have been able to bear' (Acts 15.10) nor to call impure what God had made clean (Acts 10.15). This, it is claimed, gives a biblical pattern of Spirit-led development in belief and practice which is replicated in the experience of many Christians today in relation to the full inclusion of LGBTI+ people. This argument is based in the recognition that God is at work in the life of all in the Church, including in the lives of Christians who belong to these minorities. It is argued that if God is present with them through his Spirit, then it would be quite wrong for others to put boundaries around their participation in the life and ministry of the Church. This passage also shows how what are seen as fixed God-given boundaries (here to God's people Israel) can be redrawn to include outsiders in a way similar to what is being proposed in affirming same-sex relationships and extending marriage to include same-sex couples.

Others, however, have questioned whether appeals like this fail to recognize important differences. The inclusion of the Gentiles, it is argued, was promised in the Old Testament and commanded by Jesus, yet this is not true in relation to proposed changes concerning sexual ethics. This ability to demonstrate that changes agree with Scripture – James says in Acts 15.15 (NIV) that 'the words of the prophets are in agreement with this' – shows the importance of biblical justification for any development and warns us against simply appealing to the perceived work of the Spirit in the present. The inclusion of Gentiles shows that nobody is now excluded from the reach of God's grace but it cannot resolve our disagreements over godly sexual behaviour. Indeed, the decision of the Council has been seen as adding further support for traditional teaching. This is because although certain requirements, such as circumcision, were not required of Gentile converts to Christ, they were required to avoid sexual immorality (Acts 15.20,29). This obligation, it is claimed, would have included all forms of same-sex sexual behaviour and the various conditions set down for Gentiles may even derive from the Leviticus chapters which refer to male homosexual practice. The narrative therefore, on this reading, highlights the importance of clarity concerning sexual holiness, including in relation to new converts who are welcomed into God's people.

The disagreement can reveal different underlying assumptions between those who favour these two interpretations. Those who interpret Acts 15 as supporting full inclusion tend to focus on the Gentile/LGBTI+ parallel as a question of identity. Just as Gentiles should not be excluded just because they are Gentiles, so LGBTI+ people should not be excluded or restricted simply on account of their identity. Those who do not see the story in Acts as supporting change in our present situation tend not to consider sexual and gender questions to be ones of fundamental identity, but see them as matters demanding an ethical judgement on behaviour. Just as the Gentiles are welcomed into the Church but expected to follow the Church's ethical judgements, so LGBTI+ people are welcomed into the Church but will be expected to follow those judgements – including the judgement that same-sex sexual expression is inherently immoral. The interpreters who favour full inclusion may agree that a calling to sexual morality matters, but argue that this is about faithfulness, consent and self-restraint for LGBTI+ people in exactly the same way as for anyone else.

Finally, there are those who would reject using Acts 15 in this debate today on the grounds that the situation of the book of Acts is unique, and therefore untransferable. The book of Acts chronicles the birth of the Church: first as the Spirit comes to the Jews, then as the Spirit comes to the Gentiles. This was a one-off act of God in the wake of the resurrection, which marks the beginning of a new age. Whilst there may be lessons to learn on how we disagree, Acts 15 may not give us a legitimate analogy for the disagreements before us now.

Conciliarity and communion

The gathering in Acts 15 is sometimes described as the first 'council' in the history of the Christian Church. It created a framework for subsequent Christian thinking about what ought to constitute a council of the Church: authoritative representatives drawn from different local churches, meeting together to consider matters of common concern through prayerful consultation, with the expectation that the Holy Spirit would be at work to lead them into agreement based on shared recognition of God's guidance, such guidance being always in accord with the witness of the Holy Scriptures.

What happens, however, when such councils of the Church do not lead immediately to such agreement? Who decides what is right for the Church? During the Middle Ages in the West, the question arose of where final authority lay in the Church: was it with the office of the papacy, the Pope being the successor of Peter, the chief of the apostles, or was it with an 'ecumenical' council that gathered together bishops from every church in communion with the Pope to consult together and seek the Spirit's guidance? The latter view, later termed 'conciliarism', did not prevail at the time, but the idea that authority should be located in a council of those representing all parts of the Church, rather than in a particular person, lived on in the Church of England following its break from Rome. It also found distinctive expression from the eighteenth century onwards in what we now know as The Episcopal Church in the United States, where the General Convention, a periodic gathering of bishops alongside clergy and lay representatives from every diocese, exercised final authority within certain areas. It was a model of church government that would come to influence others across the Anglican Communion, including the Church of England. It is easy to forget that bodies such as the General Synod are not simply meant to be a convenient form of organization or of managing disputes. But, as councils of the Church, they are like the gathering in Acts 15, in which it is to be expected that those meeting together to seek God's guidance will be able to say after much prayer and careful listening: 'It seemed good to the Holy Spirit and to us...' (Acts 15.28).

So what about councils that bring together representatives from across the national boundaries? Is the Lambeth Conference a 'council' for Anglicans in this sense?[323] From its beginnings in the mid-nineteenth century, there has been an ambivalence here. Conciliar bodies within the member churches of the Anglican Communion, such as the Church of England's General Synod, have the authority to make binding decisions, including passing ecclesiastical legislation. The Lambeth Conference has never had that kind of authority, but only that of being an assembly of bishops from every diocese of the Communion where the possibility exists of coming to a common understanding of God's will for a particular situation and agreeing to proceed on the basis of that understanding – much, perhaps, as was the case for the gathering described in Acts 15.

See Chapter 7 pages 147–150 to find out more about the Lambeth Conference.

In the Anglican Communion today, the Lambeth Conference is now regarded as one of four 'instruments of communion', alongside the Anglican Consultative Council, which includes representatives of the laity and of other orders of ministry, the Primates Meeting and the office of the Archbishop of Canterbury. A recent report from the Anglican–Roman Catholic International Commission recognizes the importance of conciliar bodies at local, regional and universal levels for both Communions.[324] By meeting together to take counsel for the good of the whole Church and in attentiveness to the wisdom of the whole Church, representatives of different worshipping communities, dioceses and provinces deepen their communion with one another. Due weight should therefore be given to agreed decisions and statements that emerge from such bodies – not because they carry legal force and corresponding sanctions for non-compliance, but because we trust that through such councils God is able to give guidance to the Church. It is not the same weight that is accorded to the 'ecumenical' councils of the early centuries, because Anglicans know that they are only one part of the whole Church of God. Nonetheless, through their partial, limited and often flawed councils, Anglicans today, like the disciples in Acts 15, still seek to listen to and with the whole body of Christ.

Taking counsel together

Because the body of Christ suffers separation and division here on earth, a commitment to listen to and with the whole body of Christ has to include reaching out to those parts of the Church that do not belong within our own structures of governance and oversight. As Anglicans, we therefore also need to listen to and with those who are not Anglicans but members with us of the one body of Christ.

As noted in Chapter 7 of this book, all churches in this country are responding to profound social changes around identity, sexuality, relationships and marriage, and all are seeking to be faithful to the way of Christ as they do so. Yet there is a real divergence in how they are responding. As we saw in Chapter 7, the Church of England's current teaching and practice put it in a particular place on the ecumenical 'map' – closer to the Orthodox, Pentecostal and Roman Catholic Churches so far as teaching is concerned, but with more extensive provision for 'pastoral accompaniment' in the case of church members who choose in conscience not to follow that teaching in practice. There are many in the Church of England who are hoping it can move towards one of the other approaches described in that chapter, managing difference institutionally or through doctrinal revision. Such a change would align it with a different set of ecumenical partners. We have sought to understand and learn from churches taking all three of these approaches as part of the Living in Love and Faith process, and it will be important that the Church of England continues to do this.

We also need to look beyond our national borders. The Church of England includes the Diocese in Europe and has strong relations with a number of European Churches, including the Evangelical Church in Germany, the French Protestant Churches, the Old Catholic Churches of the Union of Utrecht and the Nordic and Baltic Lutheran Churches. Moreover, as a member church of the Anglican Communion, the Church of England is involved in international ecumenical dialogues. So far, not many of these have directly addressed the questions at the heart of this book, although both the Anglican–Roman Catholic International Commission and the International Commission for the Anglican–Orthodox Theological Dialogue are currently turning their attention to questions of moral discernment and decision-making, the former in the context of ecclesiology and the latter in the context of theological anthropology. The Anglican–Roman Catholic International Commission published an agreed statement in 1994 called *Life in Christ: Morals, Communion and the Church*. This included discussion of approaches in the two Communions to marriage, contraception, divorce and same-sex relations.[325]

In 2007, another body, the International Anglican–Roman Catholic Commission for Unity and Mission, published a document summarizing areas of doctrinal agreement and disagreement between Anglicans and Roman Catholics that had been identified through the work of the Anglican–Roman Catholic International Commission, as a basis for confident partnership in mission between our churches at local level. The whole of section 8, 'Discipleship and Holiness', drawing on *Life in Christ*, is relevant for our purposes. In a paragraph outlining common ground which we alluded to in Chapter 7, it states:

> In both our Communions marriage has a God-given pattern and
> significance, entailing the life-long exclusive commitment of a

man and a woman, encompassing the reciprocal love of husband
and wife and the procreation and raising of children. Both
Communions speak of marriage as a covenant and a vocation
to holiness and see it in the order of creation as both sign and
reality of God's faithful love. It thus has a naturally sacramental
dimension.[326]

Such a statement does not have the authority of law or official
doctrine for the Church of England. As was said in the previous
section about conciliar bodies within Anglicanism, however, it
does carry a certain weight – in this case that of arising from a
process of careful listening between representatives of two global
Communions, to arrive at what they might say together about
contested questions in the light of God's revelation and continuing
guidance.

Power and inclusion

Our processes of listening and shared discernment are deeply
affected by questions of power, as we have often, sometimes
painfully, known in producing this book. There are always questions
to be faced about who is not in the room, about the different
consequences for those who are in the room, about the ways in
which our processes sometimes work to further marginalize some
whilst allowing us to tell ourselves that we have been inclusive,
and so on. The Church of England has not typically been good at
facing these questions, nor at tackling the dynamics of power and
exclusion that damage its processes of discernment – not least in the
area of identity, sexuality, relationships and marriage.

The topics that we are discussing are, of course, ones that affect
everyone. A very wide variety of people care about them deeply
and have a stake in how these discussions go. It is also true,
however, that many of the topics we discuss (and the ways in which
we discuss them) have a particularly intense impact for specific
groups of people. We are talking about marriage and singleness in
general, but also quite specifically about same-sex marriage; we are
talking about gender in general, but also quite specifically about
trans and intersex people – and so on. We need to make sure that
those of us most affected by these discussions are fully included in
the conversation. And we need to pay serious attention to the risks
that are taken by people who agree to be involved in the church's

processes of deliberation and the costs imposed on them, and
to the different ways in which those risks and costs are borne by
different participants. Our ability to hear the voice of God speaking
through the whole Body of Christ will be impaired if we fail to take
these matters seriously.

Voices from the margins

In Chapter 17 we will be looking at how, for all of us, our reading
of the Bible, our engagements with the tradition, and all the ways
in which we listen to God, are shaped by our experience. They can
be shaped, however, not just by the unique details of each person's
autobiography, but by the experience shared by a group. This idea
has been central to the development of liberation theology, and
liberation hermeneutics (i.e., liberation-focused approaches to
interpretation), over the past half-century. That development has
been powered by two insights:

- There are ways of reading the Bible and thinking theologically
  that seem normal or obvious in the Church. They are often
  shaped, in ways that might not be visible, by the experience of
  the privileged groups that do most to produce them. So what
  we take to be just *'sound* interpretation' or just *'good* theology'
  may in fact be *white, male, middle-class, affluent, and Western*
  interpretation and theology.

- The reading and thinking of marginalized groups can often see
  things in the Bible and the tradition that privileged readers miss.
  Reading and thinking from a position of poverty, or disability,
  or from the global south, or as the target of racism, makes a
  difference. And such reading and thinking can help us recognize
  the partial perspectives from which supposedly neutral reading
  and thinking comes.

This does not mean that readings from the margins are
automatically right, and readings from privilege automatically
wrong. It does mean that, if privileged readers want to be
challenged to recognize their own partial perspectives, and to
see how those have shaped their reading and thinking, and to be
enabled to read and think past them, it makes sense to engage
seriously with reading and thinking from the margins. Such
engagement invites us to read the Bible with fresh eyes and so to
hear the voice of God calling us deeper into the teaching of Jesus.

One particular area of work of this kind, relevant to our discussions, is 'queer hermeneutics'. This is an area of study focused on readings of Scripture from the point of view of LGBTI+ people. Queer readers ask how far the Church's reading of the Bible is shaped by assumptions about gender and sexuality that only seem natural or obvious because the Church privileges a cisgender heterosexual perspective. They argue that the apparently clear and stable categories that are used when the Church reads texts about sex and gender are not, in fact, natural or obvious, but the product of specific, contingent histories of thought and practice.

We also need to be aware of how our geographical locations and history with other parts of the world make us central or marginal. Voices from the global south include both voices calling for a rethinking of traditional teaching on relationships, sex and identity, and voices calling for a reaffirmation of that teaching. Those voices can alert us to the ways in which the Church of England's debates have an impact far beyond Britain, and to the ways in which the nature of that impact, as we have already noted, is entangled with our history of colonialism.

Conclusion

Listening to the voice of God is a task for the whole Church. It is a task for 'the living and growing "mind" of the church that has from generation to generation been formed and challenged by the scriptural Word in the process of appropriating that Word in liturgy, life and teaching' (Lambeth 1988).[327] It demands of us a wide variety of engagements and conversations that put us in the way of being challenged, questioned, encouraged, enlightened and surprised by the other members of Christ's body.

Canon A.1 declares that the Church of England '*belongs* to the true and apostolic Church of Christ'; it understands itself to be a true part of that Church, but not the whole. In seeking to hear what God is saying to the Church of England through the Church, therefore, we should have confidence in our own authoritative traditions and ways of exercising ecclesial authority today. We should show humility regarding our limitations and failings, and an expectation that God's guidance for us as a church will become clearer to us as we take counsel with other churches who belong with us as parts of the whole.

To attend to the '"mind" of the church' means reading the Bible together in the light of the creeds and the history of authoritative teachings from the Christian past. It means reading while alert to the challenges that our ongoing reading might present to those teachings. It means reading in the midst of worship, which directs our hearts and minds to the love of God, and shapes our imagination of the whole Christian story. It means listening to one another – to the whole community of Christ's people down the centuries and across the world today, including those often excluded from the conversations of the Church. It means reflecting on the questions about how we identify amongst them those voices that carry particular weight in conveying to us Christ's guidance to his people. The more we hear of his voice, the deeper we can be drawn into the abundant life of love and faith that God has for us.

CHAPTER 15

Creation

'We believe in one God,
the Father, the Almighty,
Maker of heaven and earth.'[328]

The God we listen to is the God
who spoke the world into being.
(Psalm 33.6; Genesis 1.3)

The whole world comes from God and
depends entirely upon God for its life,
and 'Everything created by God is
good.' (1 Timothy 4.4)

The created world is not by its nature a realm opposed to God. It is not the cold end where the radiance shining from God finally gives out. It is not even the neutral backdrop to God's action. Creation is God's good gift, freely given and lovingly upheld.

To live rightly in response to God is to live as we were created to live. Such life is not something imposed on us from outside; it is not something foreign to us. Our bodies, histories, and experience don't have to be rubbed out or ignored in order to make space for this new life – even though it does and will involve us dying to sin and rising to life in Christ. We are all being called to a life deeply in tune with what is truest about us, a life that is good for us because it is what we were made for.

Christians, therefore, don't turn to the created world as a source of independent wisdom, unrelated to the voice of God that speaks in Jesus – but nor do we turn to Jesus expecting to hear a voice unconnected to the created world. We believe that Jesus is the incarnation of the same Word that called creation into existence. He sustains and governs it, and it holds together in him (John 1.1-14; Colossians 1.15-17). We therefore expect to find the same voice that speaks to us in Jesus and in the whole history of salvation speaking through the order and beauty of creation.

Psalm 19 portrays God's voice speaking to us in these two ways. It opens

The heavens are telling the glory of God;
And the firmament proclaims his handiwork.
Day to day pours forth speech,
And night to night declares knowledge.

It continues to celebrate this until in verse 7 it turns to God's speech to Israel:

The law of the LORD is perfect, reviving the soul.
The decrees of the LORD are sure, making wise the simple.

There is no conflict here.

We also believe, however, that God's good world has been affected by sin and evil. These are not ultimate and won't have the final word; they are a corruption of God's good creation rather than an equal and opposite force standing against God. The corruption that they work in the fabric of creation is nevertheless pervasive, for creation's fall is deep. Creation as we see it is out of balance, rebellious and destructive. Similarly, our ability to *see* the good grain of creation is itself damaged by sin: we misunderstand creation and we mistake how the voice of God is speaking to us through it.

We are therefore faced with several questions:

- What claims about the world – about how it is ordered and how it works – do we make as we discuss identity, sexuality, relationships and marriage?

- What is the connection between our descriptions of how the world works and our judgements about how we ought to behave?

- What difference does it make that the world we look at is one distorted by suffering and evil?

- What difference does it make that our ability to make sense of the world is itself affected by sin?

Listening to science

If we want to learn more about the world that God has made, it makes sense to listen to the wisdom and insight gained by all those, whether Christians or not, who explore it. Turning to science does not mean turning away from the God who speaks in the Bible or through the Christian tradition. It means listening to people who use a particular set of well-developed methods to investigate the world that God has spoken into being. It means letting what we learn from them test and inform our claims.

If someone wants to explore, for example, how Christians should respond to mitochondrial transfer technology, to the chlorination of chicken, or to the epidemic of sleep-deprivation in our culture, or to the COVID-19 pandemic, it will be vital to be as well-informed as possible about the relevant science. Augustine wrote more than sixteen hundred years ago about the danger of Christians being ignorant of the best knowledge circulating in the culture around them:

> **Whenever, you see, they [i.e., those outside the church] catch some members of the Christian community making mistakes on**

> a subject which they know inside out, and defending their hollow
> opinions on the authority of our books, on what grounds are they
> going to trust those books on the resurrection of the dead and
> the hope of eternal life and the kingdom of heaven, when they
> suppose they include any number of mistakes and fallacies on
> matters which they themselves have been able to master either
> by experiment or by the surest of calculations?[329]

We need to continue following the wisdom of John Calvin. He wrote
in his *Institutes of the Christian Religion* that

> If we regard the Spirit of God as the sole fountain of truth, we
> shall neither reject the truth itself, nor despise it wherever it shall
> appear, unless we wish to dishonour the Spirit of God… Shall we
> say that the philosophers were blind in their fine observation
> and artful description of nature?… that they are insane who
> developed medicine, devoting their labour to our benefit?[330]

People today often think that there is an inherent conflict between
science and religion. Although conflicts do arise, this is a very
limited and highly distorted picture. For example, the Christian
understanding of the world as God's ordered creation and of humans
as fallen creatures was the seedbed for early modern science. It
was in part because they believed that God had given the world
a good and stable order that medieval and early modern thinkers
thought it possible and profitable to investigate that order. It was in
part because they were aware that sin clouds our reason that they
developed methods that could show us how the world that God has
made does not line up neatly with our existing desires and intentions.

When we are talking about human identity, sexuality, relationships
and marriage, we should listen to the best of what the natural and
social sciences have to tell us. They can tell us something about how
human bodies work, in all their multilayered complexity and variety.
They can tell us about the prevalence, and something about the
origin, of different kinds of orientation and identity. They can tell
us about the consequences of different patterns of action, and the
kinds of flourishing or diminished life that our interventions promote.

As we saw in Chapter 6, we need also to remember that science
itself is not exempt from problems in its attempts to understand
the world. Just as in theology, there are all kinds of possibilities for
error, bias and corruption, and our engagement with science needs
to remain critical. We should interrogate, for instance, what picture
of flourishing and diminishment is being used when a particular

treatment is said to be 'good' for us. We should ask whose bodies and lives have been attended to and whose have been ignored. We should ask whose interests have been served. It is also worth remembering, however, that many of the techniques of science are themselves tools for identifying and overcoming that error, bias and corruption.[331] The conversation between science and faith should certainly be a mutually critical one – but it is far richer and more complex than can be captured by any simple picture of science and faith in conflict.

Natural knowledge

Affirming natural knowledge?

Some Christians argue as follows:

- Creation as a whole has been given a good order by God.

- Human beings are endowed by God with the natural capacity to know that order.

- Human beings are meant to behave in ways that flow from that knowledge.

There is biblical precedent for this. Think, say, of the way that the book of Proverbs turns regularly to the natural world as a source of wisdom for life.

Within Christian tradition this good, knowable order of creation has often been given the name 'natural law'. Sometimes, natural law arguments start from reflection on what are taken to be clear basic facts about the nature of human existence, and then ask what is good for beings of this kind. Sometimes they start from the deeply rooted patterns of human wisdom – on the basis that those patterns have been laid down over centuries, as human societies have learnt to live with one another and with their natural environments. Sometimes they start from attentiveness to the patterns and possibilities that scientific exploration discovers in the world around us.[332]

Arguments like this can lead in different directions. It can be argued, for example, that heterosexual marriage is a natural response to the biology of men and women, to the way procreation works, and to the needs of children. Some will say that, since human beings have always had to respond to the same underlying biological realities, the patterns of marriage prevalent in human societies through history are pointers to this natural law. Arguments of this kind can be found, for instance, in *Men and Women in Marriage*, a document produced in 2013 by the Church of England's Faith and Order Commission. 'We cannot turn our back upon the natural, and especially the biological, terms of human existence', it says. 'Certain basic structural features' of marriage are visible in many human societies, it goes on, and we should not 'exaggerate the cultural relativity of marriage-forms'.[333]

You will also find arguments heading in a different direction, since scientific exploration is now discovering more about the complexity and diversity of human biology and the patterns of our desires and self-perceptions. Some argue that these findings challenge conventional Christian wisdom and have radical implications for our teaching and behaviour. In Chapter 6, for instance, we referred to the scientific study of intersex characteristics – including, for instance, the discovery that as well as the familiar XX (female) and XY (male) patterns, there are various other combinations: XY chromosomes in a body which looks female; one single X chromosome; or a mixture of XX and XY cells in the same individual. Does this suggest that we need to widen our understanding of the natural variability of human bodies?

Natural law arguments – leading in either of these directions, or in any other – are often combined with appeals to the Bible, to tradition, and to other sources of insight. Even if someone uses a natural law argument in favour of marriage, for instance, that doesn't stop them believing that God's revelation and the infused virtues of the Holy Spirit transform even the natural love that undergirds marriage – insisting, for instance, that married couples are called to model the love of God for one another. It also wouldn't necessarily exclude that person admitting that some correction or reorientation is needed of what we learn from the natural world, because of its fallen character or because of the effects of sin on our understanding of it. Nevertheless, those who make natural law arguments often display confidence that human beings can know the order of the world reasonably well, and that moral judgements can flow from that knowledge fairly straightforwardly.

Questioning natural knowledge?

Sometimes, in contrast to this, people make arguments where the emphasis falls much more strongly on sin's disordering of creation, and in particular on its disordering of our ability to know creation.

Someone might agree in principle that creation has been given to us by God with a good order, but insist that our capacity to know this order has become too deeply entangled with sin to be a reliable guide. They might, for instance, point to the way relations between men and women are organized in the forms of marriage prevalent across multiple human societies. They might argue that many of these forms of relationship involve the subordination of women, and that most of those forms of subordination have been justified (endlessly) as being 'natural'. These widespread patterns of human behaviour don't reveal the good order of creation so much as the unflagging capacity of human beings for oppression. We are all too good at convincing ourselves that we have a natural right to our positions of unjust privilege. One example of such an argument is provided in a critique of *Men and Women in Marriage*, where it is argued that 'We have used appeals to the "obvious" facts of biology, and appeals to the "obvious" lessons of history, to oppress and to abuse.'[334]

What is needed, in this view, is the ongoing transformation of our minds by the light of Christ – calling us away from all the distortions that we have persuaded ourselves are natural. Such a view is sometimes described as 'apocalyptic', because it stresses the dramatic revelation (in Greek: *apokalypsis*) of God's truth over against the existing patterns of our understanding, and of our world.[335]

Another version of this kind of approach can be found in much queer theology. Queer theologians and other queer theorists often argue that ideas we have taken to be 'natural' need to be 'denaturalized':

> Denaturalization renders visible the culturally constructed nature of our basic organizing categories, thus limiting their power and efficacy. Denaturalization is part of the process of destabilizing, in order to change binary and hierarchical distinctions between men and women, straight and gay, cisgender and transgender.[336]

For a wide range of critics of natural law approaches, the distortions from which we need to be freed may be in our own hearts and minds. We need God's revelation in Jesus to help us see that good order of creation, as if for the first time, so faulty is our unaided grasp of it – and we will only truly see that good order when we have been taught to live in a harmony with it that is as yet foreign to us.

The distortions from which we need to be freed may also be present in the world we see around us – because creation is in the hands of enemy powers, and so Jesus' coming has the force of an invasion, a victory over 'the cosmic powers of this present darkness' (Ephesians 6.12). God's saving work redeems and fulfils creation – but it also transfigures it. It may generate and commend patterns of life which appear, in some senses, to be 'unnatural'. The call to celibacy has sometimes been seen in this way.

See a further discussion of celibacy in Chapter 12 (pages 238–241).

Just as natural law arguments can take several different forms, so can these arguments that question natural knowledge. The emphasis can fall, for instance, on the idea that the Bible teaches us to recognize the true order of creation in ways that are likely otherwise to have been missed or denied. It can fall on the idea that this biblical revelation will tend to stand in opposition to other ways of thinking, however well rooted those ways seem to be in what people know of the natural order of things, in the long history of human society, or in the discoveries of modern science (see 1 Corinthians 1.19-21). Paul's radical statement of mutuality between husband and wife in 1 Corinthians 7.2-4 provides an example of this.

Alternatively, the emphasis can fall on the need for ongoing discovery. In the way suggested at the end of Chapter 14, someone might encounter queer readings of the Bible undertaken by LGBTI+ people and experience a transformative shock. They might come to believe that their existing readings had been shaped by problematic assumptions about what is natural, and that faithfulness to Jesus now demands that they read, and act, differently.

Conclusion

In looking for responses to the questions set out in Part Two, we are looking for ways of living well in God's world. It is inevitable that our discussion of those questions will involve claims about what that world is like. They will almost certainly involve claims about our bodies and claims about what is good for us – and some of those claims will be on topics which we can learn about from science.

Where that happens, a conversation with the relevant science is vital – but that conversation might go in many different directions.

- We might discover that we are invested in a claim about the world that we can no longer sustain in the face of the scientific evidence. There might be some, for instance, whose understanding of the biblical picture of gender or sexual differentiation is challenged by the scientific evidence about intersex characteristics.

- We might be pressed to clarify the difference between what the theological and the scientific claims are saying. Someone, for instance, who was convinced that gender transitioning was inherently harmful might need to clarify in what sense they meant 'harmful', in the face of medical evidence. Equally someone convinced of the theological case for gender transition may need to clarify at what age it can begin, given science's uncertainty about the long-term effects of some forms of treatment.

- We might participate in critiques of the scientific findings. We might, for instance, ask whether any of the findings from social psychology that we are wrestling with are affected by the 'replication crisis', in which the results of a surprising number of studies have proven difficult to reproduce.[337] This kind of questioning can be used inappropriately, as a kind of cheap 'Get out of jail free' card to wave at any result you don't like – but it can also be part of a serious mutually critical conversation.

- We might keep coming back to the difference between science's *descriptive* task, and the church's *normative* task: we are asking how things *should* be, or how we *should* behave. Those are distinct tasks, even if there is a close and complex relationship between them.

In our debates about identity, sexuality, relationships and marriage, we encounter a complex mix of appeals to science, to scriptural depictions of the natural world, to conventional wisdom, and to Christ's radical revision of what we might deem natural. There is no quick route to sorting out the differing pressures and possibilities here, nor to ordering and reconciling all these claims. There is no shortcut: listening for the voice of God demands a careful, self-critical and ongoing conversation between our faith and our knowledge of the created world. This kind of conversation is, nevertheless, unavoidable for those who believe that God made us, and that God calls us in Jesus to the redemption and fulfilment of our creaturely and sin-marred lives.

CHAPTER 16
Cultural context

When we seek to hear God's voice, we can only do so as people living in a particular time and place, embedded in a particular culture.

We have already noted some of the questions posed by the Bible's emergence from particular cultural contexts, and by the difference between those and our cultures today. We now need to understand the impact of our own cultural context.

How does that context affect how we hear God today, and how does what we hear from God challenge that context?

Church versus world?

One way into this topic is to ask how 'Church' and 'world' relate – and answers to this question can go in two broad directions.

Some will draw attention to how, in the Bible and in tradition, God's people have often shared in and drawn upon the wisdom of their wider context (e.g. in Proverbs). They might note how the God who is at work throughout the world has sometimes had to correct and change the chosen people from outside (e.g. through Cyrus in Isaiah 45.1-13). They might argue that the Church now needs to learn from our culture and repent of its errors, and that failure here damages our mission because the gospel can no longer be heard as good news by the people around us.

Others will highlight how both Scripture and tradition point to a sharp contrast between the Church and the world (e.g. 1 John 2.15-17) and also witness to the world's hostility to God's holy, called-out people. They might argue that the Church must not be ashamed of upholding its distinctive teachings, because it is called by God to be a faithful, counter-cultural community. It is called to offer a better story to the world, and to resist the misunderstandings and disordered patterns of desire that are at work in it.

Set out in this way, many Christians – whichever of these approaches they would advocate in relation to identity, sexuality, relationships and marriage – will probably recognize that on other issues they could find themselves more in sympathy with the other approach. There is no one-size-fits-all model for how we might hear and respond to the voice of God in our cultural context.

There is a problem with this way of posing the question, however. What happens when we stop using 'Church' as an abstract theological term and instead use it to refer to the real Christian communities that we participate in? We will then be referring to communities that have their own complex internal cultures, that are always embroiled in the surrounding culture in ways that are difficult to disentangle.

When we think about individual Christians, it will often be very difficult to tease out the different influences that have shaped them.

Think, for instance, about how particular Christians learn what it means to love their children, discovering the patterns of action and speech that will best embody their love, and in the process discovering more fully what that love is. Their imagination and habits are likely to have been formed by: their relationship to their own parents (in some complex stew of contrast and emulation); things they have learnt in school and through their whole education; their experience of other families around them; their consumption of novels, films, songs, television series, adverts, and any number of other cultural products; their reading of newspaper and magazine comment and advice pieces; their conversations with friends inside and outside the church; their use of the Internet and social media; the parental leave policies of their workplace; sermons; Bible reading; the unspoken but visible reactions of those around them – and so on.

It is very difficult indeed to disentangle all of these threads and to say confidently which habits and patterns of thought came from which source. It is still more difficult to separate out what came from 'Church' and what came from 'world' – and it makes no sense to suppose that all that is healthy and good in these habits came from the Church, all that is bad from the world (or vice versa). We need a better way of posing the question.

Gospel and culture

What if, rather than approaching these issues in terms of 'Church' and 'world', we think about the relationship between the gospel (the good news of Jesus Christ) and culture?

The whole world is God's, and just as God is present to every part of creation, so God relates to every human culture. But the same word by which God upholds all of creation and speaks to every human culture has been spoken to the world again, purely and truly, in Christ. The questions that face us are about the complex relationships between Christ and culture – or between Christ, the varied cultures of the Church, and the even more varied cultures of the surrounding world.

How should we view human cultures in the light of Christ – both the cultures of the world and the cultures of the Church, in all their complex intermingling? Picking up some of the themes explored in Part Three, we can see human culture as created, sinful and redeemed. As those created in God's image we are called to be fruitful and to nurture and develop God's gifts in creation (Genesis 1.28). As social creatures who live together in community (Genesis 2.18), part of fulfilling that calling involves creative culture-making. As fallen creatures, however, the cultures we develop are, like us (and as we saw in the last chapter, like creation as a whole), always a complex intermingling: life-giving and God-honouring elements found alongside elements which embody our rejection of God's good purposes and our desire to establish ourselves apart from God (as classically in the Babel narrative of Genesis 11).

The gospel, however, is the good news that God's redemption doesn't simply heal individual human beings, but their relationships, their communities and their cultures. We see this in the biblical vision of the new creation. The future God has for us is not pictured simply as a return to the garden of Eden. It is focused on a city – a glorious city filled with buildings and adornments, the products of human culture (Isaiah 60.11; Revelation 21.2-27).

As we await the realization of that multicultural vision of God's goal for humanity (Revelation 5.9, 7.9), the Church's calling, since Christ's resurrection, is to carry the gospel of Christ to all nations (Revelation 14.6) in cross-cultural mission. We see this throughout Church history from Pentecost onwards.

The mission historian Andrew Walls speaks of two principles shaping these recurring encounters between the Christian gospel and multiple, diverse cultures.

- There is a universalizing 'pilgrim principle'. The inclusive nature and missionary impulse of the gospel means it is to be continuously shared across and within ever more cultures by followers of Jesus. No culture is to be denied the gospel and no culture does not need the gospel.

- There is also a localizing 'indigenizing principle'. The gospel leads to conversion to Christ and this in turn brings about changes within every culture, and the formation of a distinctive way of being the Church in and for every culture. No culture is wholly affirmed by the gospel, no culture is wholly rejected by the gospel.[338]

Cross-cultural learning

Christian faith is global and yet should also always be local. It is transcultural and yet it should also always be inculturated. The one faith will look different in every culture, and yet its differing forms should always be in conversation with one another and recognizable to each other.

As Jesus' witnesses, when we reach new locations or encounter new sub-cultures within our existing location, we are not meant to invite the people we meet simply to take on wholesale an already formed church culture. Rather, we are meant to invite all people and cultures to be converted and go on being converted by the same Word of life that converted and continues to convert us. After all, our church cultures – all the patterns of Christian action, thought and feeling that we inhabit – are themselves not identical to the gospel. They are mixed realities, still in the process of being converted.

As response to the gospel takes root in new contexts, amongst new people, reports of that experience and discipleship can flow back to the existing centres of church life. At times this will disturb and transform them, expanding their sense of what discipleship means. In the process, those who have been sharing the gospel may discover just how much their current understanding of it is shaped by their own culture – perhaps in ways they had never before noticed. They may realize the extent to which they have been trying to pass on their own culture when they thought they were simply passing on the gospel. Seeing how, in the power of the Spirit, the good news of Jesus Christ takes root differently in the different communities we encounter may lead us into new ways of understanding, inhabiting, and communicating the gospel. The conversion of others can and should fuel our own ongoing conversion.

See the discussion about Acts 15 in Chapter 14, 'Listening to and as the whole body' on pages 320–323.

The church in any one place always needs to be listening to challenges from Christians and churches within other cultures who, from outside our culture, may see the possibilities of gospel life very differently.[339] '[T]he experience of the Church as it is lived in different places has something to contribute to the discernment of the mind of Christ for the Church' (*The Virginia Report*, 1997).[340]

In one important sense, we have already received 'the truth of the gospel' given us in Christ and in the biblical witness to him. In another important sense, however, we grow in our understanding of the gospel through obedience to the call to bring it to all nations, and to engage with all the cultures of the world. We cannot, therefore, know the fullest truth of the gospel until the end of time: 'It takes the whole world to know the whole gospel.'[341]

Anglicans and polygamy

The area where identity, sexuality, relationships and marriage have historically been most prominent within recent Anglicanism is probably in relation to polygamy. The spread of the gospel by Anglicans to polygamous cultures, especially much of Africa, raised major questions in relation to the church's teaching about monogamy.

The first Lambeth Conference in 1867 was called in part because of the teaching and ministry of Bishop Colenso of Natal. Among the problems was his more accommodating attitude to the practice of polygamy even though he was clear that it was 'at variance with the whole spirit of Christianity, and must eventually be rooted out by it, wherever it comes'. The third Conference in 1888 insisted on a strict discipline – 'persons living in polygamy be not admitted to baptism'. Significantly, Bishop Crowther was the only native African voice present at the gathering. It soon became clear, however, that, in a polygamous cultural context, this approach could lead to men divorcing wives to become monogamous, and those wives being left destitute.

By the 1920s the Conference was recognizing this context and so although reaffirming its stance it also said 'if a polygamist wishes to separate from his wives and be baptized, care must be taken that he make proper arrangements for the separated wives before he can be accepted'.

In 1958 the Conference admitted that the Anglican Communion had not yet solved the problems of introducing monogamy into polygamous societies where it brought 'a social and economic revolution'. A decade later it was recognized that 'polygamy poses one of the sharpest conflicts between the faith and particular cultures'. At last taking more seriously the need to listen to the immediate context and the church within it, it asked 'each province to re-examine its discipline in such problems in full consideration with other provinces in a similar situation'. It soon became clear, however, that there was disagreement about how to respond among African Anglicans themselves.

Finally, in 1988, after extended discussions, and as the African churches became more prominent at Lambeth Conferences, the centenary of its original decision was marked by not just revising but reversing its discipline. Monogamy was reaffirmed but the baptism and confirmation of converted polygamists was permitted on certain strict conditions (including a ban on additional wives and acceptance by the local church). However, no Anglican church ordains known polygamists, and practice in relation to them receiving communion varies.

This story is one of a long, drawn-out discernment concerning how received teaching on marriage needed to adapt in order to provide better pastoral care in a new cultural context. Eventually, while still clearly teaching monogamy on the basis of Scripture (despite famous examples of polygamy in the Old Testament) and tradition, a less strict pastoral discipline was developed. This was as a result of listening to those who knew the cultural context and the impact of current practice on the church's mission and who believed that God was calling the Communion to change its traditional stricter disciplines in relation to the pattern of married life required of those receiving baptism or confirmation.

Engaging with the cultures around us

What follows from all this for how we approach listening to God in relation to our cultural contexts?

It requires our attentiveness to the actual lived texture of the cultures which we live in. We need to look closely at their practices and their patterns of imagination. Big, blunt models of how Church and world relate can hinder this, making it harder to acknowledge what is good or to identify what is bad in the cultures around us. To do this properly we need to take and apply to our own cultural context the counsel of Max Warren in relation to cross-cultural Christian mission:

> **Our first task in approaching another people, another culture, another religion, is to take off our shoes, for the place we are approaching is holy. Else we may find ourselves treading on men's dreams. More serious still, we may forget that God was here before our arrival.**[342]

Christians' analyses of their surrounding cultures sometimes take the form of sweeping statements or simplistic 'genealogies' providing historical stories about where particular practices came from. We need, instead, to consider what our friends and neighbours actually think, say, and do, and to pay attention to the ways in which cultural practices have been repurposed and transformed over time. For instance, it is quite common to hear from Christian pulpits sweeping claims about Western individualism, and perhaps about its origins in the Enlightenment (or whichever historical period we are tempted to blame). It is less common to hear discussions that do justice to the lives of ordinary people – to the patterns of their relationship, their sense of their family and community obligations, their ways of valuing friendship.

It is only when we pursue respectful, careful listening that we will be able to discern what faithfulness to the gospel might look like in the cultures around us. We need to practise what John Stott called 'double listening': listening carefully and urgently to the world as well as listening to God.[343] It is only when we listen in this way that we might see where any particular culture could (perhaps in surprising ways) already be working with the grain of God's purposes in creation, and where it has consciously or unconsciously rejected these. The biblical distinction between the desire and way of the Spirit and the desire and way of the flesh (that is, life insofar as it is turned away from God) is a real one (Romans 8). Discerning where exactly that contrast runs in our own lives, the lives of those around us, and the complexities of any human culture is, however, no easy matter. The Spirit/flesh distinction does not cut a neat line between the visible life of the Church and the equally visible life of the surrounding cultures.

For example, sometimes the process of discernment will lead some Christians to hear God calling them to challenge something they believe to be wrong in the cultures around them. But there will not always be agreement within the Church on whether that stance is appropriate or necessary. And, given the entanglement of church culture and wider culture, taking such a stance against a tendency in the world nearly always also means taking a stance against that same tendency in the Church, and this can create conflict within the Church and even present challenges for maintaining communion.

Indeed, Christians might hear a critique of the Church arising in the wider culture, and might discern in it the voice of God, calling the Church to account. In the words of a report from the 1988 Lambeth Conference

> **the Church learns from its cultural context something about its own Gospel ... indeed, the Church may even hear its *judgement* from this context. It may be shown how restricted its vision of humanity, and of the future and hopes of humanity, has been.**[344]

Here a challenge from outside the Church, or a Christian's involvement in practices or movements beyond the Church, can send Christians to look again at their Scriptures, to look again at Christ, and to see with new eyes a distortion within the life of the church. For instance: a significant part of the impetus for recent changes in Church thinking and practice in relation to the environment, or in relation to safeguarding, has come from outside the church. Those changes are in part a response to patterns of thought and practice that have arisen in the wider culture. But in the light of the challenge posed by these developments, many Christians have recognized with new urgency and depth that their own faith calls them to take these matters far, far more seriously than they have done – and that they are called to repent of their failures.

Here again, there will not always be agreement among Christians. In fact, disagreements of this form can present even greater challenges for maintaining communion. They often lead to appeals to reorder our common life together in Christ. Those pressing for this change will understand the call to be generated by a discernment of the Spirit, blowing wherever the Spirit wills, drawing us in surprising ways deeper into the teaching of Jesus. For those Christians who disagree, it can appear that what is being proposed amounts to being blown this way and that by the winds of the prevailing culture.

These tensions can at times be heightened when the critiques are understood (or simply strongly felt) by some Christians to relate to matters which are central to the gospel and Christian identity. It might be that some well-ingrained habit of Christian speech or practice that Christians have thought part of the whole package of being Christian is now being identified by some as something not actually required by the gospel, or even as something opposed to the gospel. It might be that hallowed aspects of the church's fellowship, liturgies, or ways of reading the Bible have been found to be at fault and to be obscuring rather than communicating the good news of God's love in Christ.

The most serious difficulties arise when some people hear God calling them to make changes within their church in order to be faithful to the gospel, but those changes cannot be recognized by other Christians as consonant with what God has said in Christ and Scripture. Those other Christians might even view the proposed changes as implying a different gospel. This perspective may arise from Christians living in the same culture and wrestling with the same questions. It is even more likely to be the reaction of those living in very different cultures who may interpret what is happening as amounting to a capitulation of the church to the surrounding world.

Discussions about identity, sexuality, relationships and marriage in the Church of England are often marked by people's sweeping caricatures of others' positions. One person accuses another of being 'sectarian', or of having committed 'missional suicide'. They are accused in turn of 'cultural conformity', or of having traded the gospel for cultural relevance. The real debate here, however, is not between those who are faithful to Christian truth and those who have capitulated to the surrounding culture. Some people involved in the debate think that an insight has arisen in the culture surrounding the church that chimes with, or prompts fresh insight into, a deep truth of the gospel. They believe that, now that they have reread the Scriptures in the light of that insight, they are called by those Scriptures to penitence and change. Others involved in the debate think that the same cultural ideas are ones that, when tested against the Scriptures, turn out to be opposed to the gospel. They believe that the Church is called to resist those ideas in order to remain faithful. Both groups are seeking to be faithful to Christian truth – but they disagree about the proper understanding of that truth.

In such circumstances we find ourselves having to ask:

- how deep the rethinking of the tradition prompted by a culture's challenges and questions can go, or, in other words, how much of our inheritance is malleable and how much is unchangeable; and

- how much a church can change and adapt its teaching and practice in and for new and different cultures while remaining faithful – and being viewed from elsewhere as remaining faithful – to the one gospel for all cultures.

These are questions that need to be tackled by recourse to the Bible, to the Church's tradition, to the study of creation, to human experience, and so on – all the other sources and factors that we have been discussing in this Part. The question of how deeply a perspective has been shaped by the surrounding culture, or of how prevalent the relevant perspective is in that wider culture, might be important – but the answers to those questions by themselves will not tell us anything about how that perspective relates to the gospel.

Conclusion

The way in which Christians hear the voice of God is always shaped by the wider culture within which the Church is set, and in more ways than we will ever recognize.

Listening to the voice of God involves an ongoing process of discernment, in which we learn to recognize what in the Church and what in the wider world resonates with God's Word spoken in Jesus, and what muffles and distorts it.

In the process of that discernment, we need to attend to the way in which Christians in other contexts have learnt to respond to that Word – and to the ways in which they can enable us to hear that

Word differently. We also need to learn to recognize some of the places in which we have been mistaking our own voices for the voice of God.

One way we can do this, and discover more of what God's Word means, is by attending to the questions, challenges and possibilities of the cultures that surround us. There is no recipe for how we do this, no shortcut to discovery. There is no alternative but to listen hard to the people all around us, and to read and reread the sources of Christian faith in the light of the questions they ask, the criticisms they make, and the possibilities they present.

We may find our eyes opened to new challenges and new possibilities for the Church of England's life – as well as finding our discernments sharpened of what is healthy and what is unhealthy in those cultures themselves.

CHAPTER 17

Experience and conscience

The previous chapters in Part Four have focused on how the Church listens to God's voice in the Bible, the Church, creation and our cultural context.

All of these sources stand outside us. We can all see them.

We can draw each other's attention to them and discuss them, and test one another's claims against them.

Although we can share our understandings, each person listening
to God also does so, however, as an individual person with our own
personal experiences of God, our own deeply held convictions, and
our own conscientious moral judgements. We can report on these
to others, but only we know what we are thinking, experiencing, and
feeling. Our experience isn't available for others to view in the same
way as the other sources we have been describing.

Experience

In the Church of England's debates about identity, sexuality,
relationships and marriage, appeals to experience are often
contentious. At its crudest, we sometimes draw sharp lines between
views that we see as arising from reading the Bible, or views that
we see as being reasonable, and others that we see as depending
on experience. The implication tends to be that *some* Christians'
arguments can be defended before the independent tribunal of
rationality or the Bible but that *others* are unduly swayed by the
details of their volatile subjectivity. There's often a power dynamic to
this kind of claim, too: though people on all sides can be accused of
being emotional and experience-driven, this is an accusation more
likely to be made against people from various marginalized groups
than against people in positions of majority and privilege.

In reality, however, everyone involved in the church's deliberations
and debates is shaped by their experience. We are all deeply
shaped by our own experience when it comes to the questions we
think most important, the methods we think most appropriate, the
places we look for understanding, and so on. Our debates are never
simply a matter of intellectual arguments and the accumulation of
evidence. They are always interactions between embodied, located
human beings. And that means that all the ideas and arguments,
the questions and concerns that we bring to them come with
varying degrees of emotional investment, and varying quantities of
attached emotional baggage. We always have more reasons for our
claims than we are aware of or can express, even to ourselves.

To recognize this does not mean embracing relativism. Nor does
it mean that everyone's contribution should be seen as nothing
more than a report on their subjective experience. It does mean
though that, however objective our approaches, they are always
also *our* approaches.

Consider, for instance, our approaches to the Bible. Whatever we see in particular passages, we see because of our experience – some formation, some training of mind and imagination, some journey of life with God that has enabled us to see it. That is why we have insisted several times during Part Four that discernment of what is 'biblical' is a corporate task. Only as people with different perceptions engage with one another, try to understand one another's claims, and hold one another to account, do we discover how much our perceptions are simply our subjective responses, and how much they are more than that.

This doesn't simply affect our approach to particular passages. As we have noted in earlier chapters, our reading is shaped by our beliefs about the Bible's purpose and about the kind of reading we are meant to undertake. It is shaped by our beliefs about the Bible's unity and about the kinds of tensions or contradictions that might characterize it. It is shaped by whatever habitual ways of reading we have inherited from those who taught us. And as well as being influenced by our reading and rereading of the Bible itself, all of these beliefs and expectations will have been influenced by the company we have kept, the worship we have experienced, the cultures we have been part of, the teaching we have received, the experiences of God that we have had. These beliefs will have been influenced by the ways they mesh with (or rub against) all the other things we think we know. In other words: all of this will have been informed by our experience – and so all of it can be disturbed by our experience, or by our encounter with others whose experience is different.

Conviction

Where we feel particularly strongly – where our emotional investment is especially strong – we tend to call our ideas 'convictions'. Convictions are things we feel strongly about, often very strongly, even if we don't fully understand why. Rational argument and the careful assessment of evidence may play a role in their formation, sometimes a big role, but these are seldom if ever the whole story. We are very good at overestimating the influence of argument and evidence and ignoring or downplaying the role of society, culture, family and friends, events, personality, and multiple other factors.

We will talk in the next chapter about times when a conviction seems to arise in us unbidden, suddenly gripping and compelling us. At other times, however, our convictions will more clearly be part of a pattern of belief and feeling which we have settled into over time. This may have happened after conscious intellectual and spiritual wrestling; it may have happened subconsciously. The demands, commitments, bits of self-knowledge and knowledge of the world that we possess have somehow slowly been woven (perhaps after conscious intellectual and spiritual wrestling, perhaps more subconsciously) into a roughly coherent structure that we can inhabit, at least for now. We have found a pattern in which the way we understand God, the way we read the Scriptures, the way we experience our identity, and many other factors, all roughly cohere and reinforce one another. The sense of fit, of this being a shape that makes sense for us, can give it very deep roots in our thoughts and in our feelings. An isolated claim or argument, that seems to others to be simply something to toss around in discussion, might for us be so woven into the fabric of our minds and hearts that we find ourselves unexpectedly upset, or unexpectedly fierce, in those discussions.

Of course, convictions, however deeply rooted and closely woven or however compellingly experienced, are always fallible. As with any claims to hear God, they require processes of testing and discernment as they are related to all the other ways we have of listening for God's voice. That can involve articulating our convictions so that others can understand and respond to them, but doing this well is often a slow and difficult process.

Having deep convictions scrutinized and challenged, however, is often painful and can even feel like a deeply personal attack. But convictions can and do change in the light of new experiences, new arguments, new information, and new interactions with others. Although that may be a process that happens at the level of explicit discussion and argument, it is perhaps more often a complex resettling of all the components that have gone into their formation. This too may happen slowly and smoothly, almost imperceptibly, or it may be more sudden, as a structure which I've been living in collapses after several of the connections holding it together have weakened. This can happen after some encounter or experience that so runs counter to my current expectations that it calls into question the whole pattern of thought that underpinned them.

Conscience

The realm of conviction overlaps with the realm of 'conscience'. 'Conscience' is a word that can be used in a number of different ways. It can, for instance refer to a deep-seated sense of guilt or innocence – our hearts accusing or perhaps acquitting us before God (Romans 2.15). This might take the form of an overpowering sense of guilt or shame; it might be a persistent queasiness about the life one is leading; it might on the other hand be a cheerful confidence – an 'easy' rather than a 'troubled' conscience. In this sense, conscience is a powerful factor in the drama of salvation – as that drama takes place deep in our feelings and the ways in which we imaginatively grasp our own lives. We can be driven by a troubled conscience to repentance, and to throw ourselves on God's mercy; we can experience a guilty conscience transformed into a sense of forgiveness and grace.

In a second sense, it can refer to a conviction of the rightness or wrongness of some particular course of action or stance. That can be backward-looking: we find ourselves troubled or ashamed of some particular choice we have made, or some way in which we have ended up acting. It can be forward-looking: we find we have a deep conviction that some course of action that we are facing is acceptable or unacceptable. These convictions can be deeper than we can articulate. They are often responses of our whole selves – of feeling and imagination as much as rational deliberation.

Conscience is not infallible. We can feel guilty when we do not need to. We can feel confidently innocent when we really should not. We can be driven by an anxiety about salving our own consciences when we should be willing frankly to admit our failings and trust in God's mercy. Our consciences are shaped by all kinds of factors, and we can work together to form them well – by reading the Bible, listening to and learning from the Church's teaching and from one another, and learning to trust in God's mercy in Christ.

Because they are fallible, and because we have all been formed in different ways, our consciences differ – and our arguments about what we should and should not do as a church and individually are shaped by these different patterns of conscience. And that should have an impact on the ways in which we conduct our arguments. As well as arguing together about what is right and wrong, we need to take care with each other's consciences. As Paul shows us in 1 Corinthians 8.7-12, it is important to recognize when people's arguments and decisions are rooted in their consciences. It is important to be aware of when we are pushing someone to act in a way that runs against their conscience – and of the impact that will have on their experience of God's saving work.

The appeal to conscience in 'Issues in Human Sexuality'

Recognition of the importance of conscience has significantly shaped recent teaching regarding same-sex relationships. In 1991 in *Issues in Human Sexuality* the bishops noted that

> while insisting that conscience needs to be informed in the light of that [God-given moral] order, Christian tradition also contains an emphasis on respect for free conscientious judgement where the individual has seriously weighed the issues involved.[345]

An important question, therefore, is how the church should respond to those Christians who, after seriously weighing the issues, cannot in good conscience accept the church's teaching. The bishops were clear that this appeal to conscience could not be used to countenance 'promiscuous, casual or exploitative sex' but they viewed differently those gay and lesbian Christians who

> are conscientiously convinced...that they have more hope of growing in love for God and neighbour with the help of a loving and faithful homophile partnership, in intention lifelong, where mutual self-giving includes the physical expression of their attachment.[345]

The document concludes this paragraph with an exhortation:

> All those who seek to live their lives in Christ owe one another friendship and understanding. It is therefore important that in every congregation such homophiles should find fellow-Christians who will sensitively and naturally provide this for them. Indeed, if this is not done, any professions on the part of the church that it is committed to openness and learning about the homophile situation can be no more than empty words.[345]

Disagreements continue over whether this was a right development and application of teaching on conscience, what such respect for conscience entails for church practice, and whether greater freedom of conscience should also be recognized in relation to clergy both in ordering their own lives and in responding pastorally and liturgically to Christians in such loving, faithful same-sex relationships.

It is important to recognize that an appeal to conscience cannot be used to treat every issue as one on which Christians should simply 'agree to differ'. Questions of conscience are complex, involving psychological and sociocultural dimensions as well as spiritual ones. They also relate to and are shaped by the communities which we belong to. Disagreements about topics that are a matter of conscience for many of the people involved (on all sides) should properly make us cautious about how to proceed. We need to consider (as we have done elsewhere in this book) the psychological and sociocultural factors that shape our consciences and make us fearful of, or resistant to, the views of others. We need, as much as possible, objectively to evaluate the harms that may be associated with views on either side of a debate. We may also want to conclude that some issues are too central to the gospel to be matters on which we can agree to differ. However, that is exactly why the present debate is so difficult. Christians who take opposite viewpoints each feel strongly that the issue is central to the gospel as they understand it. Can we, therefore, find ways to respect and include those Christians who, in good conscience, we disagree with?[346]

Identity and conviction

We have already talked a lot about 'identity'. In Chapter 5, for instance, we learnt that 'identity' can refer to my sense of who and what I am, of the deep patterns of my affections and relationships, of my roles and calling.

For an exploration of identity in contemporary society, see Chapter 5 (pages 88-94). Some scientific perspectives on gender identity can be found in Chapter 6 (pages 109-110). Chapter 10 (pages 201-211) explores identity from the perspective of the Christian narrative.

In some circumstances I may have a sense of my identity that amounts to a conviction or dictate of conscience. This is especially likely for people whose sense of their identity is one that they understand as marginalized, deprecated or rejected by those around them, or that has been gained by struggling free from structures of thought and feeling that had not allowed them to be who they now know themselves to be. Someone in such a situation may come to the deeply rooted conviction that their identity is one that can be lived to the glory of God, and that has been given to them by God.

I might have a conviction that some aspect of my identity is a gift from God. That conviction might be shaped and made possible by what I have learnt about God, and that in turn might be reinforced by how I read various biblical passages. If I were to speak from this conviction, I would not simply be expressing a feeling; I would (whether I could articulate it well or not) be speaking from that mutually reinforcing collection of ideas and patterns of understanding.

As with other forms of conviction, such claims can be complex. People can have several compelling senses of identity and be unsure about how they go together. Their sense of identity can arise from complex processes of learning about themselves and about God. They can represent, whether articulated or not, serious and deep-seated claims about the possibilities of Christian living in love and faith. They are not simply whims.

That does not mean that they are to be treated as infallible and unchangeable. Wise testing and discernment are needed here, as everywhere else. Our patterns of imagination, emotion, desire and expectation, our habits of mind and heart, what we take to be normal, obvious or natural – all of these can be distorted. We all face the possibility of settling into patterns of distorted self-understanding. That can happen in relation to any and every aspect of our identity – including our gender and sexuality, but also our sense of our identity as Christians, as members of the Church of England, and as participants in the church's debates.

Two caveats should be borne in mind, however, when thinking about the testing and discernment of people's claims about their identities.

- First, it is not only the sense of identity of someone who has had to struggle for it against a hostile environment that needs such scrutiny. The Bible and the Christian tradition give us ample reason to think that similar discernment is needed in relation to those whose sense of identity comes easily and without conflict. Someone who, for instance, is heterosexual and barely thinks of it as an 'identity' at all, might well be inhabiting patterns of desire and expectation that careful Christian discernment would show to be distorted. The calling out of that distortion might be all the more difficult given how invisible those patterns have become.

- Second, to question the way that anyone experiences and expresses their sense of identity is – as we have noted several times – to handle matters that are emotionally very deep-rooted and play a significant part in people's health and happiness. Recognizing this can sometimes lead to resentment, as someone's expression of their convictions about their identity can be heard as an emotive appeal. That can be especially true where the respondents are not aware of their own complex emotional investments in the topics under discussion. Yet speaking without a deep and careful attentiveness to the people involved in these debates, however complex everyone's motivations are in speaking, is irresponsible.

In the church's debates about human identity, sexuality, relationships and marriage, we hear a variety of accounts of people's convictions about their identities and relationships. Sometimes they are presented as if they could simply settle the issues at stake. Sometimes, by contrast, such voices are dismissed as if they were irrelevant and could have no purchase set against the weight of Scripture, tradition and reason. Such accounts are, it is suggested, not the stuff of which proper theological arguments are made.

It is perhaps better to recognize that these testimonies are always complex. They express deep patterns of experience, yes – but these also draw on different patterns of thought about God, different ways of reading the Bible, different ways of relating to the Christian tradition. Rather than providing unquestionable evidence or being an irrelevance, the reports are windows into the convictions of others.

They therefore pose a series of important questions for those seeking to listen for God's voice:

- Can I imaginatively grasp the shape of this speaker's conviction – wearing their experiential shoes, at least for a moment?

- Can I imagine what it would mean to read the Bible and interpret the tradition from within that experience?

- Does imagining this then alert me to previously unseen ways in which my own approach is underpinned by my own experience or sense of identity?

- Does any of this help me to understand in new ways what is at stake between me and them?

- What would it mean to pursue the serious questions of testing and discernment in a way that did real justice to this person's self-understanding?

- How does the community of faith play a role in helping me to hear God's voice?

Such conversations will be complex and often painful. They will be shaped by awkward dynamics of power, by histories of differential inclusion and exclusion, by the reality and the threat of harassment, and by the knowledge of very different potential consequences. All of that, too, is amongst the complex experience that we bring to our arguments, and it cannot simply be set aside as irrelevant to the objective matters in hand.

Wrestling with these questions does not automatically pull us towards convergence and agreement. They may receive a variety of answers. Reports of experience are unlikely to settle the church's arguments. But they can and should act as invitations to serious questioning and self-critical attentiveness, to imagination, and to understanding. That itself might have deep and unpredictable effects upon our disagreements.

CHAPTER 18

Prayer and guidance

We said in the introduction to Part Four that 'our quest for answers needs to be rooted in prayer. We need God's help to hear God's voice. We need the Spirit's guidance and inspiration to set our feet on the right path.'

Prayer is not simply one more source of insight, or one more step
in our method of discernment. It is the water in which the whole
process of discernment swims. Everything we have been talking
about in Part Four – reading Scripture, listening to the Church,
attending to God's creation, and all the rest – we do as people
seeking to hear God's guidance for our lives. Prayer is the heartbeat
of this process. It is the place in which we focus our thoughts, our
imaginations, our affections, upon God, and upon our lives in
relation to God. It is the place in which all our deliberation, all our
conversation, all our study and reflection comes together and our
discernment is formed.

Depending on prayer

Prayer can take many forms. It can be praise, thanks, confession,
lament, contemplation, intercession, and more. Prayer is never,
however, a mechanism for generating results. It is not a technique
for ensuring the success of our endeavours, or the affirmation of our
discernments. That would make prayer a form of trust in ourselves.
Prayer, instead, should be a form of our trust in God. In intercession,
we pray for, and trust that we will receive, God's help. We pray for
God to guide our reading of the Bible, our engagement with the
tradition and with the whole church community, our attention to the
natural and cultural world around us, and our wrestling with our own
experience. We pray for God to guide our processes of deliberation
and argument – and we thank God for whatever help we receive.

We know – and, if we don't already know, our experience should
teach us – that despite all our efforts in this area we all still fail.
We get things wrong. We fail to convince one another. We
misunderstand. We depend constantly upon God's grace, and our
prayer is an expression of our dependence upon God, a confession
of our failures and inadequacy, and a petition for the grace we need.

The answers to the requests we make in prayer can come in all kinds
of forms. God's grace can work through all the activities of God's
creatures: through their thoughts, their speech, and their actions.
Our prayer might be answered through the hard work by which
someone produces a convincing interpretation of a biblical passage.
It might be answered by the development of compelling theological
and philosophical arguments. It might be answered by the slow
growth of scientific consensus, or by a new scientific perspective
that begins to disrupt it. It might be answered by the way in which

the church learns to hold fast in the face of challenge, or the slow shift of opinion in the church over time. It might be answered by the hearing in the church of voices previously marginalized or ignored. God can answer our prayer through processes that we can trace, or in ways that escape our understanding.

We are never done with the need to pray, or with the process of discerning whether and when God has answered our prayer – but we trust, in prayer, that God does not abandon us. And we surround our discernment with praise and contemplation that directs our attention away from ourselves and towards the source from which all help, all salvation comes.

Gifts of guidance

Many Christians testify that one of the ways in which God answers our prayers for guidance is in specific spiritual gifts.

Sometimes, for instance, a conviction may seem to us to have arisen in us unbidden. We can't see where it has come from or why we should be gripped by it, but we find we can't escape from it. At times, it might be quite sudden: an image or sentence or idea grows or appears within our minds. It may sometimes almost burn within us, until we feel compelled to speak. Particularly if this is in the context of prayer and worship, we may be convinced that we are (for some, quite literally) hearing the voice of God speaking to us and guiding us. We might think of Samuel hearing the voice of God in the Temple (1 Samuel 3), or Ananias hearing God tell him to go to Saul (Acts 9.10-15), among many other biblical examples.

In 1 Corinthians 14, Paul tells the members of the church in Corinth to 'strive for the spiritual gifts, and especially that you may prophesy' (v.1). In this context, prophecy is speech that encourages and consoles (v.3), or reproves and calls to account (v.24). He envisages prophecy as a gift that might be given to each member of the community, and through them to the whole body. This is the outworking of the charismatic principle that 'to each one the manifestation of the Spirit is given for the common good' (1 Corinthians 12.7 (NIV)).

Paul is not imagining a gift for infallible pronouncements. When someone has spoken, he says, 'let the others weigh what is said' (v.29). He sees it as a gift that emerges in the context of the community's worship and their reading of Scripture (v.26). Nevertheless, he clearly has a lively expectation that God can speak directly into the present. 'Do not quench the Spirit. Do not treat prophecies with contempt but test them all; hold on to what is good, reject every kind of evil' (1 Thessalonians 5.19-22 (NIV)). Such gifts may be one of the means that God uses to guide the Church.

Prayer and reason

If prayer is the place in which all our deliberation and reflection comes together, and our discernment is formed, then it is deeply connected to reason.

The word 'reason' can be used in many ways in discussions of Christian discernment. At its broadest, it can refer to the whole process by which we think through what we read in Scripture, in the light of what we hear from the Church, see in the natural world, and encounter in our cultures and in our experience. It can be a name for the whole process of our wrestling with all of that material. We work to see how all that we have been given and all that we are learning fits together. Reason is the name for our thoughtful labour with all the jigsaw pieces we have been given, working to see what picture will emerge. The Spirit infuses both prayer and reason. In that sense, the whole of Part Four has been about the exercise of reason in spiritual discernment.

Yet if reason is the name for all that thoughtful labour, prayer is the air that we must breathe as we work together. In prayer we ask God to show us how the pieces go together. In prayer we offer our work to God in penitent acknowledgement of its inadequacy. In prayer we wait patiently upon God to show us more than our own efforts have enabled us to see. All the forms of reading, listening, and conversing described throughout Part Four are ingredients in a process of prayerful reason, and reasoning prayer. Such prayer is the path we take toward wisdom, trusting in God, the source and giver of wisdom (James 1.5; 3.13-18).

The Anglican Way is a particular expression of the Christian Way of being the One, Holy, Catholic and Apostolic Church of Jesus Christ. It is formed by and rooted in Scripture, shaped by its worship of the living God, ordered for communion, and directed in faithfulness to God's mission in the world. In diverse global situations Anglican life and ministry witnesses to the incarnate, crucified and risen Lord, and is empowered by the Holy Spirit. Together with all Christians, Anglicans hope, pray and work for the coming of the reign of God.

The Anglican Way (2008)[347]

We have been exploring the various interacting ways in which Christians listen for the voice of God. We have not tried to provide a recipe for discernment, but instead to map its various dimensions: to indicate the different practices, conversations and forms of attention in which we believe Christians should be involved as they listen to the voice of God.

The Bible stands at the heart of that process. The Christian faith is uniquely revealed in its pages: God uses it to witness to the saving work that reaches its fulfilment in Jesus, and to draw us into holiness. We read the Bible in the company of a great cloud of witnesses – all the members of the Church past and present. They help us to read, challenge us to read differently, and influence what we hear when we listen to God's voice in the Bible. We read as people who inhabit the natural world; our reading is inevitably shaped by what we know or think we know of that world – and vice versa. Similarly, we read as people who inhabit the cultural world around us. Our involvement in that world presses us to ask new questions, to look again at things we thought we knew, to read and reread, sometimes with eyes opened to new possibilities or dangers. We read as people each of whom has been formed by a particular life story, and whose assumptions and convictions have been influenced in far more ways than we can see by what we have inherited, by what has happened to us, by all the people we have interacted with. We read as people who can learn, to an extent, to read the Bible through each other's eyes – mulling over, exploring, and testing different possibilities and discoveries. And, finally, surrounding all of these, we read as people who are called to pray – to throw themselves upon the grace of God in the trust that we will be led deeper into the revelation that has its heart in Jesus Christ.

As we have described this whole path of discernment, we have described some serious differences of opinion and practice across the Church of England – different attitudes to the Bible and to 'natural law', for instance. That leaves open the question of whether the variety of approaches that we have described is one that can properly be contained within the Church of England, or whether some of it – however much it might be recognized as a serious *attempt* at listening – represents an approach that takes one beyond the boundaries of the church's teaching.

Answering that question is, in turn, made complicated by another disagreement. We (and that includes the authors of this book) have differing views on whether there is such a thing as a clear Anglican approach to these questions. Some of us believe that there is. That is, some of us believe that, anchored in the canons, the Articles, and perhaps above all the liturgy of the church, and exhibited in evolving ways by faithful Anglicans over the centuries, there has been a coherent pattern to Anglican discernment of the voice of God: an 'Anglican way', which can allow clear answers to this question of boundaries. Others of us are not so convinced: we see an ongoing and evolving argument in Anglican history about the proper answer to these questions, with different sides marshalling the evidence of Anglican history in different ways, to suit their differing answers.

We differ about these matters – and those differences are serious; they make a difference to what we believe God to be saying, not least about identity, sexuality, relationships and marriage. They make a difference to the good news we believe the Church of England should be proclaiming in this area. Despite the extent of our disagreements about how to do it, however, we all remain committed to listening attentively to what God is saying – with all our heart, mind, soul and strength. We read and study the Bible, and, as we do so, listen to the tradition, to one another and to all Christ's people. We explore creation and science and engage in conversation with the wider culture, and we attend to the impact of our own and others' experience. We all believe that by these means God graciously speaks to us, leading us deeper into the Word that God has spoken in Jesus of Nazareth, and calling all people into a life of love and faith.

Encounters

Meet AMELIA

Amelia had a 'super happy' childhood. She grew up in Holland and New Zealand. Neither parent was churchgoing and even as a nine-year-old Amelia herself opted out of religious studies lessons on principle. At the age of twelve she realized she was gay and came to associate Christianity with homophobia. Her parents were easy-going, but Amelia didn't find being gay easy.

At 21 Amelia and her sister moved to London – where she soon found a new freedom since 'you have to be exceptionally weird to be considered weird in London.' She met Elsa and they were together for four or five years. These were happy years of making a home together. Neither were particularly part of the gay scene. Amelia started training as a physiotherapist. Meeting Christians who would talk about her sexuality as a lifestyle choice only cemented Amelia's antipathy to church and Christian faith: 'I just thought Christians were homophobic, bigoted, stupid.'

Elsa and Amelia broke up at the time when she began working as a physio. She was assigned to an experienced physio, Louise, who was a Christian. Amelia realized she needed to be professional, so kept her atheist convictions to herself. However, when Amelia heard Louise read Psalm 23 to a Christian patient she found herself strangely moved, against her will.

After discussing their respective convictions Louise asked Amelia if she'd like to read the Bible together. Convinced this was an opportunity to 'gather more ammo to argue against Christianity' Amelia agreed. They met regularly to read through Mark's Gospel together.

According to Amelia, this was only possible because Louise was never antagonistic towards her and made no conditions on how she should live, explaining 'I believe the Bible is God's Word and I therefore hold it as my highest authority and try and live my life in a way that honours him; if you don't even believe God exists who am I to encourage you to live for him?' Amelia was not surprised to hear that at Louise's church there was no one in a same-sex relationship but was astounded to hear that all single Christians in Louise's church, straight and gay, were celibate, holding to God's teaching that sex is for a man and a woman in marriage alone.

'I just thought Christians were homophobic, bigoted, stupid.'

In spite of her determined resistance, curiosity got the better of Amelia and she slipped into Louise's church one Sunday evening. She was surprised to find that when the Bible was explained it was interesting and very much applicable to life today. The quality of relationships and people's genuine interest in her as a person had a deep impact too. She was welcomed into the homes and lives of families.

Through reading Mark's Gospel with Louise and attending church on Sundays, Amelia started to believe that God really does exist and to see who Jesus was and why he came. She began to see how big the problem of human sin really is and understood that she would never be right before God on her own. This conviction led to a desire 'to humble myself before him and to commit to following him as my Lord and Saviour'. She realized she had inadvertently become a Christian!

It was clear to her from Scripture that God called for her to be abstinent but she was unsure of whether she was condemned merely by being same-sex attracted, a characteristic she did not feel was a choice. She met the vicar to talk about her sexuality and was relieved to hear that regardless of what we are tempted by, it is acting on those temptations, rather than the presence of them alone, that is sinful. She was baptized. Amelia meets with a group of same-sex attracted people in her church once a term. Her deep sense of belonging to a compassionate, loving church family that strives for godliness and recognizes that everyone struggles with sexual sin makes her a passionate advocate for her Christian faith as a celibate gay person.

Meet BEN

Ben is a married heterosexual vicar. His father was 'almost certainly gay or bisexual and married to my mother when homosexuality was still illegal. He never came to terms with his identity and drank himself to death at the age of 47. And was clearly frustrated and very unhappy in his marriage.'

Ben attended a Christian boarding school which was set up for children of missionaries and where homosexuality was taught as 'disgusting; it is a disgrace and an affront to God, an abomination. And would probably lead to you ending up in hell.' Ben found it difficult carrying the secret of his father's homosexuality in that environment. 'I knew there were other gay people in the school, and everything was being kept quiet. And I knew there was a master in the school who liked boys, basically. So the whole thing became incredibly confusing and unpleasant.'

Ben continues, 'I've always had a God fascination, which I don't know where and how that's been there for me. But it just has always been part of my very DNA and psyche. And I think I was in an environment, when I was a teenager, where I saw the best of Christianity and the very worst of Christianity coalescing in this deeply weird way. And I couldn't make sense of it. And so, for some time just thought, "Oh put it all to one side. I won't think about this; I'll try and get on with my own life." But you can only do that for so long, especially when you feel God's got a calling on your life to ministry.'

Ben felt a calling to ordination as a teenager but waited until his forties before following it, wrestling at length with questions of gender, sexuality and the church. He found it difficult to assent to *Issues in Human Sexuality* but did – 'on the basis that in the foreword George Carey wrote, "This is not the last word."'

Ben has two grown-up daughters. His older daughter is heterosexual, in a happy relationship with a man. She is highly intelligent and has both very mild cerebral palsy and epilepsy. 'I suppose the experience of her, although it's not to do with sexuality, was the start of a process of thinking – well, not all people are white, male, heterosexual, able-bodied, and can run marathons in their lunch hour. There are just people who are beautiful in their own way. Different in their own way. So, my experience of her shattered any kind of idea of alpha male Christianity.'

'I was in an environment, when I was a teenager, where I saw the best of Christianity and the very worst of Christianity'

His younger daughter is gay and has a relationship with 'a girlfriend who relates as both male and female'. She also has a difficult health condition that means she lives with chronic pain. When she is at home with her parents she attends church, but when she is away she is 'wary of the church... she's been to some of the churches in London. But she has to know that it's okay, and she will be okay. I think she has a living faith, but how long can that be sustained without a living church, is a moot point.'

Ben doesn't see anything qualitatively different in his children's relationships and if his younger daughter asked him for a blessing he said 'I would; I would do it in church. And that leaves me in a deeply, deeply uncomfortable place within the church.'

Meet JACK

Jack is a married father and grew up in a Christian family. Despite his mother's efforts to keep him interested in the church he drifted away while a teenager, and then again after his time at a charismatic church while at university.

Jack has very early memories of wanting to dress up as a girl which continued into his teenage years. 'I thought it was just an experiment I needed to do, or a one-off thing. I thought, "I'll just do this, and then I'll have scratched that itch, and I can get on with normal things." But it didn't really work like that.' Jack would buy women's underwear from charity shops while at university, but kept this private. A move to London for further study allowed him to enter 'a culture where no one cared. I found a wedding dress in a second-hand clothing shop for £3. A huge 80s thing with meringue, brilliant... I just put on the wedding dress and we got on the bus, walked across Hyde Park, and when I walked into the bar I just got a round of applause... So the more acceptance I had, the more free I was to do this... Now just having the clothes wasn't enough, because they didn't look right, because I have the body of a man... Every step was going deeper and deeper into a rabbit's hole. So, it just started off as wearing underwear, and then it was all the clothes, then it was the make-up, and then I was fighting my body. And I think I probably would have carried on ... and had surgery.'

While a student Jack began to feel miserable and lonely so he got back in touch with some Christian friends who invited him on a student retreat. 'It was pretty painful for the first night, and I guess there wasn't really anything to do there except listen to the Bible.' Jack started attending church. 'I kept it hidden at church, so no one tackled it head on... I think I probably would have just left and not come back... So, instead it got dissolved from the

'I don't think I've been rewired exactly, but I'm so grateful to be free'

ground up, just all my presuppositions and misunderstandings were picked away... Yeah, just hearing that you don't find freedom in sin – it leads to a bigger trap. And that just so perfectly matched my own experience. Because this is exactly what I was living.'

'All I was hearing from the world around was that you have to be yourself, and denial is a bad thing. Denying who you really are is just going to lead to psychological trauma... Whereas Jesus says, "Deny yourself and follow me."'

Eventually, Jack shared his story with someone from church who responded by saying, 'That's normal.... Everyone is struggling, everyone is sinful, everyone is fighting a fight, and that is normal.' It was a turning point. 'I just did it less and less. And then, there came a point when I thought, "I don't need this, I can get rid of it all." And I just bundled everything up into a whole load of bin bags, and I called a friend and said, "There's this area of sin that I've been struggling with, and I'm trying to get rid of it. And could you do me a favour and come and pick it up and drive it off somewhere?"

'I've been trying all my life to kick it. And I think I reached a point where I'd given up trying. And so, it was just being taught Bible by a church that didn't pull its punches and would just say the truth, which I guess a lot of people would think was terribly judgemental and non-PC ... But was just so helpful, because it opened my eyes and it was freedom. So, I haven't cross-dressed since then. I don't think I've been rewired exactly, but I'm so grateful to be free from it because it was just a trap.'

Meet ZOE

Zoe is a retired vicar with adult stepchildren. 'One of the stepchildren was a very unsettled, unhappy child. And at the age of 14 was quite sure that she was in the wrong body, as she tried to put it, at that age. [...] She was on a trans journey [and was] located with the Tavistock Clinic. Both my husband and I would be very clear that suppressing hormones and providing testosterone, whatever it is, at too young an age is devastatingly wrong. Having watched the journey, it was torturous. And I think it needs to be. It's a bit like trying to get yourself into a dog collar, really. Test it and test it and test it ...' Ten years later, aged 24, now identifying as a man, the stepchild married a woman. The church wedding was full of confidence in God's love for them. Zoe describes this story as full of hope.

In the meantime, another stepchild came out as gay at the age of 19. She has a relationship with another woman and is sad that they cannot get married in church. She and her partner, and her (now) brother and his wife are very close. As far as they are concerned, there is not much difference sexually in their two relationships, which, to them, makes the church's position difficult to understand.

Meet CHLOE

Chloe is married to a male vicar and they have small children. She was 17 when her parents told her that her dad had gender dysphoria. 'As a young girl, coming to the latter stages of puberty, why on earth would you want to break up a family just to wear a dress? As far as I was concerned what's more important is family and stuff.'

Chloe went through a tough time of questioning and pain. Her parents divorced and her father transitioned to a woman. When Chloe got married, her father – now a woman – did not walk her down the aisle. But Chloe has relied on her faith to help her find peace with the situation. 'Actually, I want to forgive her because I don't want to carry around all this stuff for the rest of my life. I think the problem with today's society is that people might even

> **'Why on earth would you want to break up a family just to wear a dress?'**

question, "What have you got to forgive? She's done nothing wrong," and yet actually for me, she'd taken away my dad, she'd broken up the family, and there is a sense she's rejecting the father/daughter relationship even though she loves me unconditionally.'

Lord, make me an instrument of your peace.
Where there is hatred, let me sow love;
where there is injury, pardon;
where there is doubt, faith;
where there is despair, hope;
where there is darkness, light;
where there is sadness, joy.
O Divine Master,
grant that I may not so much seek
to be consoled as to console,
to be understood as to understand,
to be loved as to love.
For it is in giving that we receive,
it is in pardoning that we are pardoned,
and it is in dying
that we are born to eternal life.
Amen.

Common Worship Daily Prayer:
a Franciscan prayer

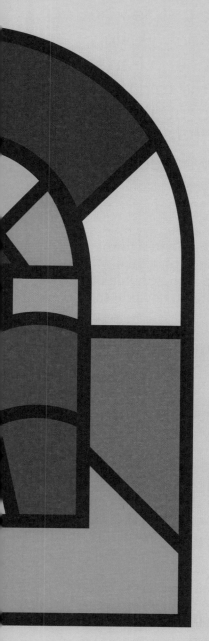

PART FIVE

Conversing: what can we learn from each other?

The purpose of Part Five is to invite you into a conversation between some of the people who have been involved in writing this book. Having engaged with and written the material in Parts One to Four, they nevertheless come to different conclusions about marriage, sex, identity and the nature of the Church. Each of the 'Scenes' is based on a live conversation that was recorded, transcribed and edited.

In **Scene 1** the conversation revolves around marriage: is marriage only between one man and one woman? Are there other forms of covenant that might be possible for other kinds of faithful committed relationships? Or should the nature of the Church of England's understanding of marriage be adapted to include same-sex couples?

In **Scene 2** we talk about sex. What boundaries should we place around sexual activity? Is its only proper place within marriage? Or are there other relationships which can find sexual expression?

Scene 3 concerns identity and gender. Is our identity entirely God-given and to be accepted? Or do we play a part in making adjustments that help us to live into the identity we believe we are called to have?

Scene 4 is a conversation about the life of the church in the context of difference, disagreement and diversity. How do we respond to Jesus' call for unity in the light of difference and disagreement? How do we hold together holiness and love?

In our journey through this book we began with God as the giver of the gifts of life, friendship and marriage. We then looked at what is happening in the world around us in relation to identity, sexuality, relationships and marriage. This raised many questions about whether what is happening in our society is a sign of God's approaching kingdom, or a walking away from the abundant life that God offers in Christ Jesus. In Part Three, we were reminded that, as Christians, we seek to walk in the way of salvation and we considered how that shapes our responses to these questions. In doing that, we learnt about what we have in common as well as what causes differences and disagreements among us about human identity, sexuality, relationships and marriage. So, in Part Four, we examined how it was that we reached these different destinations.

In Part Five, we invite you to stop for a while and to sit down together with others. We invite you to be curious: to want to find out how it is that some took different turnings and to hear about the different views their particular path led them to.

Our aim is simply to present fair and clear articulations of these different answers to the questions we have been wrestling with, albeit in very brief form. This is not a device to say that the Church of England should accept all these answers, developing a form of church life in which all of them are allowed to flourish alongside one another. We are not saying that they are all consonant with the church's doctrinal commitments, or making a judgement about the validity of the different arguments made. We are making no claims of that kind, but we are inviting you to be curious and thoughtful in learning with and about one another as members of the body of Christ.

These conversations began as real conversations among some of the people who have been involved in writing this book. We recorded and transcribed them as they talked together. We then took the transcriptions and did some work on them, making the conversations a little less meandering and easier to follow for the reader. We also changed all the names.

The groups did not claim to be representative: some have more men than women. All, however, have LGBTI+ people among them. They were real conversations among people who happened to be in the same place at the same time – and all of whom had spent time studying – or writing – the book, and working together on the other Living in Love and Faith resources. In that sense, they are like the conversations that you are invited to join as you study the book and the other resources. You won't always be in a group that is representative, but we hope that, like these groups, they will include people who see things differently.

SCENE 1

A conversation about marriage

Ashley I'd want to begin with the unique place of marriage in my understanding of the sacramental life of the Church. As we say in our contemporary liturgies, marriage is a gift of God in creation. So, unlike the other sacraments, it was part of God's plan for humankind from the beginning. In Christ, marriage acquires a sacramental character. Augustine spoke of the three goods of marriage. The faithful, loving, exclusive relationship of the couple; the gift of fruitfulness, children; and then that distinct raising of marriage to the character of sacrament so that it reveals something of the mystery of God's love for us in Christ.

We need to reflect on how far that gift of God in creation has changed and developed in the life of the Church and in what ways it can continue authentically to develop.

Emily I'm glad you talk about the development of marriage because I think it's commonly assumed that it goes back and has been set in stone since the year dot. Even if you trace Anglican liturgy we can see the different emphases, how those three goods have changed in weight and relative importance. Early on in LLF a paper from the historians about the history of marriage was eye-opening for me. It showed how the ways in which the Church of England has fostered marriage have changed deeply over time. Incremental change is the norm. That opens the door to help me see how marriage might yet change again. I'm not sure about that. But it might change without necessarily meaning a paradigm shift, an evolution rather than a revolution in our understanding of marriage.

Ian That's true, but the history of marriage is not simply one of change, let alone of just blessing any and every social context. As it has seen society's understanding of marriage change, the church has constantly gone back to its Scriptures and its tradition to evaluate those changes.

The question for me is: what is the continuity across those changes? What is essential? How does that tradition relate to so many people today living together but with real commitment and having children and nurturing them and doing all the things that marriage is meant to do? To civil partnerships? To same-sex couples? I think we need to consider how we read the Scriptures in relation to those social changes, and what differences and developments we can accept.

Max Especially now we have opposite-sex civil partnerships and we've seen a dramatic decline in the number of marriages. I think there's an irony, really, that the church is having to think quite hard about marriage now because of the fact that it's been opened up in the state to same-sex couples.

For me, one of the interesting things is that, sometimes, it's felt that the church is engaged to an excessive degree in supporting marriage. Sometimes almost at the cost of the gospel. I wonder whether there isn't a deeper question about the church's identity and relationship with marriage. Has marriage become too important in the life and teaching of the church?

Emily I've long thought that the system on the continent, where you get married under law in a registry office and then go to the church to be blessed makes total sense. It makes marriage a bit less 'religious'. And it makes the point that getting married is more of a process over time than a single event.

Ian I take your point, Emily, but for me it's not so much about making marriage less religious; rather, the continental system would give us as a church the freedom to work out what we think is really valuable about marriage. We can then promote that, regardless of whether the law does or does not treat it as marriage. Because it seems to me as if what the church wants to say about marriage and what society thinks are growing further and further apart.

Ashley Yes, I think the church has a great opportunity which could be applied to a same-sex partnership, whether or not we think that can be called a marriage. A great opportunity to help recover a sense of covenant and vow. In our world legally the direction of travel is towards a contract, something that's as dissoluble as easily as it's contracted. I think there's a great gospel opportunity here for us to speak about the nature of relationship in a way that is truly Christian. This sort of commitment isn't easy, but it is really good. At least we agree about that.

Emily And yet, as I perceive it, the sort of Disney-like dream of encountering that one other who will 'fulfil my dreams for the whole of my life' hasn't diminished in society at all. We still have – more of a fantasy, arguably – this longing for the unconditional, loyal love of a partner for life. I think there's a danger that if as a church we emphasize 'covenant loyalty' we will just end up reinforcing that romantic Disney view of marriage which is unrealistic and, frankly, unhelpful.

Max And that's what's been so interesting amongst the LGBT community. We've found ourselves able to celebrate the fact that we hope we might have found that partner for life. We've found that we now have a kind of official, state-sanctioned way of acknowledging that. I think that's changed the identity question for a lot of LGBT people. Recognizing that it's a dream but, at the same time, thinking it's a dream that we might be able to achieve. What underlies that dream is that real sense of the virtues we've talked about of constancy, commitment and faithfulness. It's opening that up to different people and the question is how we can celebrate that as a church.

Ian One of the good things in these resources is that they set marriage within the context of different patterns of loving, caring, intimate relationships. Max, I think, despite warning us against making marriage too important in the church, you are in danger of assuming that a relationship has to be called 'marriage' in order to have these things. One of the important questions for me is what is distinctive about the marriage relationship compared to other forms of relationship that we might have. We focus a lot on marriage simply as the relationship of the couple. And that's really important. But the idea of the institution of marriage as a God-given pattern of life is I think one of the key questions these resources are asking us to think about. And to ask, again, how that relates to the Scriptures. The fact that Jesus, in his debates about marriage, goes back to Genesis, to creation, and talks about a man and a woman, and becoming one flesh. I think that is essential for a Christian understanding of marriage.

Ashley Picking up what you said, Emily, one of the best bits of our recent marriage liturgies is the introduction which is very good on stressing the corporate, public, civic nature of this. Not just the relationship of the two. Not even just the immediate biological family. Entering into this state of life is a contribution to the common good. What we can offer as Christians is not only the case for loyalty, but also to resist the trend to privatize marriage, as if it's just a personal matter. It really isn't.

Emily Of course talking about 'the gift of marriage' can be difficult for the many single people in our society and churches. We need to be clear that you don't have to find that one other in order to live a fully flourishing human life. In fact, Jesus puts marriage – and the fantasies that we harbour about marriage – in its place when he speaks about not marrying. He speaks about serving God above all. Then Paul commends celibacy and arguably makes it a higher calling. I think perhaps we haven't dropped our Disney fantasies and haven't embraced seriously enough the gift of celibacy.

Max And that takes me back to my point about overemphasizing marriage in the life of the church. For me, I want to put both marriage and singleness in the context of community. What Jesus does over and over again is to create community, doesn't he? 'Who are my family? Those who do my will are my family.' He gathers the disciples and the women around him. I've spent a lot of my life as single but I've been part of a church community. That obviously hasn't necessarily taken the place of a husband but it's enabled me to feel as though I'm part of a wider whole.

Perhaps the church hasn't been very good at being community for everybody. Perhaps because it's emphasized marriage so much. There are churches where it's quite difficult for single people to be part of church. That, I think, is something we need to question. Because whatever your relationship, friendship is right at the heart of being human, isn't it? Friendship is about constancy, love and generosity and all those things.

Ashley I agree that we need to do a lot of reflecting on, 'It is not good for man to be alone' in the creation narrative. Relationship is part of God's will for us. Very few people are really called to be, and flourish in, a state of being alone. Religious communities are not about being alone, they're about lots of people living the single life but living it together in a vowed relationship.

Marriage clearly is about not being alone. So are other forms of covenanted, exclusive relationship. But the community of the church is a place where people should be able to find medicine for their aloneness. And we don't always get that right.

Ian

If I can return to the whole question of same-sex marriage... I remember Max we had a conversation after your civil partnership. You talked about it being marriage and I said, 'Why is it so important for you that it is marriage and you would like it be recognized as marriage by the church?' I think your answer was something like, 'Well, that's because it is.' That highlights the differences: some people think it obviously is and some people think it obviously isn't. Can you unpack a bit more why your relationship is, for you, marriage?

Max

I mean, we tried quite hard not to call it marriage. It was very carefully a civil partnership. It was a civil partnership with the approval of the bishop. It was a tremendous service. Everybody was full of love and light. But since then, we haven't been able to find the right language to talk about it, really.

I find it quite difficult because, actually, in reality, he is my husband. But he's not my husband because we haven't had the liturgy and we haven't gone through the legal process. So, it feels a bit dishonest to talk of 'my husband' as it feels actually not quite the right word. But there isn't another one because I don't want to talk about 'partner' because it's a different relationship.

Ian

Is that the significance of the language of marriage? The nature of the love and the commitment that you have for each other and you wish others to recognize and celebrate with you? That's the heart and the essence of what marriage is even though it's not marriage in terms of the church's teaching which is obviously difficult and painful.

For you, it's the pattern of commitment you've made to each other. The pattern of love you have for each other. That's marital love. The problem is that the church won't recognize it as that because you're both men, and that is where the real tension lies. Is that fair?

Max

I think that's right, yeah. Obviously, I was brought up with the idea of marriage as the ideal. From a very early age, it was always expected that I would get married. Then I gave up on the idea of getting married when I was about 15 or 16 and realized that that wasn't going to be possible. But I've always looked for the partner. Then, lo and behold, it became possible under the Conservative-Liberal Democrat Coalition, much to everyone's surprise. For me, this process has pointed up the virtues of marriage. It seems to me that what I have is an attempt to manifest those virtues.

Ashley   I fear this is going to sound terribly patronizing and I don't mean it to, so I apologize in advance. I want 100 per cent to celebrate your relationship, its commitment and its love. In the little phrase that Ian dropped in, 'Because you're two men'... Actually, for me, I'm still at a place where I think that little phrase takes huge unpacking.

There is something in what God has done in creation of male and female that, for me, remains something not just incidental to marriage but at the heart of it. It's that difference. I can't say this in a way that does justice to your relationship with your partner but there is that irreducible core, because of creation. I don't mean to imply anything second best about your relationship but I'm in a place, theologically, where that difference... I can't get beyond it. That's a huge question and we really need to dig into that theology of gender in creation because I think that's a way in to better understanding, perhaps, the different places that we find ourselves in.

Ian   I think one of the things I've learnt and found helpful through the process is how language of marriage in the church's teaching and Scripture, in history, and in society, is used for a whole network of different characteristics. Clearly, many of those can be seen and embodied and lived out by a same-sex couple. There isn't any doubt about that. But the question is, are there other aspects of it because of our understanding of how God has made us as human beings and the importance of our sexual differentiation into male and female? And that is part of what it means to be human as a human race. So whatever there is in those forms of love that has the pattern of marital love between the couple, it isn't actually able to be a marriage. We also can't get away from the fact that by calling a same-sex relationship 'marriage' we imply that it's the sort of relationship where sex is an important and valuable and acceptable way of expressing the love and commitment there is. But I'm not sure it is. At least the language of 'partnership' is more neutral on that.

Ashley I think what I've said about that intrinsic nature of male and female in marriage is much more contested territory than it's ever been before because gender is contested territory. I would want to argue for sexual differentiation being essential to God's creative purposes, and somehow, gender has to reflect that fact. But I'm aware that's a really contested and complex area. I don't think any of us have the answers yet.

Max I think however carefully you try to put it, it still feels as if what you're saying is that what we have is not just 'different', it's second best. We're in a position where the church can't even acknowledge what we have. There is nothing that we can do at the moment, apart from be prayed with quietly in a side chapel. Which feels very wrong, somehow unaffirming.

Emily It's interesting, 20-odd years ago, I was organizing a sermon series on hot-button issues. The question we had was, 'What about gay marriage?' and I remember being slated by the LGBT community for using the word, 'Marriage' to talk about their partnerships: 'That's a heterosexual word!' Isn't it interesting how circumstances change? Because what we were addressing was how to enable permanent, committed relationships for a community that was oppressed and forced underground and where there was a lot of promiscuity, probably related to that.

I find it so sad, the way our history in the church has related to the LGBT community. Because whatever changes now, it will feel so begrudging. I long to engage with Scripture and with the variety of those who engage with Scripture in the church to find a thrilling, positive way forward that involves promises of covenant loyalty that are publicly acknowledged and supported. The opportunity and discipline of covenant loyalty for any who are willing to risk it. Because it's actually very difficult. I just find it amazing that anybody's up for it – gay or straight.

A conversation about sex and relationships

Brad   Shall I start? I think sex is a very deep gift, a very personal thing. It's been abused so much throughout history but I think the right place for sex is in a serious commitment. That doesn't have to mean marriage for every single person, but it should not be treated lightly.

Francis To me, sex is a personal good which takes place in a social context, and there's a degree of dangerousness if that social context is ignored, if it's cut loose from socially recognized, committed relationships. The harm is quite patent, sometimes.

Jasmin   Dangerous in what ways?

Francis There's the capacity for abuse, obviously. And in terms of heterosexual sex, the potential for procreation is crucial to the social context. But we've got this concept that pregnancy is something you choose, almost an irrelevance or an afterthought. I was brought up with a basic rule: don't sleep with anyone you wouldn't be happy to marry and have kids with. That's about social responsibility. Sex is dangerous because of our need to express ourselves sexually and our individualistic temptation to ignore the social context.

Brad   For me it's about consent and harm. You can think you're offering consent, when really it's not something that you want. I've been in those situations. If you're at a certain age you go clubbing with the intention of having sex at the end of the night. That puts a lot of pressure on people and means that people are caused harm, physically, psychologically, spiritually.

Naomi   But consent can be so complicated and not just when clubbing. That's why I think we need to talk about more than commitment. I think of a young Christian I know whose girlfriend wanted him to sleep with her. He felt really uneasy but didn't know what to do. When the relationship broke up soon after that his feeling was that she wanted somehow to possess him. She knew he was committed to sex within marriage and thought that if she persuaded him to sleep with her then she owned him in some kind of way. There are so many unhealthy dynamics in relationships. That's one reason why I think the public commitment of lifelong, exclusive love in marriage – where Paul says husbands and wives belong to each other – should be made first.

Jasmin   Yes, actually, sex is about possessing somebody, isn't it? Isn't that one of the things that really changes in a sexual relationship? Part of what the Bible means by 'becoming one flesh'. Even when it's casual sex with a prostitute according to Paul. I think that passage in 1 Corinthians about sex with prostitutes says something important about the deep psychological and spiritual effects of sexual promiscuity that we ignore at our peril. The wholeness of our very identity and personality is at stake.

Brad   But surely keeping sex to marriage is not realistic is it? When I worked in university chaplaincy we often dealt with young people who had a very clear sense that sex was only for marriage, but whose parents were then saying, 'But you can't possibly get married because you won't be able to provide what you need to provide.' So they were stuck, where nothing they could do was right – they couldn't get married and they couldn't go on with their lives together without getting married.

Robin   I agree – how can we speak to people who aren't getting married now? People used to marry in their late teens or early twenties. Now they're getting married, if at all, in their thirties. What do we say to people in those 10 or 15 years?

I also think that the 'only for marriage' view just reflects the fact that the Church and sex have had an uneasy relationship right from the very beginning. I think the Church is frightened of sex, because it's a very powerful force.

Of course, there are times when sex is sinful, but there are also times when sex is creative and liberating. I think the Church has suppressed sex so much that it's forgotten to affirm how much it can be an expression of love, both within the marriage bond and for many of us outside.

Vaughan   So often for Christians sex, and talking about sex, is about fear. But for a very large number of people in our society sex is fun, recreational and casual and detached from loving commitment. My concern is that the consequences of sex are not just children but how it changes your relationship after being so vulnerable with each other. It seems to me that the reason you make a covenant with someone is because you're there for them, through thick and thin. You sort of need that depth of commitment to make sense of the sexual relationship.

Brad
Yes, although I wonder if the 'fun' of casual sex is more image than reality. And we mustn't forget that marriage is also about fun. For people having fun after clubbing, there's a certain amount of pleasure. But perhaps the fun and pleasure that you can gain when you've been married for a long time is greater even if we don't often talk about that as a church.

Francis
For me there's also the question of what we mean by sex. You get so much advice, especially for older people like me, that there are all sorts of other ways you can show physical affection with your partner. In the church, it seems that sex always equates only to penetrative intercourse, whether heterosexual or not. Is it a double standard? Or is it only later in life when you learn that sex is more than that?

Brad
I think there are lots of young Christians who think that they can do just about anything as long they don't have penetrative sex, and who are in relationships where abuse of power is massive.

Robin
I've thought for years – and more so now with Grindr and Tinder and this idea of sex on demand, which clearly is a way that some young people live now and how I lived 30 years ago - that we're in a situation where because for the church the only acceptable place for sex is within marriage we have nothing to say to anyone else.

I grew up outside the Church because I'd fallen out with God. But if I'd been in the Church, there would have been nothing to give me any kind of guidance in the way that I tried to form relationships, when they went wrong. I think the Church is being sinful in failing to speak to people where they are.

Francis
We've often, as a church, found it hard to separate the potential for the best from the conversation about when things go wrong. I find so many church conversations

about sex and marriage to be utterly unlike the experience
of anyone I know. We don't have a good theological
conversation about failure and messing up.

Naomi Yes. The church ought to be doing an awful lot more to take
the lid off the pain and the anguish that follow from the
ideas that people are being fed by society. There is a deep
cultural thing that adultery is fun, free sex with somebody
that you fancy…

We need to squash that idea and address adolescence, early
twenties. We're sexual people; I'm sexual in everything I
do. There are appropriate and inappropriate expressions
of my sexuality which obviously you navigate through life.
You can have an appropriate expression in friendship, but
it's still sexual in some kind of way. I am physically close to
my friends, I want to hug them because I'm a tactile kind
of person but certainly not have sex with them. So, finding
the appropriate expression of one's sexuality in every
relationship I think is really significant. And giving people
a lead into this within the church, within the confines of
a frank and open discussion, guided by Scripture and the
wisdom of tradition, is so important. But we don't do it.

Francis What worries me particularly, and it's a very Church of
England thing, is the immense pressure we're under to bless
what people do rather than saying that actually we have
a vision of the good, and a vision of the better, as well as a
vision of the best.

We're assumed to be saying that the best is the only thing that
God will endorse. We're always considered to be condemning
everybody who doesn't attain the best. So, the married are all
going to heaven, and the rest are damned. That's just not how
we understand being human or being sinful.

Vaughan One way through might be to talk about what it really means
to love your neighbour – what does that mean in the language
of commitment? In our society institutions are breaking
down. Pretty much 50 per cent of kids in the UK are born
outside marriage. What are we saying to those people? What's
the good news in terms of an institutional relationship which
we're saying matters, which we're saying is part of the way in

which we have come to understand God's order in society, which is about really loving each other?

Surely the question that the church has to address is 'what do we want to present as good?' We've been through some challenging stages of having to deal with that in the recent past. We've got to a point where we know that marriages can break down. And we've found a way of helping people get going again and making a new commitment. That's the sort of thing that we have to learn from to deal with the level of pluralism that has entered our society. We do want to encourage people into faithful, lifelong, stable relationships which help them to be better as human beings than they'd otherwise be.

Robin   I think partly what this whole process is about is changing the terms of the conversation. Could we get back to the Bible? There are two things I draw on from the Bible about sex. One is the Song of Solomon, right there at the heart of the Old Testament. It's about sex and about love. It's a wonderful thing to have at the heart of the Scriptures.

And the New Testament is about creating healthy Christian communities. You can't have a healthy Christian community if you don't have healthy sexual relationships going on within it. We've seen so many times that the community is broken by abusive sex, whether it's adultery or all the other things that we hear about.

It has to be the church's responsibility to help people have good relationships which are flourishing, and that's very biblical.

Naomi   And the Bible uses the word 'defiled' for what can happen in distorted sexual relationships, insisting in Hebrews that the marriage bed should be undefiled. That presumably means that this is sacred to the couple, who are committing their lives to each other and possessing each other in a way which is godly or holy. And I think that concept of an undefiled marriage bed and the sacredness of sex is a very high concept that we need to recover.

Jasmin   And it's so far from so much in our society. I worry about pornography. I have two children, turning eleven this summer. My son's already said to me, 'Mummy, what's sex like?' And he knows it's something significant, but it's like saying, 'What's it like to walk on the moon?' It's so beyond the realm of his experience but I know that at some point one of his friends will show him pornography – if they haven't already. There's this horrible sense that it's all beyond your control and a million miles from what is good and helpful.

Brad I think one of the ways to deal with it is to be more open and talk more about sex. Why are young people interested in pornography? Because sex is taboo. If we were having frank conversations about sex in society, pornography would lose its lustre.

Francis I'm not sure about that!

Robin I think there's also something about the nature of sexual desire here. I draw a parallel with travel magazines, where you see these amazing places with wonderful beaches and it 'only' costs £600 a night. We all know that's being presented as an ideal, and actually you're probably going to stay with friends because you can't afford that kind of holiday. Pornography is the same; it's kind of presented as an ideal. But it's completely artificial and stops you making the most of what you have.

I think if we could even just have a frank conversation about how sexual intercourse isn't nearly as common as people think it is both in heterosexual and homosexual relationships that might open things up a bit. If we are honest and say that, in a relationship, there are times when you have sex and it's amazing, and there's times when you have sex and it's kind of quite routine. Why don't we just talk about that? And say, 'Okay, fine.'

Vaughan I'm more reserved about opening this conversation up and saying we'd all be much better if we were able to talk about it. Because there's a bit of me that thinks…

Naomi It's private.

Vaughan Yeah, actually.

Jasmin We've strayed quite a bit from the Bible but, on pornography for example, I think Genesis has a lot that's really relevant. The eating of the apple and how they became ashamed of their nakedness. And that self-consciousness and shame could also be a consequence of engaging with pornography and feeling really polluted. It's what Naomi was saying about sex being defiled.

Naomi And then by contrast you do have wonderful models of friendship where there is an emotional and physical intimacy, an appropriate sexuality actually, but without sex as such. Like the beloved disciple leaning on Jesus. Or David and Jonathan.

Brad I think that what the Bible says about our individual bodies and our social bodies as a temple of the Spirit is also helpful here. The temple is a space of worship that's decorated and made beautiful, which is sometimes my response when people criticize my tattoos.

I think about how that plays out in sex as well. Am I treating my body as a temple? And respecting and enjoying it? The same goes for other people's bodies: am I treating other people as temples of God?

Jasmin Jesus and Paul also say a lot about something we haven't really talked about at all: singleness. I wouldn't want it to sound like we're saying if you never enter a sexual relationship, you have missed something of God's grace and goodness. Saying sex is a necessary good could come across as difficult for people who are single, celibate or asexual.

Vaughan If you have a vocation to be single, or if it just happens by chance that you're single you can make something really good of that. I wouldn't want what was said to be a judgement on that.

Naomi I know we need to draw to a close but I think we can forget how although singleness and celibacy and keeping sex for marriage all might seem weird they can also be attractive to people. I think of a celibate young man I know in his late twenties, a youth leader, who is a great actor. At the end of a theatrical production he was horrified to discover they played a party game where each person names something they had done and thinks nobody else has done. Within 30 seconds he realized it was all about sex – where people had sex, how many people in a night, and so on. When it came to him he said, 'Well, I've never had sex anywhere, with anybody.'

What happened next was fascinating. A woman who had bragged about her sexual exploits looked horrified and there was total silence. Then somebody said, 'So, you're gay and not out yet?' and he replied 'No. I've just not had sex.' More silence. Then the woman said, 'Well, actually, it wasn't quite like I said... In fact, most of that was really quite exploitative, and in fact I felt raped by this second bloke.' And people started being real about their sexual experiences. Very different from the bragging game. Some stayed until two or three in the morning and at the end one bloke said to him, 'I just regret everything now and just wish I could be like you.' Thankfully the youth leader said, 'You can. Tomorrow is a new day. And from where I am, we start afresh with God every day. You can actually start again.'

SCENE 3

A conversation about gender identity and transition

Colin

Can we begin with probing differences between gender dysphoria and gender ideology? I feel there's a difference between people struggling deeply with gender identity and those making statements about their body for ideological reasons. In the one case we're still learning why that happens and how we can best support people, but the other involves a whole complexity of things going on.

Gabriel

It's very difficult though, because you can't really know how anyone else understands their identity until you meet them and talk to them, so it can be hard to draw those distinctions. I had both physical and psychological suffering before I transitioned and that's part of the reason I transitioned. It's not just, 'I'd quite like to be a boy today.'

Kerry

I'm also uncomfortable with the word 'ideology' here. There's a whole range of different kinds of experience leading people to transition. In talking to trans friends and in other discussions, I've encountered very few people who just decide to be something different today.

Gabriel

I think it would be very hard to do it, actually. It's very hard to be something you're not. I just can't imagine psychologically how one could pretend to be trans. Spiritually, I believe God speaks to each person and calls them into who they are. Going against that is very, very difficult.

Kerry

A lot of discussion operates with a kind of dualism where we separate what we say about bodies from what we say about minds. We think that trans experience is real if you can tie it to something in the body, but it's not real if it's just in the mind. Scientifically, philosophically, that doesn't work. If someone has a deep-seated, long-term pattern of experience, that is a fact about something going on in their body, just as much as a hormone imbalance.

Olivia

Yes, but that does not mean that we simply celebrate whatever is present in a person's body. Not everything that goes on in our minds and bodies is healthy. It is important to be able to identify mental illnesses as well as physical illnesses; to identify patterns of behaviour that are not normal – however we define normality – and to respond appropriately. I don't have any time for mind/body dualisms but I do recognize that not all that goes on in our mind is healthy and able to be celebrated.

Gabriel What you're describing is exactly how trans people are treated – in this country at least. There's psychological diagnosis of gender dysphoria, and we go through a long, long period of psychotherapy before anyone transitions in any physical way.

A lot of our treatments for various mental health conditions are biological. We do something biological to people's bodies in giving them medicines. Sometimes it feels like we treat transitioning as worse than anything else we do to our bodies as a reaction to something that's going on in our minds. The idea that we're just allowing people to change their bodies because we're celebrating something wrong with them isn't what really happens in our health system at all.

Sarah Are some of the medical procedures that people undergo irreversible?

Gabriel Some are, but lots of medical procedures are irreversible. Decisions are made about whether to amputate a limb, or pursue cosmetic surgery. Often that's not a life-or-death decision. It's a quality-of-life decision. Yet it's irreversible. Trans people should think very carefully about every surgery they have. I haven't had what would be seen as the full set, because I've made careful decisions about what I need to live well in my body and respect the body that God's given me. It's complicated, making decisions. I don't think our current system allows anyone to just say, 'Okay, I'm just going to have the surgery.' The amount of psychological work you have to go through. I've had friends who have been turned down for surgeries because the surgeon's psychologist hasn't been sure about their motivation. The way it's presented in the media is very different from what happens in reality.

Kerry Yes, the determination that one of my close friends has needed in order to transition, and stuff she's had to go through (worst in the church!) has been incredible. The strength and support necessary for any of this to happen shows there's nothing easy or quick about it.

Sarah   We do have people whose biological sex is ambiguous. And then there are those showing 'opposite' gender behaviour. I went through a tomboy stage, hated being with boring girls, climbed trees, had a sword, sat with boys. At puberty I got very, very cross I was going to be like those boring, drab women who didn't interest me. But now I'm a completely different person and love the company of women. We're all going through life stages where our identity, our Christian faith, is playing out in different kinds of scenarios. I worry about young teenage girls today being encouraged to think they are trans.

Gabriel   Yet I find it really difficult when people compare what we feel to being a tomboy and what toys kids like playing with. In fact, I never was a tomboy. Being trans is such a deep and real thing.

Sarah   I get that, Gabriel, but alongside gender dysphoria, there is a political kind of legal-cultural movement for people to be able to choose their gender. I'm not saying that all trans people ascribe to that cultural movement, but it does exist, very evidenced in the media. There were some interesting statistics in the book that seemed to point to almost three times the number of young people referred are assigned female at birth, compared to male. Is there a reason for that? Is it just harder to be female? Or is it a reflection of social changes?

Olivia   If you look at the distribution of gender realignment across a number of decades, and back into the last century, predominantly it used to be male to female, distributed amongst all the age groups. Very few in comparison transitioned from female to male. More recently, a reversal has taken place and there are far more girls to boys, and they're younger – as the statistics earlier in the book show.

We have to question what's going on within culture as a whole and within male-female relations, as well as ask questions about individuals. We're never just individuals. As the book's discussion of identity suggests, we're 'situated' persons, in social contexts, and our situated-ness matters enormously as to how we understand ourselves. As well as personal, deep-seated psychological angst about identity that some people have, other issues can be involved. For instance, feminist sociologists look at the negative experiences of women's identity: being attacked, undermined, ridiculed and so on – and ask, who wants to carry on being a girl? They suggest women are rejecting their female identity, but are opting to being trans because of cultural disapproval towards lesbianism.

Gabriel The trans-positive sociologists offer an opposite view of what's behind these shifts. They point to greater visibility of trans people and the way women and men are seen. Because of the rise in visibility, young trans guys have felt able to transition, but that has created a backlash – largely against trans-women because of the controversial idea of a man wearing a dress in a female bathroom. So, things have sociologically completely reversed. It's much harder now to come out as a trans woman than as a trans man. In terms of: 'I don't want to be a girl, because it's too difficult' my own experience is completely opposite. I don't think anyone would be given hormone therapy or surgery just for sociological reasons. We have to prove extreme dysphoria.

Colin Can I turn this discussion back to the Bible? It seems to me that one of the things that the Bible is saying is that we don't really understand ourselves. Even the way we think about our own circumstance and situation can be flawed. We're sinners, so we need some external help to know what it means to live life as a human. When I say that, I don't mean in any way to undermine the experience of gender dysphoria. We absolutely need to learn from science, and from people's accounts of their experiences. I don't want to diminish or undervalue that. This problem is true of everyone, whatever their gender or sexual identity. It does seem to me that the Bible lays out a picture of what it means to be human, and of how we should think about our own identity.

It gives us normative categories. It shows us God's purposes in creating us. We're made in the image of God; we're made male and female. Yes, there is more going on in the spectrum of God's creation than male and female, but male and female are significant categories in the way that God has shaped the universe. We are developing all sorts of new

thinking about trans in our society but I think the Bible
gives us some other frameworks that we need to think about
and hold on to as the church.

Gabriel　Honesty is also a biblical norm throughout the Bible. For
me, honesty does mean describing my identity as trans.
I will never describe myself completely as male: that
would be technically incorrect. It's an ongoing journey for
me. I have experienced certain things as a woman that a
biological man cannot experience. And I don't want to be a
stereotypical man, pressed to act, believe or think in ways
that aren't healthy and don't fit me. So I hope that what some
new generation trans people are doing is trying to unsettle
those things and saying, 'It's more complicated.'

In the Old Testament we have really strict rules, most
of which, by the end of the New Testament, have been
dismantled. Jesus fulfils the law by saying, 'The law is self-
sacrificial love' and that's different from, 'You must, and you
must not.'

Colin　I think this shows our disagreements here are not just about
how we understand experience and science and society but
about Scripture and theology. I'm not keen in principle on
the idea that we start with rules and finish just with love.
The Ten Commandments, for example, are sometimes
explicitly restated in the New Testament. And on gender,
it's more than the law – it's about God's work as Creator.
Jesus himself reaffirms that God made us male and female,
quoting Genesis 1, Paul suggests that marriage is a picture
of Christ and the Church and something set in creation, and
John uses the imagery of bride and bridegroom for the new
creation. The male-female binary runs consistently from
Genesis to Revelation.

Kerry　Actually, I think that there is more than one way to go with
the biblical material and the creation of men and women. If
you ask, 'Where in the Bible do we find people that don't fit
into that pattern?' there are eunuchs – not the same category
as trans, but people who didn't fit the gender system of the
time. The comments we have about those people, both
in Isaiah and from Jesus (in Matthew 19.12) are positive
and welcoming. So one possibility is to say that, even in

the Bible, there is an acknowledgement that male/female doesn't cover everyone, and those excepted are celebrated.

Possibly also, when talking about male and female, the Bible is giving us a decent approximation. 'Men' and 'women' covers most people, most of the time, but when we delve in, it's complicated as to who is in or outside those two categories.

Gabriel   Yes, in Genesis we have these very clear binaries – night and day, waters and land, for instance. But that doesn't mean God didn't make dawn and dusk, or marshes and beaches.

Sarah   There's a danger that we take some of those Bible verses out of context for the time we're living in now.

Olivia   I think a lot of Bible verses were revolutionary for the time, given the way women were viewed. It's a wake-up call, really, in terms of how God values everyone. We're all made in the image of God, both female and male… I'm reminded of that verse in Corinthians that talks about how men and women are connected – woman was made from man, but man is born of woman. So, we're different but not independent of each other.

Gabriel   That brings us back to marriage, and that's another difficult area. My legal marriage was what is called a 'same-sex wedding'. That's because legally I'm female, even though, very clearly to all of you, I'm male. That meant that I had to get married in a registry office and we had to be called 'wife and wife'. That hurt so much. I find it so difficult that when I hear my old name or see old photos I feel physically unwell. It's distressing.

Colin   I think that's really important for us to hear. As a church it feels like we haven't begun to think through how what we are saying about trans and celebrating transition connects with what we are saying about marriage as between a man and a woman. If you had legally transitioned you could have married in church. But why does the church think legal transition makes that difference? I'm not sure we've got a coherent Christian understanding here and so we are causing hurt and confusion.

Olivia   Perhaps, though, we are learning that we need to tread really carefully when we talk about these things. Also, isn't behind it all something about the church needing to model ever better the liberating news of Jesus Christ liberating us from what society sometimes imposes on us, but all sorts of other factors? And don't we need to be saying that the most important thing is that we're in Christ? When talking about issues of identity, whether to do with race, or gender, we need to be saying, 'This is important, but not as important as the fact that we are Christians together, bought by the blood of Christ, united with him.' That has to be the first thing. Wouldn't it be wonderful if we modelled that better than we do now?

SCENE 4

A conversation about the life of the Church

Derek   One of the things that has come home to me through our work is that questions of identity, sexuality and marriage rest on all sorts of other deeper disagreements. Some of them are historic that we've managed to live with or find ways through and some of them are new. Sadly, I've come to the conclusion that we are in the sort of high-middle to high range of disagreement because it has to do with issues of holiness.

We all say that the Scriptures are there to guide us into a way of holiness. But if we can't agree on what the Scriptures give us as a way of holiness, then we've got a serious challenge for our common life together.

Harry   It's a massive challenge. This is, for me, fundamentally about whether we are faithful to the Bible or not. And I can't get round what the Bible seems to me clearly to be teaching in this area.

Lorraine   But then we have seen the variety of ways to interpret the Scriptures. I've got no wish for us not to attend to the Bible as our first authority. But I do get frustrated with people saying biblical teaching is absolutely clear because I don't think it is, Harry.

Pat   Yes, there's a kind of understanding that one view is Bible-based and the other view isn't. I think allowing that to develop traction is really sad. It doesn't reflect the way in which all of us, wherever we are on the spectrum of views on this, ground everything in Scripture, but we understand it differently. Why can't we accept the different interpretations we come to in good faith?

Harry   You are right that there's a strong mood to say, 'Well, there's different ways of interpreting Scripture. We live with lots of kinds of difference and that's alright.'

But I don't think that's ultimately sustainable. If you look at Acts 15 or 1 Thessalonians, teaching about marriage and relationships is critical to how the Church reaches out and draws the nations into the kingdom of God. Whatever you think, to try to make it marginal or secondary, I think, is just not really faithful to Christian tradition.

If sexual activity outside marriage is sinful then to say 'it's not, it's alright' is to do harm to people. If we come to a different view and it's not, say, sinful for people of the same sex to have sexual relationships, then to teach that it is sinful is deeply harmful. Either way, some people in the church are doing serious harm to some other people.

Pat   Sure, marriage and relationships are part of what the church originally taught but it was much more about the community that Jesus built up around him, which was very much *not* about a particular kind of domestic relationship. Perhaps the tradition has been wrong in giving these questions such a central significance? They are important, but they are not *that* important.

Lorraine   I'd want to say, 'yeah, vital for mission but the sort of committed, monogamous, permanent same sex relationships of today weren't an option.' If what matters is monogamy and permanent covenantal commitment, then I think your argument wobbles a little bit. Even with something as clearly problematic as polygamy we have learnt that insisting rigorously on church members ending all polygamous relationships was actually an obstacle to mission.

Derek   But even if you don't think that, the only possible reading of the scriptural evidence is the conservative view – marriage and sexual morality are really important biblically and there has to be very clear teaching on these things. And, Lorraine, there's a world of difference between tolerating polygamy and celebrating it.

Pat   But people have dealt with disagreements in the Church throughout history. Things which have seemed extremely challenging to one generation have been less challenging to the next. The classic example is the remarriage of divorced people, isn't it? People were very serious about remarriage of divorced people while a former spouse was still living, but now it's become one of those things which we just live with.

Derek   But divorce is something where you can see debates going on in the biblical canon. On same-sex relationships there is a much more uniform biblical pattern. What, exactly, Scripture refers to may be tricky but that Scripture is uniformly negative isn't in dispute.

What's more, as a church, we've got to a certain position on divorce and remarriage but a) we haven't changed our doctrine of marriage and b) it took a long time with a careful process in which the church came to a mind that it would be possible in certain circumstances for this to be acceptable. It then took a long time to work out how it could be done in such a way that the teaching wasn't undermined but proper pastoral care and support was given. No one says that divorce is good. When it comes to same-sex relationships we are a long way back on that track.

Sam   I am not sure we are so far back on the track, Derek. Since *Issues in Human Sexuality* in 1991, we've been living with permission for lay people to live faithfully together in sexually active same-sex relationships. Not everyone's comfortable with that but it has kept us together. What's wrong with that approach?

Derek   You're right, the Church of England's approach is a particular, quite expansive version of pastoral accompaniment – or we might call it pastoral accommodation. As a church we maintain our doctrine and our liturgy expresses that doctrine. But we make allowances for people who do not follow the lines set out in that doctrine to participate in the church and we don't push them away.

That's now seen as very unsatisfactory. For some our discipline is already too lax. For others we need to be more accommodating or change our doctrine and liturgy. The gap between formal church teaching and the beliefs and practices of many, perhaps most, members of the church, clergy, Synod members, even bishops, has just grown bigger and bigger. I think we're at the point where it's unsustainable.

Harry   Perhaps the church needs to get serious about self-discipline again across the whole range of sexual behaviour?

Pat   But Harry, that implies we agree on the standards, and we don't. Pastoral accommodation has just papered over the cracks. And not just in terms of homosexuality but also heterosexual sex outside of marriage. There have also been major developments in how we understand human identity, gender and sexuality. We recognize people who are lesbian or gay or trans are equal in value before God in a way that wasn't widely perceived 50 years ago. The LLF book and resources are about the gift of life and how we come to celebrate the gift of life for everybody regardless of gender identity or sexuality. That's a different understanding that the church now has from 50 years ago.

Sam
The Church of England has changed on the ministry of women too. It's been difficult but we have managed to find structures which keep us together. Can't we find a similar way here as well?

Derek
I think it's more difficult than over the ordination of women because the harm is of a sort of moral order. I don't want to believe it's impossible. It seems to me that the differences are part of the life of the Church of God and whatever happens that's not going away.

If we can hold that in one church, that would be an amazing thing. But I don't want to underestimate how difficult it is and I don't think it helps us trying to say it's no big deal. I think it really is a big deal.

Wayne
In terms of the history of the Church of England, and the way the Anglican Communion is set up, there's huge room for working out the life of the gospel differently in our different cultural and historic contexts. We have to recognize that we cannot sit here in England and legislate for a Nigerian or let a South African or South American province legislate for us.

Of course, we are affected by what we each do, and for me there is huge pain in that were we to change our practice here in the way I would want to, I know the cost that that could potentially be, for example, for my fellow Christians in Muslim-majority contexts. But I'm also aware of the pain of gay people in those contexts and the huge pain of gay people in this context who feel we're being kind of held hostage to an ecclesiology coming out of another particular context.

Lorraine
The Anglican Communion is not a church but it demonstrates a structure that has allowed quite a bandwidth for doctrinal as well as practical pastoral diversity. That's partly why negotiation and argument has been a hallmark of Anglican holiness. It hasn't been a peaceful consensus at any point.

Sam
I'm wondering whether that 'bandwidth' can take a change in the doctrine of marriage. And if it can't, might, might it include something else…

Lorraine A recognition, a blessing of same-sex relationships?

Pat I think one of the most important things that's come out of LLF is that the bishops are not of a common mind on this. That's really, really crucial because it opens up the kind of conversations we are having about structures.

Lorraine Well, the bishops are wrestling with what it means to guard the unity of the Church in that situation, which is why the House of Bishops has sought to function as one.

Wayne But there's a difference between unity and uniformity... Couldn't communion be held and separation avoided if the questions were more in the category of what can faithful Christians practise according to their conscience and not in terms of formal liturgy, never mind a change in canons or doctrine? I know that taking marriage services out of the liturgy would be a massive change, but wouldn't it help us manage our disagreements better?

Sam It seems to me that there's agreement that the bandwidth of practice needs to be pretty wide to hold the Church of England together. But even if you couldn't have church marriages, you'd still have people requesting some sort of church blessing. Or look at what happened over the reaffirmation of baptismal vows in the context of gender transition. There's disagreement about the sanctioning of all sorts of practices, be that by formal changes of doctrine or through some form of liturgical recognition.

Derek For me, it's about what the church does. I think if we have an authorized service for the blessing of people in committed same-sex relationships, that becomes something the church does. And what the church does, the whole church does.

Lorraine Even if an individual priest out of conscience does or doesn't do something?

Derek There's a move that wants to lower the temperature by saying it won't be an action of the church, just be an action of those priests who take this view, just something that happens in those congregations that take a particular view, and those clergy who don't take that view and those congregations that don't take that view can kind of disassociate themselves from it. And I think if you have a more congregationalist style of church life you can make that move. But I'm not really sure that as Anglicans we can do that. Even with alternative episcopal oversight.

Pat It's such a knotty question, isn't it? Because we do live with difference, we live with all sorts of difference. We live with all sorts of structural injustices. Take nuclear weapons or fossil fuels, we have very different views. Or the Eucharist.

So, we do live with fundamental differences and the church can cope with that. I know that this is seen as a first order moral issue by some people. I actually don't think it is. I think this question is not about what marriage is but who can be married.

Harry And I think that there are fundamental points that we're agreed on about human flourishing and honesty, constancy, faith, prayer and love and all those things.

Sam Aren't we back in John 17 and Jesus' insistence on the essence of Christian identity as being in Christ together, a togetherness in him, a unity that brings us into the oneness of the Son and the Father? What does Jesus' insistence that above all things we must be one mean for the church today? I agree with Wayne that unity is not uniformity, but it must have some real meaning.

Wayne I think it's really important because I hear some people talking about our differences being like between different religions, and I think it is just not that. Whatever anybody is doing or believing, if they believe in Jesus and are baptized in a trinitarian understanding, then they are my sister or my brother and we are one in that sense.

That doesn't necessarily mean that we can be part even of the same church denomination, but it does mean there is a deep unity, that I am pained when they suffer and when that unity is broken.

Sam Jesus does say 'that the world may believe'; it doesn't look too convincing if we start splitting up.

Harry Jesus also said in John 17.11, 'Holy Father, protect in Your name those which You have given to Me, that they may be one as We are one.' It is only by abiding in the name given to us in revelation in Christ that we are one. I think to come to a judgement that anyone is no longer in that place is a very, very serious thing and I would never want to do it. But there are places in the New Testament where that happens. And in relation to sex too. So, our prayer for unity with each other can't be detached from the prayer that we remain in the truth.

Lorraine I also want to say, we need to get over ourselves and not act as if we're holding the unity of Christendom in the Church of England. A bit of me wants to say, 'The body of Christ is invisible and what actually matters is that we dwell with one another in prayer on the journey of pursuing discipleship together.' I just wonder whether there's unity on the ground that is being prevented by unity through the structures.

Pat That's right. We come together to do things, and the story of food banks, night shelters and things brings together people regardless of their differences. Perhaps we need to get better at working together. The other thing which has really come to me out of this whole process is the recognition that the eye cannot say to the hand, 'I do not need you.'

Sam I agree that there is more unity on the ground and in practice. Although perhaps that's because for many it's not such a big issue. But how does unity on the ground work itself out in the structures – the actual governing and leading relationships – in the life of the church?

Wayne I just want to say that I would hope that as we face deep disagreements we do so with a frankness and an openness and, I hope, a kindness and a respect that haven't always marked these things in the past. That itself can be an occasion for the deepening of communion and the deepening of our unity in Christ with one another. And it doesn't just have to be a situation we have to manage by walking a bit further apart from each other. It can be a challenge that we face in Christ together, that draws us closer together, closer to the reality of the name that he has been given, and makes Christ more manifest.

In this final Part of the book you were invited to eavesdrop on a series of conversations among people who disagree about the matters discussed in this book. It may be that you identified with some of the 'characters' in the discussions. You may have picked up insights, or heard perspectives you hadn't thought about before.

In different ways, all of the speakers in these conversations drew on material that we have explored earlier in the book. If you began your journey here, the earlier Parts of the book will help you delve more deeply into the claims that the different characters made, and the arguments they used.

If this Part is the end of your journey through this book, then the next step might be to join in conversations like this. In 'An Appeal by the Bishops of the Church of England' that closes the book, you will find out what part you might play in the church's discernment about identity, sexuality, relationships and marriage.

Encounters

Meet some people at ST PHILIP'S UPPER FRINTON

The vicar, Neil, collected me at the nearest railway station. We drove through the countryside to the small town of Upper Frinton in the East of England. There, in the church hall, a group of six parishioners had already gathered and were making cups of tea and coffee. We sat around a large table and began our conversation.

'The whole dynamic of worshipping here is around, "Hooray, you're with us, welcome!"' says Daniella, a relative newcomer. The others agree that St Philip's policy is to be welcoming and 'absolutely accepting' to all. 'It should just be a non-issue, shouldn't it, really?' says Colin, whose friends are put off the Church of England because same-sex marriage is not allowed. 'I find it so frustrating, because there are so many wonderful things this church does... and all of that is undone, to some extent, by this discriminating policy which is so indefensible.'

'I'm quite excited that we're part of a process that's actually talking about this now', says Georgie. Her gay friends hope she will be able to change the church from the inside: 'One of them said "Please sort it out, so that I can marry my partner!"'

The group is concerned that the church moves 'painfully slowly' on issues of sexuality, lagging far behind the rest of society and becoming removed 'from reality, from real life and people's own experiences'. 'I think it's really important that we start reflecting what there is out there within our church', says Georgie.

'I am excited that we're moving forward', says the vicar, Neil, 'and I can see from my own life and my own experience of the church that it is, because it's just not an issue anymore.' He describes being offered his current job and asking the PCC to double-check that people would be happy for him to accept, given he is in a same-sex civil partnership. 'They came back and just said, "That's fine"', he says, noting that wouldn't have been the case 20 years ago.

'The important thing is that the gospel shapes us. When that happens, things change.'

Gillian believes that people's opinions and views can be changed by good leadership and modelling a better way: 'People are very frightened of things they don't understand and have no knowledge of.' Reading the Bible interpretatively rather than literally can also change people's stance, especially, says Daniella, if we read asking 'What is it telling us about how we live now?'.

'We're not saying, "Let's forget [the Bible], lead immoral lives"', adds Georgie. 'That's what people are scared of. There are basic elemental truths that will always remain the same on a moral level – how we deal with each other.'

Colin points out that some people think being non-heterosexual is a decision or a lifestyle choice 'rather than just being part of who you are.' 'I don't minister as a gay person', says Neil. 'I minister as Neil and because I believe in Jesus. The important thing is that the gospel shapes us. When that happens, things change.'

'I think it's up to us to live by example, to be a daily living sacrifice and go out and behave how we want the church to be', says Ruth. 'We won't change things by complaining and browbeating. We've got to do it by being a positive influence.'

Meet some people at ST PAUL'S CHURCH HOWTON HILL

St Paul's is in the London suburb of Howton Hill. Four parishioners meet in a family living room to talk – together with two babies and the occasional toddler. Lydia is a married mum; Jacob is married; Sasha is a single mum and Elly is single and works for the church.

The talk is about St Paul's diversity, welcome and emphasis on being family to each other. Elly shares 'I came into St Paul's knowing that I was quite clear on what the Bible says about sexual ethics. That marriage is one man, one woman for life. I'd made a decision very early on in my Christian walk that that therefore meant not acting on my same-sex attraction. And that was a tough decision; it was really hard and continues to be very hard. But the joy of coming to St Paul's [is] they really celebrated the fact that I'd made that decision.'

'not finding my identity in my sexuality but finding my identity in Christ is so much more freeing'

They discuss the importance of a few brave people talking honestly about struggles – both upfront and between each other: Elly says 'That encourages everyone that it's a good thing to be open, honest and caring to each other.' Lydia adds, 'It's wanting to point people to Jesus in whatever situation they're in. So as opposed to making [same-sex attraction] the issue it's "What's your identity in Christ? Your whole life."' Jacob observes that 'the ideal is not set. The ideal is not husband, wife and 2.4 kids [...] Whatever circumstance you're in, it's being a disciple of Christ. And I guess that's the ideal to strive towards.'

Elly continues 'We're at a church that trusts the Bible, that wants to listen to what God says, perhaps particularly the hard bits or the bits we don't instantly agree with. And we're trying to listen to God's word, not the culture, not our feelings, not what other people say life should be like.' Sasha goes on 'But I think that's because the gospel is good news, and so actually not finding my identity in my sexuality but finding my identity in Christ is so much more freeing.'

Sasha lived some of her adult life in same-sex relationships before coming to faith. She became a Christian at St Paul's. Early on in her Christian life, she became pregnant through IVF treatment ('as a single woman, not my wisest decision'). While the church has reservations about the ethics of IVF, they nevertheless wholeheartedly support Sasha, saying 'We're family and we're going to support you in it.' After having her daughter, Sasha then had to consider what to do about the remaining frozen embryos. Thinking about it from a Christian perspective, she made the tough decision to use the embryos 'knowing that I would then be a single parent of three'.

She knew it was not something everyone could agree with and felt supported when the church said 'Look, it's great. We believe in the sanctity of life and therefore, we're going to support you in that.' She continues 'I've had nothing but love and support' and says the vicar emphasized that 'We are family. Some people aren't going to agree with this, but we are family.'

She finished 'And so, that's actually been bigger than [the fact] I'm attracted to people of the same sex.'

Meet some people at ST MILDRED'S CHURCH

St Mildred's Church serves the small town of Upper Mallowpool with a population of nearly 15,000. Six parishioners had gathered at the back of the church to take part in the conversation: Richard, the vicar; Duncan and Miriam, an older couple who also attend a Baptist church; Jenny, a lesbian woman in a partnership; Owen, a gay youth worker; and Noah, a heterosexual married man. In the background a group was clearing up after the midweek coffee and craft session.

Richard got the conversation going. 'So, my theology has changed over time. As an evangelical, I'm quite clear on the need for the Scriptures to lead the way. But my thinking has changed. Being divorced and remarried, the theology I take for myself on divorce is that divorce is not God's ideal plan but that when I read the Scriptures, it's allowable. And when I look at the Scriptures' teaching on sexuality, the conclusion I've come to is that same-sex relationships are not God's ideal plan, but that they are allowed. And so, I feel like I'm in a position to say that because I'm willing to criticize myself over divorce and remarriage. That has enabled me to reach out so we have gay people involved in positions of responsibility within our church family. We have to find a way, though, of including those who see it differently.' Noah chipped in, 'It's interesting, we're not out for overt inclusion. But we welcome anybody, and we don't exclude anybody.'

It soon became apparent that not only did everyone agree that being truly inclusive meant including people with opposing views, but this little group embodied this very reality. Although Duncan and Miriam were clear that same-sex marriage was not an option, they were happy to join in the conversation – a conversation that combined deep and overt affection with spontaneous honesty.

Owen pitched in with his story: 'As someone who is gay, my theology has been left, right and centre. I've gone, is abstinence the correct way? But then, come to the conclusion that if God is love, then it says, "Whoever does not love, does not know God." And therefore, I must be able to love, to know God. But yeah, I can understand both sides, because my theology has gone all the way round. I love this sort of conversation.'

Jenny spoke movingly about how difficult she had found it to cross the threshold of the church eight years ago and what it meant for her to be welcomed in by Richard. She had been thrown out of her Christian family home at the age of 16 when she came out. Even now, only one sister is willing to be in touch with her.

But the conversation kept coming back to how each of them had come to their convictions. 'Is there actually any gender in the afterlife, in heaven? Is gender only a concept for a tiny fraction of our existence? And that, maybe, puts it a little bit in perspective,' said Noah. 'By trying to say that we know all of the rights and wrongs, I'd say we're putting ourselves almost in the position of God over humanity. God tells us to let him judge, because it's in our nature to get things wrong.' Richard agreed: 'But he *will* judge, and, therefore, it's important that if we become convinced that something we thought before wasn't right, then we must change. As long as we're open to the possibility that we might be wrong, then I think that's what will qualify us, when we meet God.'

An appeal

by the Bishops
of the Church of England

We began this book with an invitation to every reader: an invitation to engage with the book, the Living in Love and Faith Course and accompanying resources together with others in faith; to be nourished together in hope and to discover the love of God among us even in our differences.

Now, as we lead the Church of England into making whatever decisions are needful for our common life regarding matters of identity, sexuality, relationships and marriage, we appeal to you to join us in the period of discernment that follows their publication. The timetable for this discernment and decision-making process can be found at **www.churchofengland.org/LLF**.

Our strong hope is that people and communities all around the country – everyone who looks to the Church of England as their spiritual home – will engage with this book and its accompanying resources and, as far as possible, do this together with those who have different perspectives and lived experiences. This work demands from us that together we face our differences, divisions and disagreements honestly, humbly and compassionately, and that together we stand against homophobia, transphobia and all other unacceptable forms of behaviour, including demeaning those whose views are different from our own. It requires us all to serve, honour and love one another as we seek the face of Christ in each other. It calls us all to enter into the suffering of Christ's body as we embrace the pain of differences and see the harm that some of our disagreements cause. It implores us to seek the inspiration of the Holy Spirit that we may be led more deeply together into the mind of Christ.

Therefore, we exhort you to walk with us in a new stage of our common life in Christ so that, 'speaking the truth in love', godly discernment and right decisions can be made over contested matters of identity, sexuality, relationships and marriage, for 'we must grow up in every way into him who is the head, into Christ' (Ephesians 4.15).

Our invitation at the beginning of the book drew on the Gospel of John. Now, as we conclude with this call to take part in the period of discernment, we turn again to the wisdom of John's Gospel to guide our way.

In John chapter 17 we are brought into the intimacy of Jesus' prayer to his Father shortly before he lays down his life for the world. Jesus prays for his disciples whose feet he had earlier washed and with whom he had shared a meal and spoken intensively about many matters. It is a prayer that Jesus extended to all those who would believe in him because of what they would hear about him through these first disciples. It is a prayer for us in our life together as Jesus' followers today. It is a prayer which we find ourselves as bishops relating to very closely, not least because it speaks of the unity of Christ's people which is dear to our hearts and central to our calling.

Jesus knew that following him would not be easy. His disciples would be hated by the world. They will need guarding from the evil one. So he prayed for their protection. Jesus also knew that there would be many pressures that would try to force them apart. So he prayed that they will be one. As we read the Letters of John later in the New Testament, we can sense some of those pressures at work in the communities to which John was writing. The letters call them to believe in Christ, to confess that Jesus 'has come in the flesh', to resist any deception that denies that 'God sent his only Son into the world so that we might live through him' (1 John 4.3,9; 2 John 7-11).

The life that Jesus leads us into has a distinctive character to it, bearing the stamp of the kingdom of God, for it is 'eternal life' (John 3.3). Hence, the principles and practices that shape Christian life cannot be expected to coincide entirely with those of society at large, even in those times of greater alignment between the Christian faith and human culture. Indeed, they are not always fully evident even in the Church, and so we go on praying for God's will to be done on earth as in heaven.

The sexual ethics of the early Christian communities, shaped by their Jewish inheritance, were distinct from many of the prevailing customs of the wider world in which the Christian faith first spread. In the discussions that we have encountered in this book and the disagreements they have exposed, together with the stories that have been told in all their diversity, the desire to be obedient to Christ and deeply Christian in sexual ethics and personal lifestyles is a common theme across our differences.

Those same discussions, though, have also exposed the depth of disagreement between Christians on exactly how we are called to be distinctive in our ways of life in obedience to Christ, and about what it means to be those who, according to Jesus' prayer, have received his 'word' and have been '[sanctified] in truth' (John 17.14,17,18). Those disagreements are to be found among us as bishops. We do not agree on a number of matters relating to identity, sexuality, relationships and marriage. Some of those differences of view relate to the ethics and lifestyle of opposite sex relationships and some relate to questions around gender and pastoral provisions for transgender people. Most pressing among our differences are questions around same-sex relationships, and we recognize that here decisions in several interconnected areas need to be made with some urgency.

The disagreements among us reflect those of the Church at large. It remains clear that all of us – bishops included – need to go on learning from each other and from all who seek the way of truth. That is the purpose of the Living in Love and Faith learning resources – to help us to learn and discern together so that right judgements and godly decisions can be made about our common life.

This sort of learning and discerning relies upon the work of the Spirit of God, for – as Jesus said – it is the Spirit who takes what is true to Christ and declares it fully to us (John 16.13). Our hope is that the Holy Spirit will use these learning resources to open a way for us to find our deepest convictions about Jesus Christ also affirmed by those who we presently disagree with. If the work of the Spirit is to lead us to new vistas on our disagreements and new perspectives on our differences, it will be through enabling us to ascend the summit of Jesus' prayer in John 17.

Father, I desire that those also, whom you have given me, may be with me where I am, to see my glory, which you have given me because you loved me before the foundation of the world (John 17.24).

Shortly before he was to be 'lifted up' on the cross to give his life for the world (John 3.14; 12.32), Jesus prayed that his followers would not only see the glory of the eternal love that the 'righteous Father' has for him, but also that truly knowing God's name, this love 'may be in them' because the risen Christ is 'in them' (John 17.25,26).

When we were ordained as bishops we were asked, 'Will you promote peace and reconciliation in the church and in the world; and will you strive for the visible unity of Christ's Church?'.[348] And each of us replied, 'With the help of God, I will'. As we have acknowledged, we do not all agree over some matters of great importance for the well-being of Christ's church and how they relate to another question our ordination put to us: 'Will you teach the doctrine of Christ as the Church of England has received it?'. We feel the tension among ourselves between uniting the church in its differences and pressing for decisive decisions in the contested areas about which each of us feels strongly. Nevertheless, we are united as bishops in our commitment to promote peace in the Church and to strive for the visible unity of the church. Jesus prayed that we may be one, so that the world may believe that he was sent by the God of life, through the Spirit of life, to bring the world to fulness of life.

Finally, as this book closes and the work it sets in motion begins, we turn to John chapter 21, the final chapter of John's Gospel, sometimes called the epilogue.

John 21 tells of how Jesus appears again to his disciples. There are three scenes in the appearance of Jesus that John recounts. First the disciples, going about their work, set off to fish on the Sea of Galilee. They work through the night but catch nothing. At daybreak someone calls out to them from the shore, 'Cast the net to the right side of the boat'. They do so and their catch is so large it seems to overwhelm them. One of the disciples declares – the one 'reclining next to Jesus' at the supper and 'standing near the cross' with his mother at Jesus' death – 'It is the Lord!'. With their nets now brimming over, perhaps the disciples remember Jesus' earlier words, 'apart from me you can do nothing' (John 15.5).

In the second scene, Jesus invites the disciples to eat breakfast with him. They do so gladly not even daring to ask their host, '"Who are you?", because they knew it was the Lord' (John 21.12).

In the third, Jesus speaks with Peter and asks him three times, 'Do you love me?'. Peter, who a few days before had denied three times that he knew Jesus, now replies, 'Yes, Lord, you know that I love you', on the third, saying, 'Lord, you know everything, you know that I love you'. In response to Peter's reply, Jesus says to him, 'Feed my sheep' (John 21.15-17). It is an exchange of love for the purposes of love. Jesus, in love, gives Peter the chance to affirm his love for Jesus. Their relationship, scarred by Peter's earlier denial, is restored and Peter is commissioned to love, tend and feed Christ's people and to walk in the way of Christ, even to death.

At our ordinations the Archbishop reminded us in words that resonate with John's that 'Bishops are called to serve and care for the flock of Christ. Mindful of the Good Shepherd, who laid down his life for his sheep, they are to love and pray for those committed to their charge, knowing their people and being known by them'. During this period of discernment and beyond it, we commit ourselves to 'knowing our people and being known by them' in the love of Christ, 'to serve and care for the flock of Christ' in the faith of Christ and 'to promote peace and reconciliation in the church' in the hope of Christ.

We desire greatly that the whole Church of England will take part in this period of discernment. We offer you this book, the Living in Love and Faith Course and accompanying resources, as well as the 'Pastoral Principles' we have already commended, for this common call and purpose. We are confident that 'It is the Lord' (John 21.7) who will be with us all, his people, speaking his word to us together in the reality of his risen life, saying to us together 'Follow me' (John 21.19) and saying to each of us personally – as he said to Peter – as the Gospel comes to an end: '*You* follow me!'.[349]

Lord Jesus,
write the story of your grace and truth
into the lives of your people
that, believing in you,
the world may have life in your name.
Amen.

Glossary

Language shapes our understanding of ourselves and others. It is particularly important to use words with care when we are talking about sex and gender. Sexual and gender identity are intimate aspects of human self-understanding, in relation to which we are all vulnerable. It is easy to hurt others by using the wrong words. It is also easy to misunderstand one another when terms have multiple possible meanings, some of which have changed significantly over time.

There is no neutral terminology available. The use of a particular term can be experienced by someone as having to accept a label that imposes a qualification of their identity that marginalizes them. Some will interpret the use of certain terms as an indication of accepting a particular understanding. In this book choices have had to be made but they are not intended to close down the questions or pre-empt the discussions that these matters raise.

This glossary is offered primarily to aid in the reading of this book and focuses on terms used within it. A fuller and more detailed glossary is available on the Living in Love and Faith website (**www.churchofengland.org/LLF**).

Asexual – lacking sexual desire or attraction.

Bigender – a gender identity encompassing two different gender identities, either as a blended identity, or else alternating over time.

Bisexual – capacity for attraction to both male and female, and possibly also other gender categories.

Cisgender – a term introduced to refer to people who identify exclusively with the sex assigned to them at birth. Most people who identify with the sex/gender assigned to them at birth do not think of themselves as cisgender (but only as male or female), and some may actively object to the use of this term. It is therefore less about self-identification and more about the need for a gender identity term complementary to transgender.

Cross-dressing – at the simplest level, dressing in the clothes of the opposite gender, based on a binary gender distinction between male and female. In reality, this may involve a complex variety of behaviours which, to different degrees and in diverse ways, transgress gender boundaries in relation to dress.

DSD or dsd (Differences of Sex Development) – A term used to cover a range of conditions, including chromosomal variations, different development of the genitals and reproductive system, and variations in secondary sex characteristics; see also Intersex. The medical preference for expanding the abbreviation as Disorder of Sex Development is contested and many people with intersex characteristics consider it stigmatizing. Within medical language there is a tendency to use 'DSD' and in psychosocial approaches, 'dsd'.

Gay – A man who is sexually attracted, primarily, towards other men; a homosexual man. The term is also used inclusively by some women, who refer to themselves as gay rather than lesbian. See also entry for 'homosexual'.

Gender – cultural constructions associated with being male/female or other gender categories, as distinguished from biological sex.

Gender binary – understanding of gender as a binary variable (male vs female); many people now prefer to understand gender as non-binary.

Gender dysphoria – distress associated with discrepancy between sex assigned at birth and experienced gender identity; controversially retained as the name for a diagnostic category (replacing gender identity disorder) within the Diagnostic and Statistical Manual of the American Psychiatric Association (DSM 5).

Gender expression – physical manifestations of gender identity (clothing, hairstyle, voice, etc.).

Gender fluidity – this term is used in different ways; it may refer to change in gender identity across time, or else to recognition of a multiplicity or continuum of gender categories.

Gender identity – self-identified gender; in addition to male/female this may be, for example, as transgender, bigender, or another category.

Gender incongruence – category within the International Classification of Diseases (eleventh revision) but classified under 'conditions related to sexual health' and no longer considered to be a mental disorder.

Gender reassignment – legal or surgical change of gender; whilst this is preferred medical and legal terminology amongst most authorities in the US/UK, it is not the preferred terminology amongst trans people (for whom gender confirmation is considered more appropriate).

Gender transition – the process by which a transgender person assumes the gender role and gender expression consonant with their experienced sense of gender identity; this may or may not include surgical or other medical procedures.

Heterosexual – a term used since the early twentieth century as the binary opposite of homosexual.

Homophobia – sexual prejudice against gay/lesbian people; it is not a phobia in the strict sense and fear may be only one of the negative feelings experienced or expressed towards gay/lesbian people. Homophobia may be internalized by gay/lesbian people so that they experience negative feelings and attitudes towards themselves in relation to their sexual identity.

Homosexual – this term first appeared in Germany in 1869; it may be used to refer to sexual behaviour, sexual attraction, sexual identity, or sexual arousal. There is debate about whether it is best used as an adjective or noun, but it is not the preferred term amongst gay/lesbian people (who would rather be referred to as gay or lesbian). E.g. 'He is a gay man', not 'He is a homosexual'.

Intersex – An umbrella term used where someone is born with sexual and reproductive anatomy that means their body does not fit typical binary definitions of male or female: this can include variations of the genitals, reproductive system, chromosomes or other sex characteristics. Alternative terms for intersex include DSD (see above) and VSC (Variations in Sex Characteristics).

Lesbian – A woman who is sexually attracted, primarily, towards other women; a homosexual woman. See also entry for 'homosexual'.

LGBTI+ - stands for lesbian, gay, bisexual, trans and intersex. We have used the term LGBTI+ throughout this document to refer to people who identify as lesbian, gay, bisexual, transgender or intersex; as well as others who identify in similar ways but use differing terms. Some people prefer to use the term 'sexual and gender minorities', but neither is this a universally accepted term.

Queer – This term, originally a slur which has subsequently been reclaimed, is used in various ways. For some, it is used as an affirming self-descriptive and inclusive term for all LGBTI+ people. For others, it is more concerned with rejecting stereotypes and labels associated with gender and sexuality. This has extended into academic discourse, with growing bodies of literature on Queer Theory and Queer Theology which take a broadly inclusive approach to the study of sexual and gender diversity.

Questioning – An exploratory approach to one's own sexual and gender identity.

Sex – typically used to refer to biological status as male/female but may refer to genetics, anatomy, physiology, psychology, or legal status.

Sexual fluidity – refers to context dependence of sexual attraction for some people (especially women); it is sometimes taken to suggest that sexual orientation is not fixed and may vary across time.

Sexual orientation – reflects the gender/sex towards which attraction is primarily experienced; traditionally understood as heterosexual, homosexual or bisexual, but now seen by some as on a continuum rather than a series of discrete types.

Sexuality – the human experience of being sexual. This includes gender and gender identity, sex and sexual orientation, amongst other things.

Trans – short for transgender; a form of self-identification preferred by many transgender people e.g. 'I am a trans woman'.

Trans man – a man who was assigned female at birth but identified and lives as a man.

Trans woman – a woman who was assigned male at birth but identifies and lives as a woman.

Transgender – gender identity of those who do not exclusively identify with sex assigned at birth; should be used as an adjective and may be experienced as offensive by trans people if used as a noun. 'She is a transgender woman', or 'She is a trans woman', not 'She is a transgender'.

Transition – a process of change, social and/or medical, from gender corresponding with sex assigned at birth to the gender which the person self-identifies with.

Transsexual – This term has been used variously in the past but is not commonly used now and is not preferred either in medical circles or amongst trans people. It has been replaced by the preferred term 'transgender' (for which, see entry above).

Transvestism – cross-dressing; dressing in the clothes of the opposite binary gender category. There are a variety of reasons why people may do this, and the term has been used in diverse ways historically. In contemporary usage it would be inappropriate to use this term in relation to a transgender man wearing male clothes, or a transgender woman wearing female clothes.

Endnotes

1. As signalled in the 'Note to the reader' on page vii, for simplicity we have adopted the convention of using 'Church' to refer to the universal Church and 'church' to refer to the Church of England and to local congregations.

2. Church of England, *Pastoral Principles for Living Well Together* (London: Church House Publishing, 2019); available at https://www.churchofengland.org/about/leadership-and-governance/general-synod/bishops/pastoral-advisory-group/pastoral-principles (accessed 06/07/2020) and can be purchased at https://www.chpublishing.co.uk/books/9780715111550/pastoral-principles-cards (accessed 06/07/2020).

PART ONE

3. Aelred of Rievaulx, 'The Pastoral Prayer', trans. Mark DelCogliano, *Cistercian Studies Quarterly* 37.4 (2002), p. 464.

4. Augustine, *The City of God: De Civitate Dei (Books 11-22)*, trans. William Babcock, Boniface Ramsey (ed.) (New York: New City Press, 2013); see Book 19, Chapter 17, p. 375.

5. 1 John 4.16 which is given as an optional biblical sentence at the beginning of the Common Worship Marriage Service. See The Archbishops' Council, *Common Worship: Pastoral Services* (London: Church House Publishing, 2000), p. 104. The Common Worship Marriage Service can also be found at https://www.churchofengland.org/prayer-and-worship/worship-texts-and-resources/common-worship/marriage (accessed 05/03/2020).

6. 'The Form of Solemnization of Matrimony' in *Book of Common Prayer, Standard Edition* (Cambridge: Cambridge University Press, 2004), pp. 301-11. The *Book of Common Prayer* (1662) is referred to as the Prayer Book in this chapter. The Prayer Book service can be found at https://www.churchofengland.org/prayer-and-worship/worship-texts-and-resources/book-common-prayer/form-solemnization-matrimony (accessed 05/03/2020). The status of the *Book of Common Prayer* in the Church of England is described in Chapter 14, pp. 232-4 and some of the developments of the Church of England's Marriage liturgies are described in Chapter 9, pp. 144-5.

7. The Archbishops' Council, 'Declaration of Assent' in *Common Worship: Ordination Services* (London: Church House Publishing, 2007); available at https://www.churchofengland.org/prayer-and-worship/worship-texts-and-resources/common-worship/ministry/declaration-assent (accessed 10/03/2020).

8. The Archbishops' Council, *Common Worship: Pastoral Services* (London: Church House Publishing, 2000), p. 105.

9. The Archbishops' Council, 'Section B' in *Canons of the Church of England* (London: Church House Publishing, 2012, 2015, 2016); available at https://www.churchofengland.org/more/policy-and-thinking/canons-church-england/section-b (accessed 14/01/2020); see Canon B30.

10. Lambeth Conference 1958, *The Lambeth Conference 1958: The Encyclical Letter from the Bishops together with the Resolutions and Reports* (London: SPCK & Seabury Press, 1958), Part 1, p. 56.

11. Augustine, *De Bono Coniugali and De Sancta Virginitate*, trans. P. G. Walsh (Oxford: Oxford University Press, 2001); see section 17.21. Augustine regarded the pledge made between husband and wife to be indissoluble, a view shared by many Anglicans today.

12. Church of England, *The Two Books of Homilies Appointed to be Read in Churches* (Oxford: Oxford University Press, 1859), p. 500.

13. 'The Form of Solemnization of Matrimony' in *Book of Common Prayer*.

14. 'The Form of Solemnization of Matrimony' in *Book of Common Prayer*. The Prayer Book lists two causes of marriage before this one. Although that order was reversed in the revised liturgies which came into use from the 1970s when 'mutual society' was placed first, not too much should be made of this. They do not propose an ordering of priority. Augustine seemed to set his goods of marriage – *proles* (offspring), *fides* (faithfulness) and *sacramentum* (sacrament) – in what he regarded in his time to be an ascending order of importance.

15. 'The Form of Solemnization of Matrimony' in *Book of Common Prayer*.

16. However, the church's teaching on the necessity of consent has not always been fully honoured in practice. For example, the Hardwicke Marriage Act (1753) was enacted to outlaw clandestine marriages, including those of underage spouses, conducted by some Church of England clergy.

17. The Archbishops' Council, *Common Worship: Pastoral Services* (London: Church House Publishing, 2000), p. 106.

18. The Archbishops' Council, *Common Worship: Pastoral Services* (London: Church House Publishing, 2000), p. 106.

19. The Archbishops' Council, *Common Worship: Pastoral Services* (London: Church House Publishing, 2000), p. 108.

20. The Archbishops' Council, *Common Worship: Pastoral Services* (London: Church House Publishing, 2000), p. 108.

21. The Archbishops' Council, *Common Worship: Pastoral Services* (London: Church House Publishing, 2000), p. 109.

22. The Archbishops' Council, *Common Worship: Pastoral Services* (London: Church House Publishing, 2000), p. 136.

23. The Archbishops' Council, *Common Worship: Pastoral Services* (London: Church House Publishing, 2000), p. 157.

24. The Archbishops' Council, *Common Worship: Pastoral Services* (London: Church House Publishing, 2000), p. 111.

25. 'The Form of Solemnization of Matrimony', *Book of Common Prayer*, 1662; available at https://www.churchofengland.org/prayer-and-worship/worship-texts-and-resources/book-common-prayer/form-solemnization-matrimony (accessed 23/07/2020).

26. The Archbishops' Council, *Common Worship: Pastoral Services* (London: Church House Publishing, 2000), p. 164.

27. The Archbishops' Council, *Common Worship: Pastoral Services* (London: Church House Publishing, 2000), p. 157.

28. *The booke of the common prayer and administracion of the Sacramentes, and other rites and ceremonies of the Churche: after the use of the Churche of England* (London: Edward Whitchurche, 1549); see Part VIII. This edition of the Prayer Book was the precursor to the 1662 version, published shortly after the Reformation.

29. *The Lambeth Conference 1958*, Part 1, p. 56.

30. The Archbishops' Council, *Common Worship: Pastoral Services* (London: Church House Publishing, 2000), p. 159.

31. The Archbishops' Council, *Common Worship: Pastoral Services* (London: Church House Publishing, 2000), p. 127.

32. The Archbishops' Council, *Common Worship: Pastoral Services* (London: Church House Publishing, 2000), p. 159.

33. The Archbishops' Council, *Common Worship: Pastoral Services* (London: Church House Publishing, 2000), p. 112.

34. The Archbishops' Council, *Common Worship: Pastoral Services* (London: Church House Publishing, 2000), p. 105.

35. The Archbishops' Council, *Common Worship: Pastoral Services* (London: Church House Publishing, 2000), p. 159.

36. The Archbishops' Council, *Common Worship: Pastoral Services* (London: Church House Publishing, 2000), p. 113.

37. Pope Francis, *Amoris Laetitia: On Love in the Family* (Huntington, IN: Our Sunday Visitor Publishing Division, 2016); section 53, p. 43.

38. The Archbishops' Council, *Common Worship: Pastoral Services* (London: Church House Publishing, 2000), p. 105.

39. The Archbishops' Council, *Common Worship: Pastoral Services* (London: Church House Publishing, 2000), p. 136.

40. 'The Form of Solemnization of Matrimony' in *Book of Common Prayer.*

41. Debates about the sacramental status of marriage in the Church as a whole, and the Church of England in particular, have run over many centuries. Different assessments can be found in the sixteenth century reform of the English Church with, on the one hand, the 39 Articles of Religion saying that Matrimony among other 'commonly called Sacraments' is not to be 'counted' a sacrament with the same 'nature' as baptism and Holy Communion, and with, on the other, the Homily on Perjury and Swearing comparing marriage with baptism saying, 'By like holy promise the Sacrament of Matrimony knitteth man and wife in perpetual love'. *The Two Books of Homilies Appointed to be Read in Churches*, p. 75.

42. 'The Form of Solemnization of Matrimony' in *Book of Common Prayer.*

43. 'The Form of Solemnization of Matrimony' in *Book of Common Prayer.*

44. 'The Form of Solemnization of Matrimony' in *Book of Common Prayer.*

45. The Archbishops' Council, *Common Worship: Pastoral Services* (London: Church House Publishing, 2000), p. 111.

46. 'The Solemnization of Matrimony (1928)' in *The Shorter Prayer Book*. The preface referenced here has subsequently been authorized within *Common Worship* as an alternative preface and can be found here: 'A Form of Solemnization of Matrimony (Alternative Services: Series One)' in The Archbishops' Council, *Common Worship: Pastoral Services* (London: Church House Publishing, 2000, 2005); available at https://www.churchofengland.org/prayer-and-worship/worship-texts-and-resources/common-worship/marriage/form-solemnization-matrimony (accessed 14/01/2020).

47. The Archbishops' Council, *Common Worship: Pastoral Services* (London: Church House Publishing, 2000), p. 136.

48. Lambeth Conference 1930, 'Resolutions of the Lambeth Conference, 1930' in *The Lambeth Conferences (1867–1930)* (London: SPCK, 1948), pp. 163–78; see p. 166.

49. The Archbishops' Council, *Common Worship: Pastoral Services* (London: Church House Publishing, 2000), p. 109.

50. The Archbishops' Council, *Common Worship: Pastoral Services* (London: Church House Publishing, 2000), p. 105.

51. The Archbishops' Council, *Common Worship: Pastoral Services* (London: Church House Publishing, 2000), p. 109.

52. The Archbishops' Council, *Common Worship: Pastoral Services* (London: Church House Publishing, 2000), p. 113.

53. 'The Form of Solemnization of Matrimony' in *Book of Common Prayer.*

54. The House of Bishops, *Marriage: A Teaching Document* (London: Church House Publishing, 1999); available at https://www.churchofengland.org/sites/default/files/2017-10/marriage%20-%20a%20teaching%20document.pdf (accessed 14/01/2020).

55. The Archbishops' Council, *Common Worship: Pastoral Services* (London: Church House Publishing, 2000), p. 156.

56. The House of Bishops, *Marriage: A Teaching Document* (London: Church House Publishing, 1999); available at https://www.churchofengland.org/sites/default/files/2017-10/marriage%20-%20a%20teaching%20document.pdf (accessed 14/01/2020).

57. The Archbishops' Council, *Common Worship: Pastoral Services* (London: Church House Publishing, 2000), p. 107.

58. 'The Form of Solemnization of Matrimony' in *Book of Common Prayer.*

59. 'The Form of Solemnization of Matrimony' in *Book of Common Prayer.*

60. The Archbishops' Council, *Common Worship: Pastoral Services* (London: Church House Publishing, 2000), p. 136.

61. The Archbishops' Council, 'Declaration of Assent' in *Common Worship: Ordination Services* (London: Church House Publishing, 2007); available at https://www.churchofengland. org/prayer-and-worship/worship-texts-and-resources/common-worship/ministry/ declaration-assent (accessed 10/03/2020). See the Preface, which is made by deacons, priests and bishops of the Church of England when they are ordained and on each occasion when they take up a new appointment.

PART TWO

62. Éva Beaujouan and Máire Ní Bhrolcháin, 'Cohabitation and Marriage in Britain since the 1970s', *Population Trends* 145 (2011), pp. 35-59; available at https://link.springer.com/ content/pdf/10.1057%2Fpt.2011.16.pdf (accessed 03/03/2020), p. 41.

63. Beaujouan and Bhrolcháin, 'Cohabitation and Marriage in Britain since the 1970s', p. 43.

64. **Relationships in numbers**

Marriage

Office for National Statistics, *Marriages in England and Wales: 2016* (2019); available at https://www.ons.gov.uk/peoplepopulationandcommunity/ birthsdeathsandmarriages/marriagecohabitationandcivilpartnerships/bulletins/ marriagesinenglandandwalesprovisional/2017 (accessed 05/07/2020).

Office for National Statistics, *Population estimates by marital status and living arrangements, England and Wales: 2018* (2019); available at https://www.ons.gov.uk/ peoplepopulationandcommunity/populationandmigration/populationestimates/ bulletins/populationestimatesbymaritalstatusandlivingarrangements/2018 (accessed 03/03/2020).

Office for National Statistics, *Marriages in England and Wales: 2017* (2020); available at https://www.ons.gov.uk/peoplepopulationandcommunity/ birthsdeathsandmarriages/marriagecohabitationandcivilpartnerships/bulletins/ marriagesinenglandandwalesprovisional/2017 (accessed 05/07/2020).

Single people

Office for National Statistics, *Families and Households: 2019* (2020); available at https:// www.ons.gov.uk/peoplepopulationandcommunity/birthsdeathsandmarriages/families/ bulletins/familiesandhouseholds/2019 accessed 05/07/2020).

Divorce

Office for National Statistics, *Divorces in England and Wales: 2017* (2018); available at https://www.ons.gov.uk/peoplepopulationandcommunity/birthsdeathsandmarriages/ divorce/bulletins/divorcesinenglandandwales/2017 (accessed 03/03/2020).

Office for National Statistics, *Divorces in England and Wales: 2018* (2019); available at https://www.ons.gov.uk/peoplepopulationandcommunity/birthsdeathsandmarriages/ divorce/bulletins/divorcesinenglandandwales/2018 (accessed on 05/07/2020).

Marriage Foundation, *Back to 1969: Lifetime divorce risk is now 34 per cent* (2019); available at https://marriagefoundation.org.uk/back-to-1969-lifetime-divorce-risk-is-now-35-per-cent/ (accessed 03/03/2020).

Cohabitation

Office for National Statistics, *Families and Households: 2018* (2019); available at https:// www.ons.gov.uk/peoplepopulationandcommunity/birthsdeathsandmarriages/families/ bulletins/familiesandhouseholds/2018 (accessed 05/07/2020).

Office for National Statistics, *Marriages in England and Wales: 2017* (2020); available at https://www.ons.gov.uk/peoplepopulationandcommunity/birthsdeathsandmarriages/ marriagecohabitationandcivilpartnerships/bulletins/marriagesinenglandandwalesprovisi onal/2017#type-of-ceremony (accessed 05/07/2020).

Same-sex couples

Office for National Statistics, *Families and Households in the UK: 2019* (2019); available at https://www.ons.gov.uk/peoplepopulationandcommunity/birthsdeathsandmarriages/ families/bulletins/familiesandhouseholds/2019#same-sex-married-couples-are-the-fastest-growing-type-of-same-sex-family (accessed 05/07/2020).

Children

Office for National Statistics, *Births in England and Wales, 2018* (2019); available at https://www.ons.gov.uk/peoplepopulationandcommunity/birthsdeathsandmarriages/livebirths/bulletins/birthsummarytablesenglandandwales/2018 (accessed 13/01/2020).

Office for National Statistics, *Families and Households: 2019* (2019); available at https://www.ons.gov.uk/peoplepopulationandcommunity/birthsdeathsandmarriages/families/bulletins/familiesandhouseholds/2019 (accessed 05/07/2020).

Office for National Statistics, *Families and Households: 2018* (2019); available at https://www.ons.gov.uk/peoplepopulationandcommunity/birthsdeathsandmarriages/families/bulletins/familiesandhouseholds/2018 (accessed 05/07/2020).

65. See Jana Marguerite Bennet, *Water is Thicker than Blood: An Augustinian Theology of Marriage and Singleness* (Oxford: Oxford University Press, 2008) and Philip B. Wilson, *Being Single in the Church Today: Insights from History and Personal Stories* (New York: Morehouse, 2005); see also two short papers by Julie Gittoes, 'Alone Together' and 'Loneliness and Ethics' (both 2016), published on her blog at https://juliegittoes.blogspot.com/2016/04/alone-together.html and https://juliegittoes.blogspot.com/2016/12/loneliness-and-ethics.html (accessed 05/03/2020).

66. 'Love Island, dating apps and the politics of desire', *Analysis* [radio programme] BBC Radio 4, 27 May 2019; available at https://www.bbc.co.uk/sounds/play/m0005f5m (accessed 03/03/2020).

67. Ruth H. Perrin, *Changing Shape: The Faith Lives of Millennials* (London: SCM, 2020), pp. 81ff.

68. Bob Erens et al, *National Survey of Sexual Attitudes and Lifestyles II: Reference Tables and Summary Report* (2003), www.natsal.ac.uk/media/2083/reference_tables_and_summary_report.pdf (accessed 05/07/2020), p. 14.

69. Church of England, 'Generation Y still hope to walk down the aisle', 2018, www.churchofengland.org/more/media-centre/news/generation-y-still-hope-walk-down-aisle (accessed 05/07/2020).

70. Office for National Statistics, *Marriages in England and Wales: 2014* (2017), www.ons.gov.uk/peoplepopulationandcommunity/birthsdeathsandmarriages/marriagecohabitationandcivilpartnerships/bulletins/marriagesinenglandandwalesprovisional/2014 (accessed 05/07/2020).

71. Office for National Statistics, *Marriages in England and Wales: 2015* (2018), www.ons.gov.uk/peoplepopulationandcommunity/birthsdeathsandmarriages/marriagecohabitationandcivilpartnerships/bulletins/marriagesinenglandandwalesprovisional/2015 (accessed 05/07/2020).

72. Office for National Statistics, *Marriages in England and Wales: 2016* (2019), www.ons.gov.uk/peoplepopulationandcommunity/birthsdeathsandmarriages/marriagecohabitationandcivilpartnerships/bulletins/marriagesinenglandandwalesprovisional/2016 (accessed 05/07/2020).

73. Office for National Statistics, *Families and Households in the UK: 2019* (2019); available at https://www.ons.gov.uk/peoplepopulationandcommunity/birthsdeathsandmarriages/families/bulletins/familiesandhouseholds/2019 (accessed 05/07/2020).

74. Office for National Statistics, *Marriages in England and Wales: 2017* (2020); available at https://www.ons.gov.uk/peoplepopulationandcommunity/birthsdeathsandmarriages/marriagecohabitationandcivilpartnerships/bulletins/marriagesinenglandandwalesprovisional/2017#type-of-ceremony (accessed 05/07/2020).

75. Office for National Statistics, *Marriages in England and Wales: 2015* (2018); available at https://www.ons.gov.uk/peoplepopulationandcommunity/birthsdeathsandmarriages/marriagecohabitationandcivilpartnerships/bulletins/marriagesinenglandandwalesprovisional/2015#religious-ceremonies-continued-to-decline-in-popularity (accessed 05/07/2020).

76. Church of England, *Statistics for Mission 2018* (2019), https://www.churchofengland.org/sites/default/files/2019-10/2018StatisticsForMission_0.pdf (accessed 05/07/2020); Statistics for Mission 2017 (2018), https://www.churchofengland.org/sites/default/files/2018-11/2017StatisticsForMission.pdf (accessed 05/07/2020).

77. John Eekelar, 'Why People Marry: The Many Faces of an Institution', *Family Law Quarterly* 41:3 (2007), pp. 413–31; see p. 421.

78. Claire Crawford et al., *Cohabitation, marriage, relationship stability and child outcomes: final report* (London: Institute for Fiscal Studies, 2013); available at https://www.ifs. org.uk/comms/r87.pdf (accessed 03/03/2020); and Alissa Goodman and Ellen Greaves, *Cohabitation, Marriage and Relationship Stability* (London: Institute for Fiscal Studies, 2010); available at https://www.ifs.org.uk/bns/bn107.pdf (accessed 03/03/2020). See also the response by Graham Stacey: Marriage Foundation, *IFS have completely misconstrued their own evidence* (2013); available at https://marriagefoundation.org.uk/ifs-have-completely-misconstrued-their-own-evidence/ (accessed 03/03/2020).

79. Ann Mooney et al., *Impact of Family Breakdown on Children's Wellbeing: Evidence Review (Research Report No. DCSF-RR113)* (London: University of London Institute of Education, 2009); available at https://dera.ioe.ac.uk/11165/1/DCSF-RR113.pdf (accessed 04/03/2020).

80. Sara McLanahan and Isabel Sawhill, 'Marriage and Child Wellbeing Revisited: Introducing the Issue', *The Future of Children* 25:2 (2015), pp. 3–9. This edition of the journal, entitled 'Marriage and Child Wellbeing Revisited', attempts to provide a broad overview of available research:
The Centre for Social Justice, *Family Structures Still Matter*, (August 2020); available at https://www.centreforsocialjustice.org.uk/core/wp-content/uploads/2020/08/CSJJ8372-Family-structure-Report-200807.pdf (accessed 12/09/2020).

81. Office for National Statistics, *Births in England and Wales: 2018* available at https://www. ons.gov.uk/peoplepopulationandcommunity/birthsdeathsandmarriages/livebirths/ bulletins/birthsummarytablesenglandandwales/2018 (accessed 05/07/2020).

82. Claire Crawford et al., 'Cohabitation, marriage, relationship stability and child outcomes', *IFS Commentary C120*, (London: Institute for Fiscal Studies, 2011); available at https://www. ifs.org.uk/comms/comm120.pdf (accessed 26/03/2020).

83. Audrey S. Koh et al., 'Predictors of mental health in emerging adult offspring of lesbian-parent families', *Journal of Lesbian Studies* (2019) DOI: 10.1080/10894160.2018.1555694; available at: https://www.tandfonline.com/doi/full/10.1080/10894160.2018.1555694 (accessed 26/03/2020).

84. Kate Leaver, *The Friendship Cure: A Manifesto for Reconnecting in the Modern World* (London: Duckworth Overlook, 2018).

85. Francesco Alberoni, *Friendship* (Leiden: Brill, 2016), pp. 22–3.

86. Kath Weston, *Families We Choose: Lesbians, gays, kinship* (New York, Columbia University Press, 1997).

87. Francesco Alberoni, *Friendship* (Leiden: Brill, 2016), pp. 33–6.

88. Church of England, *The Two Books of Homilies Appointed to be Read in Churches* (Oxford: Oxford University Press, 1859), p. 500.

89. Eleanor Wilkinson, 'Single people's geographies of home: intimacy and friendship beyond "the family"', *Environment and Planning* A46:10 (2014), pp. 2452–68.

90. Alistair Sutcliffe et al., 'Relationships and the social brain: Integrating psychological and evolutionary perspectives' *British Journal of Psychology* 103 (2012), pp. 149–68.

91. Anne M. Cronin, '"Domestic friends": women's friendships, motherhood and inclusive intimacy', *The Sociological Review* 63:3 (2015), pp. 662–79.

92. Francesco Alberoni, *Friendship* (Leiden: Brill, 2016), pp. 127–73.

93. Rosemary Blieszner, 'Friendships', in Susan K. Whitbourne (ed.), *The Encyclopedia of Adulthood and Aging* (Oxford: Wiley-Blackwell, 2015).

94. Keith D. M. Snell, 'The rise of living alone and loneliness in history', *Social History* 42:1 (2017), pp. 2–28.

95. John T. Cacioppo and Stephanie Cacioppo, 'The growing problem of loneliness', *The Lancet* 391 (2018), p. 426.

96. Zhiming Cheng and Russell Smyth, 'Sex and happiness', *Journal of Economic Behaviour and Organization* 112 (2015) pp. 6–32; David G. Blanchflower and Andrew J. Oswald, 'Money, sex

and happiness: An empirical study', *Scandinavian Journal of Economics* 106:3 (2004), pp. 393–415.

97. For an insightful discussion, see Sam Brewitt-Taylor, *Christian Radicalism in the Church of England and the Invention of the British Sixties, 1957–1970: The Hope of a World Transformed* (Oxford: Oxford University Press, 2018).

98. **Sexual activity in numbers**

The outcomes of the latest survey (Natsal-3, 2010-2012) can be found in *The National Survey of Sexual Attitudes and Lifestyles;* available at https://www.natsal.ac.uk/home.aspx (accessed 05/07/2020).

The statistics in this section are taken from *Natsal, Sexual Attitudes and Lifestyles in Britain: Highlights from Natsal-3;* available at www.natsal.ac.uk/media/2102/natsal-infographic. pdf (an infographic giving key findings). For more detail, see the set of articles published in *The Lancet* 382 (Nov 30, 2013), 1781–1855.

For information about pre- and extra-marital sex, see Bob Erens et al, *National Survey of Sexual Attitudes and Lifestyles II: Reference Tables and Summary Report* (2003) p. 12; available at www.natsal.ac.uk/media/2083/reference_tables_and_summary_report.pdf (accessed 05/07/2020).

The findings of a more recent British social attitudes survey (2018) can be found in John Curtice et al. (eds), *British Social Attitudes 36* (London: The National Centre for Social Research, 2019), 120; available at https://www.bsa.natcen.ac.uk/media/39363/bsa_36.pdf (accessed 05/07/2020).

Abortion statistics can be found in Department of Health and Social Care, *Abortion Statistics, England and Wales: 2018* (2019); available at assets.publishing.service.gov.uk/ government/uploads/system/uploads/attachment_data/file/808556/Abortion_Statistics__ England_and_Wales_2018__1_.pdf (accessed 05/07/2020).

The Abortion Act 1967 (as amended) is available at https://www.gov.uk/government/ publications/abortion-act-1967-as-amended-termination-of-pregnancy (accessed 05/07/2020).

99. See, for instance, Jean M. Twenge et al., 'Sexual Inactivity During Young Adulthood Is More Common Among U.S. Millennials and iGen: Age, Period, and Cohort Effects on Having No Sexual Partners After Age 18', *Archives of Sexual Behavior* 46:2 (2017), pp. 433–40. It is unclear whether a similar picture holds in the UK.

100. Shira Tarrant, *The Pornography Industry: What Everyone Needs to Know* (Oxford University Press, 2016).

101. Camilla Herbert et al., *Capacity to Consent to Sexual Relations* (British Psychological Society, 2019); available at https://www.bps.org.uk/sites/bps.org.uk/files/Policy/Policy%20 -%20Files/Capacity%20to%20consent%20to%20sexual%20relations.pdf (accessed 04/03/2020).

102. Home Office, *Modern Slavery Awareness and Victim Identification Guidance* (London: Home Office, 2017); available at https://www.gov.uk/government/publications/modern- slavery-awareness-booklet (accessed 04/03/2020); Home Office, *2018 UK Annual Report on Modern Slavery* (London: Home Office, 2018); available at https://www.gov.uk/government/ publications/2018-uk-annual-report-on-modern-slavery (accessed 04/03/2020).

103. End Violence Against Women, *Attitudes to Sexual Consent* (London: End Violence Against Women Coalition, 2018); available at https://www.endviolenceagainstwomen.org.uk/wp- content/uploads/1-Attitudes-to-sexual-consent-Research-findings-FINAL.pdf (accessed 04/03/2020).

104. See the report cited in note 111 for public understanding of rape legislation. For conviction rates, see Alexandra Topping and Caelainn Barr, 'Revealed: less than a third of young men prosecuted for rape are convicted', *The Guardian*, 23 September 2018; available at https:// www.theguardian.com/society/2018/sep/23/revealed-less-than-a-third-of-young-men- prosecuted-for-are-convicted (accessed 04/03/2020).

105. Thames Valley Police, *#Consentiseverything* (2015); available at http://www. consentiseverything.com/ (accessed 04/03/2020). See also their video 'Consent: It's Simple as Tea', found on the home page.

106. The Serious Crime Act 2015 made coercive and controlling behaviour a criminal offence in the UK: see UK Parliament, *Serious Crime Act 2015* (London: 2015); available at http://www. legislation.gov.uk/ukpga/2015/9/introduction/enacted (accessed 04/03/2020). Further legal responses to domestic violence are included in the proposed Domestic Abuse Bill: see UK Parliament, *Domestic Abuse Bill 2017–19* (London: 2019); available at https:// services.parliament.uk/bills/2017-19/domesticabuse.html (accessed 04/03/2020). See also: Evan Stark, 'Coercive Control', in Nancy Lombard and Lesley McMillan (eds.), *Violence Against Women: Current Theory and Practice in Domestic Abuse, Sexual Violence and Exploitation* (London: Jessica Kingsley Publishers, 2013), pp. 17–33.

107. This definition relates to the UK government definition of domestic violence and abuse: see Home Office, *Domestic abuse: how to get help* (2018); available at https://www.gov.uk/ guidance/domestic-violence-and-abuse (accessed 04/03/2020). See also: *Women's Aid, What is domestic abuse?* (2019); available at https://www.womensaid.org.uk/information-support/what-is-domes (accessed 04/03/2020).

108. ONS, *Intimate Personal Violence and Partner Abuse* (London: Office for National Statistics, 2016), 3.

109. Lori L. Heise, 'Violence Against Women: An Integrated, Ecological Framework', *Violence Against Women* 4.3 (1998), 262–90; Lori L. Heise, *What Works to Prevent Partner Violence: An Evidence Overview* (London: STRIVE, 2011), Figure 1.2; available at http://strive.lshtm. ac.uk/resources/what-works-prevent-partner-violence-evidence-overview.

110. The Crime Survey for England and Wales; available at https://rapecrisis.org.uk/get-informed/about-sexual-violence/statistics-sexual-violence/ (accessed 11/05/2020).

111. IICSA, *Interim Report of the Independent Inquiry into Child Sexual Abuse* (London: IICSA, 2018); available at https://www.iicsa.org.uk/publications/inquiry/interim (accessed 04/03/2020); see section 3.3.

112. NSPCC, *29% increase in counselling sessions on peer sexual abuse* (2018); available at https:// www.nspcc.org.uk/what-we-do/news-opinion/rise-childline-counselling-sessions-peer-sexual-abuse/ (accessed 04/03/2020).

113. The question about children identifying as trans is discussed briefly in Chapter 6, 'The science of gender identity; Transgender and gender diverse children and adolescents'. This and the other questions mentioned here are regularly the subject of news stories and public discussions sparked by specific incidents. Recent examples include the tragic death of Charlie Gard which is discussed in detail in Dominic Wilkinson and Julian Savluescu, *Ethics, Conflict and Medical Treatment for Children: From Disagreement to Dissensus* (London: Elsevier, 2018); available at https://www.ncbi.nlm.nih.gov/books/ NBK537987/pdf/Bookshelf_NBK537987.pdf (accessed 04/03/2020). See also Sarah Marsh and Jim Waterson, 'Instagram bans "graphic" self-harm images after Molly Russell's death', *The Guardian*, 7 Feb 2019; available at https://www.theguardian.com/technology/2019/ feb/07/instagram-bans-graphic-self-harm-images-after-molly-russells-death (accessed 04/03/2020).

114. See Shoshana Zuboff, *The Age of Surveillance Capitalism: The Fight for a Human Future at a New Frontier of Power* (London: Profile Books, 2019).

115. Sarah Marsh and Jim Waterson, 'Instagram bans "graphic" self-harm images after Molly Russell's death', *The Guardian*, 7 February 2019; available at https://www.theguardian.com/ technology/2019/feb/07/instagram-bans-graphic-self-harm-images-after-molly-russells-death (accessed 05/07/2020).

116. Office for National Statistics, *Sexual Orientation, UK: 2018* (2020); available at https:// www.ons.gov.uk/peoplepopulationandcommunity/culturalidentity/sexuality/bulletins/ sexualidentityuk/2018 (accessed 05/07/2020).

117. We have drawn below on the 'Trans & Genderqueer Studies Terminology, Language, and Usage Guide', forthcoming in Alicia Spencer-Hall and Blake Gutt (eds.), *Trans and Genderqueer Subjects in Medieval Hagiography* (Amsterdam: Amsterdam University Press, forthcoming 2020); and in the LLF Online Library *Human Sexuality: A Lexicon of Terms and Definitions* by Chris Cook.

118. See Sari van Anders, 'Beyond Sexual Orientation: Integrating Gender/Sex and Diverse Sexualities via Sexual Configurations', *Archives of Sexual Behaviour* 44(5) (2015), pp. 1177–1213; Janet Shibley Hyde et al., 'The Future of Sex and Gender in Psychology: Five Challenges to the Gender Binary', *American Psychologist* 74:2 (2019), pp. 171–93. See also

Anne Fausto-Sterling, 'Gender/Sex, Sexual Orientation, and Identity Are in the Body: How Did They Get There?', *The Journal of Sex Research* 56:4–5 (2019), pp. 529–5.

119. Mercedes Allen, 'Transgender History: Trans Expression in Ancient Times', *The Bilerico Project*, 12 February 2008; available at http://bilerico.lgbtqnation.com/2008/02/transgender_history_trans_expression_in.php (accessed 04/03/2020).

120. L. Griffin et al., 'Sex, gender and identity: A re-evaluation of the evidence', *BJPsych Bulletin*, 21 July 2020; available at https://www.cambridge.org/core/journals/bjpsych-bulletin/article/sex-gender-and-gender-identity-a-reevaluation-of-the-evidence/76A3DC54F3BD91E8D631B93397698B1A (accessed 31 July 2020).

121. Norman P. Spack et al., 'Children and adolescents with Gender Identity Disorder referred to a pediatric medical center', *Pediatrics* 129:3 (2012), pp. 418–25;
Maureen D. Connolly et al., 'The mental health of transgender youth: Advances in understanding', *Journal of Adolescent Health* 59 (2016), pp. 489–95;
J. Olson et al., 'Baseline physiologic and psychosocial characteristics of transgender youth seeking care for gender dysphoria', *Journal of Adolescent Health* 57 (2015), pp. 374–80;
Thomas D. Steensma et al., 'Behavioral and emotional problems on the teacher's report form: A cross-national, cross-clinic comparative analysis of gender dysphoric children and adolescents', *Journal of Abnormal Child Psychology* 42:4 (2014), pp. 635–47;
Abbeygail Jones et al., 'Anxiety disorders, gender nonconformity, bullying and self-esteem in sexual minority adolescents: Prospective birth cohort study', *Journal of Child Psychology and Psychiatry* 58:11 (2017), pp. 1201–9; Anneliese A. Singh et al., '"I am my own gender": Resilience strategies of trans youth', *Journal of Counseling & Development* 92:2 (2014), pp. 208–18.

122. World Health Organization, 'HA60 Gender incongruence of adolescence or adulthood' in *ICD-11 for Mortality and Morbidity Statistics* (2019); available at https://icd.who.int/browse11/l-m/en#/http://id.who.int/icd/entity/90875286 (accessed 04/03/2020).

123. The reasons for a relatively low number of applications for a Gender Recognition Certificate include the view that it is too expensive, too difficult, too long or that it is too intrusive and demeaning. See the government's report on the consultation regarding a Review of the 2014 Gender Recognition Act, available at https://www.gov.scot/publications/review-gender-recognition-act-2004-analysis-responses-public-consultation-exercise-report/pages/1/ (accessed on 03/07/2020).

124. K.J. Conron, M.J. Mimiaga and S.J. Landers, 'A Population-Based Study of Sexual Orientation Identity and Gender Differences in Adult Health', *American Journal of Public Health* 100:10 (2010), pp. 1953–60; available at https://www.ncbi.nlm.nih.gov/pmc/articles/PMC2936979/ (accessed 03/07/2020); G.N. Rider et al., 'Health and Care Utilization of Transgender and Gender Nonconforming Youth: A Population-Based Study', *Pediatrics* 141:3 (2018); available at https://pediatrics.aappublications.org/content/pediatrics/141/3/e20171683.full.pdf (accessed 03/07/2020).

125. See, for example, Jamie Doward, 'High Court to decide if children can consent to gender reassignment', *The Guardian*, 5 January 2020; available at https://www.theguardian.com/society/2020/jan/05/high-court-to-decide-if-children-can-consent-to-gender-reassignment (accessed 23/03/2020).

126. See Kerith J. Conron et al., 'A Population-Based Study of Sexual Orientation Identity and Gender Differences in Adult Health', *American Journal of Public Health* 100:10 (2010), pp. 1953–60;
G. Nicole Rider et al., 'Health and Care Utilization of Transgender and Gender Nonconforming Youth: A Population-Based Study', *Pediatrics* 141:3 (2018);
Bernard Reed et al., *Gender Variance in the UK: Prevalence, Incidence, Growth and Geographic Distribution* (2009, Gender Identity Research and Education Society); available at http://worldaa1.miniserver.com/~gires/assets/Medpro-Assets/GenderVarianceUK-report.pdf (accessed 04/03/2020);
Gender Identity Research and Education Society, *The Number of Gender Variant People in the UK – Update 2011* (Gender Identity Research and Education Society, 2011); available at https://www.gires.org.uk/wp-content/uploads/2014/10/Prevalence2011.pdf (accessed 04/03/2020);
Gender Identity Development Service, *Referrals to GIDS, 2014–15 to 2018–19* (Tavistock and Portman NHS Foundation Trust, 2019); available at https://gids.nhs.uk/number-referrals (accessed 04/03/2020).

127. Geraldine Bedell, 'Coming out of the dark ages', *The Guardian*, 24 June 2007; available at https://www.theguardian.com/society/2007/jun/24/communities.gayrights (accessed 04/03/2020).

128. See the discussion in House of Commons, Hansard's Parliamentary Debates: The Official Report (10–21 Oct 2016, volume 615), columns 1073–4. (London: Hansard, 2016); available at https://www.parliament.uk/documents/publications-records/House-of-Commons-Publications/HCBV615.pdf (accessed 11/05/2020).

129. See legislation.gov.uk, available at http://www.legislation.gov.uk/ukpga/2004/7/pdfs/ukpga_20040007_en.pdf (accessed 11/05/2020).

130. See Equality and Human Rights Commission, available at https://www.equalityhumanrights.com/en/equality-act/protected-characteristics (accessed 11/05/2020).

131. Government Equalities Office, *Reform of the Gender Recognition Act 2004*; available at https://www.gov.uk/government/consultations/reform-of-the-gender-recognition-act-2004 (accessed 03/07/2020).

132. Deparament for Education, *Statutory Guidance: Introduction to Requirements* (2019); available at https://www.gov.uk/government/publications/relationships-education-relationships-and-sex-education-rse-and-health-education/introduction-to-requirements (accessed 04/03/2020).

133. Department for Education, *Primary school disruption over LGBT teaching/relationships education*, (2019); available at https://www.gov.uk/government/publications/managing-issues-with-lgbt-teaching-advice-for-local-authorities/primary-school-disruption-over-lgbt-teachingrelationships-education (accessed 04/03/2020).

134. LGBT+ History Month, *First Gay Rights March in Britain* (2007); available at https://lgbtplushistorymonth.co.uk/2007/11/first-gay-rights-march-in-britain/ (accessed 04/03/2020).

135. Robert Booth, 'Acceptance of gay sex in decline in UK for first time since Aids crisis', *The Guardian*, 11 July 2019; available at https://www.theguardian.com/society/2019/jul/11/acceptance-gay-sex-decline-uk-first-time-since-aids-crisis (accessed 11/05/2020); Peter Tatchell, 'This is how LGBT Pride began in 1972', *Huffington Post*, 7 July 2017; available at https://www.huffingtonpost.co.uk/peter-g-tatchell/lgbt-pride_b_17418306.html (accessed 04/03/2020); Colin Drury, 'London Pride 2019: Partying against prejudice as 1.5 million people sing and dance at rainbow-filled parade', *The Independent*, 6 July 2019; available at https://www.independent.co.uk/news/uk/home-news/london-pride-2019-lgbt-rights-equality-prejudice-party-a8991631.html (accessed 04/03/2020) and BBC; available at https://www.bbc.co.uk/news/av/uk-48898066/london-pride-2019-highlights-from-this-year-s-parade (accessed 15/06/2020).

136. Government Equalities Office, *LGBT Action Plan: Improving the Lives of Lesbian, Gay, Bisexual and Transgender People* (London: Government Equalities Office, 2018); available at https://assets.publishing.service.gov.uk/government/uploads/system/uploads/attachment_data/file/721367/GEO-LGBT-Action-Plan.pdf (accessed 04/03/2020).

137. J. Curtice, E. Clery et al., (eds), British Social Attitudes: The 36th Report, *Relationships and Gender Identity* (London: The National Centre for Social Research, 2019); available at https://www.bsa.natcen.ac.uk/media/39358/5_bsa36_relationships_and_gender_identity.pdf (accessed 05/07/2020).

138. See, for example, Brian S. Barnett et al., 'The Transgender Bathroom Debate at the Intersection of Politics, Law, Ethics, and Science', *Journal of the American Academy of Psychiatry and the Law* 46 (2018), pp 232–41.

139. See, for example, Sean Ingle, 'IOC delays new transgender guidelines after scientists fail to agree', *The Guardian*, 24 September 2019; available at https://www.theguardian.com/sport/2019/sep/24/ioc-delays-new-transgender-guidelines-2020-olympics (accessed 24/03/2020).

140. See, for example, Janice Turner, 'Giving puberty blocker to "trans" children is a leap into the unknown', *The Times*, 21 February 2020; available at https://www.thetimes.co.uk/article/giving-puberty-blocker-to-trans-children-is-a-leap-into-the-unknown-x3g37sb7f (accessed 24/03/2020).

141. Talia Mae Bettcher, 'Intersexuality, Transgender, and Transsexuality' in Lisa Disch and Mary Hawkesworth (eds) *The Oxford Handbook of Feminist Theory* (New York: OUP, 2016).

142. Sarah Marsh et al., 'Homophobic and transphobic hate crimes surge in England and Wales', *The Guardian*, 14 June 2019; available at https://www.theguardian.com/world/2019/jun/14/homophobic-and-transphobic-hate-crimes-surge-in-england-and-wales (accessed 04/03/2020).

143. BBC, 'Transgender hate crimes recorded by police go up 81%', *BBC News*, 27 June 2019; available at https://www.bbc.co.uk/news/uk-48756370 (accessed 04/03/2020); Chaka L. Bachman and Becca Gooch, *LGBT in Britain: Hate Crime and Discrimination* (London: Stonewall, 2018); available at https://www.stonewall.org.uk/system/files/lgbt_in_britain_hate_crime.pdf (accessed 04/03/2020).

144. Government Equalities Office, *National LGBT Survey: Summary Report* (London: Government Equalities Office, 2018); available at https://assets.publishing.service.gov.uk/government/uploads/system/uploads/attachment_data/file/722314/GEO-LGBT-Survey-Report.pdf (accessed 04/03/2020).

145. Wendy Norton et al., 'Gay men seeking surrogacy to achieve parenthood', *Reproductive BioMedicine Online* 27:3 (2013), pp. 271–9; available at https://www.rbmojournal.com/article/S1472-6483(13)00180-6/pdf (accessed 07/03/2020).

146. BBC, '"Seahorse" transgender man loses challenge to be named father"', *BBC News*, 25 September 2019; available at https://www.bbc.co.uk/news/uk-49828705 (accessed 07/03/2020).

147. J. Michael Bailey et al., 'Sexual Orientation, Controversy, and Science', *Psychological Science in the Public Interest* 17:2 (2016), pp. 45–101.

148. See the LLF Online Library: 'The Causes of Sexual Orientation' by Chris Cook.

149. Bailey et al., 'Sexual Orientation, Controversy, and Science'; Simon LeVay, *Gay, Straight, and the Reason Why: The Science of Sexual Orientation* (Oxford: Oxford University Press, 2011).

150. Andrea Ganna et al., 'Large-scale GWAS reveals insights into the genetic architecture of same-sex sexual behaviour', *Science* 365:6459 (2019).

151. Royal College of Psychiatrists, *Royal College of Psychiatrists' statement on sexual orientation* (2014); available at https://www.rcpsych.ac.uk/pdf/PS02_2014.pdf (accessed 04/03/2020).

152. Ray Blanchard, 'Fraternal Birth Order, Family Size, and Male Homosexuality: Meta-Analysis of Studies Spanning 25 Years', *Archives of Sexual Behavior* 47:1 (2018), pp. 1–15.

153. Ray Blanchard and Philip Klassen, 'H-Y Antigen and Homosexuality in Men', *Journal of Theoretical Biology* 185 (1997), pp. 373–8.

154. See What We Know, *What does the scholarly research say about the effect of gender transition on transgender well-being?* (New York: Cornell University What We Know, 2020); available at https://whatweknow.inequality.cornell.edu/topics/lgbt-equality/what-does-the-scholarly-research-say-about-the-well-being-of-transgender-people/ (accessed 04/03/2020).

155. Cecilia Dhejne et al., 'Long-Term Follow-Up of Transsexual Persons Undergoing Sex Reassignment Surgery: Cohort Study in Sweden', *PLoS ONE* 6:(2), pp. 1–8; available at https://doi.org/10.1371/journal.pone.0016885 (accessed 22/11/2019).

156. Bernard Reed et al., *Gender Variance in the UK: Prevalence, Incidence, Growth and Geographic Distribution* (GIRES, 2009); available from https://www.gires.org.uk/wp-content/uploads/2014/10/GenderVarianceUK-report.pdf (accessed 07/03/2020).

157. Johanna Olson-Kennedy et al., 'Research priorities for gender nonconforming/transgender youth: gender identity development and biopsychosocial outcomes', *Current Opinion in Endocrinology, Diabetes and Obesity* 23:2 (2016), pp. 172–9; available at https://www.ncbi.nlm.nih.gov/pmc/articles/PMC4807860/ (accessed 07/03/2020).

158. See the LLF Online Library: 'Transgender and Gender Diverse Children and Adolescents' by Michael King and references therein.

159. Thomas D. Steensma et al., 'Factors Associated With Desistence and Persistence of Childhood Gender Dysphoria: A Quantitative Follow-Up Study', *Journal of the American Academy of Child & Adolescent Psychiatry* 52:6 (2013), pp. 582–90.

160. Michele Moore and Heather Brunskell-Evans (eds), *Inventing Transgender Children and Young People* (Newcastle upon Tyne: Cambridge Scholars Publishing, 2019).

161. See note 157.

162. Leonidas Panagiotakopoulos. 'Transgender medicine – puberty suppression'; *Reviews in Endocrine and Metabolic Disorders* 19:3 (2018), pp. 221–5.

163. Michelle Telfer et al., *Australian Standards of Care and Treatment Guidelines for Transgender and Gender Diverse Children and Adolescents* (Melbourne: The Royal Children's Hospital, 2018); available at https://www.rch.org.au/uploadedFiles/Main/Content/ adolescent-medicine/australian-standards-of-care-and-treatment-guidelines-for-trans- and-gender-diverse-children-and-adolescents.pdf (accessed 07/03/2020).

164. Editorial, 'Gender-affirming care needed for transgender children', *The Lancet* 391 (2018), p. 2576; available at https://www.thelancet.com/action/ showPdf?pii=S0140-6736%2818%2931429-6 (accessed 07/03/2020).

165. Richard Byng et al., 'Gender-questioning children deserve better science', *The Lancet* 392 (2018), p. 2435; available at https://www.thelancet.com/pdfs/journals/lancet/PIIS0140- 6736(18)32223-2.pdf (accessed 07/03/2020); and Marcus Evans, 'Freedom to think: The need for thorough assessment and treatment of gender dysphoric children', *BJPsych Bulletin*, 21 July 2020; available at https://www.cambridge.org/core/journals/bjpsych-bulletin/article/ freedom-to-think-the-need-for-thorough-assessment-and-treatment-of-gender-dysphoric- children/F4B7F5CAFC0D0BE9FF3C7886BA6E904B (accessed 31 July 2020).

166. See the paper by Sari van Anders in endnote 118 for a discussion about the complexities of the language of 'alignment'.

167. Tove Lundberg et al., 'Making sense of 'Intersex' and 'DSD': how laypeople understand and use terminology', *Psychology and Sexuality* 9:2 (2018), pp. 161–73.

168. Susannah Cornwall, *Sex and Uncertainty in the Body of Christ: Intersex Conditions and Christian Theology* (London: Equinox, 2010).

169. Government Equalities Office, *Variations in Sex Characteristics: Technical Paper January 2019* (London: Government Equalities Office, 2018); available at https://assets.publishing. service.gov.uk/government/uploads/system/uploads/attachment_data/file/771468/VSC_ Technical_Paper_Web_Accessible.pdf (accessed 07/03/2020); see p. 8.

170. Cited from S. Faisal Ahmed et al., 'Society for Endocrinology UK guidance on the initial evaluation of an infant or an adolescent with a suspected disorder of sex development (Revised 2015)', *Clinical Endocrinology* 84:5 (2016), pp. 771–88; available at https://www. ncbi.nlm.nih.gov/pmc/articles/PMC4855619/ (accessed 07/03/2020). The basis of the estimates are S. Faisal Ahmed et al., 'Regional & temporal variation in the occurrence of genital anomalies amongst singleton births, 1988–1997 Scotland', *Archives of Disease Childhood* 89 (2004), F149–F151; and U. Thyen et al., 'Epidemiology and initial management of ambiguous genitalia at birth in Germany', *Hormone Research* 66 (2006), pp. 195–203.

171. United Nations Officer of the High Commissioner for Human Rights, *Fact Sheet: Intersex* (2015); available at https://www.unfe.org/wp-content/uploads/2017/05/UNFE-Intersex.pdf (accessed 07/03/2020).

172. David G. Blanchflower and Andrew J. Oswald, 'Money, sex and happiness: an empirical study', *Scandinavian Journal of Economics* 106:3 (2004), pp. 393–415; available at https:// www.nber.org/papers/w10499.pdf (accessed 07/03/2020).

173. Zhiming Cheng, 'Sex and happiness', *Journal of Economic Behaviour and Organization* 112 (2015), pp. 26–32.

174. Kristin R. Mitchell et al., 'Sexual function in Britain: findings from the third National Survey of Sexual Attitudes and Lifestyles (Natsal-3)', *The Lancet* 382 (2013), pp. 1817–29; available at https://www.thelancet.com/journals/lancet/article/PIIS0140-6736(13)62366-1/ fulltext (accessed 07/03/2020); and Nigel Field et al., 'Are depression and poor sexual health neglected comorbidities? Evidence from a population sample', *BMJ Open* 6:3 (2016), pp. 1–15; available at http://eprints.gla.ac.uk/118818/1/118818.pdf (accessed 07/03/2020).

175. Terrence Higgins Trust, *Sexually Transmitted Infections in England: The State of the Nation* (London: Terrence Higgins Trust, 2020); available at https://www.tht.org.uk/our-work/our- campaigns/state-of-the-nation (accessed 02/03/2020).

176. John A. Terrizzi Jr. et al., 'Disgust: A predictor of social conservatism and prejudicial attitudes toward homosexuals', *Personality and Individual Differences* 49:6 (2010), pp. 587–92.

177. Alfred C. Kinsey et al., *Sexual Behaviour in the Human Male* (Bloomington: Indiana University Press, 1948); Alfred C. Kinsey et al., *Sexual Behaviour in the Human Female* (Philadelphia: W B Saunders, 1953).

178. Bruce Voeller, 'AIDS and heterosexual anal intercourse', *Archives of Sexual Behavior* 120:3 (1991), pp. 233–76; Daniel T. Halperin, 'Heterosexual Anal Intercourse: Prevalence, Cultural Factors, and HIV Infection and Other Health Risks, Part I', *AIDS Patient Care and STDs* 13:12 (1999), pp. 717–30; available at https://www.liebertpub.com/doi/10.1089/apc.1999.13.717 (accessed 07/03/2020);
Joshua G. Rosenberger et al., 'Sexual Behaviors and Situational Characteristics of Most Recent Male-Partnered Sexual Event among Gay and Bisexually Identified Men in the United States', *The Journal of Sexual Medicine* 8:11 (2011), pp. 3040–50.

179. See note 178 and Mark Berry et al., 'Risk Factors for HIV and Unprotected Anal Intercourse among Men Who Have Sex with Men (MSM) in Almaty, Kazakhstan', *PLoS ONE* 7:8 (2012), e43071; available at 10.1371/journal.pone.0043071 (accessed 24/03/2020).

180. Kimberly R. McBride and J. Dennis Fortenberry, 'Heterosexual Anal Sexuality and Anal Sex Behaviours', *Journal of Sex Research* 47:2–3 (2010), pp. 123–36.

181. ICD-10 did retain a controversial category of ego-dystonic sexual orientation. In ICD-11 (2018) sexual dysfunctions are no longer classified as mental disorders and sexual orientation is not included as a sexual dysfunction of any kind.

182. See the LLF Online Library: *Mental Health and Fluidity of Sexuality and Gender* by Michael King.

183. Studies of completed suicide are especially difficult as it is not always clear retrospectively whether or not someone was homosexual or heterosexual. It is therefore difficult to quantify the exact increase in risk – but it is fairly clear that there is an increase in risk.

184. Foreign and Commonwealth Office, Policy paper 2020, *Equal Rights Coalitions (ERC) statement on coronavirus (COVID-19) and the human rights of LGBTI persons*; available at https://www.gov.uk/government/publications/coronavirus-and-the-human-rights-of-lgbti-people-equal-rights-coalition-statement/equal-rights-coalitions-erc-statement-on-coronavirus-covid-19-and-the-human-rights-of-lgbti-persons (accessed 30/06/2020); and Stonewall 2020, *How COVID-19 is affecting LGBT communities*; available at https://www.stonewall.org.uk/about-us/news/how-covid-19-affecting-lgbt-communities (accessed 30/06/2020).

185. Andrew Kohut et al., *The Global Divide on Homosexuality: Greater Acceptance in More Secular and Affluent Countries* (Washington: Pew Research Centre, 2013); available at https://www.pewresearch.org/global/wp-content/uploads/sites/2/2014/05/Pew-Global-Attitudes-Homosexuality-Report-REVISED-MAY-27-2014.pdf (accessed 07/03/2020).

186. Mark L. Hatzenbuehler et al., 'The Impact of Institutional Discrimination on Psychiatric Disorders in Lesbian, Gay, and Bisexual Populations: A Prospective Study', *American Journal of Public Health* 100:3 (2010), pp. 452–9; available at https://www.ncbi.nlm.nih.gov/pmc/articles/PMC2820062/pdf/452.pdf (accessed 07/03/2020).

187. April Guasp, *The School Report: The Experiences of Gay Young People in Britain's Schools in 2012* (Cambridge: University of Cambridge Centre for Family Research and Stonewall); available at https://www.stonewall.org.uk/system/files/The_School_Report__2012_.pdf (accessed 07/03/2020).

188. Within medical language there is a tendency to use 'DSD' and in psychosocial approaches to use 'dsd', with the latter denoting 'differences of sex development'.

189. Nita G. de Neve-Enthoven et al., 'Psychosocial well-being in Dutch adults with disorders of sex development', *Journal of Psychosomatic Research* 83 (2016), pp. 57–64.

190. Katrina Roen, 'Intersex or Diverse Sex Development: Critical Review of Psychosocial Health Care Research and Indications for Practice', *The Journal of Sex Research* 56:4–5 (2019), pp. 511–28.

191. J.M. Serovich et al., 'A Systematic Review of the Research Base on Sexual Reorientation Therapies', *Journal of Marital and Family Therapy* 34(2):227–38 (2008); available at https://doi:10.1111/j.1752-0606.2008.00065.x
Douglas C. Haldeman, 'Gay rights, patient rights: The implications of sexual orientation conversion therapy', *Professional Psychology: Research and Practice* 33(3), 260–64 (2002); available at https://doi.org/10.1037/0735-7028.33.3.260
Talen Wright et al., 'Conversion therapies and access to transition-related healthcare in transgender people: a narrative systematic review' *British Medical Journal Open* 8:12 (2018); available at https://researchonline.lshtm.ac.uk/id/eprint/4653835/ (accessed 27/03/2020).
See also the LLF Online Library : *Mental health and wellbeing of sexually and gender diverse people* by Michael King.

192. British Association for Counselling and Psychotherapy, 'Memorandum of Understanding on Conversion Therapy in the UK' (2015); available at https://www.psychotherapy.org.uk/wp-content/uploads/2016/09/Memorandum-of-understanding-on-conversion-therapy.pdf (accessed 27/03/1010).
Church of England General Synod 2017: The motion agreed was: 'That this Synod:
(a) endorse the Memorandum of Understanding on Conversion Therapy in the UK of November 2015, signed by The Royal College of Psychiatrists and others, that the practice of gay conversion therapy has no place in the modern world, is unethical, potentially harmful and not supported by evidence; and (b) call upon the Church to be sensitive to, and to listen to, contemporary expressions of gender identity; (c) and call on the government to ban the practice of Conversion Therapy.'; available at https://www.churchofengland.org/more/media-centre/news/general-synod-backs-ban-conversion-therapy (accessed 27/03/2020).
For the supporting documents see GS2070A and 2070B:
Church of England General Synod GS 2070A (https://www.churchofengland.org/sites/default/files/2017-11/GS 2070A Conversion Therapy, A note from Ms Jayne Ozanne.pdf) and Church of England General Synod GS 2070B (https://www.churchofengland.org/sites/default/files/2017-11/GS 2070B conversion therapy a note from the Secretary General.pdf) (accessed 27/03/2020).

193. British Association for Counselling and Psychotherapy, 'Memorandum of Understanding on Conversion Therapy in the UK: Version 2' (Lutterworth: BACP, 2017); available at https://www.bacp.co.uk/media/6526/memorandum-of-understanding-v2-reva-jul19.pdf (accessed 07/03/2020).

194. See, for example, James E. Phelan, *Successful Outcomes of Sexual Orientation Change Efforts (SOCE): An Annotated Bibliography* (Charlestown, SC: Practical Application Publications, 2014); Ignatius Nugraha, 'The compatibility of sexual orientation change efforts with international human rights law', *Netherlands Quarterly of Human Rights* 35:3 (2017), pp. 176–92; available at https://journals.sagepub.com/doi/pdf/10.1177/0924051917724654 (accessed 07/03/2020).

195. Stanton L. Jones and Mark A. Yarhouse 'A Longitudinal Study of Attempted Religiously Mediated Sexual Orientation Change', *Journal of Sex & Marital Therapy* 37:5 (2011), pp. 404–27.

196. Paul W. Hruz, 'Deficiencies in Scientific Evidence for Medical Management of Gender Dysphoria', *The Linacre Quarterly* 87:1 (2019), pp. 34–42.

197. Janice Turner, 'Giving puberty blocker to "trans" children is a leap into the unknown', *The Times*, 21 February 2020; available at https://www.thetimes.co.uk/article/giving-puberty-blocker-to-trans-children-is-a-leap-into-the-unknown-x3g37sb7f (accessed 02/03/2020).

198. NHS England, *Update on gender identity development service for children and young people* (2020); available at https://www.england.nhs.uk/2020/01/update-on-gender-identity-development-service-for-children-and-young-people/ (accessed 07/03/2020).

199. John Curtice et al. (eds), *British Social Attitudes 36* (London: National Centre for Social Research, 2019), 21; available at https://www.bsa.natcen.ac.uk/media/39363/bsa_36.pdf (accessed 05/07/2020), pp. 17ff.

200. Rabbi Jeff Goldwasser, *Judaism, Homosexuality and the Supreme Court*, 24 June 2013; available at https://reformjudaism.org/blog/2013/06/24/judaism-homosexuality-and-supreme-court (accessed 05/07/2020).

201. Aaron Lerner, *Judaism and Homosexuality Orthodox, Conservative and Reform Sources*; available at https://www.sefaria.org/sheets/20552?lang=bi (accessed 05/07/2020).

202. Ephraim Mirvis, *The Wellbeing of LGBT+ Pupils: A Guide for Orthodox Jewish Schools* (September 2018); available at https://chiefrabbi.org/wp-content/uploads/2018/09/The-Wellbeing-of-LGBT-Pupils-A-Guide-for-Orthodox-Jewish-Schools.pdf (accessed 03/07/2020).

203. J. Jhutti-Johal, *Sikhism Today* (London: Continuum, 2011), pp. 77–9.

204. Sarbat, *Sikhism and Same-Sex Relationships*; available at http://www.sarbat.net/wp-content/uploads/Sarbat-Leaflet-v2.pdf (accessed 05/07/2020).

205. https://www.washingtonpost.com/national/religion/indias-debate-can-hinduism-and-homosexuality-coexist/2015/07/08/3e124270-25a5-11e5-b621-b55e495e9b78_story.html

206. 'Hinduism does not condemn gay people: UK Hindu Council', *The India Express*, 3 July 2009; available at http://archive.indianexpress.com/news/hinduism-does-not-condemn-gay-people-uk-hindu-council/484563/ (accessed 05/07/2020).

207. Human Dignity Trust, *Criminalising Homosexuality and Understanding the Right to Manifest Religion* (2015); available at https://www.humandignitytrust.org/wp-content/uploads/resources/9.-Criminalisation-Freedom-of-Religion.pdf (accessed 22/06/2020).

208. *Contextualising Islam in Britain II* (Centre of Islamic Studies, Cambridge, 2012), pp.65–6.

209. See www.inclusivemosque.org (accessed 22/06/2020).

210. See https://www.keshetuk.org (accessed 05/07/2020).

211. See https://www.galva108.org/about-galva-108 (accessed 05/07/2020).

212. See http://www.sarbat.net (accessed 05/07/2020).

213. See Shanon Shah, 'Religion and Sexual Minorities: The Experiences of Lesbian, Gay, Bisexual and Transgender (LGBT) Muslims', *Temple Tracts*, 5:2 (2016); available at https://williamtemplefoundation.org.uk/wp-content/uploads/2017/02/Religion-and-Sexual-Minorities-Shanon-Shah-.pdf (accessed 05/07/2020).

214. See for example, *Muslims for Progressive Values;* available at http://www.mpvusa.org/sexuality-diversity (accessed 05/07/2020).

215. https://www.royal.uk/queens-speech-lambeth-palace-15-february-2012 (accessed 05/07/2020).

216. Department for Education https://www.gov.uk/government/publications/relationships-education-relationships-and-sex-education-rse-and-health-education (accessed 15/06/2020).

217. Although there are some parallels, pastoral accompaniment – which is about an ongoing relationship between one person and others in the context of the church's pastoral ministry – is not the same as pastoral accommodation, which concerns specific responses that may be made by the church to a situation where church teaching has in some way not been observed by members of that church. For a discussion of pastoral accommodation, see the Pilling Report: The House of Bishops, *The Report of the House of Bishops Working Group on Human Sexuality* (London: Church House Publishing, 2013); available at https://www.churchofengland.org/sites/default/files/2018-01/GS%201929%20Working%20Group%20on%20human%20sexuality_0.pdf (accessed 09/03/2020).

218. The Methodist Church, 'God in Love Unites Us: The Report of the Marriage and Relationships Task Group 2019'; available at https://www.methodist.org.uk/media/12606/3240-10-amended-marriage-and-relationships-report.pdf (accessed 20/03/2020).

219. The House of Bishops, *The Report of the House of Bishops Working Group on Human Sexuality* (London: Church House Publishing, 2013); available from https://www.churchofengland.org/sites/default/files/2018-01/GS%201929%20Working%20Group%20on%20human%20sexuality_0.pdf (accessed 09/03/2020) see paragraphs 59-63.

220. 5.6 and 5.23 in *Issues in Human Sexuality*.

221. Church of England, *Can I Marry in Church?* (undated); available at https://www.yourchurchwedding.org/article/can-i-marry-in-church/ (accessed 07/03/2020).

222. See IICSA Research Team, *Child Sexual Abuse within the Catholic and Anglican Churches: A Rapid Evidence Assessment* (2017, revised 2018); available at https://www.iicsa.org.uk/

key-documents/3361/view/iicsa-rea-child-sexual-abuse-anglican-catholic-churches-nov-2017-.pdf (accessed 07/03/2020).

223. Anglican Consultative Council, *The Lambeth Conference: Resolutions Archive from 1888* (London: Anglican Community Office, 2005); available at https://www.anglicancommunion.org/media/127722/1888.pdf (accesed 07/03/2020); see Resolution 4.

224. Randall Davidson, 'Encyclical Letter of 1908' in *The Five Lambeth Conferences* (London: SPCK, 1920), pp. 294–317, see p. 309.

225. The Lambeth Conference 1920, *Resolution 67 – Problems of Marriage and Sexual Morality* (2020); available at https://www.anglicancommunion.org/resources/document-library/lambeth-conference/1920/resolution-67-problems-of-marriage-and-sexual-morality.aspx (accessed 9 March 2020). Lambeth Conference 1930, *Resolution 11 – The Life and Witness of the Christian Community – Marriage* (2020); available at https://aco.org/resources/document-library/lambeth-conference/1930/resolution-11-the-life-and-witness-of-the-christian-community-marriage (accessed 9/03/2020).

226. Church of England, *Year Book of the National Assembly of the Church of England* (London: SPCK, 1938); see pp. 250–1 and pp. 259–61.

227. The 1947 Act of Convocation of Canterbury, *Chronicles of Convocation*, Session XIX (1 October 1957), iii–iv.

228. Archbishop of Canterbury's Group on the Divorce Law, *Putting Asunder: A Divorce Law for Contemporary Society* (London: SPCK, 1966).

229. Howard Root, *Marriage, Divorce and the Church: The Report of a Commission Appointed by the Archbishop of Canterbury to Prepare a Statement on the Christian Doctrine of Marriage* (London: SPCK, 1971).

230. Church of England General Synod 2002 GS 1449; available at https://www.churchofengland.org/sites/default/files/2018-11/gs1449-marriage%20in%20church%20after%20divorce%3A%20report%20from%20the%20hob.pdf (accessed 08/05/2020).

231. Church of England, 'Civil Partnerships – for same sex and opposite sex couples. A pastoral statement from the House of Bishops of the Church of England'; available at https://www.churchofengland.org/sites/default/files/2020-01/Civil%20Partnerships%20-%20Pastoral%20Guidance%202019%20%282%29.pdf (accessed on 08/05/2020).

232. Church of England, 'Statement from Archbishop Justin and Archbishop Sentamu following the College of Bishops meeting'; available at https://www.churchofengland.org/more/media-centre/news/statement-archbishop-justin-and-archbishop-sentamu-following-college-bishops (accessed 08/05/2020).

233. Matthew Grimley, 'Law, Morality and Secularisation: The Church of England and the Wolfenden Report, 1954–67', *Journal of Ecclesiastical History* 60:4 (2009), pp. 725–41.

234. UK Parliament, *Historic Hansard: Lords Sitting* (12 May 1965); available at https://api.parliament.uk/historic-hansard/sittings/1965/may/12#lords (accessed 09/03/2020); see series 5, Volume 266, columns 80-81.

235. *Homosexuality: A Review of the Situation after the Passing of the Sexual Offences Act 1967* (London: Board for Social Responsibility, 1970).

236. June Osborne et al., *Report to the House of Bishops on Homosexuality* (1989); available at http://thinkinganglicans.org.uk/uploads/osborne_report.pdf (accessed 09/03/2020); see paragraphs 33 and 324.

237. A Working Party of the House of Bishops, *Some Issues in Human Sexuality: A Guide to the Debate* (London: Church House Publishing, 2003).

238. The House of Bishops, *Issues in Human Sexuality: A Statement by the House of Bishops* (London: Church House Publishing, 1991); see paragraphs 5.3 and 5.4.

239. Church of England, *Issues in Human* Sexuality (1991), see paragraph 5.6.

240. Church of England, *Issues in Human* Sexuality (1991), see paragraphs 5.13 and 5.22.

241. The House of Bishops, *Civil Partnerships – A Pastoral Statement from the House of Bishops of the Church of England* (2005); available at https://www.churchofengland.org/sites/default/

files/2017-11/House%20of%20Bishops%20Statement%20on%20Civil%20Partnerships%20 2005.pdf (accessed 09/03/2020); see paragraph 27.

242. *Civil Partnerships – A Pastoral Statement*, see paragraphs 17 and 18.

243. *Civil Partnerships – A Pastoral Statement*, see paragraph 21.

244. The House of Bishops, *The Report of the House of Bishops Working Group on Human Sexuality* (London: Church House Publishing, 2013); available at https://www.churchofengland.org/sites/default/files/2018-01/GS%201929%20Working%20Group%20 on%20human%20sexuality_0.pdf (accessed 09/03/2020).

245. Church of England, http://www.sharedconversations.org/ (accessed 24/04/2020).

246. The House of Bishops, *House of Bishops Pastoral Guidance on Same Sex Marriage* (2014); available at https://www.churchofengland.org/more/media-centre/news/house-bishops-pastoral-guidance-same-sex-marriage (accessed 09/03/2020); see parapgraph 18.

247. The House of Bishops, *Pastoral Guidance on Same Sex Marriage*, see paragraphs 20 and 21.

248. The House of Bishops, *Pastoral Guidance on Same Sex Marriage*, see paragraph 27.

249. Church of England General Synod GS 2055; available at https://www.churchofengland.org/sites/default/files/2017-11/gs-2055-marriage-and-same-sex-relationships-after-the-shared-conversations-report-from-the-house-of-bishops.pdf (accessed 08/05/2020).

250. Church of England General Synod GSMisc 1158; available at https://www.churchofengland.org/sites/default/files/2017-11/gs-misc-1158-next-steps-on-human-sexuality.pdf (accessed 08/05/2020).

251. Church of England, 'Sending Candidate to BAP: A Guide to the Selection Process' (2017), section 1.14, p. 12; available at https://www.churchofengland.org/sites/default/files/2017-10/Sending%20Candidates%20to%20BAP.pdf (accessed 09/06/2020).

252. The House of Bishops, *Some Issues in Human Sexuality* (2003). See also Evangelical Alliance Policy Commission, *Transsexuality* (London: Paternoster, 2000).

253. The House of Bishops, *Some Issues in Human Sexuality* (2003), pp. 248–9.

254. HB(03)M1 – House of Bishops: Summary of Decisions from the meeting of the House held 13-16 January 2003; a summary reference to this paper is provided in GS2071A Diocesan Synod Motion, *Welcoming Transgender People* (2017); available at https://www.churchofengland.org/sites/default/files/2017-11/gs-2071a-welcoming-transgender-people.pdf (accessed 09/06/2020).

255. Church of England, *Pastoral Guidance for Use in Conjunction with the Affirmation of Baptismal Faith in the Context of Gender Transition* (2019); available at https://www.churchofengland.org/sites/default/files/2019-06/Pastoral%20Guidance-Affirmation-Baptismal-Faith-Context-Gender-Transition.pdf (accessed 09/03/2020).

256. Resolution 41; available at www.anglicancommunion.org/resources/document-library/lambeth-conference/1908/resolution-41.aspx (accessed 08/05/2020).

257. Resolution 68; available at www.anglicancommunion.org/resources/document-library/lambeth-conference/1920/resolution-68-problems-of-marriage-and-sexual-morality.aspx (accessed 05/07/2020).

258. Resolution 15; available at www.anglicancommunion.org/media/127734/1930.pdf (accessed 05/07/2020).

259. Resolution 115; available at www.anglicancommunion.org/media/127740/1958.pdf (accessed 05/07/2020).

260. The Lambeth Conference 1978, 'Resolution 10' in *The Lambeth Conference: Resolutions Archive from 1978* (London: The Anglican Communion Office, 2005), p. 8; available at https://www.anglicancommunion.org/media/127746/1978.pdf (accessed 09/03/2020).

261. The Lambeth Conference 1988, 'Resolution 64' in *The Lambeth Conference Resolutions Archive from 1988* (London: The Anglican Communion Office, 2005), p. 29; available at https://www.anglicancommunion.org/media/127749/1988.pdf (accessed 09/03/2020).

262. *The Kuala Lumpur Statement on Human Sexuality – 2nd Encounter in the South, 10 to 15 Feb 1997*; available at www.globalsouthanglican.org/blog/comments/the_kuala_lumpur_statement_on_human_sexuality_2nd_encounter_in_the_south_10 (accessed 05/07/2020).

263. Global South Anglican Online, *The Kuala Lumpur Statement on Human Sexuality – 2nd Encounter in the South, 10 to 15 Feb 97* (1997); available at https://www.anglicancommunion.org/resources/document-library/lambeth-conference/1998/section-i-called-to-full-humanity/section-i10-human-sexuality (accessed 09/03/2020).

264. The Lambeth Conference 1998, *The Lambeth Conference Resolutions Archive from 1998* (London: The Anglican Communion Office, 2005); available at https://www.anglicancommunion.org/media/76650/1998.pdf (accessed 09/03/2020).

265. Gerald Beaumont et al., *A Pastoral Statement to Lesbian and Gay Anglicans from Some Member Bishops of the Lambeth Conference* (1998); available at http://justus.anglican.org/resources/Lambeth1998/paststmnt.html (accessed 09/03/2020).

266. International Anglican Conversations on Human Sexuality, *A Final Report* (2005); available at https://www.anglicancommunion.org/media/189015/conversations_on_human_sexuality.pdf (accessed 09/03/2020).

267. The Lambeth Commission on Communion, *The Windsor Report* (London: The Anglican Communion Office, 2004); available at https://www.anglicancommunion.org/media/68225/windsor2004full.pdf (accessed 09/03/2020).

268. Philip Groves (ed.), *The Anglican Communion and Homosexuality: A Resource to Enable Listening and Dialogue* (London: SPCK, 2008).

269. The Lambeth Conference 2008, *Section I: The Scriptures* (2020); available at https://www.anglicancommunion.org/resources/document-library/lambeth-conference/2008/section-i-the-scriptures (accessed 09/03/2020).

270. ACNS, 'Statement from Primates 2016', *Anglican Communion News Service*, 14 January 2016; available at https://www.anglicannews.org/news/2016/01/statement-from-primates-2016.aspx (accessed 09/03/2020).

271. The Global South Fellowship of Anglican Churches, 'A Proposal on the Global South Fellowship of Anglican Churches Structure', 11 October 2019, page 29, paragraph 16; available at http://www.globalsouthanglican.org/images/uploads/GSA_Covenantal_Structure_(adopted_on_11_Oct_2019).pdf (accessed 24/03/2020).

PART THREE

272. Friedrich Nietzsche, *Thus Spoke Zarathustra: A Book for Everyone and Nobody*, Graham Parkes (trans.) (Oxford: Oxford University Press, 2008), p. 79.

273. The Archbishops' Council, *Common Worship: Services and Prayers for the Church of England* (London: Church House Publishing, 2000), see Eucharistic Prayer F on p. 199.

274. Gabrielle Thomas, 'The Human Icon: Gregory of Nazianzus on Being an *Imago Dei*', *Scottish Journal of Theology* 72:2 (2019), pp. 166–81.

275. Frances Young, *God's Presence: A Contemporary Recapitulation of Early Christianity* (Cambridge: Cambridge University Press, 2013), p. 197.

276. Rowan Williams, *Being Disciples: Essentials of the Christian Life* (London: SPCK, 2016); see p. 64.

277. Gregory of Nyssa, 'On the Love of the Poor, 1: On Good Works' in Susan R. Holman (ed. and trans.), *The Hungry are Dying: Beggars and Bishops in Roman Cappadocia* (Oxford: Oxford University Press, 2001), pp. 193–9; see p. 195. Translation slightly altered.

278. Richard Baxter, *The Poor Man's Family Book* (London: Nevill Simmons, 1674), p. 307.

279. See, for example, 'Jesus' teaching on marriage' in Chapter 12 pp.246–52.

280. Church of England, *Issues in Human Sexuality* (1991), see paragraphs 5.3 and 5.4.

281. See, for instance, John M. Hull, 'The Broken Body in a Broken World', *Journal of Religion, Disability & Health* 7:4 (2004), pp. 5–23.

282. See, for instance, Nuffield Council on Bioethics, *(Un)natural: Ideas about Naturalness in Public and Political Debates about Science, Technology and Medicine* (London: Nuffield Council on Bioethics, 2015); available at https://www.nuffieldbioethics.org/wp-content/uploads/Nuffield_Council_Naturalness_booklet.pdf (accessed 10/03/2020).

283. Justin Welby and John Sentamu, *Letter from the Archbishops of Canterbury and York following General Synod* (Church of England, 2017); available at https://www.churchofengland.org/more/media-centre/news/letter-archbishops-canterbury-and-york-following-general-synod (accessed 10/03/2020).

284. For the discussion in this sub-Part, see Faith and Order Commission of the Church of England, *Communion and Disagreement: A Report from the Faith and Order Commission* (London: The General Synod of the Church of England, 2016); available at https://www.churchofengland.org/sites/default/files/2017-10/communion_and_disagreement_faoc_report_gs_misc_1139.pdf (accessed 10/03/2020).

285. The Breaking of the Bread in *Common Worship* Order One for Holy Communion.

286. Diocese of Winchester, *Sharing God's Life* (Winchester: Diocese of Winchester, 2018); available at https://cofewinchester.contentfiles.net/media/assets/file/Rule-of-Life-Brochure.pdf, accessed 10/03/2020).

287. 'The SCL journey' (2014), www.singleconsecratedlife-anglican.org.uk/journey.php (accessed 05/07/2020).

288. The exception is in *The First Book of Homilies* (1547) 'Against Swearing and Perjury': 'By ... holy promise, the Sacrament of Matrimonie knitteth man and wife in perpetuall love.' See *The Two Books of Homilies Appointed to be Read in Churches*, p. 73. Also available online, see Ian Lancashire (ed.), *Homily on Swearing and Perjury* (Toronto: University of Toronto, 1994; HTML version The Anglican Library, 1999); available at http://www.anglicanlibrary.org/homilies/bk1hom07.htm (accessed 10/03/2020).

289. Jean Porter, 'Chastity as a Virtue', *Scottish Journal of Theology* 58:3 (2005), pp. 285–301; see p. 285.

290. See Rowan Williams, 'The Body's Grace', in Eugene F. Rogers, Jr. (ed.), *Theology and Sexuality: Classic and Contemporary Readings*, Blackwell Readings in Modern Theology (Oxford: Blackwell, 2002), p. 313.

291. 'The Body's Grace', see p. 317.

292. 'The Body's Grace', see p. 315.

PART FOUR

293. 'Collect for the 5th Sunday after Easter' in *Book of Common Prayer*; see p. 142. Also available online at https://www.churchofengland.org/prayer-and-worship/worship-texts-and-resources/book-common-prayer/collects-epistles-and-gospels-39 (accessed 10/03/2020).

294. Gerald Bray (ed.), 'A Fruitful Exhortation to the Reading and Knowledge of Holy Scripture', *The Books of Homilies: A Critical Edition* (Cambridge: James Clarke and Co., 2015), pp. 7–13; see p. 7.

295. 'Articles of Religion' in *Book of Common Prayer*, pp. 607–29; see Article 20, p. 619. Also available online at https://www.churchofengland.org/prayer-and-worship/worship-texts-and-resources/book-common-prayer/articles-religion (accessed 10/03/2020).

296. The Anglican Consultative Council, *The Virginia Report: The Report of the Inter-Anglican Theological and Doctrinal Commission* (London: Anglican Consultative Council, 1997); available at https://www.anglicancommunion.org/media/150889/report-1.pdf (accessed 10/03/2020); see paragraph 3.6. Quotations from Anglican/Roman Catholic Join Preparatory Commission, *Elucidation* (1981); available at https://www.anglicancommunion.org/media/105227/ARCIC_I_Elucidations_on_Authority_in_the_Church.pdf (accessed 10/03/2020); see paragraph 2.

297. John Webster, *Holy Scripture: A Dogmatic Sketch* (Cambridge: Cambridge University Press, 2003); Douglas Burton-Christie, *The Word in the Desert: Scripture and the Quest for Holiness in Early Christian Monasticism* (New York: Oxford University Press, 1993); Chris E. W. Green, *Sanctifying Interpretation: Vocation, Holiness, and Scripture* (Cleveland, OH:

CPT, 2015); Mark McIntosh, *Mystical Theology* (Oxford: Blackwell, 1998); see Chapter 3; Lewis Ayres, 'Augustine on the Rule of Faith: Rhetoric, Christology, and the Foundation of Christian Thinking', *Augustinian Studies* 36:1 (2005), pp. 33–49.

298. Richard Hooker, *Of the Laws of Ecclesiastical Polity: A Critical Edition with Modern Spelling*, ed. Arthur Stephen McGrade (Oxford: Oxford University Press, 2013); see section I.14.4, p. 92. Punctuation and capitalisation altered.

299. 'Articles of Religion' in *Book of Common Prayer*; see Article 6, p. 613.

300. Rowan Williams, *Archbishop's Presidential Address – General Synod November 2010* (2010); available at http://aoc2013.brix.fatbeehive.com/articles.php/919/archbishops-presidential-address-general-synod-november-2010 (accessed 10/03/2020).

301. John Sentamu, *Presidential Address to General Synod July 2019* (York: Archbishop of York, 2019); available at https://www.archbishopofyork.org/news/news-2019/presidential-address-general-synod-july-2019 (accessed 20/03/2020).

302. 'Articles of Religion' in *Book of Common Prayer*; see Article 20.

303. The definition of adultery is widened substantially in the intertestamental period, in a way that then shapes the teaching of Jesus (Chapter 12, Jesus' teaching on marriage, pages 246–252) and therefore, taken as a whole, we can argue Scripture promotes monogamy as argued in the text box on the teaching of Jesus on marriage.

304. Most of the scholarship referred to has been focused on Western studies, but scholars in other parts of the world have also argued for affirming interpretations. See, for example, Adriaan van Klinken, *Kenyan, Christian, Queer* (Pennsylvania State University, forthcoming 2020).

305. William P. Le Saint, S.J., S.T.D. (trans.), *Ancient Christian Writers: The Works of the Fathers in Translation* (New York: Newman Press, 1951), p. 98.

306. Augustine, *De Doctrina Christiana*, trans. R. P. H. Green (Oxford: Clarendon, 1995); see section I.86.

307. The Archbishops' Council, *Canons 7th Edition* (London: Church House Publishing, 2012, 2015 and 2016); available at https://www.churchofengland.org/more/policy-and-thinking/canons-church-england/canons-7th-edition (accessed 10/03/2020).

308. 'Articles of Religion' in *Book of Common Prayer*; Article 20.

309. The Lambeth Conference 1930, *Encyclical Letter from the Bishops with Resolutions and Reports* (London: SPCK / New York: Macmillan, 1930).

310. Archbishop's Commission on Doctrine, *Doctrine in the Church of England: The Report of the Commission on Christian Doctrine Appointed by the Archbishops of Canterbury and York in 1922* (London: SPCK, 1938), p. 29.

311. The Lambeth Conference 1958, *The Encyclical Letter from the Bishops together with the Resolutions and Reports* (London: SPCK / Greenwich, CT: Seabury, 1958); see Resolution 1.

312. 'Articles of Religion' in *Book of Common Prayer*; see Article 20 and Article 21, p. 620.

313. Inter-Anglican Theological and Doctrinal Commission, *For the Sake of the Kingdom: God's Church and the New Creation* (1986); available in *Inter Anglican Theological and Doctrinal Commission: Meetings Communiqués and Documents* (2008) at https://www.anglicancommunion.org/media/107645/IATDC-Inter-Anglican-Theological-and-Doctrinal-Commission.pdf (accessed 10/03/2020).

314. The Lambeth Conference 1988, 'Dogmatic and Pastoral Concerns' in *The Truth Shall Make You Free: The Lambeth Conference 1988: The Reports, Resolutions & Pastoral Letters from the Bishops* (London: Church House Publishing, 1988), pp. 79–122; see section 89, p. 104.

315. *The Virginia Report*; see section 3.12.

316. Church of England Doctrine Commission, *Subscription and Assent to the 39 Articles: Report of the Archbishops' Commission on Christian Doctrine* (London: SPCK, 1968); see section 89.

317. See Colin Podmore, 'The Church of England's Declaration of Assent', *Ecclesiastical Law Journal* 5.25 (1999), pp. 241–51.

318. Arches Court of Canterbury, *In Re St Alkmund, Duffield: Judgement* (2012) Fam 51; available at https://www.ecclesiasticallawassociation.org.uk/judgments/reordering/duffieldstalkmund2012appeal.pdf (accessed 10/03/2020). Citing also *Re St Thomas, Pennywell* (1995) Fam 50, section 58; and *Re Christ Church, Waltham Cross* (2002) Fam 51, section 25.

319. 'The Form of Ordaining or Consecrating of an Archbishop or Bishop' in *Book of Common Prayer*, pp. 584–95. Also available online at https://www.churchofengland.org/prayer-and-worship/worship-texts-and-resources/book-common-prayer/ordaining-and-consecrating-1 (accessed 10/03/2020). Similar language is found in both the modern service in *Common Worship* and in *Canon C18.1*.

320. The Archbishops' Council, 'The Ordination and Consecration of a Bishop' in *Common Worship: Ordination Services* (London: Church House Publishing, 2007); available at https://www.churchofengland.org/prayer-and-worship/worship-texts-and-resources/common-worship/ministry/common-worship-ordination-services (accessed 10/03/2020).

321. In recent years, there have been Reports of the House such as *The Ordination of Women to the Priesthood: The Second Report by the House of Bishops* (London: Church House Publishing, 1988); Occasional Papers of the House of Bishops such as *Bishops in Communion: Collegiality in the Service of the Koinonia of the Church* (London: Church House Publishing, 2000); and Theological Statements, such as *Eucharistic Presidency: A Theological Statement by the House of Bishops of the General Synod* (London: Church House Publishing, 2014).

322. *The Virginia Report*, see section 5.21.

323. See Part Two Chapter 7 to read about the Lambeth Conference.

324. Anglican–Roman Catholic International Commission, *Walking Together on the Way: Learning to Be the Church – Local, Regional, Universal. An Agreed Statement of the Third Anglican–Roman Catholic International Commission (ARCIC III)* (London: SPCK, 2018).

325. Second Anglican–Roman Catholic International Commission, *Life in Christ: Morals, Communion and the Church* (Vatican: 1994); available at http://www.vatican.va/roman_curia/pontifical_councils/chrstuni/angl-comm-docs/rc_pc_chrstuni_doc_19930906_life-in-christ_en.html (accessed 10/03/2020).

326. International Anglican–Roman Catholic Commission for Unity and Mission, *Growing Together in Unity and Mission: Building on 40 Years of Anglican – Roman Catholic Dialogue* (Vatican: 2007); available at http://www.vatican.va/roman_curia/pontifical_councils/chrstuni/angl-comm-docs/rc_pc_chrstuni_doc_20070914_growing-together_en.html (accessed 10/03/2020); see paragraph 85.

327. The Lambeth Conference 1988, 'Dogmatic and Pastoral Concerns' in *The Truth Shall Make You Free: The Lambeth Conference 1988: The Reports, Resolutions & Pastoral Letters from the Bishops* (London: Church House Publishing, 1988), see section 80, p. 102.

328. The Nicene Creed, for example, can be found in 'Holy Communion Service' in *Common Worship: Services and Prayers for the Church of England*; available at https://www.churchofengland.org/prayer-and-worship/worship-texts-and-resources/common-worship/holy-communion (accessed 10/03/2020).

329. Augustine, *The Literal Meaning of Genesis* I.19.39, in Augustine, *On Genesis*, trans. Edmund Hill (Hyde Park, NY: New City Press, 2002), p. 187.

330. John Calvin, *Institutes of the Christian Religion*, II.2.15, ed. John T. McNeill, trans. Ford Lewis Battles (Philadelphia: Westminster Press, 1960), spelling Anglicised.

331. For a good guide to both scientific problems and scientific solutions in one area, see Ben Goldacre, *Bad Pharma: How Drug Companies Mislead Doctors and Harm Patients* (London: Fourth Estate, 2012).

332. For discussions of references to natural law in the history of Anglican moral theology, see Peter Sedgwick, *The Origins of Anglican Moral Theology* (Leiden: Brill, 2018).

333. Faith and Order Commission, *Men and Women in Marriage* (London: Church House Publishing, 2013), §§10, 19; available at www.churchofengland.org/sites/default/files/2017-10/marriagetextbrochureprint.pdf (accessed 08/05/2020).

334. Mike Higton, 'Gender, Nature, Culture', *Kaì Euthùs*, 19 March 2014; available at mikehigton.org.uk/gender-nature-culture/ (accessed 08/05/2020).

335. Apocalyptic readings of various biblical texts, especially Paul's epistles, have become increasingly prominent in recent years. See, for example, Ben C. Blackwell, John K. Goodrich and John Maston (eds), *Paul and the Apocalyptic Imagination* (Minneapolis, MN: Fortress Press, 2016) and Beverly Roberts Gaventa (ed.), *Apocalyptic Paul: Cosmos and Anthropos in Romans 5–8* (Waco, TX: Baylor University Press, 2013).

336. Linn Marie Tonstad, *Queer Theology: Beyond Apologetics* (Fair Lawn, NJ: Cascade Press, 2018), p. 56.

337. See Edward Diener and Robert Biswas-Diener, 'The Replication Crisis in Psychology' in Biswas-Diener and Diener (eds.) *Noba Textbook Series: Psychology* (Champaign, IL: DEF, 2019); available at https://nobaproject.com/modules/the-replication-crisis-in-psychology (accessed 10/03/2020).

338. Andrew F. Walls, 'The Gospel as Prisoner and Liberator of Culture' in *The Missionary Movement in Christian History: Studies in the Transmission of Faith* (New York: Orbis Books, 1996), pp. 3–15.

339. See the discussion about Acts 15 in Part Four Chapter 14.

340. *The Virginia Report*, see section 3.11.

341. The saying is usually attributed to Max Warren who led the Church Missionary Society from 1942 to 1963.

342. Max Warren, 'General Introduction to the Christian Presence Series' in Kenneth Cragg, *Sandals at the Mosque: Christian Presence Amid Islam* (London: SCM Press, 1959), pp. 9–10.

343. John Stott, *The Contemporary Christian: An Urgent Plea for Double Listening* (Downers Grove, IL: InterVarsity Press, 1992).

344. The Lambeth Conference 1988, 'Dogmatic and Pastoral Concerns' in *The Truth Shall Make You Free: The Lambeth Conference 1988: The Reports, Resolutions & Pastoral Letters from the Bishops* (London: Church House Publishing, 1988), see section 37, p. 90.

345. Church of England, *Issues in Human Sexuality* (1991), paragraph 5.6.

346. See this exchange: Joshua Hordern and Loveday Alexander, 'Communion, Disagreement and Conscience' in *Supporting Papers for the Faith and Order Commission Report, Communion and Disagreement* (Archbishops' Council, 2016), pp. 6–18; available at https://www.churchofengland.org/sites/default/files/2017-10/communion_and_disagreement_supporting_papers.pdf (accessed 10/03/2020).

347. TEAC Anglican Way Consultation, 'Introduction' in *The Anglican Way* (Singapore: 2007); available at https://www.anglicancommunion.org/theology/theological-education/the-anglican-way.aspx (accessed 10/03/2020).

PART FIVE

348. *Common Worship: Ordination Services*.

349. In verse 19 Jesus says to Peter, 'Follow me' – *akolouthei moi* in Greek. The dialogue moves on and Peter, distracted by 'the disciple whom Jesus loved', asks Jesus, 'Lord, what about him?' Jesus' last words to Peter, his last words in the Gospel of John here at verse 22, are *su moi akolouthei*, literally: 'You me follow'.

Index of biblical references

General index

Note: Page numbers referring to infographics are in *italics*; those referring to Glossary items are in **bold** type.